studies in jazz

Studies in Jazz No. 5

Metuchen, N.J., & London, 1987

The Scarecrow Press and the Institute

Pee Wee Erwin

This Horn for Hire

as told to

WARREN W. VACHÉ, SR.

of Jazz Studies, Rutgers University

Library of Congress Cataloging-in-Publication Data

Erwin, Pee Wee, 1913-1981.
   This horn for hire.

   (Studies in jazz; no. 5)
   Discography: p.
   Includes index.
     1. Erwin, Pee Wee, 1913-1981.   2. Trumpet players—United
States— Biography.   3. Jazz musicians—United States—Biography.
I. Vache', Warren W., 1914-   II. Title.   III. Series.
ML419.E8A3 1987   788'.1'0924 [B]   87-4842
ISBN O-8108-1945-7

To Madeline

ACKNOWLEDGEMENTS

Nobody produces a book of this kind without a helping hand, and I gratefully extend my appreciation to the following nice people for the time and efforts in my behalf:

Bill Weinberg for his editing and suggestions;

Dan Morgenstern, most especially for his great work in editing and extending the discography;

Ed Berger for his able assistance and guidance;

Doris Raskin, for her patience and fortitude in the typesetting and page make-up;

And the entire editorial staff of Scarecrow Press for their invaluable help.

In addition, thanks to all those who lent moral support and encouragement; particularly the good friends who have been waiting for so long to see this volume become a reality. Their patience and loyalty helped me over the rough spots.

Warren Vache' Sr.

CONTENTS

FOREWORD

THE AUTOBIOGRAPHY of Pee Wee Erwin is the ultimate self-portrait of a most representative jazz musician. He participated in almost every aspect of jazz from the 1920s well into the 1970s. Starting out with local and territory bands, he quickly achieved full recognition. Playing with some of the most important swing bands of the 1930s, notably Benny Goodman and Tommy Dorsey, he became a star. His career shifted to the studios, where he achieved stability of income and had the opportunity for varied supplementary work. Eventually, he led his own groups and participated in countless pickup bands and recording dates. There was little in the way of jazz performance that eluded Pee Wee. He was a musician's musician. That story alone, the life of an itinerant jazz musician, would be enough to guarantee interest in his memoirs.

There is another facet to this book, however, one often missing from the biographies of performing artists—the human dimension. Pee Wee Erwin presents his whole self. He had a photographic memory, and the dates, personnels, itineraries and details of the interplay of musicians, bands, and audiences are all there. But also there are the intimate details of the life of a sensitive artist and man. The tensions of his relationship with parents, especially his father, the failure of a marriage, and the problem with alcohol are not glossed over.

Pee Wee was truly a nice guy, loved by all. It was his just reward to meet Caroline, who helped him through adversity and who could restore him to a productive professional career and a loving personal life. His children also played an important role, and he writes openly of his affection and anxieties.

This is a beautiful story, even if you are not an avid jazz fan eager for its wealth of details about the jazz life in the heyday of swing. Perhaps its most important contribution is that it delineates fully the professional life of a sideman. Pee Wee was not among the band leaders who achieved broad popular acclaim. He was not a superstar, but he was one of those unsung heroes without whom no leader could have achieved stardom, the gifted, flexible and reliable players who were the backbone of the bands. No other musician of that era has told his story in such richness of detail and with such integrity and love.

A special thanks must go to Warren Vache', Sr., who urged Pee Wee to write and talk for the record, and who shaped the material without losing the Pee Wee Erwin tone and touch. Without the persistance and devotion of his collaborator, Pee Wee's story would not have been told. Warren's affection and admiration for Pee Wee glows throughout the book; it is a true labor of love. The special friendship between these two has had yet another legacy: Warren Vache', Jr. was greatly influenced by Pee Wee as a teacher and a friend.

Warren Vache', Sr. has made it possible for us to see the span of many decades of jazz performance through the eyes of Pee Wee Erwin. This is a rare book.

WILLIAM M. WEINBERG

PREFACE

PEE WEE ERWIN was one of those rare people who is liked by everybody. If he had an enemy, I haven't heard of him. On the other hand. Pee Wee had friends without limit, male and female, young and old, near and far, and from all walks of life—and he never forgot them. He remembered their names, no matter how long it had been since he last saw them, and in most cases could tell you something about their background. Pee Wee loved people, and they loved him.

He was a modest man. He had a tendency to downplay his own accomplishments with one of his wry jokes, but he was always ready to praise the abilities of others and to lend a helping hand to a talented youngster getting started. So taking Pee Wee at his own evaluation, as you will find it in this book, is a bit misleading. He mentions only in passing accomplishments that testify to his amazing talent and quick wit, so the reader has to judge the facts for himself.

To start with, he was a musical prodigy, pushed by his father, of course (who seems to have been aware of the commercial aspects of his son's talent from the start), but without question an exceptionally talented boy. Then, if we analyze the episode of his high school junior and senior years, it becomes pretty obvious he was unusually self-disciplined as well as far above average in intelligence. Not many youngsters could have maintained such a rigid schedule, and hardly any would have elected to study much more than was required—as he did. There is also the barely mentioned decision to forego an appointment to West Point in order to continue his musical career. Pee Wee made this decision, from what he says, entirely on his own and seems never to have regretted it, but it points up several aspects of his situation at the time. First, it testifies to his self-reliance, but also shows how his family has disintegrated as a unit, because choosing a career—or, more to the point, passing up such a coveted plum as an appointment to West Point—is a momentous occasion in any young man's life, the kind of thing most families discuss and examine for months, sometimes years. It's evident that whatever Pee Wee was to accomplish from this point foreward, he would have to do on his own.

Something else must be kept in mind while Pee Wee talks about his musical adventures in New York during the 1930s. This was the worst period of the Great Depression, yet Pee Wee never lacked for work in the most highly competitive market in the country. The truth is that he was already recognized as an exceptional trumpet player, with an unusually wide range, a beautiful tone, and the ability to play practically anything, with or without written music. Probably the outstanding example of this is that Glenn Miller picked him to be a member of the star-studded Ray Noble Orchestra at the Rainbow Room, while at the same time, John Hammond and Benny Goodman sought him out as the replacement for Bunny Berigan in Goodman's band. For a while, until Goodman went on the road, he played in both bands. At this late date this may not seem to be a great accomplishment, but if you stop to reflect that both bands were considered the cream of the crop, with Noble playing the most prestigious spot in New York, and the Goodman band broadcasting from coast to coast on a major network show, you begin to get an idea of how enviable a niche Pee Wee had carved out for himself.

Aside from the essential ability to hold down a job in just about any kind of musical organization, Pee Wee was also fortunate to be in the right place at the right time. Thus he was able to move from one great band to another with hardly a break, and ultimately go on to pursue a lucrative career in the studios. But this fine timing failed him at a critical stage of his career, when he tried to launch his own band. It is futile now to conjecture how far he might have gone as shareholder in the Glenn Miller band, but hindsight shows that was the time when he should have considered going out on his own. This was when new bands were still a novelty, business was good, and the war was still far enough ahead to allow time for a band to develop and gain recognition. As it was, he waited too long. The war-time restrictions and effects of the draft ground his band into pieces. It is synonymous with the music business that bandleaders become more famous than sidemen. Whatever eminence Pee Wee achieved as a great trumpet player is as nothing compared to the fame he might have earned as leader of a successful band, like Harry James, Charlie Spivak, Bunny Berigan, Gene Krupa, or Glenn Miller, all of whom jumped from the ranks of sidemen into the spotlight, as leaders, managed to do. They made their moves at the right time. Pee Wee, for once in his life, did not.

Regardless of the uncertainties of a musician's life, and the pressures that finally forced him to retreat into a bottle, almost ending his career and life prematurely, Pee Wee never had any doubts about the rightness of his choice to pursue a musicial career. He enjoyed it. He loved to talk about it. And for the most part, music was good to him. He gave it all he had, and in return his name has to be considered among the great ones—not only as a musician, but as a fine human being.

WARREN W. VACHE'
Rahway, N.J. 1985

Pee Wee at age 15. Kansas City, 1928.

This Horn For Hire

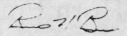

Apr. 6, 1934

PLACE OF BIRTH

County of *Richardson*

Township of ....
or
Village of ....
or
City of *Falls City*   (No. *1066 Stone*

FULL NAME OF CHILD *George Francis Erwin*

E-650

Department of Commerce and Labor
BUREAU OF THE CENSUS
STANDARD CERTIFICATE OF BIRTH
State of Nebraska
Registered N. *10720*
St.: *32*   Ward)

If child is not yet named, make
supplemental report, as directed

| Sex of Child *Male* | Twin, triplet, or other ...... | Number in order of birth *first* | Legitimate *Yes* | Date of birth *May 30* 19 1... |

	FATHER		**MOTHER**
FULL NAME	*James O. Erwin*	FULL MAIDEN NAME	*Chloe Maxine Prtes*
RESIDENCE	*Falls City Nebr*	RESIDENCE	*Falls City Nebr*
COLOR *White*	AGE AT LAST BIRTHDAY *23* (Years)	COLOR *White*	AGE AT LAST BIRTHDAY *21* (Years)
BIRTHPLACE	*Hamlin Kans*	BIRTHPLACE	*Falls City Nebr*
OCCUPATION	*Barber*	OCCUPATION	*House wife*
Number of children born to this mother, including present birth *One*		Number of children of this mother now living *One*	

CERTIFICATE OF ATTENDING PHYSICIAN

I hereby certify that I attended the birth of this child, who was *Born alive*   at *11* P M
on the data above stated.   (Here alive or Stillborn)

* When there was no attending physician then the father, householder, etc., should make this return. A stillborn child is one that neither breathes nor shows other evidence of life after birth.

(Signature) *M. L. Wilson*
Address *Falls City*

Given name added from a supplemental report

REGISTRAR   * Filed *June 3rd 19/13 Edna A Brown*   REGISTRAR

Facsimile of birth certificate

2

ONE

MY FATHER, James Erwin, was a trumpet player. On Memorial Day, May 30, 1913, he was playing in a church in Falls City, Nebraska, when suddenly he had a vision of a little guy dancing on the bell of his horn and he knew I had arrived.

Well, anyway, it made a good story. Falls City, just in case you have never been to Nebraska, was an important division center for the Missouri-Pacific Railroad, and in those days had a population around 7,000. Come to think of it, it's still around 7,000—not a very big town, but because it was a division center just about everything that took place in it had something to do with the railroad. One of the earliest sounds I remember hearing is that of train whistles, and as a schoolkid one of my big thrills was visiting the locomotive repair shops.

By the time I was old enough to have some idea of what was going on around me I was living with my mother's parents, George and Josephine Prater, and I can still recall how confused I was when somebody tried to explain to me that the people I called Dad and Ma were my grandfather and grandmother, and the lady who came to visit us each evening was my mother. I also had a father, they told me, and this made no sense at all because I didn't know what a father was and had never seen one. I was three or four years old at the time, and neither my mother nor my invisible father were important to me because I was very happy with things as they were, that is, basking in the doting care of my grandparents who—now that I can look back—were doing a beautiful job of spoiling me.

Something else I didn't understand, even though I overheard people talking about it, was a thing called war that was going on. My father was in the navy, stationed at the Philadelphia Navy Yard, and my mother was working as a telephone operator for the Southeastern Nebraska Telephone Company, which to this day is one of the few privately owned telephone companies in the country. She and my Aunt Hazel, who played piano in silent-movie theaters and later on earned my respect for having a terrific left hand, were actually living with us, but because they both worked I didn't see much of them. Consequently, the most important people in my limited world were the ones I

3

called Ma and Dad. When the situation changed later, in a way that seemed to me pretty drastic, I had a bit of trouble trying to adjust.

As I've said, Falls City was a railroad town. But it was in the middle of farm country, and while I've often heard people talk about shortages of certain food items during the first World War, I don't think this bothered us much. As long as I can remember, good food has always been very important to me. I love to eat. So I can recall vividly my grandmother canning fruits and vegetables from the garden, and my grandfather stocking the storm cellar with provisions for the long Nebraska winters—meat from the two hogs he would order slaughtered for him in the fall, flour for the baking of our own bread, sugar, and the preserves my grandmother put up. We weren't rich but we ate well, and we weren't anything unusual in Nebraska because we had a storm cellar. In tornado country just about every house has one: an underground cave-like place well away from the main house where the family can wait out a twister. In those days, though, they often doubled as refrigerated storehouses—natural ones.

Since radio and TV were still in the future, I imagine the war must have seemed very remote to the people of Falls City, but they couldn't help being reminded of it in many ways, especially by the absence of the men who had gone away. Listening to the stories, they all became heroes to me. Sometimes when I visited my mother at the telephone exchange I was allowed to go into an outer booth and place a call to "Billy," one of the local boys who had gone to France. Somebody on the other end would pretend to be Billy talking, and I would be all thrilled and excited by the conservation. It was all done in a spirit of fun, of course, just grown-ups amusing themselves and a small boy, but the tragic aspect is that the real Billy never came back.

I don't know how long my mother worked at the exchange, but somewhere near the end of the war she gave it up and went to work for a drugstore in town. Maybe she found it more convenient or something, but she could not have picked a busier time to make the change because a flu epidemic was sweeping the country and a lot of people were down with it. One night on the way home she stopped off at a house to deliver some medicine, as a neighborly favor, I guess, and caught the flu herself. And about a week later I had it too. But the remarkable thing was that my grandmother and grandfather, who took care of us, never caught it. They walked around the house with masks over their faces, and kept an asafetida bag around their necks at all times, so maybe the stink scared away the bugs, but they stayed healthy. After awhile my mother began to get better. But they were worried about me, and after some discussion I heard them decide to send for Grandfather Erwin.

Judging from what I have learned about my grandfather, Frank Erwin, he was quite a guy and a typical country doctor. He was born in Rock Hill, South Carolina, in 1860, but my grandmother was born in Louisville, Kentucky, and they were married there. Then they migrated west so he could establish a practice and he became one of the most respected and highly regarded men in the area.

This was prior to the time of the handy corner drugstore, so Frank Erwin mixed his own prescriptions. I still have his instruments, which were passed on to me when he died in 1926. At one time I also had his medical books, but years ago I gave these to an old friend, a doctor in Falls City, who was one of the many babies delivered by my grandfather.

A well-worn family story about Grandfather Frank concerns an episode that took place at my father's wedding party. Like a couple of other Erwins you're due to hear about, Frank was a drinker, so he showed up at the wedding with a bottle in his pocket because he had been forewarned that my mother's people were tee-totalers and there would be no booze. He did his nipping discreetly, and all went well until the wedding party was seated around the dining table, and all of a sudden the cork left Grandpa's bottle with a loud pop, and he had to make an embarrassed retreat outside so he could put it back.

Regardless of his drinking habits he had a well-earned reputation as a fever specialist, and after a couple of days under his care I started to come around, only to become more confused than ever trying to sort out grandfathers, dads, and fathers. I was still trying to figure out what a father was—this guy I had never seen but was always hearing about—and now I suddenly discovered I had two grandfathers and one was a doctor. He looked like a giant with bushy eyebrows, and I was a little afraid of him although he treated me kindly enough.

Then, along with a lot of excitement and fanfare, came the announcement that my father was getting a furlough, because my mother and I had been so sick, and was coming home. I don't know what I expected, but a short time later in walks this sharp-featured, blue-eyed character in a sailor suit, and I'm told he's my father. With him was a duffel bag loaded with toys for me, including a battery-powered electric train from Wanamaker's in Philadelphia. That wasn't hard to take, and I was fascinated by the wondrous tales he told of the fabulous pipe organ at Wanamaker's. But when he left again a few days later to go back to base, I was glad to see things settle down to the way they had been before he came. For some reason he seemed to expect something from me, but whatever it was I wasn't about to give it, and if somebody had asked me to choose I would have readily picked grandfathers over fathers.

Of course, in time I got to know my father pretty well, and, piecing together some of the things he told me later, I learned something about his time in the navy. For one thing, although he was a trumpet player when he went into service, he switched to baritone horn, but just why he did this I have never been sure. Maybe he did it because of the important role the baritone has in a brass band, or because the baritone is a countermelody instrument and offers the player wide latitude to improvise on his parts (something my father was very good at), or maybe just because the larger mouthpiece made it easier to play in a marching band. Whatever his main reasons, I'm sure he had an ulterior motive—he could carry the baritone out of its case while somebody else carried the case full of booze. And a baritone horn case holds a lot more booze than a trumpet case.

Nevertheless, judging from what he told me, and from what I heard from others later, he must have been a very fine musician. He played in the band during his early training at Great Lakes and afterwards was assigned to groups put together for John Philip Sousa, traveling around the country playing for Liberty Bond rallies. In fact, he put in quite a number of stints under the direction of Sousa during the war. Knowing what I know now, I believe he must have been a very powerful player with the qualities that would have classified him in those days as a "street screamer." In other words, when a band was still off in the distance you could hear the trumpet, and later on it seemed the rest of the band would join in. That was a street screamer trumpet player you heard, and it took great power and a tone that could carry a long way. In later years Harry James reminded me of this kind of player. His tone has the same penetrating, piercing quality. I don't know where my father received his early training, but whoever taught him knew his business and turned out an excellent legitimate musician, which he would have had to be to work with Sousa. But on top of this, he had a great ear, excellent improvisational ability, and could fake very well, and in the bargain somewhere along the line he had been exposed to ragtime. For those days—1917—he was pretty good at it.

My recollections of the ensuing period are very sharp. My grandmother was active in the women's suffrage movement and played a prominent role on the local scene. Grandfather always owned a Model T Ford. She would decorate it with streamers, dress me up in an Uncle Sam suit to sit in a box on one side, and we'd drive off to join a parade, the women wearing hats with ostrich plumes and decked out in their best Sunday-go-to-meetin' clothes. A name that kept cropping up in conversation was that of Carrie Nation, who went around chopping up saloons.

I remember when Prohibition and the Volstead Act came in, too. At the time I didn't think about it too seriously, but I'm sure that later on it would have been a traumatic experience for me to stand watching, as I did, while people literally emptied the saloons and poured barrels of good whiskey into the street. All that good booze down the drain!

Also around this time I vaguely recall my father making a permanent appearance on the scene, and that I considered it a rather disagreeable arrangement. I realize now that he must have had a disciplinary problem with me. I had been thoroughly spoiled by grandparents who never said "no," and I had the manners of a pig. One evening we were sitting at the dinner table and I did something he didn't approve of—probably putting my bread in the sugar bowl. He hit me so hard I was almost knocked off my chair. He was right, of course, even if his method was a bit drastic, but I didn't like anybody interfering with what I wanted to do at any given time, and I probably hated him ever after. In fact, this was the beginning of considerable animosity on my part, but I was very careful not to let him know.

TWO

BEFORE I GET too wrapped up in telling you about my days as a little kid in Falls City, I think I should tell you something about my family so you know who I'm talking about when I mention certain members from time to time.

On the maternal side my grandfather was George Prater, who was born in Mt. Moriah, Missouri, on August 1, 1869. He moved to Falls City in 1872 with his parents, and as a youth worked for his father in his blacksmith and carriage shop. He also raised greyhounds, and tried his hand as a part-time jockey. Then, while still a young man, he purchased a barbershop which he operated until he was well along in his eighties. In the meantime he served on the Falls City Council as police commissioner and representative for the Third Ward, from 1922 until 1929.

I have more respect for this man than any other I have ever known. He tried to teach me the importance of education (of which he had little), friends, and honesty. I never saw him lose his temper, and he never made an enemy. Despite the fact that he never made a lot of money, he always owned his own home, lived well, provided for his family well, and counted his friends in scores. I might have fared better if I had been able to follow his example more closely.

He married my grandmother, the former Josephine Bentley, in Falls City on July 25, 1891. She was born in Mound City, Missouri, on July 22, 1872, so they just missed getting married on her nineteenth birthday. They had two children, both girls: my mother, Chloe, who was born January 31, 1892, and my aunt, Hazel, February 24, 1895. They were given musical training at a local convent and became accomplished pianists—and they still play. They have mentioned those convent music lessons many times, and it seems the nuns were pretty strict. A wrong note brought a crack on the knuckles from a ruler. But say what you will about the teaching method, the main point is that my mother and Aunt Hazel have excellent legitimate musical backgrounds and both play very well. Aunt Hazel, though, had more of a natural feel for ragtime. She really took to it and developed a tremendous left hand, and played piano in silent-movie houses well into the Twenties.

My grandmother, Josephine Bentley Prater, had one of the most phenomenal memories of anyone I have ever known. She spent her girlhood in the farm country and was completely equipped with all the know-how of a farm woman of the last century, which was considerable. She would take me on a trip along the creek bank or in the woods and identify and pick every edible green that grew in the wild—such things as lamb's lettuce, sour doch, and young, tender dandelions—and make the most delectable dish you could possibly want, plus her home-baked bread which would melt in your mouth. She spent a lot of every summer and fall canning countless jars of vegetables and fruits, and jams and jellies for the hard winter months, and could while away a long, bad-weather afternoon with interesting stories about the Indians that still abounded in the area, and the quilting bees and box suppers that were a part of her early life.

My paternal grandfather, Frank H. Erwin, told stories about hiding in storm cellars when he was a tiny lad during the Civil War. He graduated from medical school in Louisville, Kentucky, in 1883, and upon graduation married Elizabeth Oglesby of that city. They moved to Brown County, Kansas, and there he established his practice. They had three children, two girls, Jean in 1885, and Bess, in 1887, and my father, James Oglesby Erwin, in 1890.

In the 1890s Frank Erwin took part in one of the great land rushes in the Oklahoma Territory and claimed a homestead, later giving it up to return to his medical practice in Hamlin, Kansas. Among other things, he raised his own tobacco and on occasion was known to drink rather heavily. Nonetheless, he delivered a great number of babies in Brown County, and to this day I still meet people in the area who tell me he was their family doctor.

My grandmother was Elizabeth Oglesby, born in 1864 into the southern aristocracy of Louisville, Kentucky—and no one in the family was ever allowed to forget it! She was a niece of Mary Todd Lincoln, closely related to President Zachary Taylor, and descended from the family of Dolly Madison. There are other family ties too, which I have never been able to truly clarify because I was never that close to them. But I do know that one of my father's cousins became a successful newspaperman with the *Chicago Tribune* and my grandmother had a brother, Dick Oglesby, who was a successful shipowner on the Great Lakes. Her other brother, Joseph Oglesby, M.D., was a nice, story-telling doctor from La Grange, Kentucky. I know nothing about his medical ability, but he could write marvelous prescriptions for that great Kentucky whiskey during Prohibition.

My father, James Oglesby Erwin, was born March 4, 1890, in Hamlin, Kansas, where he went to school and also studied music. I gather he became a pretty good cornet player at an early age, because he was playing in the Hamlin band at age ten. I don't know who her teachers were, but my Aunt Jean had a very good training on piano.

According to family history, my father was spoiled by his mother and after quite a bit of delinquent behavior was shipped off to a military school. (The story goes he made one of the local girls pregnant.) He attended Wentworth Military Academy in Lexington, Missouri, where he played football at 135 pounds and wound up each season with a broken nose. Sometime during his schooling he took off (a trick that became a habit for most of his life) and rode the rails, as it was known at the time. In other words, he bummed rides on freight trains to California, where he did more considerable traveling before finally returning to his home and obligations. He used to tell me fascinating tales about making meals from a loaf of bread and a can of beans and sharing "Mulligan Stew" in the hobo jungles.

While my father was still courting my mother, he rode a motorcycle 14 miles from his home in Kansas to Falls City, and one day the motorcycle stalled on a railroad crossing. He was hit by a passenger train and so severely hurt that he had to be packed in ice, and it was six weeks before they could tell whether or not his back was broken. Typically, the aftermath of this includes stories of his sneaking out of the hospital on crutches and driving a horse and buggy to visit his fiance'e, (my mother).

They were married in Falls City on January 20, 1912. During the first two years of their marriage they lived in St. Joseph, Missouri, and were active in the two theaters there, especially one called the Tootle Theater, after the people who owned it. When my mother went to the theater she took me along, and the interesting thing about it is the orchestra conductor was Leo Forbstein, later the titular head of Warner Brothers. His brother, Louis Forbstein, conducted the orchestra in the other theater and afterwards changed his name to Lou Forbes and became musical director and coordinator for Columbia Pictures.

My parents also lived for awhile in Abilene, Kansas, about 60 or 70 miles west of St. Joe. I guess I was about two years old. Abilene is close to Salina, the hometown of Willard Robison, one of the finest composers we've ever had, and in later years we were close friends. Anyway, midway between Abilene and Salina there's a well which the natives claim has the purest water in the United States. Willard and I used to joke about how much smarter we would have been if we had stuck to drinking that water instead of the stuff we were on.

Well, getting back to Falls City, when my father came home to stay he wasted no time in starting to teach me the scale on a cornet he brought with him. However, I was more attracted to the baritone horn because when I stood upright I was just the right height to reach the mouthpiece with the baritone resting on the floor. As a matter of fact I made my first public appearance on it. This took place at some sort of memorial service held at the Christian Church in Falls City, in the company of a girl named Gwendolyn Schultz and a boy born one week apart from me, Albert Maust. Albert was dressed as a soldier, and I guess because my father had been in the navy, I was a sailor. Gwen was a Red Cross nurse, a very popular figure after the war. I don't remember exactly what we did, except I blew a few notes on the baritone horn. Much more important, this was the beginning of a lifelong friendship with Albert, who is now the county judge in Falls City and married me to my present wife on July 17, 1957.

I visit Albert whenever I go back home. Although he decided to go legitimate and became a lawyer and a judge instead of a musician, he is an excellent tenor sax player. While he was a student at the University of Nebraska he played in Jimmy Joy's band, but never made music a full-time career. Nevertheless, he blows in the style of the great Kansas City tenormen and sounds a lot like Ben Webster. I once took Lou McGarity to hear him and Lou was very impressed. Albert still plays for local dances, and nobody seems

9

to find anything wrong with the county judge tooting a tenor on Saturday nights, altough Albert sometimes finds it a little strange to play for dancers one night and the next day find one of them in his court.

Shortly after my father came home from the navy, we moved—the first of many moves—to a house on Chase Street. The pace of musical activity picked up considerably. My father returned to playing trumpet and joined the town band (in those days every town had one), which was under the direction of a man who became one of his close friends, Claude Crandell. Every Wednesday night was band-concert night, and the Falls City band was pretty big, about 50 members. In addition to this, my father developed two other intense interests, jazz and the banjo, although in 1919 he was hardly unique because there were a lot of other people with similar interests. And by the way, I don't recall anybody calling it "jazz" in those days—although maybe they did.

Anyway, my father put a group together with the idea of playing for local affairs, and they would rehearse at our home. I can still remember some of the people involved—Joe Reavis, who played saxophone (C-melody, of course), his brother Dave, who played piano and was sometimes replaced by his sister Nellie, and Edward Tibbets Jr., who was a drummer. There may have been others, too, and probably were. As I recall, they wasted a lot of rehearsal time discussing the procurement of instruments. You've seen those old pictures with all the instruments piled in front of the band? Well, the general idea seemed to be that the more instruments you had, the better the band. Of course, I was always hanging around, and I developed the ability to pick up tunes or make them up, and my father encouraged the trick by letting me sit in and play.

On the subject of instruments, though, the Erwin family suffered a temporary setback. My father at this time was working in my grandfather's barbershop, and he was nothing if not friendly. My father was one of the friendliest men you would ever want to meet, and he became friendly with a handyman and porter who also worked for my grandfather. I don't remember the man's name, but my father felt sorry for him because he had no family and invited him to join us for Thanksgiving Day dinner. Shortly after this kind act, the porter took off, with my cornet and my father's favorite banjo. Needless to say, we never got them back.

To the best of my recollection there were two good drummers in Falls City at that time. One was a man named Tracey LaForge, who became my idol, and the other was Ed Tibbets, who I never got to know very well. There was always a dance on Saturday night at the Eagles Hall, and everybody went, unless he was too decrepit or otherwise unable. My mother and grandmother would take me. Like most kids I was fascinated by the drummers, and, in particular, Tracey's technique on the snare drum.

Frankly, at this stage I don't know how good or how bad he really was, but I thought then that he had the utmost in finesse. Then again, my opinion may have been influenced by the fact that in the daytime Tracey drove a horse-drawn laundry wagon, and because he knew my father and was a friend of the family, he would let me ride on the seat beside him, and in the winter allow other kids to hitch their sleds to the back of the wagon. Tracey was my hero.

10

Also of fond recollection during the period we lived on Chase Street is the large family that lived next door, the Herlings. This included four brothers and they were the best outdoorsmen I can remember. They always had several cages in their large yard holding various specimens of wild animals and birds native to our area: raccoons, possum, coyotes. Whenever they went rabbit hunting they would come home with plenty for themselves plus some for the neighbors.

I developed a lot of admiration for these men, especially when one of the brothers, while fishing on the Nemaha River, dove under a submerged door and came up with a 25-pound catfish that he caught barehanded.

The brother I knew best was Elmer, who was gifted with one of the most magnificent baritone voices I've ever heard. He sang popular music with some of the bands my father played with, and his voice always retained its quality. You must remember this was before the day of microphones, and a voice had to have power as well as tone. I still see Elmer occasionally.

THREE

I MUST ADMIT that one thing my father did right was to give me a good foundation on the trumpet. Besides teaching me the fundamentals himself, he sent me to his friend Claude Crandell for lessons. Crandell was a violinist and cornetist and well qualified to teach a youngster the rudiments of the horn. So I was on my way.

About 12 miles straight east from Falls City was a summer resort called Missouri Lakes—a ten-mile trip down to Rulo, on the Missouri River, which was crossed by ferry. My father's band got a job playing every Friday, Saturday, and Sunday at the Missouri Lakes Pavilion, and my mother and I would go with him. Missouri Lakes was quite a place. It consisted of two large lakes, probably a half-mile across, and lots of shoreline with cottages. It had a baseball diamond and several large picnic areas. By now his interest in the banjo was so strong that he had just about given up playing the trumpet. I think this was one of the main reasons he wanted me along, just so I could sit in and he could play the banjo. Actually, all I did was play choruses on the tunes I knew. "Smiles," I recall, was my big number, and I also did "Ja Da," and "Hindustan." I'm not sure that what I played was jazz, but it probably came out with a jazz feel at any rate. Another tune that was extremely popular but couldn't be considered jazz by any stretch of the imagination was "K-K-K-Katy." My father's big moment was a banjo solo on "The World Is Waiting for the Sunrise," but I doubt very much if he originated it, more likely he heard it someplace and copied it.

It was at Missouri Lakes that I witnessed my first Indian powwow, in reality just an excuse for the tribes to get together and have a huge outdoor barbecue. There were quite a few Indian tribes in that area of Nebraska, the Nemahas to the north, the Potawatomies to the south, and, nearby, the Sac-Foxe, and always a large number of them, from 800 to 1,000, would attend the powwows. The events were very colorful and I was quite impressed, so much so that it wasn't until I went to school with Indian kids that I realized Indians didn't always dress as they did at powwows.

I gained quite a bit of practical experience playing at Missouri Lakes, thanks to my father's preoccupation with the banjo. But to this day I have never been able to figure out why a guy who could play trumpet as well as he did wanted to play the banjo. The only possible reason I can think of is the importance he attached to rhythm in a dance band. He may have had the idea that nobody else could keep time as steady as he could. He was always harping on it, and used to resort to all kinds of tricks for keeping time in the band. In this connection, he was always working toward getting more volume out of the banjo so nobody could get away from him. One of his rituals was soaking the banjo heads in milk to soften them up, after which he would roll them on the hoops himself. Why milk, I don't know.

Before we go any further, let me say this about my father: he was a very talented man, quick-witted, and well-liked. But he had a restless, unpredictable nature and this, along with a few other problems in his make-up, sometimes sent him shooting off on tangents that were against his own best interests and those of his family. Some things he did very well. Had he concentrated on them a little more he could have been very successful. But he was his own worst enemy. The banjo thing was typical.

He worked at other things besides music. I guess he had to do a lot of things to scratch out a living. For one thing, and I haven't any idea where he learned the trade, he was an excellent barber. Whenever we made one of our moves, or he was in a strange town and needed work, he could always get a job in the local barbershop cutting hair.

We always had a phonograph and a lot of records. I can still remember some of the titles of the ones I used to play. "Chile Bean" was a very popular tune of the day, but in all the years since then I've only found one guy who remembered another one that sticks in my mind, "I Found a Rose in the Devil's Garden." We also had a lot of Ted Lewis records. Many years later I mentioned this to him and he told me that as early as 1910 he was making sides that sold over a million copies.

Around 1920 we moved into a second floor apartment in the Wall Building in Falls City. Quite often on weekends, dances were held in a combination armory and dance hall on the third floor, which made it pretty convenient—all we had to do was walk up one flight. I well remember the pop tunes: "Dardenella," "I'm Forever Blowing Bubbles," "Oh, What a Pal Was Mary," "Feather Your Nest," "Margie," and "San." In addition to playing at Wall's Hall, my father would play for dancing in neighboring areas, sometimes going into Kansas for jobs, as well as Nebraska towns. Since these jobs were relatively close to Falls City, usually a bunch of friends and dancers would follow the band to the job, which made it great to be playing for regulars as well as people from other towns. One of the regulars was a close friend and drinking buddy of my father's named Vic Gutz, who repaired electrical automotive parts. Sober he was a great guy, but when he attended these dances he usually wound up roaring drunk and hard to handle. At a dance in Linn, Kansas, he created such a disturbance he was thrown in jail. He was still wearing his work clothes, which were saturated with oil. So he peeled them off, stacked them in a corner of his cell, and set fire to them and the jail. Another time he drove his car over a half-mile railroad trestle, bouncing from tie to tie, in order to escape the local constable.

13

Usually I was allowed to sit in and play only on the local jobs. They would sit me on top of the piano to play trumpet. As I see it now, my extrovert father probably considered it good showmanship to feature me the way he did. He had another trick of bringing friends home to the house and making me play for them while he accompanied me on the banjo.

On the other hand, we often played at home for our own amusement, with my mother on the piano. She was probably the best musician in the family, but she had a hang-up about steady rhythm. She could never quite get the hang of it, for some reason. After a while this would send my father into one of his long tirades about the importance of keeping time. As I said before, he made a big thing out of it.

I'm not sure, but I think my Aunt Hazel may have been in show business at one time. I seem to recall a story that she met my uncle, Harry Bivens, when they were both appearing in a show around 1915; in 1916 they were married. Aunt Hazel was a very outgoing person, and an excellent and experienced pianist. Since we were all people of moderate circumstances, the wives in my family worked as well as the husbands. In 1920 my aunt and uncle moved to Kansas City. This was the beginning of a chain of events that was to affect all of us. My uncle owned a large automobile which he converted into a taxi, an easy way to start your own business. My aunt went to work playing piano in the movie theaters.

Kansas City has always been very active musically, and especially so from the days after the first World War. Sheet music was the big thing then. Every Woolworth store always had a piano player (better still, one who could sing) to demonstrate the popular tunes of the day. Sheet music sales in the millions were not unusual.

Well, Aunt Hazel was not only a good pianist, she had a find soprano voice, and with her personality she had all the qualifications of a good demonstrator. So she got a job in a song shop that was located at 12th and Main Streets in Kansas City, a location that was right in the middle of the action in town. (This 12th Street, by the way, was the inspiration for the "12th Street Rag.")

The place was called "Eddie Kuhn's Song Shop" and all it sold was sheet music. It got to be quite a hangout for the many musicians who were working in the area. All of the big hotels had ten- and twelve-piece bands, and there were at least a dozen other large bands working around the city. What's more, Eddie Kuhn—who played piano along the lines of Vincent Lopez—was in a band-booking business with two other musicians, Emil Chaquette, a violinist, and Johnny Campbell, a drummer. Between the three of them they cornered some of the best jobs in town and kept quite a stable of musicians working for them. Chaquette's big asset as an orchestra leader was his strong resemblance to Douglas Fairbanks (no mean advantage at that period) and Kuhn and Campbell had the big band which played at the Hotel Baltimore.

Eddie Kuhn was a mixer and a good salesman with the right political connections, another big asset in the Kansas City atmosphere of the Pendergast era. The Kuhn-Chaquette-Campbell office kept a lot of musicians busy doing party work, playing hotel jobs, etc., so the song shop was a hub of

14

activity and it was only natural that Aunt Hazel began to meet many of the musicians. In particular, she often spoke of the first time Joe Sanders, known as "The Old Lefthander," walked into the shop wearing one of those billed caps that were so popular in the early Twenties and asked if he could try out a new tune on the piano. His playing created quite a sensation and made a big impression on Aunt Hazel. He and Carleton Coon, who played drums and always had a bottle of gin stashed behind them, were coleaders of the Coon-Sanders Orchestra, which became the house band for WDAF, the radio station owned by the *Kansas City Star*. More about this later.

It was only a matter of course that word of all this musical activity should filter back to us in Falls City and my father, sensing an opportunity to make it big on the musical scene, decided to move the family to Kansas City. His ambition was to prove himself on banjo, not the trumpet, which was sort of tragic because, as a trumpet player, he was certainly good enough to hold down a chair in any band in the city. I don't believe he was ever too great as a jazzman—although it's hard for me to evaluate this because I was so young—but I don't remember being very impressed by his jazz playing (called "hokum" choruses then; "jazz" was still a term that wasn't used very often). On the other hand, as a banjo player he definitely wasn't anything spectacular. I'd say offhand there must have been 400 or more banjo players in Kansas City who were better. This is where the tragic part comes in, because, in spite of this, he wouldn't even take jobs doubling on trumpet. He was going to make it on the damn' banjo, come hell or high water!

So we relocated on a street close to Mercy Hospital in the north end of the city. To tide us over until he set the world on fire with his banjo, my father got a job in a barbershop nearby. Then, as if the move to Kansas City wasn't enough, the family was subjected to a second traumatic experience. My mother decided to let him cut her hair. She had always had beautiful, dark-brown hair that fell to her knees, but the move to the big city had made up her mind to go modern and have it bobbed. It was quite a family event, believe me.

Through Aunt Hazel, who introduced him around, my father began to make contacts with the local musicians. He managed to get a few playing jobs on banjo, but before long it must have become pretty obvious even to him that he was not making a great stir in musical circles. Whether he decided to use me as a wedge to get jobs for himself, or just because he wanted to show me off, he started taking me around with him. By then, 1921, I could play a pretty good melodic semblance of jazz, and he made a big thing out of it.

In the meantime, Aunt Hazel had become good friends with Joe Sanders. The Coon-Sanders band was rapidly gaining a national reputation because of its radio broadcasts. With an announcer at WDAF, Leo Fitzpatrick—who I was to meet again years later in Detroit—they had formed a show, "The Kansas City Nighthawks," which went on the air every night at midnight, and they were being heard all over the country. WDAF was a powerful station for those days before network radio, probably rated about 50,000 watts. The battery-operated radios—the Atwater-Kents and the Fried-Eismanns (two names that stick in my mind)—had no trouble picking it up late at night. DX-ing, as they called tuning in long-distance stations, had become a national pastime. A lot of people were losing sleep just so they could brag to each other the next day about the distant stations they had pulled in. Consequently, the "Nighthawks" show was becoming very popular.

I don't know how he promoted it, although I suspect that Aunt Hazel had something to do with setting it up, but my father took me to the radio station and we went on the air. On the first broadcast I played a tune called "Tuck Me to Sleep in My Old Kentucky Home," and he backed me up on banjo. It wasn't jazz, of course, but I guess it was pretty well received because while we were in Kansas City broadcasting got to be a habit. My father, always the opportunist, made sure he maintained a close association with the station. For that matter, I guess the experience didn't hurt me either.

But the Kansas City period didn't last too long. My father, probably because he wasn't making the big success on banjo he had expected and couldn't establish himself with any of the better working bands, began drinking heavily. Every Saturday night he would get completely stoned. I remember one instance when my uncle and I walked a couple of blocks one night to pick him up off the streetcar tracks.

While we were there, though, Kansas City made a big impression on me, especially the food. On hot summer evenings the air was filled with the cries of the pushcart peddlers selling hot tamales. Maybe hot tamales do not sound like food for a hot summer night, but they sold plenty. Then there were the barbecue pits, like no place else I've ever been, turning out meat flavored with a sauce that is the most unique in the country. Nowhere have I ever tasted sauce like the stuff they made in Kansas City. They used to say that if it was left overnight in a metal pan it would eat a hole right through the enamel. The pits were located in the black sect: ans of the city, great stone ovens about eight feet square, or even larger, with only a small opening in front in order to hold in the smoke. The bottoms were always loaded with hickory logs, never any other kind, which were dampened to make them smoke. The meat was slow-cooked on iron grates. After a long period of time some of the ovens had soot on the wall several inches thick. There was one pit called the "Old Kentuck" at 17th and Vine that barbecued a ton of meat a week, mostly ribs, but also beef for sandwiches. The short end of the ribs was the best because they had the most meat. But the unique quality of the Kansas City barbecue was the sauce. I don't know how they made it, but I have never tasted anything like it anywhere else.

My Aunt Hazel quit her job at the song shop, and went back to playing in the theaters. This brought about another interesting phase of the Kansas City stay. I was now eight years old, and my aunt and uncle started a running gag of entering me in amateur contests. These were very big at the time as a means for the outlying theaters to stimulate business. We would look in the papers for a theater that was running a contest. Then my aunt would take me there and enter me as a contestant. Since the other contestants were usually singers and dancers and the audiences were pretty fed up with these, all I had to do was play trumpet and a little banjo and I usually won.

It got to be a nice source of income, although I don't remember exactly how much I got for winning first prize—maybe fifteen or twenty dollars. My uncle, who wasn't a musician but nevertheless got quite a kick out of what we were doing, would look at me with a big grin as my aunt and I would be leaving to enter another contest, and ask, "Well, are we going to bring home the bacon again tonight?"

After awhile, we began to run out of theaters, and they got wise to us when we showed up at the same one twice. But later on in Falls City I made an appearance at a local theater and won what I considered to be a tremendous prize—a free pass to the theater for a year! To me this was the greatest thing that ever happened because those were the great days of the silents, Pauline Stark, William S. Hart, Douglas Fairbanks! I had it made!

It was around the end of 1921 when my family returned to Falls City. My father's drinking had become a real problem and he wasn't getting anywhere in Kansas City, so we went back home for a fresh start. For a while my father behaved himself. He went to work in the music department of a furniture store, gave up drinking, and started a boys' band.

This last was no small enterprise, because it grew into a project the whole town became interested in, with about 50 kids in the band. We lived in a large house on Harlan Street, and it became a mecca for young people. I made a lot of friends, and my father was instrumental in starting several kids on musical careers. It seems to me that somebody was always playing music at our house.

FOUR

IN THE FALL of 1921 I started third grade at Central School in Falls City, the third generation of my family to attend this elementary school. My mother had gone to school there, as had my grandfather.

It was an interesting and exciting time in my life. I was eight years old, I loved movies and popcorn, and I had a free pass to see all the pictures I wanted to. I idolized Douglas Fairbanks in "Robin Hood" and "The Four Horsemen" and spent my spare time making bows out of hickory wood and arrows tipped with spent rifle shells. With some friends close to my age, I kept busy playing Robin Hood and the war games that had temporarily replaced cowboys and Indians, enjoying the place I lived.

To me Falls City was a fascinating place. I still remember that winter when after the sidewalks had been cleared of snow it was stacked so high on Main Street that a small guy like me couldn't see from one side to the stores on the other. The pop tunes I was playing included "Ain't We Got Fun," "Peggy O'Neil," "Wang Wang Blues," and "When Francis Dances with Me."

The boys' band my father started proved to be a great experience for me, as well as all the other people involved in it. My father was working for Reaves and MacComber, who owned the music store, and in addition was teaching a large number of music students at home. The band did a lot of rehearsing, but it also played some concerts which were very well received by the townspeople (only to be expected since these were the parents and friends of the musicians). It also gave me some experience in reading brass-band parts, something I hadn't had prior to this.

In addition to the boys' band, ostensibly organized as a civic project, but obviously a promotion to sell more instruments for the music store, my father began to expand his danceband operation. He augmented it into a larger group, for one thing, and although I can't remember their names, it seems to me we had a couple of the musicians staying at our home on Harlan Street, and we had musical instruments all over the place. I distinctly recall a xylophone and a baritone sax, plus several C-melody saxes, which were the big thing in those days. As I look back, I would say my father was developing what later came to be called a "territorial" band, although the lack of paved roads made a trip of 30 or 40 miles a pretty good jump. Nevertheless, the band played an area

18

that included towns as far away as Horton, Kansas, Nebraska City, and Auburn, which meant that they ranged as far as 50 miles away from Falls City.

The circuits these traveling bands played during the spring and summer months, when the weather and the roads were good, probably developed along with the bands themselves, because in the beginning some of the facilities were primitive. A typical spot was called Burke's Park, owned and operated by two brothers named Burke. The word "Park" made the name sound impressive, but actually the place was just a pavilion for dancing, made of wood. This particular pavilion had a roof and was a pretty fair establishment of its kind, but it wasn't unusual for some to be only dance floors without a roof. Burke's Park was a Sunday-night dance hall.

Other places in other towns held dances on different nights of the week— Sunday in Horton, Wednesday in Wymore, Friday in Falls City—and this was the beginning of the circuits which later became the regular routes of the territorial bands. People in the area were familiar with the schedules and they would come from all over to the various towns to dance. Probably the main reason Burke's Park stands out in my memory is because I always associate it with a story my father liked to tell about a gig he played there with his band.

The piano player working in the band was a competent musician, I imagine, but he had something of a shady background. At any rate, the story relates he had been in jail, or something on that order. The band was booked to play Burke's Park, but when they got there they found out there was no piano. My father brought this to the attention of one of the Burke brothers, who told him it presented no problem. All they had to do was walk across the road to his house, get the piano in his livingroom and bring it over to the pavilion. How they accomplished this is vague, but the point of the story is that along around the middle of the evening, while the band was playing and the piano player was pounding away on the keys, the other Burke brother, who had been out of town for some reason, came home and found the piano missing.

He probably guessed what had taken place, but the first indication the band had of anything out of the ordinary was when he rushed up on the bandstand, shoved the piano player out of the way, and proceeded to remove the bottom panel from the piano and take out a metal strongbox. According to the story the box held $8,000 in cash. Afterwards the band got many a chuckle over speculating what their piano player might have done if he had known what was inside his piano.

I was still too young to work with the band on a regular basis, but I sat in with them once in awhile and I rehearsed with them. I never played with the Falls City Band directed by Claude Crandell. More than likely I could not read well enough (if I could read at all at that time) but aside from that, my interest was in playing the popular songs of the day. I did not care too much for marches or the semiclassical things turned out by the Falls City Band, although I was exposed to some of this when I played in the boys' band. Then, somewhere around 1922 one of those unexpected incidents took place that seem casual and unimportant at the time but can have a long-term influence that stays with you forever.

19

As it is, I have no idea where the man came from, or where he disappeared to afterwards, and I don't know the circumstances under which my father met him, except it's a fair guess that since both of them liked to drink, this is how they became acquainted. However it came about, they started talking and during the conversation it came out that the stranger, who was only staying in town for a couple of days, was living with his wife and two kids in a tent he had pitched in the city park . . . and he was a trumpet player. I'm pretty vague about the particulars, but according to the story he was not just any trumpet player of the run-of-the-mill variety, but a fine, legitimate musician who had worked with Sousa and several others of the big-name brass bands. As I believe I've mentioned, my father liked to brag, and he told him about me and brought him home to hear me play.

So I played for the man, and he played for me. Afterwards he said to my father something like: "Tell you what I'll do, if it's all right with you. You let me have this young man for a full afternoon, and I will give him a sound that will remain with him for all of his life."

My father agreed, so the stranger sat me on a piano bench and spent all that afternoon teaching me to play with an open throat and a lip vibrato. He gave me all the mechanics, at the same time forewarning me against getting too wide a vibrato or too slow, and especially emphasized keeping an open throat while blowing. At the time I was not aware of what he was talking about, but I must have absorbed enough of what he said about playing with an open throat (he was implying an unrestricted air column), because I've played that way ever since.

This man's name was W. D. (Bill) Dorsey. Through the years I have made a number of attempts to find out more about him from other brass-band musicians that might have played with him—or at least have heard of him—but without success.

Along about this time I also developed another faculty in playing the horn which was considered pretty unusual then, but not much of an accomplishment in this day of high registers: a pretty fair pedal register, or an octave below low C. It was probably due to the thinness of my lips at that age, but at 9 or 10 I could play five octaves on the instrument, the usual middle C, low C, high C, and could skip an octave from low C to pedal C and play somewhat accurately in the register from pedal C down to a full octave to double pedal C. This ability inspired my father to regard me as something of a freak.

My experiences with accomplished trumpet players of the era were not all as benign as the one with Bill Dorsey. I have in mind an incident that took place around this same period. My father was performing on trumpet with the Falls City concert band at a large outdoor picnic being held in a nearby resort called Sun Springs. He suggested I go along with my horn and play with the band for experience. I did. I played the first third of the concert, really enjoying myself, and thought I was doing fine.

Then during the first break, while all of the band members were enjoying refreshments and mingling with the crowd, my father met an old friend, a well-known cornetist with the bands of surrounding towns. His name was George Willey. I'm sure he was a good cornetist and a nice man, but after

20

meeting him my father told me, "Let Mr. Willey use your horn. He's going to play the rest of the concert with our band."

Needless to say, I deeply resented being displaced, and I didn't care how important the intruder was. It wouldn't have made any difference if it had been Herbert L. Clarke. I was burned.

The band was set up on an open platform with the conductor in the middle, and all of the band chairs arranged so they faced the conductor. This meant the musicians had their backs to the audience. When the band started playing again I had a bright idea to soothe my injured feelings. I went around collecting a good-sized pile of dry grass, heaped it under Mr. Willey's chair, and set fire to it. Fortunately, my father discovered the blaze and kicked it out before any serious damage was done, but he took a pretty dim view of my action. Although I don't recall the punishment, I'm sure it suited the crime.

Many years later the story had an interesting postscript in the hey-day of Ripley's "Believe It Or Not," cartoons, when he depicted George Willey as a musician who played actively for 75 years.

FIVE

SOMEWHERE BETWEEN 1923 and 1924 we moved again. This time it was to Horton, Kansas, about 30 miles south of Falls City, where my father opened a branch music store for a company in Atchison, Kansas, called the Carl Latinzer Music Company.

Horton was another railroad town, similar in size to Falls City, and was also a division point for the Rock Island Railroad in the same way Falls City was for the Missouri-Pacific. It had a large Mexican population who worked for the railroad, and a lot of the local business was tied in with the railroad. Like Falls City, it was located in the middle of an agricultural area and not too far from Indian reservations. I seem to remember it was considered pretty lush selling territory, even though Horton was only about 30 miles from Atchison. A short distance today; you have to take into consideration that in the Twenties it was just the opposite, therefore the necessity for a branch store.

I must admit my father was a good salesman. He knew all the rules about openings and closings, and he never met a stranger. He was a very amiable guy to talk to, so he could sell. The only trouble with his sales technique, as far as I was concerned, was that he had a fund of stock phrases which he used over and over, and when you heard them as often as I did they got pretty tiresome. Things like, "Anyone who doesn't like children and music—there's something wrong with them." Or "Listen to my son play, and he's only been playing about six months."

I heard these remarks pretty often, because if it meant making a sale he would take me (and my mother) along to cinch a prospect. One of his pet tricks was to put a piano (in those days, very often it was a player piano) into a house on trial, and then make an appointment to visit the people in the evening, taking us along to entertain. When he would spring his, "Listen to my son—" line, it was the signal for me to whip out my horn and go into some cornball thing. Sometimes it was a trio, with my mother on piano and my father on banjo, and sometimes duets, with the two of us on trumpets. Mostly it depended on what instruments he was trying to sell. He made the entertainment fit the situation.

22

I recall too that he made a lot of sales to the Indians on the nearby reservations, especially pianos. I would not be surprised if a lot of these deals involved some hanky-panky because there was some kind of an arrangement whereby anything the Indians bought was paid for by the government. I know my father visited the Indian agents regularly to collect his money. Anyway, one way or another he made a lot of sales.

When we moved to Horton we lived in a large apartment on the second floor of the same building that housed the music store. This was very convenient for my parents, because my mother helped out quite a bit in the store, especially when it was necessary for my father to go on the road for his sales efforts in the neighboring rural areas.

The building was a great place for a ten- or eleven-year-old. For one thing, in the basement were stored 20 or 30 old-fashioned pump organs, and with their many stops and different sounds they were fascinating for a guy to play. For another, the "backyard" was actually a block-square city park, complete with bandstand. And most important of all, there was the music store itself, well stocked with a large supply of musical instruments and just about every important accessory.

The store featured the Conn line of band instruments. I still remember a complete display which I have never seen duplicated. The major instruments—saxophone, clarinet, trumpet, and trombone—were finished in bright red, blue, and green lacquer, and studded with varicolored imitation stones in a variety of patterns. I'm sure none were ever sold, but they made a great display.

A full line of pianos, with Gulbransen and Ampico as the featured lines, was carried by the store, and most of these were players. My father was especially successful in placing ready music in homes. And in addition, available was a full line of sheet music, phonographs, and an extensive selection of radios. Outstanding was the Edison phonograph with the reproducer arm controlled by an arm at the side of the console.

Great emphasis was placed on the sale of radios and the accessories needed to run them. Radio was a fascinating medium in 1924, with everyone caught up in the race for more power and long-distance reception. (It was also the year my uncle, Charles G. Grau, who had just married my Aunt Jean in Montana, sent a crystal set he had made for me.) I vividly remember my father setting up the complicated installations for those radios in the houses of the purchasers, all kinds of wires for the wet and dry batteries needed to operate them.

I don't know who designed it, but my father had one of the most efficient and unique systems to facilitate the delivery of a piano I have ever seen. He had a flatbed Model T truck, and a crank tilted the bed to an upright position, so a piano could be rolled right up against it and anchored by heavy straps. Then the truck bed could be cranked back into position, so the piano lay on its back. In this way one man, with the aid of wheeled dollies, could deliver a piano.

The music store itself was large and took in a lot of floor area, but a portion of the front was partitioned off and was operated as a millinery shop by a lady named Miss Emma Kral. Miss Kral was proud of her German

23

heritage and did her best to teach me some of the German language.

I attended school in Horton for the fourth, fifth, and sixth grades. In retrospect I view it the most advanced school system academically of any I attended . . . and I attended quite a few. I can still remember the names of my three teachers for those years—Mary Ruth, Daisy McKee, and Mrs. Simpson. The last had married a local druggist, William Simpson. When you consider they were teaching students between the ages of 10 and 12, the current events topics we were made aware of are rather astounding. We learned all about the Bonus Bill, the Teapot Dome Scandal, Naval Armaments Limitations, and the Coolidge presidency.

In those years I began to seek out information on my own, too. "The American Weekly" (the Hearst scandal sheet) became a regular source of stimulation for me. Disregarding the constant screaming about the "Red Menace," the Hearst trademark, the stories about the French Surete used to hold my interest, and a feature I followed closely was the reports on Goddard's experiments with rockets. A trip to the moon was suggested at this early stage, but I doubt if anyone really believed it to be possible. Eckner's ill-fated dirigibles, the *Los Angeles* and the *Shenandoah*, were big news. Jack Dempsey, Babe Ruth, Red Grange, Bobby Jones, and the Four Horsemen of Notre Dame were the sports heroes. The hit tunes were the Berlin waltzes ("All Alone," "What'll I Do?," etc.), "Charlie My Boy," "Always," "Dinah," "Five Foot Two," "Yessir, That's My Baby" and "The Prisoner's Song." They were certainly interesting and exciting times.

My musical activities during this period brought me into association with some very talented young people. These included two children from a family in the dry-goods business, Jack (Vincent), and Betty (Tarr); Janet and James Hacker, whose father was a doctor; the daughter of a violinist, Margaret Farley; and the children of a druggist, Mary Jo, Catherine, and Camille Lindsy, were some of those I played with in school or civic performances.

We were all under the guidance of a very colorful band director, leader of the city band, W. C. "Bud" Nadeau, who had been a fixture on the scene and at the center of music in Horton going as far back as 1886. During his early career he had toured with circus and tent shows as a cornetist in the bands. I learned a great deal from being under "Bud's" supervision.

For the most part I played with a group of boys who were a little older than I was, Joe White on trombone, Ray Whaley, piano, Jim Harker, saxophone, and Norman Schuetz on drums. We played together for more than a year, and of course had a lot of musical fun. The best thing to come out of my association with the group was my friendship with Norman Schuetz. Norman came from a large family. His father, John Schuetz, operated a farm in Mercier, Kansas, a community not far from Horton. Some of the greatest experiences I remember from this time were when I would be invited to visit. They gave me a chance to roam the fields, hunt with the boys, ride the horses, and play in the haymow. There must have been eight people in that family, and I'll never forget the great meals and the warm friendliness.

About this time I heard a couple of bands that would forever influence my future musical concepts. Up until then I had never played in a band that used a bass. One evening I heard a group called the "K. U. Footwarmers," and a short time later another, "The Coloradoans." Each had a tuba in the lineup. Listening to them opened up a whole new vista of sound to my ears. My sense of what is right in music told me that nothing could ever be quite right in a rhythm section that did not include the low frequencies. From this point on it became my ambition to join a band with a tuba (string bass was yet to come into the picture).

Aside from musical associations, I had a couple of close friends in Horton who were with me in the Boy Scouts. One, LaVerne Graves, lived close by, and the other, Henry McNary, lived on a farm outside of town. We conducted our own electrical experiments and took part in all the other activities common to boys our age. Years later, in the Forties, I met them both in New York. LaVerne had became a very successful hair stylist, and Henry was an executive with Boeing Aircraft.

Incidentally, one of the things I remember about Horton was listening to William Jennings Bryan make a speech in the park behind the music store. Not that I had any real knowledge or understanding of who he was or what he stood for, but I was told he was a person of importance and I should go see him, so I did. I believe this was a short time before the famous Stokes case.

On September 28, 1925, my brother, James Erwin Jr., was born. He was something of a surprise but a welcome stranger to an active twelve-year-old, and he stepped up the family activities considerably.

We were in the middle of the Charleston era, and although I was still too young to be working with dance bands, except for sitting in at Burke's Park, I did play onstage in a theater with a kid's band with a whole line of Charleston dancers in front of us. As for Burke's Park, by then some of the fine black bands out of Kansas City and St. Joe were coming through. I can't be sure now who they were, but I do know that one fellow, now in New York, whose father also worked for Carl Latinzer in Atchison, had a very good band that played in a park outside of Atchison. His name is Jesse Stone, and he had an eight- or ten-piece outfit that was really fine.

Most of the towns in Kansas and Nebraska had small black populations. They were treated with the same respect and consideration as anybody else. In fact, I played occasional dates with a mixed band that operated out of Hiawatha, Kansas, around 1924, led by a local baker. In the band were two cousins who were black—one, an excellent sax player far ahead of his time, named Earl Graves, and the other, a trombonist, a wonderful man named Hawkins. I have often wondered if he was somehow related to Coleman, who came from St. Joe. Anyway, the point is there was never any criticism of the fact we had a mixed band.

While we lived in Horton I continued to pick up quite a bit of experience in various musical activities around the Horton-Hiawatha area. Hiawatha had a promoter named Billy Schenkleberger who had been pretty active in

25

theatrical productions, carnivals, and motion pictures, and he opened three ballrooms. In one of them, The Red Mill, I played quite a bit. Then the theater in Horton, which had started out as a movie house, began playing repertory companies who would come to town for a week or two and put on plays. I took what they did pretty much for granted then, but now I'm very impressed when I realize these companies were capable of presenting a new play every night—or at least every other night. I remember one, in particular, the North Brothers, because in the company were a couple of professional musicians who traveled with the show. These men, along with some local musicians, made up a small orchestra to play for the stage presentations. It was my first meeting with a trumpet player who had false teeth. This man with the North Brothers had figured out a way to put a rubber lug between the plates on each side of his mouth so he could blow without loosening the plates.

There were all kinds of musical affairs taking place in those days, such as dances after the rodeos, which were pretty common, and I recall my father bringing in the Coon-Sanders band from Kansas City to play for some kind of fair. This was quite an accomplishment, and I imagine it was a bright feather in his cap. He spent the day in renewing acquaintances in the band, especially with Fitzpatrick, the chief himself, who came along too. They had a few snorts together.

In spite of the fact that those were the days of Prohibition, there was a considerable amount of heavy drinking. One of my heroes was a piano player named Min Holland, who I played a few dates with at Burke's Park. He played a whale of a piano and I enjoyed playing with him, but he usually wound up the night getting stoned. My father's weekend drinking was developing too, and when he really got going he became a roaring, helpless drunk. He used to buy a pint of grain alcohol from the local bootlegger and dilute it by pouring half of it into another pint bottle filled with water. He didn't bother to flavor it as some people did, and sometimes after he was loaded I saw him make the mistake of taking a nip from the undiluted bottle. Loaded or not, that shook him up. Grain alcohol burns like fire.

His drinking grew more prevalent as time went on, and the usual things began to take place. He neglected the business and debts began to pile up. Shortly after my brother was born, and my Grandfather Erwin died of dropsy (predicting his own demise about 30 days before), he simply disappeared. He left my mother with a new-born baby and me, a pile of unpaid bills, and no means of support. So once again my mother's father came to our rescue and took us all back to Falls City. The Horton period was at an end.

SIX

IN THE SUMMER of 1926 I began one of the most active and extended periods of playing I ever put in with the Falls City musicians. Albert Maust always took an active role in our musical organizations. He was a thorough musician and a good saxophonist even then. Donald Hysell was an excellent drummer, and with Hollis Putnam on piano we had the nucleus of a good band and began to get quite a few jobs. We worked the area near to Falls City, Horton, and Hiawatha, and by the time fall came around we had a regular night each week at High's Hall in Falls City for public dancing, and another in a hall on the fair grounds in Hiawatha called the Green Mill. This was operated by our friend Billy Schenkleberger, who also found occasions to use us in his theater in downtown Hiawatha.

In almost every place we played the audience was made up of friends and people we knew. Half of the fun was everybody collecting at one of the local hangouts after the job for a hamburger or a dish of chili. Due to the size of the towns involved, only one restaurant stayed open all night, and these also served as stops for the overnight buses. Falls City, in particular, was often used as a stop because it was exactly midway between Omaha and Kansas City and on the main highway.

The spa in Falls City was "Brown's Cafe," operated by a Mr. Brown who had migrated to Falls City from Nova Scotia and who knew the secret of preparing good food that appealed to young customers. This made his restaurant just as popular in the daytime as a meeting-place for the coke-and-burger set. There wasn't any great excess of drinking among the young people in our area for a number of reasons. Prohibition, of course, was in full force, but bootleg booze, while available, was very expensive. More important, though, drinking just didn't seem to be the most popular pastime. For my part, during this period I was having a great time both socially and musically, and the best part about it was that in spite of my youth I knew it.

That Fall I started school at the Falls City Junior High, which I enjoyed a lot. It was the first time I had different teachers for each subject, and the ones I remember best were Miss Gagnon, Miss Fish, and my manual-training teacher, Mr. Smith, who also played the clarinet in the Falls City

27

band. I struggled in a declamation class to deliver the oration "The Return of Regulus" and was awarded a blue ribbon for it. I remember the beginning of the work to this day.

There were two other musical groups in Falls City. A good trumpet and tuba player, Harry Seegar, was always active in music and sometime played with us, but he had his own group too. The other was a territorial band led by John Whetstine. This was an eight-piece unit that traveled a wide area and had a busy schedule.

As for our band, we were having personnel problems. Hollis Putnam left Falls City in the fall, and for a short time we had a fellow named Carson on piano. Then he moved to Idaho, and we were left with a critical hole in the band. Maust, always enterprising, took inventory of our situation and then decided which instrument we needed the least. He centered on the fellow who played third alto in some of our sessions, Jack Hutchings, and informed Jack that from that point on he would be our piano player. Of course, you have to understand that the type of piano player we needed was only required to play the right chords in the rhythm section.

The Fall of '26 was notable for another development, the beginning of a regular season of burlesque at a Falls City theater formerly used as the opera house. This was the "Gehling Theater," and our group was chosen to be the house orchestra. The manager was a man affectionately known as "Muggins" Nedro, and a house piano player, Frank Vaughn, took care of that situation for us. For the rest we had three saxes—Maust, Jack Hutchings, and John Falter (later to become known as one of America's top artists)—and our drummer, Don Hysell, who enjoyed the show he was playing a great deal. Bob Graham, another friend, joined us as a utility man and filled in wherever he was needed.

We really had a great time on this job, even if we didn't make musical history. I arranged a system of signals with John Falter, which he has recalled even recently, using our feet when it was time for him to play or to lay out. He contends, however, that he got fired from the band, and I can't recall this or who would have the authority to fire anybody. On the other hand, he's correct in pointing out that one of the burlesque comedians, Bozo Davis, only a few years later joined one of those splinter political groups in the West and was actually nominated for vice president of the United States.

The situation which sticks most vividly in my recollection of our burlesque stint is that of one of the girls. After she finished with her stripping and shaking onstage, she went back to her dressing room to nurse her baby, who traveled with her on the road.

On the whole, I guess we did a pretty good job at the Gehling, because we were told a new theater was being built, and that Mr. Carver, the manager of the new "Rivoli Theater," wanted to employ us since a limited vaudeville and presentation policy was being planned. So we were in the Rivoli when it opened in 1927. The vaudeville acts were typical of those used in the smaller theaters around the country, using localized people rather than the topflight (and expensive) acts from the big-time circuits. This helped us because the music was less critical than in the more complex theaters. But I still

28

remember one tune that was almost a standard for fast-action acts like jugglers and dog acts. This was the "Russian Rag"—which I was never able to play. I was always reminded of this in later years whenever fast moving acts insisted on working to "The Sabre Dance." I could never play that one either.

Like the Gehling, the Rivoli solved our piano problem by providing a really good piano player, Sterling Grabin, who played with us and then doubled on the organ during the showing of the moving pictures, still silent during the early days at the theater. Grabin, I believe, came from Sioux City, Iowa, and was a slightly built, extremely well-dressed, and excellent musician, but on occasion he had a tendency to drink too much. We used to have lots of fun at his expense when he was stewed—in retrospect, this is sad. Like so many people he was more than likely doing himself a lot of harm and this is not funny. But I can remember a couple of times when he passed out on the organ during the picture with his arms pressing down the keys, and someone had to go into the pit and pull him off.

For our grand opening at the Rivoli we put our all into a production number. We decided on the new song hit "Moonlight on the Ganges," not only for its popularity but because its structure of block chords descending in half tones made it a perfect vehicle for our three-man sax section, and implied just enough mysterioso for us to get the most out of the great lighting facilities in the new theater. Donald Hysell had seen several stage shows presented by Waring's Pennsylvanians, so he knew how to set up an attractive display of percussion equipment on a riser in the back of the band. To enhance this, our artist saxophone player, John Falter, did a great painting on the front of the bass drum. It depicted a sailing ship foundering in a stormy sea, dramatically intensified by lights inside the drum which flashed on and off. John's artistic effort has always been true to his hometown. In 1975 the U.S. Post Office issued a postage stamp of his design, a portrait of the Falls City water tower which was close to his boyhood home.

As for our Rivoli opening, our presentations were well received by the patrons and management alike, and we had a very successful and interesting musical season.

Toward the end of the school season in the spring of 1927 we heard from my father. He was in the area of Waukeegan, Ill., and he launched one of his deceptive campaigns preparatory to returning to his family. As usual, my mother believed his lies about going straight, giving up drinking, and working hard, and, by the time summer came around, it had been decided that we would be reunited.

We moved to a Missouri suburb of Kansas City called Liberty, a college town about ten or twelve miles from the big town and half way on the route to a lovely resort and health spa called Excelsior Springs, where people came from all over in large numbers to take advantage of the mineral springs. We moved into a pretty grubby apartment. My father went to work selling roofing and siding, and other construction materials, for a Kansas City firm—a career he was to follow for most of his remaining years—commuting between Liberty and K.C. Liberty is not far from the former home of the James brothers, Jesse and Frank, and at that time some people still claimed to remember them—or at least they were familiar with their exploits. The courthouse in Liberty still had a bullet hole in it as a souvenir of a James raid on a local bank, during which a little boy was killed. There was a lot of indignation over this episode, but it seemed that otherwise the James boys weren't regarded too badly.

I don't recall how it came about, but I was asked to play with a band consisting of a group of students from William Jewel College, which is located in Liberty. The leader was a premed student, Bud Carr, and his most active associate was a saxophone player named Avery D'Arnold. I worked with them first in a College Tea Room in town, and also played some fraternity parties. I don't remember if the band was good or bad, but the exposure was good for me because it was through a piano player on one of Bud Carr's jobs that I met two very good musicians, George and Norman Patterson, who had good connections and played a lot of jobs within driving distance of Liberty.

Norman Patterson, an excellent sax player, had been chosen, a short time before I met him, to join a youth band in Kansas City organized and conducted by Leo Forbstein called the "Newman Junior Orchestra." I knew this to be a terrific group, and later on I met some other fine musicians from it—a bass player named Wilson, a sax player named Hempill, and a trumpet player, Les Boyer.

The Newman Junior Orchestra played some at the "Isis Theater" in Kansas City, located on 31st and Troost Streets (where I also played while working with the Pattersons). The only reason I mention this is because Joan Crawford, as Lucille LeSueur, once performed there as a chorus girl, and a man named Edward Hickman, who was later convicted of murder, worked there as an usher.

The important thing is, my musical activities expanded into some interesting work with the Pattersons in addition to the college dates with Bud Carr about the same time I became a freshman at Liberty High School in September of 1927. I don't recall too much about the academic side but remember playing in the school orchestra, mainly because one of the violin players was a beautiful girl named Dorothy Black. Many years later I met her with her husband in New York, and as Mrs. Leach she is still a very beautiful lady.

I made some other good friends in school too. One, Sammy Woodson, was a clever guy who built short-wave radio equipment, and it was Sammy who first played for me the Paul Whiteman record of "When Day Is Done," featuring the classic muted trumpet chorus by Henry Busse. I was very impressed, both by the record, which was the only one I had heard which featured a trumpet solo unhampered by other instruments, and by Sammy's marvelous radio set-up. My other friend was a terrific auto designer and mechanic, Alvin Lightfoot. He used to take me for rides in a car he built which was mostly open chassis with heavy roll bars. It could be used for playing polo.

30

Liberty was a college town and a lot of Kansas City bands came through to play for dances and house parties, and this gave me the opportunity to hear what the others were doing besides the ones I played in. "Who" was a very popular song, and it seemed to be standard procedure for it to be played as a trombone solo through a megaphone, which gave the horn a very resonant sound. I first heard the great Kansas City trombonist Merlin Shreve playing in this fashion.

Meanwhile, I was gaining a lot of experience with the Patterson band. Our piano player was usually a good one, Harold Boyd, who operated a dry goods business in Smithville, Missouri, and we had a darn good group for the times. Our repertoire, of course, included, "Dinah," "Rain," "Me and My Shadow," and "Among My Souvenirs," but the big tune of the day was "My Blue Heaven." I had also learned "Song of the Wanderer," which I heard played by Emil Chaquette, the violinist, who was working at a roadside dance hall between Liberty and Kansas City.

The Patterson band worked what amounted to pretty much of a regular circuit for awhile. Every Sunday night we played in a town north of K.C., Edgerton, Missouri. It was a small town but drew a good-sized dancing audience. The dances were held in an upstairs hall. Every week we had to wait to start the dancing until the movie was over that was shown in the same hall.

Some of our wildest experiences in those days were the result of travel. The Patterson boys owned an old Hudson which was as strong as a locomotive, but at one stage the brakes were bad. Coming home from a job one night we had to go down a pretty steep hill, and by the time we were at the bottom we were moving at quite a clip and heading into a curve. Rounding the curve was hairy enough, but after we got around it we saw a slow freight train pulling across the road in front of us. Whoever was driving stood up on the brakes and we slithered to a stop with the hood under a box car. Fortunately, no one was hurt.

Another time we were on the way home in the area around Platte City in 30° below zero weather and the car froze. We had to have water badly but we were out on a deserted highway at one a.m. and nothing was open or moving except an air-way beacon light which seemed to mock us in making its rounds. After stumbling around awhile we found a frozen lake. After chopping through the 8-inch ice, we managed to fill the radiator with water, using my metal derby mute for a bucket.

In this age of modern interstate highways, it's a little difficult, I suppose, to imagine what roads were like a comparatively short time ago. We used to play jobs in towns like Hamilton and Cameron, Missouri, and these were at least 40 or 50 miles north of Liberty by country roads. Unpaved dirt roads were just fine in clear, dry weather, but if we had a heavy rain—and if that rain lasted long enough—the roads could become impassable. On the road we used the paving ended just before a little town called Breckenridge. When we were caught in Breckenridge in a heavy rain we automatically knew it was useless to try to travel any farther. Lucky for us, the Pattersons knew Ben, the local marshal, who had a night office in the firehouse. He would let us sleep in the firehouse, or if we didn't feel like sleeping we had the alternative of sitting around the pot-bellied stove listening to Ben read poetry. He and his wife were both poets.

One winter night we were booked into a roadhouse on the outskirts of Kansas City, called (ironically) "The Fireside Inn." This was one of those places which are usually empty every night except Friday or Saturday. It was where I first heard the old musician's gag line, "Let's play—a car just drove into the driveway." After our cold trip we were pretty chilled when we got there, and so were our instruments. We were delighted to find that the place had a big fire in the fireplace. We piled the instruments in front of the fire to warm them up and stood around talking and getting warm ourselves. Afterwards nobody could say just how it happened, but most likely somebody in adding wood to the fire accidentally kicked Norman Patterson's clarinet into the fire and it got pretty badly scorched.

This incident came to mind years later when almost the same thing happened to Pee Wee Russell. In his case, he was fit to be tied and kept grumbling about it all night long, but whatever damage was done to his clarinet it didn't affect his playing. I remember the night as one of the best I ever worked with him, and if getting him mad made him play that way, he should have stayed mad all the time.

Working with the Patterson boys was more than a great musical experience, it was also the beginning of lifelong friendship with some fine people. I used to be invited to Bremer, Missouri, where the boys' father was a physician, and have a wonderful time visiting with the Toomey family. Mike Toomey, the son, had lived in Falls City and worked with John Whetstine's band.

SEVEN

ALL THROUGHOUT THE YEAR my unfortunate father had been gradually but steadily slipping back into bouts with alcohol. In spite of the fact that he was doing quite well in his new field of work, his heavy drinking was making life miserable for the rest of the family. Just around the finish of my school year, it go so bad my mother could not stand it any more, so she took my brother and me back to Falls City—a practice that was becoming a ritual.

As things turned out for me the move made it possible to take advantage of another opportunity. In that June of 1928 John Whetstine asked me if I wanted to join his band and go on the road for the summer. And I was very happy to accept the offer. I had just turned 15, and some people might think I was a bit young to go off on my own (especially if they believe the stories about musicians that enjoy such wide circulation), but anybody familiar with the situation knew better. My mother never objected to my playing with any of the local bands, especially Whetstine's, because the musicians were all wellknown in Falls City and were recognized as reliable people. As a matter of fact, because of my age my fellow players had a tendency to keep too close a watch over me. I would have had a hard time getting into trouble.

Whetstine's was a seven-piece unit, with three saxes, a trumpet, trombone, piano, and drums, and all of the members were residents of Falls City—at least, as long as they were in the band. The personnel included Ralph Bolejack, first alto; Tiny Wickheiser, second alto; Al Cockerill, tenor; Theodore Moore, trombone; Claire "Sock" Yarger, drums; and John Whetstine, the leader, on piano. During the summer road tour we were also joined by a singer-entertainer from Omaha, Mac Ohman.

This was the first band I ever joined on a regular basis, and I believe it was a typical, good territorial band. We didn't read music—not unusual in those days when probably nobody could read anyhow, and when printed arrangements for such a combination still didn't exist—but we wanted to sound like an organized group. We rehearsed at least once a week, working out head arrangements and committing them to memory. It was a simple process, but effective.

33

When we wanted to learn a new tune, first the saxes would work it out with the piano, developing and memorizing a three-part harmony pattern, and when they had it down, the trumpet and trombone would be added. Variety was achieved by splitting choruses and releases. The result was a practical head arrangement, or at any rate, a good dance-band routine. After we had done this a number of times, we had a pretty extensive repertoire, and Whetstine's band rated well among the territorial outfits. I have often wished we had made some records so I could hear what we really sounded like.

As mentioned earlier, John Whetstine played piano. He was also a semipro ball player, as strong as an ox, and, along with most piano players in those days, he had a highly developed left hand. His left hand worked quite well as a substitute for a bass, but he beat the hell out of a piano. Sometimes he played so hard he would break the hammers on the piano, and as anybody who plays can tell you, that isn't easy to do.

Our sax players all doubled on clarinet, and, as was the custom, the tenorman played an Eb clarinet. To this day I can't understand the popularity of this instrument, because it seems to me the frequency is too high. Nevertheless, some guys even played jazz on it.

But we would try anything for the sake of variety in the sound of the band and were always experimenting. This was the first one I played in that had a good trombonist. Ted Moore played his horn with a nice solo sound, using the popular megaphone for especially pretty solos. He was a very serious young man with very high moral standards. For that matter the men in the band were either married or had steady girlfriends, and I have no recollection of any "one-night romances," during our travels.

Our singer, Mac Ohman, had some really good routines and was well received by the patrons. He had a fine sense of showmanship, and I remember a number he did with props and a broom, called "Keep Sweeping the Cobwebs off the Moon," that never failed to be a sensation with the customers.

Whetstine's band worked a regular circuit, traveling in automobiles that were fitted with outside racks on the roofs to carry the luggage and instruments—usually big cars like Hupmobiles and Hudsons. Seven men could travel very comfortably in two cars that way, and I don't recall any inconvenience. Of course, it was all done during the spring and summer months when people were able to dance in those pavilions. Our winters were far too severe for long hauls, but all travel in those days was dependent on the condition of roads that were either dirt, or at best just gravel. Both could be treacherous, especially in bad weather. It didn't help the situation that many of the bridges over streams and culverts were only wide enough for one car. The graveled roads were the first improvement over the old dirt tracks. They offered the advantage of a harder surface and better drainage, but the loose gravel thrown on top after the first layer packed down could be pretty slippery.

It was on a gravel road of this kind when one of the Whetstine cars skidded at the bottom of a hill and overturned, killing our drummer, Claire

John Whetstine's Band, photographed in a theater at Fremont, Nebraska, August, 1928. L to R: Ted Moore, trb; Pee Wee Erwin, tpt; Claire "Sock" Yarger, drms; John Whetstine, pno; Mac Ohman, vcls; Tiny Wickheiser, alto; Ralph Bolejack, alto; Al Cockerill, tnr.

35

Yarger. I don't remember who we got to replace him, but as always in these cases the band kept going.

Our circuit, for the two or three months we were on the road, covered towns within a radius of 100 miles or more, with sometimes a jump of 75 miles between towns like Beatrice, Nebraska, and Wymore, after which we would have to rush back and play Nebraska City and Auburn. A typical swing would be Sunday night in Horton, Monday in Wymore, Tuesday in Beatrice, Thursday in Nebraska City, Friday in Auburn, and still another town on Saturday. On some occasions we traveled well up into northern Nebraska, crossing paths with Lawrence Welk's group, which would be working its way south. Welk, as I recall, was very popular with the middle-European population and specialized in polka music.

East of Omaha in southwestern Iowa are two towns located smack in the middle of the agricultural region called Red Oak and Shenandoah, and in each one was a large seed house. In Shenandoah it was the Henry Fields Seed Company; in Red Oak, the Earl May Seed Company. Both owned and operated radio stations which, for those pre-network times, were the most lavishly outfitted imaginable. Whetstine's band would broadcast from both of them periodically. The Fields station was the first building I had ever seen that had a moving-cloud ceiling. Some years later I came across the same thing in the Aragon Ballroom in Chicago, but it seems to me that in those early years the idea must have been unique. It was certainly impressive.

Actually the radio station was a large theater, with the usual arrangement of seats for the audience, but the stage was separated and soundproofed by a tremendous sheet of plate glass. The audience could see and hear the broadcast, but any sounds they made were completely insulated from the broadcasting area. These were powerful radio stations—more than likely, 50,000 watt transmitters—and they did a good job of blanketing the area, so broadcasting over them was a big help in buildig popularity for the band. As for me, it was really my first experience in serious broadcasting, because I don't believe you can include those things I did in Kansas City with Coon-Sanders in the same category.

In fact, I consider the season or so that I played with Whetstine a very important period for me from the standpoint of experience. Playing every night taught me a lot about endurance and how to last out a job. Although I was lucky this way to some extent, the dances we played for were generally only three hour gigs. We'd play more or less continuously until 10:30 or 10:45 and then, after an intermission, go back to finish the night. Which wasn't bad. But there were other times when we played for "jitney" dances, which took eight times the stamina of ordinary jobs and, when they were over, my lip had just about had it. Jitney dance halls charged 5¢ a dance, and a dance was one minute long—plus a 30-second encore. The encore was to make the customer feel he was getting his money's worth, I guess.

And if you're wondering how much I got paid for working with this band, I believe it was 15 bucks a night which, multiplied by seven nights, was pretty good money in the Twenties, especially since it only cost us a dollar apiece for a room in a hotel, if we doubled up, and meals were inexpensive. With a little careful planning we could even save our dirty laundry until we got home.

Of course, Whetstine's wasn't the only band in the area. There were quite a few operating out of the different towns. At least two were from Beatrice, one under the leadership of a man named D'Atherton, and the other the Lamberti brothers. In Lincoln there was Adolph Simonic, and probably others. Incidentally, the most impressive trombonist I ever heard, up to this point, was George Herman, who played with the Lamberti brothers. Years later I met him in Philadelphia. He was going to college and majoring in Greek.

The guys in the band, following the customs of the times, drank a lot. John Whetstine used to buy a 4-ounce bottle of 190-proof grain alcohol from a bootlegger for a dollar, and then dilute it in an 8-ounce bottle. There were all kinds of tricks for spiking drinks; they varied according to the different sections of the country. In some places you could buy home-brew that was pretty good, but even the near-beer they sold had just enough room left in the bottle so you could add an ounce of alcohol. Some people did it with soft drinks. You could even buy a rubber cap that fit over a bottle so you could turn it over and mix the alcohol with whatever was in it.

Ralph Bolejack, who played sax with Whetstine, still lives in Falls City, and whenever I see him and we talk over old times, he reminds me of the time we came across a barnstorming pilot who was taking people for airplane rides at $5 apiece. This was a pretty common thing. Some guy with an airplane would pay a farmer a few bucks for the use of his pasture for a couple of days and then take a couple of people at a time for a short hop around the field. Maybe the whole thing would last five minutes. Anyway, I wanted to go up, but I couldn't talk any of the guys in the band into going with me. I kept pestering, though, and finally Bolejack agreed to go. Well, I thought it was a great thrill and enjoyed every minute of it, but it scared Bolejack away from planes for the rest of his life. He has never been up in one since and has never forgotten the incident.

37

EIGHT

IN AUGUST of 1928 I was still with Whetstine when I received a telegram from Eddie Kuhn. To this day I don't know what prompted him to contact me. Even though my aunt had worked for him in the music shop, I doubt very much if she had ever mentioned me. Although I knew who he was, I had never met him. But you can imagine how excited—and delighted—I was to get that telegram! It was an invitation to join the band Eddie had at the Kansas City Athletic Club. I jumped at the chance, even though it meant that certain complications had to be ironed out first, such as where I would live and how I would get to school. I'm not sure, but I think somebody went to see Kuhn, and arrangements were made for me to live at the Athletic Club so he could look out for me. They gave me a room on the 21st floor.

So, wearing the new tuxedo I had to buy for the job, I joined the band that August, and for awhile worked with them on the roof garden, a completely enclosed area on the 22nd floor. It was a beautiful room, but those were the days before air-conditioning, and the windows were open. When the wind was in the right direction I can't begin to describe the odor that drifted in from the extensive Kansas City stockyards. Unless you have experienced it yourself, you've never smelled anything like it.

During my first week I had a traumatic experience. I took a nap in the afternoon and woke up 15 minutes after the dinner session had begun. My fears that I was about to lose my good job proved groundless, but I had learned a lesson. For that matter, in spite of my experience playing with Whetstine and the other bands, I was very concerned abut whether I was good enough to hold down the job with Kuhn. I still couldn't read and I felt insecure. But I soon found out I had no trouble faking the second trumpet parts. I got a lot of help from the lead trumpet player who, strange as it may seem, was a regular army man from Fort Leavenworth who used to commute every day from the base. I can't recall his name, because in a comparatively short time he was replaced by a student from Kansas City Junior College named Louis Forman.

We played two sessions nightly—the dinner session from 7 p.m. to 9 p.m., when we played subdued music designed not to get into the way of polite conversation, and the dancing session, from 10 p.m. to 1 a.m. On Sundays we only played the concert session, and for these we added a string section. They were conducted by a fine violinist, Sol Bobrov, and one of the others was Jack Tarr, whom I had known in Horton and who was now living in Kansas City. We played show music—things like "The Desert Song," and "Play Gypsies."

As I recall we had a pretty good band. At least I thought so then. We had three saxes, three brass, drums, piano, and probably one or two fiddles. In addition, Kuhn sometimes added an accordion. We had one for awhile anyway, an itinerant player from Detroit named Frank Uvarro, but he didn't stay long and was replaced by Mel Hoffman, who also did some arranging. I'm a bit hazy about the trombonists, but we had a good one in Charles McCamish, whose father was a judge in Kansas City. He was eventually replaced by Byron Nicholson.

I don't remember the sax men who were in the band when I joined it, but I do recall those who replaced them—John Sheridan, who played lead alto; Kenny White, tenor; and Joe Snodderly, third alto. Sheridan and Snodderly still live in Kansas City.

Eventually we had a banjo-guitar player, Francis Williams, and a man named Pop Walker on tuba, but at that impressionable age of 15 the man I most admired was the drummer, Perrin MacElroy.

Mac was not only a good drummer, he was a good-looking guy who dressed well, knew a lot of important people, and had a sharp wit. As far as I was concerned, he was a perfect example of the polished gentleman. In other words, he was a pretty powerful personality. Besides playing drums at the Athletic Club he had some kind of affiliation with a steel company in Kansas City, possibly Kansas City Structural Steel. He had a good-sized block of stock in the company and was involved in labor relations. At any rate, he had some important connections and was friendly with a lot of important people at the club. Indirectly this helped me because Mac took a fatherly role toward me and kept an eye out for my welfare. He also, incidentally, gave me my nickname. At one point he talked about getting an offer to join the Royce Taylor Orchestra, a unit affiliated with Don Bestor, which included me. We debated about taking it, but somehow this never materialized.

In October the band moved out of the roof garden into the main dining room on the 6th floor for the winter, and we no longer used fiddles. In the meantime I had started high school in the north end of Kansas City. While living at the club was convenient to the job, getting to school involved quite a trek. Nevertheless, I was determined to do what had to be done, because I wasn't about to give up my job for love, money, marbles or chalk, so, although I was playing dinner sessions from 7 to 9 and supper sessions from 10 to 1, I was up early each morning to take the street car from 11th and Baltimore. I rode this trolley to a point where I had to change to a smaller streetcar—I still think of it as the Toonerville Trolley—and ride this for another five miles to the high school. After a few months of this I was fed up and decided to look around for a better arrangement.

39

My aunt and uncle had started a chicken farm a few miles north of Kansas City and were struggling to make it go. They bought 10 acres of land near Nashua, built a garage, which they partitioned off for use as a temporary home, and put up five good-sized chicken houses, with the facilities to keep 1,000 chickens in each one. They also had an ice house and an incubator house. I don't believe they ever did get around to building a house for themselves. Nevertheless, they had all the conveniences—with the exception of modern plumbing—and were quite comfortable. They even kept a cow. Nothing is more indelibly emplanted in my mind than the memory of scooping the heavy cream from the milk buckets for use at the breakfast table. On investigation, I discovered that moving out of the Athletic Club and in with my aunt and uncle offered an almost perfect solution to my problem of getting to school. My uncle was a machinist with a night job at a machine shop in Kansas City, and he drove back and forth to work. By riding with him in the evening I had easy transportation to the Athletic Club, and in the daytime I only had a short distance to travel to school. It was an arrangement that made life a whole lot easier during the winter months.

NINE

THERE WERE TWO aspects about the Kansas City of those days I was not aware of at the time—or more than likely, merely accepted as conditions normal to the city without thinking about them. The first was racial discrimination. As far as jazz musicians were concerned, in the long run it probably worked out to the detriment of the whites. Every now and then somebody asks me why it is that in view of all the great black musicians that have come out of Kansas City, so few of the white musicians became famous. I can only explain, by way of an answer, that there was very little opportunity for a white musician to mingle with blacks. Until fairly recent times there were even two separate union locals—one for blacks and one for whites—so there were no mixed bands, and actually very little opportunity for a white musician to hear the great bands that were playing in the black part of town. This applied to me, too, in spite of my expeditions in search of the barbecue pits. Black musicians played with black musicians, and white musicians played with white musicians, each in their own area.

The other thing was the political climate in the city under the Pendergast regime, which brought bossism to a new peak but at the same time created a lot of social activity and functions which were good for bands and musicians. Just how good the musical picture was you can judge for yourself as I try to describe it.

The Kansas City Athletic Club was located at 11th and Baltimore, in the heart of downtown. Two blocks down on Baltimore was the Kansas City Club. A band similar to Eddie Kuhn's worked there, but I never got to hear it, and very few outsiders ever did, because the club was very exclusive. "Exclusive," in this instance, meant that the club excluded Jews, as opposed to the Kansas City Athletic Club, which accepted anybody as long as they were white and could afford it. In between the two clubs was the Muehlebach Hotel, the best in town. For me the most important part of it was the Plantation Grill where all the MCA bands (those operating out of the Music Corporation of America booking office) played. Every day at noon WDAF, the *Kansas City Star* station, would broadcast a half-hour session from here, and this is where I first heard many of the better-known bands—Ted Weems,

41

Bernie Cummins, Guy Lombardo. I used to stand outside the door in the outer foyer and listen.

There were three large theaters in town, all with orchestras. The Newman was a presentation house, with an orchestra under the direction of Leo Forbstein. The Midland was a newer theater with a concert orchestra under the initial direction of the violinist Dave Rubinoff, later to become a popular radio conductor. The third was the Mainstreet Theater, where they usually offered vaudeville acts backed by a stage band. For an extended period, the band was Walter Davidson and the Louisville Loons, a fine stage band of at least 16 men. Sometimes it would alternate with a traveling stage band. It was at the Mainstreet I first heard the Vincent Lopez Red Caps, a Lopez unit under the direction of Bernie Dolan, with two of my future good friends, Herman Fink and Charles Margulis. It was also where I saw Bob Hope's vaudeville act. In addition to these more or less legitimate theaters, there was a very popular burlesque house on 12th Street. Kansas City was a great town for entertainment.

Across from the Muehlebach, and also on 12th, was the Phillips Hotel, which had a band, and two blocks south on Baltimore was the Aladdin Hotel with a roof garden and a band. In other words, there were five fair-sized bands within a radius of two or three blocks. The only exception to this big-band policy was the Baltimore Hotel, across the street from the Muehlebach, which used small groups in the various rooms but had so many social functions, especially political and civic affairs, that it provided work for a lot of musicians.

I used to work extra gigs there quite often. They had the best-tasting coffee and butter in town. It was while I was playing for a show there that I first met Velva Nally, a very attractive, talented girl who played piano and sang blues vocals. She was working for a promoter named Jolly Jones, who maintained a stable of entertainers. Later on she and two others in this same group made quite a reputation on WGN, the Chicago radio station, and still later, when I was playing with Joe Haymes and Roy Wager came into the band, she was Roy's wife. She left him to marry Jack Crawford, a bandleader known as the "Clown Prince of Jazz," but when I met her again, she was married to Lou McGarity.

Besides the theaters and hotels Kansas City maintained two important radio stations, WDAF, and KMBC, an independently owned station, and both had fair-sized staff orchestras. Innumerable small nightclubs and 10¢-a-dance places were scattered all over the city.

Most important of all, there were two big and very active ballrooms in town. The El Torreon Ballroom was opened with a great fanfare and promotion in 1928, featuring Spanish decor and a floating-cloud ceiling like the one in the seed company radio station. It was located on Gladstone Boulevard near 31st and Troost. The opening band, which also served as the house band for quite awhile, was previously known as Phil Baxter and His Texas Tommies, but after the ballroom opened they dropped the Texas Tommy part of the name. But it was a much better than average band. When

I was with Joe Haymes later on I got to know Phil Baxter quite well, a natural association, because Baxter had written "Piccolo Pete," which was Haymes' first hit arrangement for the Ted Weems band. In fact, Phil Baxter, a piano player, was also a prolific songwriter with quite a few hits to his credit. Several of the guys in his band came from Arkansas, including a trombonist named Al Jennings, who was a personable entertainer and the original "Ding Dong Daddy From Dumas." Dumas was a town in Arkansas, and Baxter wrote the tune as a feature for Jennings. The tune became a big hit and as a result Dumas was practically immortalized in song. Baxter decided to try it again, using the name of another Arkansas town, Hoxey. This one was "Heavy-laden Hester From Hoxey." It told the story of a 300-pound lady who was taken with appendicitis, but instead of operating the doctors had to blast.

Baxter had a pretty fine band, with some good musicians. Several of them, including Jennings, later played with Joe Haymes. Another was the lead alto man, K. T. Naylor, and a trumpet player whose last name was Weiser (pronounced Wiser) and, of course, was automatically nicknamed Bud. He was on the road with Haymes before Roy Wager joined.

Another band that played the El Torreon in 1929, and then stayed around to work dates in the area, was a band from New York, the Cass-Hagen Orchestra, a pretty high-powered outfit and my first real contact with an eastern band. I got to know the members pretty well, including Red Nichols, who was with them on second trumpet. The rest of the brass team included Itch Schulkin on lead, Fred Van Eps Jr., on third, and Al Philburn—featured later by Bert Lown on his hit theme song, "Bye Bye Blues"—on trombone. The saxes were Larry Tice on lead alto, Pete Pumiglio (later with the Raymond Scott Quintet) on third, and a star on tenor sax named Pee Wee Russell. Bobby Van Eps played piano, and they had a drummer named Gray, but I can't remember the bass player. This group impressed me quite a bit and was one of the high spots of my Kansas City stay.

The other ballroom, the Pla-mor, was also opened by a good unit which was affiliated with the Jean Goldkette office. The musical director was Paul Sells, and the musicians were mostly from Detroit. Pee Wee Hunt was in the band, and so was Nat Natoli and several other men from the Casa Loma Orchestra.

I also heard Paul Whiteman's concert orchestra at the Pla-mor. It was some time after they had made the movie "The King of Jazz," so many of the musicians I would have liked to see and hear were no longer in the band, but it still included stars like Chester Hazlet, Charles Strickfadden, and Bill Rank. Playing trumpets were Nat Natoli and Andy Secrest (the jazz trumpeter who followed Bix Beiderbecke in the band). But the only guy I really got acquainted with was Fud Livingston. Fud wanted to buy some booze, so I took him to a bootlegger after the job. I remember this clearly because he had the fattest roll of twenty-dollar bills I had ever seen—a bit ironic, because I saw a lot of Fud in his last year of life, 1957, and he was

Eddie Kuhn's Band at the Kansas City Athletic Club, Nov. 1928. John Sheridan, Kenny White, Joe Snodderly, saxes; Louis Forman, Pee Wee Erwin, tpts; Byron Nicholson, trb; Mel Hoffman, acc; Francis Wallace, bjo; Pop Walker, tuba; Perrin MacElroy, drums; Eddie Kuhn, pno.

practically destitute.

Later on the Pla-mor went to a more or less local band policy, although the leader, Chick Scroggins, wasn't from Kansas City. But he did have an excellent house band with some fine musicians, in particular, a trumpet player named George Bridenthall.

All of which should give you some idea of what a busy musical town Kansas City was in those days. You still must keep in mind that this only represents white musical activity. The black side of town, in the meantime, was making musical history with bands like those of Bennie Moten, Jay McShann, George E. Lee, Andy Kirk, and Count Basie, but as I mentioned earlier, I wasn't close to this action.

Actually, from my own standpoint, I must admit that as a 15-year-old kid, playing at the Athletic Club suited me fine. I thought I had it made. I can't be exact, but I must have been making 60 or 70 bucks a week, and the fringe benefits were great. Everybody at the club treated me very well, including Eddie Kuhn, and even the busboys were my friends. They were always bringing me food—just about anything I asked for—and when I was going to school they made sandwiches for my lunch on huge slabs of bread that were a meal in themselves. I lived and ate well.

I enjoyed playing with the band. As I recall, it was a pretty good one—except for Eddie Kuhn, who wrecked it with his right-handed piano-playing. But he was a good leader, a good mixer, and he obviously knew his business and how to deal with the management and the patrons. In fact, he had one trick which all by itself promoted a lot of friends. About every two weeks he would buy two five-gallon bottles of distilled water and a ten-gallon can of grain alcohol, and mix them together, half and half. This gave him a pretty good supply of home-made gin to use in cementing political relations, that is, whatever he didn't drink himself. I never knew whether he sold the stuff or gave it away, but he probably did both. For that matter there was never a shortage of booze at the club, because the members always brought their own bottles and set-ups were available. It was a private club, so nobody questioned this.

The members included some very important people, especially politicians. I was not particularly interested in politics myself (what kid is?) but I remember being very impressed with the club's facilities for reporting the returns of the 1928 presidential election which, of course, was the year Al Smith ran against Herbert Hoover. For the occasion the club somehow rigged up a system of projecting the results on a big screen on one entire wall of the main diningroom. In comparison with modern methods of reporting on elections, this doesn't sound like much, but it does give an indication of how far the club management was willing to go to please its members.

Some of the politicians and influential people maintained a suite of rooms on the 21st floor—the same one my room was located on—which was a sort of club-within-a-club called The Boar's Nest. They entertained a lot, and sometimes I was invited in to play a little or just join the party. In this group were people like Roy Natsiger, who owned a chain of bakeries, and members of the Muehlebach family, who owned breweries and the Kansas City Blues baseball team. There was another club member, a man originally from Falls City, who trained horses for the extensive Pendergast racing interests. His name was Milo Shields. There was one instance where he won so much money on one horse race that he was able to buy a pretty good-sized farm on the Missouri River where land, even then, was selling at $300 an acre.

It wasn't unusual for many of the star athletes of the day to use the club's gym facilities on the 6th floor. One I distinctly remember is still rated as one of the greatest wrestlers of all-time, Ed "Strangler" Lewis, and another was a well-known wrestler, Wayne Nunn. I seem to recall that the former Notre Dame football star Joe Savoldi also trained there. Baseball players from the Kansas City Blues were around a lot too, especially Joe Kuehl, who went on to make a name playing with the Washington Senators. The Blues, incidentally, was the white team in town. There was a black team called the Kansas City Monarchs, and the great Satchel Page was with them at one time.

Well, after all my talking about the drinking that went on and repeated references to the fact that most musicians I was working with went at it pretty heavily, you're probably wondering when I finally yielded to the temptation of trying it myself. It was about this time that I began feeling my oats and took to drinking a bit. I struck up a friendship with a night chef at a place called Fowler's Steak House, between 11th and 12th on Baltimore. On Saturday nights we would split a pint of "red-eye," or bootleg booze. We used to go in the back room and set up the drinks on a meat-chopping block. I was still very friendly with Don Hysell, who was attending the music conservatory in town, and he and I would make the rounds of the speakeasies. Sometimes when I made a visit by train back to Falls City to see my family I would get a ride back to Kansas City with Don, and we'd do quite a bit of drinking on the way. Incidentally, I don't recall anybody in those days drinking for taste. Most of the stuff tasted pretty awful. When you drank, you drank for one reason—to get bombed.

Another indication that I couldn't wait to grow up and ruin myself were my feelings about a situation that bothered me a lot. I was very much aware that all day and every night I was only one block away from the notorious 12th Street, which was a promenade for hundreds of hookers. I did not take into account that to them I would have seemed one step out of the cradle. I just thought these bug-infected creatures should at least proposition me.

TEN

I WAS VERY HAPPY at the high school in north Kansas City. It gave me an opportunity to enjoy some social life, plus providing everything I needed academically. Probably because of the respect for education that my grandfather had instilled in me, I always took a schedule of subjects as full as I could handle. Right from the start I planned for college preparation, so I took the subjects I felt would be useful. Every year I elected English, history, Latin, and math, figuring this combination would cover all future requirements for college entrance. These, plus the required physical education and playing in the school orchestra made up a very busy schedule. As a matter of fact, working every night at the Athletic Club and going to school with a full schedule in the day time I was actually living two separate lives at the same time.

Nevertheless, school gave me the chance to form marvelous friendships that have remained for my entire life. My closest school friends were Wilbur Bartels and his family, James Davison, who lived in a rural area north of Kansas City, and George Atterberry. The school had a maximum of 300 students at any time, so it was possible to know practically every student in the school, which I was lucky enough to do. We never had enough music students to have a very large orchestra, and never enough for a band, but we tried hard with the people at hand.

Around January of 1929 my mother and father decided to move to North Kansas City, where they took an apartment close to my school. I moved in with them which made commuting a lot easier. My father was on his good behavior again, not doing any heavy drinking, and making out quite well at earning a living. I never did understand too well how he operated his business, but I got the impression he rode around looking for houses that obviously needed roofing or siding. Then he would approach the owners and if he succeeded in selling them either a new roof or siding, or both, he would turn the contract over to people who would do the actual work. He'd immediately collect his commission because the paper was financed by banks who held a promissory note. Unfortunately, his term on the wagon only lasted until near the end of the school year, when he felt the urge to take off again.

My mother and brother, as usual, went back to Falls City, but I had to stay in Kansas City. It was a tough move for me to make but I even went so far as to make inquiries about getting a court order to keep my father from appearing at my school or at the Club and bothering me. It's impossible to describe how insecure he made me feel or how upsetting and embarrassing his behavior could be. I was working in a public place with a well-known band so he could find me very easily.

Knowing my position, the family of our first trumpet player, Louis Forman, invited me to stay at their home. These are among the nicest people I have ever known. They accepted me as another son, and my stay with them was one of the best times of my life.

Mr. and Mrs. Forman had walked 300 miles behind a dog cart to escape from Russia and the pogroms of 1911 under the Czar. Their experiences had been hard, which no doubt had a lot to do with their being so understanding and considerate and such gentle people. A great deal of their characteristics brushed off on their son Louis, who at the time was studying hard toward a medical career. Upon finishing his medical training, he contributed his efforts to army field hospitals during the second World War, since then devoting his practice to the field of psychiatry. With his great desire to help his fellow man, he has been instrumental in helping many people.

My sojourn with the Formans has always been an oasis of pleasant memories. I remember standing with Louis Forman in the front yard and watching the dirigible Graf Zeppelin pass by on its trip around the world. It was my first exposure to a closely knit family in which there was a great love for each other—as a matter of fact, a love for all people—which was conducive to a marvelous feeling of well-being and happiness. Mrs. Forman, who always seemed to be smiling, was a wonderful cook. I used to live on edge, waiting for the classic Friday evening meals she would prepare. But above all, I enjoyed the sense of stability in the home, something I never got from my father's feeble attempts to establish one.

Louis Forman was a well-trained, legitimate trumpet player. Knowing my problems along these lines, he took me to his teacher, Ferdinand Jacobs, who was the son of Otto Jacobs, a prominent cornet and baritone soloist who conducted various brass bands. Both Otto and Ferdinand had been trained in the Conservatory of Brussels, Belgium, and were the best-equipped trumpet and lower brass authorities in Kansas City. Ferdinand Jacobs had been the principal trumpet player with Leo Forbstein at the Newman Theater before an automobile accident made him a paraplegic. I remember him as a nice guy who tried very hard to give me a basic foundation in the Arban Method, but the legit approach didn't brush off on me too well. Mainly, I'm afraid, I was just lazy, and I had been playing wrong too long. Since the jazz I was required to play utilized so much pressure I was afraid to let up for the more sensible reliance on more air column.

Living in central Kansas City was a new experience for me socially, and it provided a chance for new activities. I started playing tennis, but since this required some effort it didn't last long, but at least I tried it. Most important of all I was close to the fellows I was working with. For some reason our tuba player was replaced by a zany character from Kansas City Junior College named Kenneth Fink, a fun guy who lived close by. We also started working with a good sax player, Phil Miller, who joined our inner circle. John Sheridan was always a close friend, as was Byron Nicholson, the trombonist. I also spent a lot of time with John Falter, who was studying at the Kansas City Art Institute.

In the spring Eddie Kuhn opened a chain of waffle shops throughout Kansas City, and small groups of us started playing in the shops to stimulate the lunch business. They were called "The Red Robin Waffle Shops." Naturally our theme song was "When the Red Red Robin Comes Bob-Bob-Bobbin' Along." We usually had three to five men in these groups, and the jobs provided extra income. The overall idea of the waffle shops may have been a good one, but the trouble seemed to be that Eddie opened too many of them too quickly. This spread the profits so thin that the whole thing folded in a short time. And I don't remember exactly what happened—perhaps it was due to his losses in the waffle shop venture, but the job at the Athletic Club either stopped altogether or it dropped down to weekends. At any rate, late that summer I returned to Falls City and once more rejoined Maust and Hysell on playing jobs

In September I entered the Falls City High School and immediately ran into academic trouble. I don't remember the teacher's name who taught physics, but her instruction method was completely beyond my comprehension. I had a correct feeling that I was getting further and further in trouble the more I attempted to understand what was going on. In my own defense I have to say that I never took my studies lightly. I had aspirations to increase my knowledge in academics despite my musical interests, but this one was whipping me for sure.

On the other hand, all was not study or seriousness at this point either. Like my peers I was involved in co-ed associations, and, since I was in my hometown and knew everybody, I was having a lot of fun in the usual teen-age pursuits. Most of my friends had automobiles and a lot of time was spent in joy riding, as well as playing dance jobs. I thought we were growing up, but I can remember one horrendous deed that Donald Hysell and I participated in that throws some doubt on it. We had a teacher we were not fond of—she was probably only guilty of trying to teach us something. One day before class we each ate several cloves of raw garlic and then tried to approach the teacher at close range. She must have been nauseated, poor thing.

That October I was offered a job playing with a band that was based about 50 miles south of Falls City, the Roland Evans Orchestra, from Atchison, Kansas. They had just returned from an extensive tour of Canada, going as far as Winnipeg, and had also worked territory jobs and traveling carnivals. It was a good band but there was a bonus involved for me. By joining it I was able to transfer to Atchison High School and get away from the physics class that was giving me so much grief. So I took the offer and moved on to a new challenge.

The entire Evans band was quartered in the large Atchison home of Roland Evans and his family. The third floor of the house was like a dormitory, and I moved in with the other musicians. One of the sax players was Al Cockerill, whom I knew from Whetstine's band, and the others were Bert Andrus from New Orleans, and Ken Smith, a fine musician who later became very active in the Kansas City musician's union. The guitar player's name was Val (his last name slips my memory), the drummer was "Snooks," from Tuskaloosa, Alabama, and the piano player was a local man named Glenn Willis, and I still correspond with him on occasion.

It was a good band and we did very well in the territory surrounding Atchison—even traveling as far as Falls City to play jobs. The musicians had a lot of travel experience and a vast fund of fascinating stories to tell. It was listening to these that started my desire to travel and see new places.

Roland Evans at this time was courting a very lovely lady, Lucia Langon, whose family lived in Lancaster, a small community just west of Atchison. They were married later. Their son, Philip R. Evans, is co-author with Richard M. Sudhalter of *Bix, Man & Legend*, the definitive book on Bix Beiderbecke.

I transferred my credits and started attending Atchison High. Fortunately for me, I enrolled in a physics class where I could follow the instructor. I began turning in some constructive work on the subject of the physical aspects of man's environment, something always of interest to me, in spite of the fact that nothing I learned has been of any use in my life's work.

Like any average young man of 16 I had a dream girl. She went to Atchison High too, but she was completely unaware of my regard. Her name was Eleanor Bailey, and I really knew her sister Gwen much better. I understand that in later years Eleanor had some success in Hollywood, but by then I would have been long gone—as if it would have made any difference.

I joined the school orchestra, under the direction of a fine conductor, Mr. Altemeyer. It was in this orchestra that I made the acquaintance of a younger trumpet player, William Muchnic, who to this day remains my closest friend and confidant. Once a week Bill made a trip into Kansas City to study with the father of my teacher, Otto Jacobs. He was a very serious student and got a firm foundation from Jacobs. Now, long after the days of his daily trumpet playing, he can still multiple-tongue along with the best soloists to be heard.

Bill helped me get acquainted with other of our schoolmates. One, Ralph Brewster, was also a very good trumpet player, and later on he became quite famous as a member of the original Glenn Miller vocal group, the Modernaires.

Because of the time involved in traveling with the Evans band working with them proved to be more than I could handle as a high-school student, so I had to leave them. Luckily I was able to return to the Kansas City Athletic

Club where the job had been reactivated on a weekend basis. This also enabled me to return to North Kansas High School where I could resume my classes and my association with many of my friends.

I took a furnished room with a very nice family named Denny, who lived close to the school, and since I worked late quite often I had an arrangement worked out with the youngest boy, Riley Denny. Riley delivered papers very early in the morning, and when he returned from his route he would wake me up in time for school. Years later I was walking down New York's Sixth Avenue when suddenly a huge 6' 3" man stepped in front of me, blocking my way, and when I looked up I was staring into that same familiar face I had seen bending over me so many mornings. Riley was now a successful executive with a major cosmetic firm.

For some vague reason I find hard to explain now, when I planned my school subjects I attempted to work them out so I would have most of my majors completed after three years. I think this is a psychological short-coming of mine, based on laziness as much as anything else. If I do wood work, wash dishes, study, practice, or whatever, I try to do it as fast as possible. The theory being that by getting the job done in a hurry I'll have leisure time at the other end. It seldom works out that way, but to some extent it did in high school. After a conference with the administration it turned out that I only needed one academic credit to graduate. I could probably have taken courses during the summer to meet the requirement, but I elected to wait until the fall term.

During the second half of my junior year I became involved in another completely one-sided romance. This time I decided I was desperately in love with a young lady named Marguerite Collins, who was very nice to me and quite sympathetic. The trouble was she was going steady with another trumpet player, Bill Gilbert, the son of a good friend of mine, the Reverend Gilbert, a local minister. In other words, it was a pretty hopeless case, and I contemplated all of the usual infantile answers to unrequited love, such as suicide, taking to drink, etc., none of which offered happy solutions, so I finally gave up.

Reverend Gilbert, in addition to his church ministry, served as the orchestral director in my school. He was a well-prepared teacher and spent quite a bit of time with me, telling me stories of his days at Columbia University. It was his suggestion that, since I spent every night playing trumpet, I should study another instrument, so I wound up playing string bass in the orchestra. I never gained much technique, but it saved my embouchure.

ELEVEN

THAT SUMMER OF 1930 the band again left the Athletic Club. We took a job at a park south of Kansas City called Wildwood Lakes. The park, with a very attractive, rustically styled dance pavilion and a large swimming pool, was a popular resort. We spent a lot of time adding to our repertoire. It included copies of many such Red Nichols classics as "Dinah," "Ida," and the new Archie Bleyer arrangement of "Business In F." We also gave special treatment to the popular new hit "Stardust."

The ballroom pavilion was equipped with one of those Venetian-glass revolving balls which reflect countless colored lights around the room. The dancing crowd consisted of the young set of Kansas City, and business was always good. Radio still had not captivated everyone to the point where it replaced other entertainment. The younger crowd still considered dancing the number one social activity.

When we started playing at Wildwood Lakes that June my parents took an apartment at 3501 Paseo, in Kansas City, and this put me much closer to the job, but since there was no public transportation to the Lakes I had to ride with one of the musicians. The band included three saxes, Phil Miller, Kenny White, and Joe Snodderly, Byron Nicholson on trombone, James Schull on piano, Perrin MacElroy, drums, and Charley Knox on bass.

Besides the dance pavilion, the other big attraction at Wildwood was the swimming pool. On special occasions we would play a matinee by the side of the pool. On one of these days I noticed a very attractive young lady, and when I pointed her out to one of the musicians he promptly said "Oh, I know her, I'll introduce you."

Her name was Roberta Greding, and we became friendly to the extent that I believe we had one date, but I was too busy playing so it never went any further than that. But I was to meet her again in Chicago when I was working with Benny Goodman, and she became my first wife.

I went back to the high school in north Kansas City for my senior year. Now we were living in the center of Kansas City. My parents had moved one block further south to 3601 Paseo—which was interesting because our neighbors in the building included our tenor sax player, Kenny White, and his brother and family. We all became quite friendly, but I do not remember how I made that long haul to school every day. I have no idea at this late date what I used for transportation, but somehow I made the trip.

In addition to the long trip, I didn't take advantage of the fact I only needed one subject to graduate. This didn't seem to me that I would be taking advantage of all the school had to offer, so I filled up my schedule with four major subjects. During my terms in high school I took four years of English, Latin, history, and math.

I had some marvelous teachers, and the school had a great feeling for the students. One very special teacher I kept in touch with until she passed away a few years ago; her name was Hazel Carter and, of course, she taught music. Mrs. Carter had a lot of confidence in me and decided I should enter the regional instrumental contests. So after much practice and preparation on a classical solo I accompanied Mrs. Carter and her chorus of 20 girls to the regional contests held in Maryville, Missouri—about 65 or 70 miles north of Kansas City—where I won a gold medal as a cornet soloist. Winning the gold medal wasn't all that difficult, since I was the only cornetist in the contest, but I'll never forget the comment of the judge, a symphonic oboe player: "You play very well, but you will never be able to earn a livelihood in music unless you eliminate the vibrato you play with."

With the typical overconfidence of the young I thought my body was indestructible, and instead of returning to the Athletic Club that fall I took a roadhouse job in the south end of Kansas City at a place called Meyers Barbecue. We had a five-piece band. I remember my friends Mel Hoffman, who was the leader, and Donald Hysell were in it with me. We worked long hours, but the heavy schedule finally caught up with me—I developed a spot on one lung.

I was grounded at home for over a month, and, either out of sympathy or because he also was sick, my father stayed home with me. All I remember of the incident is taking tonics with milk shakes to build up my strength and playing cribbage by the hour with my father or pinochle with members of the White family. Most important of all, for the first time in my life I was able to concentrate on listening to the radio. Amos 'n' Andy were big and also a giant orchestra led by B. A. Rolfe, sort of an early version of the later Hit Parade. (If anyone had been able to tell me that only four or five years later I would be playing with many of the men from that show—Phil Napoleon, Manny Klein, the Dorseys—the idea would have been unbelievable. But the program that impressed me the most was played by a brass band on Sundays and was sponsored by Enna-Jetick Shoes. On each show Walter Smith, one of the great classical soloists, would play two cornet solos.

We also had recently been exposed to the movie "The King of Jazz," featuring Paul Whiteman and his great concert orchestra. The Duke Ellington orchestra was a feature on radio, and during this period I was lucky to hear the band in person at the Newman Theater and again later at a black dance at 15th and Paseo.

At night the radio waves were flooded with the music of good bands,

Graduation picture—North Kansas City High, 1931.

Coon-Sanders from the Blackhawk, Fred Hamm had a good band at the Mounds in St. Louis, and Henry Theis a great band at the Sentin Hotel in Cincinnati. And it was from Cincinnati that I first heard the Joe Haymes band, broadcasting from the Gibson Hotel. This was also the day of the great Kansas City black bands. Bennie Moten was at Fairyland Park, Andy Kirk at Winwood Beach, and George E. Lee was playing in a roadhouse, the "Blue Hills Gardens." Good music was very much the order of the day.

After I recuperated from my illness I returned to playing at Meyers Barbecue, but on a lighter schedule. Also I went back to school. It was while I was at Meyers an incident took place which I never knew about, or I had forgotten, until Charley Knox, the bass player, told me about it in 1979.

Charley and Joe Haymes, the bandleader, were both from Springfield, Missouri, and were close friends. Charley had played with Joe in their early days, so it was only natural for Joe, on a scouting trip to Kansas City for talent, to contact Charley. Joe's band was still in its first year of development and he was always on the lookout for possible replacements should he need them. Charley told him, "I'll take you to hear this kid trumpet player, and you can see how you like his style." Charley says he brought Joe to Meyers Barbecue to hear me play. I'm sure he did, even though I don't remember it, because in May of 1931 when the Joe Haymes band was playing at the Muehlebach Hotel in Kansas City, I was asked if I would be interested in joining the band.

I graduated from high school that month and had quite an important decision to make. It had always been understand that when I graduated from high school Congressman Moorhead, my grandfather's good friend, would give me an appointment to West Point. But after a lot of serious thought and soul-searching I came to the conclusion that at heart I was first a trumpet player, and, assuming I could pass the physical and academic exams for entry to the Point, I would probably turn out to be the worst example of a soldier in their history. So I agreed to join the Joe Haymes band in June.

My first dates with the band were one-nighters. They had been broadcasting every noon from the Muehlebach, so they made a sweep through the Kansas wheat belt to cash in on the resultant popularity. That was tough country! When some of those farmers came to town on a weekend for a good time they expected to get it, and there were always a few wise guys. A few snorts of corn and they were ready for a fight.

I joined the band on lead trumpet. The second trumpet player was a fellow named Claude Love. I remember him as a very amiable guy, but I honestly can't recall how well he played, although Johnny Mince tells me he was good. Our trombonist was Al Jennings, quite a colorful character and entertainer who had been with Phil Baxter's Texas Tommies and was known as the original "Ding Dong Daddy From Dumas." He sang novelty vocals, including "Ding Dong Daddy," and was a big asset to the band. Our lead alto man, K.T. Naylor, had also been with Baxter. I still don't know what the initials stood for; in the South they have a habit of calling people by initials instead of a name. Johnny Mince, featured on clarinet, was from Chicago

55

The Erwin family in 1931. Pee Wee with mother, father, and younger brother.

Heights, Dick Clark played tenor, and John Langsford, baritone sax, doubled on bassoon. He was only a half inch under seven feet tall, and was billed as the world's tallest sax player, but whenever anyone marveled at his height he would tell them about his grandfather, who, he claimed, had been over eight feet tall.

The band manager was a dapper young guy of German descent, Carl Snyder, an alleged guitar player. I never heard him play. But he had a good business head and handled the band well. I think he came from Ash Grove, Missouri, and I vaguely recall hearing a story about him that indicated a tragic childhood—something about his father being shot and killed in front of him. Anyway, he was a nice guy and stayed with the band throughout its existence. Stanley Fletcher was our bass player, on both tuba and string bass. Paul Mitchell was the pianist with the original band, and a guy from Detroit, Jimmy Underwood, was the drummer. He also did vocals. In addition to the musicians we had a vocal trio, the McMichael brothers, Judd, Ted, and Little Joe—three great guys who, unlike most vocalists, were as much a part of the band as the musicians. I was very friendly with Judd and sometimes roomed with him on the road. In later years they made quite a name for themselves as "The Merry Macs."

Joe Haymes was a very talented guy, in many ways far ahead of his time. He and Phil Baxter had collaborated on some tunes which did fairly well (they were good friends) and he had arranged for the Ted Weems band before organizing under his own name. So he had some good solid experience under his belt. He was not much of a piano player, but he needed a piano when he arranged. He drank a lot and seemed to be walking around in a daze much of the time, although he never got staggering drunk. He was such a foggy character that we never knew if the glassy look came from booze or if he was dreaming up ideas. He'd go off into hiding when he was working on an arrangement, and after a long period he'd emerge with the results. They would be good. He was always striving for new effects in his writing— new voicings, new ways of phrasing—and was really ahead in his conceptions. Typically, he used clarinet or trumpet lead concerted with saxophones very early in his arranging career, a device used much later and credited to Glenn Miller.

In Kansas we played towns like Salina and Junction City. In those days when most radio stations had only 5,000 watts there was one in Kansas owned by a surgeon named Dr. Brinkley that had 50,000. It blanketed the whole area and as a result was very influential. Its house band was a marvelous outfit directed by Steve Love and Joe Harris played trombone in it. Dr. Brinkley eventually wound up in trouble with the government and the station had to go out of business. Brinkley would go on the air selling and promoting his operations—he specialized in rejuvenation, using monkey glands. A lot of people were horrified by the idea and complained. Maybe he could have gotten away with it if he had been a little quieter, but with the help of 50,000 watts he was broadcasting to the entire country. Uncle Sam stepped in and told him to stop, took away his broadcasting license, and supposedly put him out of business.

Instead the doctor moved his operation to Mexico and built a radio station about ten miles south of the border, which was capable of transmitting on 500,000 watts, and proceeded to blanket the Southwest with his broadcasts. Before leaving Kansas he had the nerve to run for Lt. Governor, and he enjoyed lots of popularity in the rural sections.

After the Kansas tour Joe Haymes took the band back to Springfield, Missouri, where it had first started. We went into a place called the Half-a-Hill Tea Room for two weeks, while Haymes did some intensive writing and the band some extensive rehearsing. Besides providing good dance music the band was an excellent entertaining unit, because in addition to Al Jennings and his "Ding Dong Daddy" routine and the other things he did, we had the McMichael brothers and another showstopper in K.T. Naylor. K.T., a lovable character who bore an amazing resemblance to the comic-strip figure Major Hoople, could put on a turban, stand out in front of the band, and wiggling one finger like a snake do a fantastic version of "Egyptian Ella."

K.T. told a story I have always considered a classic. He was a heavy drinker and, like everybody else in the area, he bought a lot of grain alcohol (a perfectly clear liquid) and used it to spike his near-beer or soda pop. While

57

Under-rated genius, Joe Haymes.

he was playing with a band at Missouri University he was buying his alcohol from a student who was working his way through school as a bootlegger. All went well until one day he noticed some strange-looking little white flakes floating in his alcohol. After some investigation he discovered the student had been draining alcohol from the tanks holding cadavers in the medical school. The flakes were human skin from the poor stiffs.

I guess the first major job I played with Haymes was The Colosseum in Tulsa, Oklahoma, where we worked every night from Monday through Saturday. I don't know if it was because there was so much oil money in the area, but there didn't seem to be any sign of the Depression. I was extremely impressed with how clean the city was. We stayed at the Alvin Hotel and, directly opposite our room on the second floor, was the studio of the Tulsa radio station, KVOO. We got very friendly with the musicians in the house band, which was very good, especially a trumpet player named Walt Tupper. Another fine local band was that of Tracy Brown, with Les Jenkins on trombone, drummer Riley Scott, and an excellent trumpet man, T.J. Dean.

Our room was immense. It wasn't the usual hotel bedroom, but one of those they used to call "Salesman's Sample Rooms." When a salesman came to town he would rent one of these rooms to display his line and then invite dealers from the area to come in and view his samples. So our room had three beds in it. John Langsford and Johnny Mince were my roommates. Mince practiced a lot, whenever the mood hit him, sometimes at three in the morning. The room had one of those old-fashioned overhead ceiling fans and when he stood under it and played, it somehow played tricks with the soundwaves so the result was some very peculiar sounds.

Johnny lugged along a phonograph and records wherever we went. This was my first real introduction to the wonderful world of records, especially those of Louis Armstrong. It was thanks to Johnny and his phonograph that I became aware of what was going on in music. Since I had played all the way through school, I seldom got the chance to hear other bands, even on the radio, and Johnny's records were a revelation. Among the records we played in Tulsa were Jimmy Dorsey's solo record of "Beebe" and lots of Louis' classics. It was a new world to me. I was also beginning to enjoy my new freedom and the relief of no longer maintaining a heavy school schedule. Now all I had to do was play the job.

Another thing that sticks in my mind about Tulsa was the meals. We ate breakfast at the hotel, but somebody discovered that we could do much better on other meals by eating out at places that served in boarding-house style. You paid one price—50 or 75¢—and they'd have one meat dish along with tremendous bowls of vegetables, and you helped yourself. We lived well—and cheap.

We played to good crowds at The Colosseum. We played some pops, tunes like "Sweet and Lovely," but mostly we concentrated on Joe's arrangements of things like "Get Cannibal." Our theme song at the time was "Linger Awhile." The one Joe wrote and everybody remembers, "Not For Sale," didn't come along until 1932 when we were at The Nut Club in New

York. The spirituals were later too.

I remember the thing that impressed me most about the Colosseum crowds was the prevalence of weed. This was long before it received all the publicity we hear today. In Oklahoma it was known as "loco weed," and it grew all over the place. When a crowd gathered around the bandstand we were enveloped in big clouds of smoke and the strong smell of weed. Nobody seemed to think anything of it; there was nothing illegal about it. It was around this time that I began smoking it myself. It appealed to me and I took to it for a period that lasted for the next few years.

Oklahoma, by the way, was a dry state. You bought booze from bootleggers. I once bought a pint from a bellhop at the hotel for $5, and the thing that was surprising about it for those days was the quality. It was the best tasting booze I'd ever had.

While in Tulsa I teamed up with Judd McMichael. He and I hit it off pretty well, and he used to take me with him when he went to visit a girlfriend who lived in Sapulpa, a town about 15 miles away. (Joe Haymes's mother had a millinery store there. She had remarried, and her name was Mrs. House. Once Joe's sister came to see us at The Colosseum. She looked like Joe.) And looking back, that was one of the wildest summers of my life. We'd head for Sapulpa on Saturday night after the job. When we got there a house party would already be in progress. There would be fifteen or twenty people, gallons of booze—plus all the home brew you could drink—tons of food, and the party would last until Monday evening. To put it mildly, we had very attractive weekends.

Altogether it was a very interesting eight-week engagement, but it came to an end that September. We were booked to play the Pla-mor Ballroom in Kansas City, with a one-nighter between, in Columbia, Missouri. When we left Tulsa, Judd was driving his girlfriend's sky-blue Buick. She was in the front seat with Judd and I was in back with a girl named Lorina Moore. Just across the state line, near Joplin, we ran into a violent rainstorm, and the torrents of water washed a lot of mud onto the road. When Judd tried to pass another car we went into a wild skid that ended up with the car doing cartwheels. When it was all over we finished right-side-up, but poor Lorina Moore was lying prone on the floor of the car . . . *and I was standing on her!* Miraculously, nobody was hurt.

TWELVE

WHILE THE JOE HAYMES BAND was at the Pla-mor Ballroom we were besieged by a series of changes. First, I developed a sore throat, and when I went to the doctor he told me I had an abscess on my tonsils. It was pretty painful and I was running a light temperature. The doctor gave shots of grain alcohol to kill the pain and told me not to play for awhile, so my old buddy Louis Forman filled in for me with the band. Also around the same time Al Jennings decided to leave. He had a very attractive wife, Louise, who had once led a band, and he may have had plans to start up another with her. Then Claude Love was leaving too—or had already left, so we needed replacements for both of them . . . only to find out that K.T. Naylor had decided to quit, too.

Our tenorman, Dick Clark, was from North Dakota, an area noted for good bands and good musicians. When we got the word that Naylor wanted to leave, Clark contacted Mike Doty, who had been leading a band in Tacoma, Washington, for a year or so, with Roy Wager in the lineup. Meanwhile we went back to Springfield and the Half-a-Hill, Joe's home base, to work a couple of weekends and while we were there Doty joined the band. He showed up wearing the broadest-brimmed hat I ever saw. A heavy, chunky man weighing close to 275 pounds, he was an even-tempered, down-home kind of guy, and he played excellent lead alto, doubling on bass clarinet and flute.

We still needed a trumpet player and a trombonist, so Bud Weiser from Kansas City came in on trumpet—a fine player and a very nice guy—and Joe Harris joined on trombone. Joe Harris was something special. Without a doubt, he was the best trombone player I had ever heard up to that point. He played and sang like Jack Teagarden and already had a pretty varied career before he came with us. He was born in Sedalia, Missouri, but his wife, Juanita, came from Shawnee, Oklahoma, where the Teagardens also lived for a while (not to mention Les Jenkins, who was to enter the picture a bit later), so maybe Joe met Jack there. Joe admired Jack tremendously and at one time played with him in the oilfields. They used two trombones, a clarinet player, Sidney Arodin (the man who wrote the music for "Lazy

61

River"), and a piano man named Brooks Pruitt. Joe had some pretty heady tales to tell about those days; he was quite a storyteller.

Harris was a great asset to the band. His approach to the trombone was the same as Teagarden's—closed position slide work, all kinds of execution using his air column and lips instead of the slide. Tea had this system perfected, and so did Joe. Before joining us he had been playing with a jazz band on a riverboat called the *Idlewild*, out of Kansas City. After he came in we began to play things like "Basin Street Blues," and he'd work up special choruses on tunes like "Alice Blue Gown," along the same lines as Tea did on "Diane," and "Lover." I still play a lot of Joe's chorus on "Alice Blue Gown," which I will never forget.

So now the band was intact again, and the personnel was to remain stable for some time. We also had a lot to offer, particularly in the distinctive sound of Joe Haymes's arrangements. His long suit was writing for the saxophones—noty, fast-moving choruses that took a lot of rehearsing, even with Mike Doty, to get them down, but once this was accomplished the sound was pretty exceptional. And we were still strong in the vocal department. Joe Harris and Mike Doty both sang, and we still had Jimmy Underwood and the McMichael brothers.

Rehearsing the band left lots of time for social activity around town, and I met a couple of very nice girls. One of them was Jean Covi. I saw her again years later, and her son came to visit me when I was playing at Nick's in the Village. I was also very fond of a girl named Jean Lightfoot, a statuesque, very attractive and very bright girl. She knew so many big words that when I got back east and she wrote me letters I had to get the dictionary to find out what she was talking about.

We worked around the Kansas City-Springfield area for awhile, but we were getting itchy to move and finally we were booked into Norfolk, Virginia, by a young fellow who owned a hobby craft business. He got me interested in building model airplanes. For some time after, I spent my spare time in hotel rooms building them, starting out with those that had rubber-band engines and finally graduating to one that was powered by a real gasoline engine. The very first time I tried it out it took off for parts unknown and I never saw it again. I also built a special sling in the car we used on cross-country hops so the planes wouldn't get broken during travel.

We made a big sweep across the country—traveling by car; I rode in a big Hupmobile driven by Carl Snyder. We passed through St. Louis, Indianapolis, and Cincinnati, on our way to Norfolk, and it was all very exciting and a big thrill. Our first date was at William & Mary College. Norfolk was my first introduction to the seacoast, and I couldn't get enough of it. I wandered around, admiring the navy installations and marveling at the ocean off Virginia Beach, and was greatly impressed by the size of the Chesapeake Bay oysters.

We played some school dates, and then for a time worked a location. Here we ran into trouble. We did a radio broadcast from Norfolk to advertise the place and unwittingly broke a rigid union rule. For some reason, it developed, a band couldn't go in collectively to broadcast, while advertising they were playing somewhere else. The Norfolk local filed charges against us. I don't remember the extent of the charges, but they spelled serious trouble, and the worst part was that we had no defense; we were guilty. Carl Snyder saved us. He undertook the considerable job of writing what amounted to a small book that presented the band's position in a favorable light, and forwarded it to the International Board. As a result of the excellent job he did, the charges were dropped, even though we were guilty. They had us cold, but they let us go.

Once in the Virginia area we stayed and began to work for a local booker named Holtzschmeider. This involved making fast trips through the territory, hitting spots in Roanoke, Lynchburg, Richmond, Bristol, and across the Tennessee border. Other swings took us as far as Huntington, West Virginia, Harrisonburg, and Luray. I remember going on at a place in Ashland, Kentucky, right after some young guy had been shot.

We worked through October and into November and finally wound up in Greensboro, North Carolina, a memorable place for a couple of reasons. For one thing, at one point I got hold of a half pint of applejack and proceeded to combine it with a half pint of the local corn whisky (which was sold in mason jars) and drink it. I was no good for anything the rest of the night. But far more serious, our bookings suddenly ran out, and the booker took off with the money he owed us. All at once we were in a panic. Completely broke and with no food except for some canned goods that Joe Harris's wife, Juanita, had stored in their car.

We were living upstairs in the hotel where we had been playing, but now we had no job and barely enough money between us to live on. Luckily, a man who owned a restaurant learned about our plight, took pity on us, and sent us food. In the meantime, the guys in the band wired home for emergency money; Joe Haymes contacted Ted Weems for help; and while we were waiting for something to happen we amused ourselves playing pool.

I don't know who bailed us out. Maybe Ted Weems sent money to Joe. Anyway, somebody helped, and we were able to get out of Greensboro so we could play a job at the Richmond Country Club. The Club was closed for the winter, but somehow arrangements were made to open it for one night and we played the date. But whatever the money settlement was supposed to be we still wound up without any. There we were again, broke and with no jobs and no food. Somebody allowed us to stay on at the Club for three or four days, but there was nothing to eat. We tried scrounging in the closed kitchen for anything edible, but all we came up with was a bag of onions.

Things looked so bad and we were so hungry that we reached the desperation stage. Judd McMichael and I decided to try our hands at chicken stealing. We went cruising around listening for the sounds of chickens, but when the chips were down neither of us had enough nerve to climb a fence or go near a barnyard.

I don't know how we got out of that situation either, but again some unknown benefactor came to the rescue and we came up with a string of bookings in central Pennsylvania. My guess is Carl Snyder managed to contact some local bookers, because at the time we were still not connected with a regular agency. We left Richmond with no regrets.

● ● ●

This seems as good a place as any to tell you what I know of the history of the Haymes band before I joined it, and maybe give you a better insight into what the band business was like in the Twenties. In the first place, there were some pretty good musicians around the Springfield, Missouri, area. One who comes to mind immediately is the late Stan Wrightsman, an excellent piano player who already had quite a reputation then and was often mentioned by the Haymes men with admiration. Others included John Langsford, Paul Mitchell, and two brothers. Skeeter and Tappy Palmer. These men were in the little band that Joe Haymes had at the Half-a-Hill Tearoom when Ted Weems brought his band—a typical MCA road unit— through Springfield. Springfield was on the way from Dallas to Chicago— the two main centers of activity for MCA—and Weems probably stopped off long enough to play a one-nighter. Just how it happened is anybody's guess at this point, but it seems logical to assume that Weems heard the band at the Half-a-Hill, liked the sound of Joe's arrangments, and offered him a job. One thing is definite, when Weems left Springfield Joe was with him as a second pianist and was with the band when it opened in Chicago at the Granada Cafe.

It was 1929, and Weems spent the better part of the year playing at the Granada Cafe, which was located in the heart of Chicago's gang territory and was run by a tough character named Al Quodbach, reputed to have underworld connections. The story goes that it was a good location for building a band, and Weems gave Joe Haymes permission to do anything he wanted in choosing material and writing for it. Ted also had talented men in the band who were capable of being fine entertainers, like Elmo Tanner, Parker Gibbs, and Country Washburn. So Joe picked a tune written by his old friend Phil Baxter, called "Piccolo Pete," arranged it as a showcase number for the Weems band, and they recorded it for Victor. It made a tremendous hit.

From then on Joe Haymes could do no wrong as far as Ted Weems was concerned, and he continued to write most of the special material for the band. He also became a good friend of a trumpet-playing vaudevillian, Phil Dooley, a great guy and one well equipped for show business. Phil knew the right people and had the right connections; and he had a knack for writing novelty material like "Little Nell," which the Haymes band recorded later. More than likely it was Phil who first suggested to Joe that he start his own band, and then he was supported in the idea by a guy from Ventnor, New Jersey, Al Zugsmith, who also began pushing Joe. I have no doubt either that the whole thing had Ted Weem's blessing, because he and Joe always remained good friends.

Anyway Haymes started auditioning musicians in Chicago. I believe he had intentions of augmenting the little band at the Half-a-Hill, because to a large extent that's what he did. When he did organize his band it was in Springfield. But he found a fine clarinetist in a kid from Chicago Heights, 17-year-old Johnny Muenzenberger (better known as Johnny Mince), and an excellent tenorman, Dick Clark, and took them back to Springfield and the Half-a-Hill. Then he put together a band that included Paul Mitchell, John Langsford, and Tappy Palmer on bass—three members of his original group. I suppose he got help from Phil Baxter, who sent two more men over from his band, K.T. Naylor and Al Jennings.

Their first job was at the Mayo Hotel in Tulsa, and for the rest of the year they played locations like the Radison Hotel in Minneapolis, the Gibson Hotel in Cincinnati, and probably made a sweep through the Pennsylvania coal region. (This I surmise because they all seemed familiar with the area when I played it with them later.) I understand too that some time in the middle of this tour they were farmed out to Zez Confrey, who fronted the band for two weeks in Baltimore. They also played a steady gig at the Bamboo Gardens, a Chinese restaurant in Cleveland, a big music town in those days.

By this time the band was well launched. All of the engagements had been successful money makers and good places to work. Dooley and Zugsmith, who always seemed to hover in the background like guardian angels, were very close to the band and probably had a lot to do with paving the way for it. Phil Baxter probably helped too. This was the band I joined at the Muehlebach.

• • •

I imagine it was Al Zugsmith who pulled us out of our second panic in Richmond and got us booked into Pennsylvania in December 1931. We still had a good band and most of it was intact, although the McMichael brothers had had enough and left us. We worked our way north through Luray into the south Pennsylvania York-Lancaster area, and I recall that one of our stops was at the Valencia Ballroom in York.

In spite of our difficulties there was a lot of spirit in the Haymes band. The musicians liked each other, they liked the band, and they were happy to be working in it. Joe Harris always griped a lot, but his griping was part of his character and all done in fun, and it helped a lot on those panic jobs that the Harrises always carried along a supply of canned fruits and vegetables.

Like a good many of the road bands of that era, we eventually gravitated to the Plaza Hotel in Scranton, and it became our headquarters for the next year or so. The Plaza was the hub for all the bands and musicians working the territory. Sometimes there would be as many as 15 or 20 bands staying there at one time. It had a small lobby, but the place was always jammed with musicians, so I got acquainted with a lot of the men working with outfits like Casa Loma, Phil Emerton's Diamonds, Ace Brigode, Tal Henry, Rudy Vallee, Ben Bernie, and Cab Calloway. I even met one lead trumpet player who claimed he was making $135 a week, big pay in those days.

The Detroit crews came through too—outgrowths of the Goldkette days. One was led by Freddy Bergen, a pianist, and a whale of a musician. Another was Hank Biagini's band, with Bob Zurke on piano. That was the same year, by the way, that I heard Art Tatum for the first time in some upstairs beer joint in Cleveland. Either one of those guys—Zurke or Tatum—when you heard them for the first time, it was unbelievable.

I also met a lot of the local musicians at the Plaza—sax player Gene Fowler, piano player Hal Gibbons, Gabe Gelenas, who later played with Gene Kardos, and the Stevens brothers—Bob, who played trumpet and became an A & R man for Decca, and Haig, who went on to become a contractor for Harry Sosnick, and their younger brother Roy, who also played trumpet.

Working out of the Plaza we played up and down the valley—Nanticoke, Sunbury, York—they all had ballrooms. Then up to Binghamton to play the George F. Pavilion in Johnson City, or the Orlando Ballroom in Wilkes-Barre, or the two ballrooms situated dead center of the coal-mining district south of Sudbury called the Lakewood and the Lakeside. Another ballroom I distinctly remember was in Hazelton, called the Winter Garden and run by a Mr. Shiffler. A stairway led down from the ballroom to a room he called the Brauhaus, where they served beer supposedly piped in right from the brewery. At any rate, Mr. Shiffler looked like the prototype of the German brewmaster and, besides the beer, they served wonderful limburger sandwiches with raw onions.

Incidentally, if you're wondering why musicians were so fond of the Plaza Hotel, the reason was very basic—it was cheap. We usually teamed up two to a room, and this meant it cost a buck apiece for the night. Several of our guys were traveling with their wives—Harris, Underwood, Weiser, Langsford—so they had to pay the entire $2 charge, but the rest of us could get away for half. Holding down expenses was important because we weren't making a lot of money. In Haymes's band everybody got the same salary, which I think was around $70 a week.

We sometimes played a place in the center of Scranton called The Town Hall, run by a manager and promoter named Art Cohen. The place drew tremendous crowds. One day Cohen had to make a business trip into Manhattan and he agreed to take me with him. I was all excited. I had always wanted to see New York, and I was delighted at the chance. Just what business Cohen transacted I'm not sure, but it seems to me that Joe Haymes also went along, so it's possible that the two of them were paving the way for our first engagement at Roseland Ballroom, which was to come along in the spring. We stayed overnight in the Big Town, so I had time to roam around and look it over. I can still remember my first impressions. The Times Square area was exciting, and I was impressed by the compactness of the tall buildings. But the thing that is stamped indelibly in my mind was my surprise at the varied colors of the taxicabs that darted around the streets. In other cities they were always yellow.

The Joe Haymes Orchestra at the Riverside Club in Utica, N.Y., 1932. Front row L to R: Paul Mitchell, pno; Dick Clark, tnr; Pee Wee Erwin, tpt; Joe Haymes, ldr; Carl Snyder, gtr, mgr; Joe Harris, trb/vcl; Bud Weiser, tpt. Back Row: Johnny Mince, alto/clnt; Mike Doty, lead alto/vcl; John Langsford, bari; Stanley Fletcher, st bass/tuba; Jimmy Underwood, drms/vcl.

We played a weekend at a theater in Carbondale and then we began to hit spots in New York State. One of the saddest affairs I've ever played was a date at the women's prison in Auburn. They enjoyed the music, but it took us some time to get over the looks on their faces.

New Year's Eve we worked at a place called Ryan's in Shenendoah, Pennsylvania, and it was my first introduction to a swinging-door saloon with beer on tap. Then, early in January, we went into a steady job at the Riverside Club in Utica, N.Y., run by two gentlemen named Emanuel Salzman and Dan Verelli. Several things are vivid in my memory of this place. For one thing, while we were there the Lindbergh baby was kidnapped. For another, I recall making the rounds of Salzman's string of houses in Utica while he made his collections. Then there was the night I got so stoned that I walked the five miles from the Riverside Club into Utica center in the middle of a snowstorm. And last, but hardly least, business at the Club fell off so badly that part of the band's pay was made in the house whiskey. My share was seven bottles. It was probably made in somebody's bathtub, but the Golden Wedding label was on the bottles.

We were scheduled to go further into New York State at the end of this engagement, but things were looking so panicky that Bud Weiser decided to leave the band. Joe Harris was getting shaky, too, Mike Doty got in touch with his friend Roy Wager, and Roy joined us at the Majestic Hotel in Utica. This was around March of 1931.

We moved on to a date in Johnstown, and I remember playing the Finger Lakes region. Then we played Oil City and Erie, on a lake near the Ohio border, circling around to work Myers Lake in Canton, Ohio, and moving on to Steubenville. These were dates booked by a local promoter friend of ours, Ray Wingerter from Erie.

In Steubenville Joe Harris left us, and we had to wait around for his replacement, Les Jenkins. I suspect that Harris lined him up for us. Jenkins turned out to be a big six-footer from Oklahoma. Before joining Haymes he had been playing a job in Bermuda with John Riley Scott. The two of them were great rounders and they had enjoyed the great booze they were able to get there, but the job blew up on them as the result of a practical joke. A sax player in the band found a dead shark on the beach. He took an oar and bashed it into a bloody mess and then dragged it into the lobby of the Hamilton Hotel. The hotel management wasn't amused, and the band was sent back to the States.

When Jenkins arrived in Steubenville, all he had with him was a very small bag containing three or four shirts. He was very concerned because his trunk hadn't arrived on the same train. For the next day or so he hung around the railroad station looking for his trunk, and when it finally arrived—a small, footlocker kind of thing—he brought it back to the hotel. We all figured he had a change of clothes in it, but when he opened it up it was half-filled with phonograph records—mostly 12" symphony sides but some jazz. The rest was weed.

There were quite a few people in the bands who smoked marijuana before it was put on the federal narcotics list, but it wasn't until after Bop came in that I ever knew junk to be used. The only narco I ever recall knowing before then was a guy who lived at the Plaza Hotel, and he wasn't a musician. In the greatest contradiction of all time, he made his living lecturing against dope and had an arm punched full of holes.

With Jenkins in the band we went on to play Altoona, Washington, and Pittsburgh. Then, after a week or so, we started heading back East. That trip from Pittsburgh to Harrisburg over the old blacktop roads of the time was a real chore—a demon of a ride over the mountains. In bad weather it was dangerous, and at best it was a miserable drive. We were all glad to get back to Scranton.

As you may know Scranton was famous for something else in those days besides music. It had the most notorious redlight district in the East called "The Alley," which is what it was: a two-block alley between the main streets of the town. A series of houses—perhaps 20—faced the alley, and each house had a half-a-dozen girls or so. This was an important aspect of the night life of the people in the coal industry, and the coal miners blowing off steam after a hard week's work were important business factors in the town. They loved dancing, drinking, and women. The girls were as much a part of the scene as the dancing in the ballroom, and a trip with a chick was one buck—pretty cheap lovemaking.

I made the acquaintance of one of the madams in The Alley, and for some reason, maybe because I was just a kid, she took a shine to me. She brought me into her kitchen, introduced me to her husband, and treated me like one of the family. This gave me a marvelous opportunity to meet some of the girls and listen in on shop talk that went on in the kitchen after the girls were finished with their tricks. I remember one night I was sitting in the kitchen drinking with the madam and her husband, when one of the girls—a big blonde, strong as an ox, named Babe—came in, plopped herself down, propped her feet up, and announced with justifiable pride that the last guy she'd had was number 50 for the day. I never heard the duplicate of that: all in all, a pretty good day's work. On another occasion the madam used my sympathetic ear to pour out her grievances against the local chief of police. It seemed she owned a lovely home in a residential area of the city, but the police chief wouldn't let her live in it because of her business.

Whatever the chief's opinion of the madam, I liked her and she liked me. When it came time for us to leave Scranton she gave me a going-away present, a hand-embroidered laundry bag she made for me while she sat around the kitchen stove. Madams had a lot of time on their hands.

I had a knack, I guess, if you want to call it that, for making odd friends. Making sorties into the night in Wilkes-Barre I stumbled on a black cathouse and got pretty friendly with the black guy in charge, who did a little bootlegging on the side. One night a drifter came through, a young black kid who had been riding the rails—in the lap of luxury. He had hopped a boxcar in the western part of New York State, and it turned out to be a sample car for furniture, including a completely assembled and set-up bedroom. He took off his clothes, had a beautiful night's sleep, got up in the morning, dressed, and got off at Scranton.

THIRTEEN

MAY 4, 1932, was a very important date for the Joe Haymes band, and somewhat of a milestone in my own career, because that was the day we made our first record for Victor in the old church studio in Camden, N.J.

To this day I don't know who arranged for the band to record, although I suspect that Zugsmith had something to do with it. We were all excited and keyed up for the thing, as you can well imagine, since I don't believe any of us had ever seen the inside of a recording studio before. It was a new experience for us. We all knew there was a lot of prestige attached to the fact you could say you were a recording band, especially if you recorded for Victor.

The recording director for Victor was Eli Oberstein. I always found him to be a likeable guy, but he had a reputation for being a shrewd operator with his fingers in a lot of pies. Just how he maneuvered his deals I guess no one will ever know, but the ultimate result was that a lot of bands and artists wound up recording for Oberstein rather than Victor. He always seemed to have an interest in the destinies of bands like Haymes's, Gene Kardos, and the lesser known outfits that came under his thumb. His full name, for the history books, was Eliot Everett Oberstein, which is where "Eliot Everett and His Orchestra" came from, if you have ever come across it on a record label. I know some of the Haymes sides came out this way, and the name was used on records for other bands too.

Our first record was a good one. We played a Joe Haymes arrangement of the James P. Johnson tune, "Old Fashioned Love." It is a fine example of what the band could do and especially an indication of how far ahead Joe's musical ideas were. Actually, as the record illustrates, he was anticipating the Glenn Miller format by several years, utilizing a trumpet lead in unison with the saxophones, although an octave lower. According to the discographical data which are so readily available today, we did it in one take. But I remember running it through—I suppose they were checking for recording balance—and really belting it out. When we were finished, Oberstein came out of the control booth, looked straight at me with a big grin, and said, "This is a band recording, not a trumpet solo." I guess I was trying to blow the filament out of his microphone.

We made three other sides that day, all of them arrangements by Joe of the novelty things that were great crowd-pleasers but at the same time served as showpieces for the band—"He's the Life of the Party," "Pray For the Lights to Go Out," and "Let's Have A Party."

Don't ask me why, but for some reason "Old Fashioned Love" was issued on Victor under the name Radio Rascals Orchestra and as the Harlem Hot Shots on Bluebird, names that were as meaningless then as they are now. As a result Joe was cheated out of any credit for his fine arrangement, and any benefit the band might have gotten for an exceptional performance was completely nullified. Maybe it wouldn't have made any difference if the side had been issued under his name, but Joe and the band were victimized by this kind of foolishness quite a few times.

After the record date we headed for New England and our first series of dates for the Schribman office. Charlie Schribman was the active brother at that time; I don't remember Si getting into the act until some time later when I was with Miller and Spivak. This was the big booking office for the New England area and they controlled it. We headed for Boston and, believe me, those of you who drive there from New York today have no idea of what a murderous trip it used to be. The Hutchinson River Parkway today is still a twisting, winding, snarling road, but at that time it was the super highway of all highways, which should give you some inkling of what the rest were like. Usually we went to Boston on Route 1 as far as New Haven, then on Route 15 to Hartford, and from Hartford to Massachusetts through Stafford Springs. This meant two-lane blacktop all the way and through the center of every city and town, so it was a ten- or twelve-hour trip, an all-day deal.

Sometimes we were lucky and the jump to Boston was broken by a stop in Norwalk, where we played one of the famous big-band locations called Roton Point (better known to musicians as "Rotten Point"). Or maybe we'd play the Ritz Ballroom in Bridgeport, or a place named Lake Compounce. These were all on the Schribman circuit. We usually played them on a Sunday. New England had many dance spots in those days.

When we got to Boston we holed up at another of those hotels which catered to musicians, the Metropolitan, located on Huntington Ave., one block down from the Bradford, which is still there. Across the street and down a ways was the Metropolitan Theater, a big presentation house which featured a line of girls and a full orchestra. Later on it became another stop for name bands on the order of the New York Paramount.

The Metropolitan Hotel wasn't quite a fleabag, but neither was it first class; it was adequate for our needs. The important thing was the rates—a buck apiece for a night. You could live pretty well on the road if you were making from $50 to $75 a week and only had to pay a buck a night for a hotel room, so there was always more than one band staying there; we were seldom alone. Like the Plaza, the place was usually crawling with musicians. Some years later Gene Krupa met his wife, Ethel, there. She was the telephone operator in the hotel.

Another Boston landmark was located on the next corner from the

Metropolitan Hotel. It was called The Little Club, and later it became the first musical home of Bobby Hackett and Brad Gowans. They had a great little jazz band there, probably Hackett's first major job, or at least the first one I remember him on. I think I met him playing guitar in a Providence ballroom called Roads-on-the-Pawtucket, but I identify him best with The Little Club.

Down in the center of the block was a delicatessen, another hangout for musicians, most of them ate breakfast and lunch there. Professional wrestlers liked the place too. At any rate, it was here we bumped into a fast-talking Irish kid named Larry Murphy who said he was a singer, and Haymes hired him. He was with us on our next recording session. Larry was a great guy with a wonderful Irish sense of humor. The only trouble was he was also a kleptomaniac and he would steal anything that wasn't nailed down. Before the band caught on to him, he even used us as props for some of his gimmicks. He'd ask a couple of guys to go with him into a jewelry store. There he would start talking to the sales clerk about his upcoming engagement, or some other event he dreamed up on the spot. It was all a front so he could pocket a ring or two now and then. On a return trip to Boston (by now everyone was wise to him) in the same little delicatessen where we met him, Larry Murphy stole my overcoat. He came around wearing it, and told me a big story about the great overcoat he had found in the street.

In spite of his idiosyncrasies, he was a very likeable guy. He wasn't very good-looking, but he was tall, slender, and made a nice impression on the bandstand. He had a real Boston accent and since there were no other Easterners in the band we had a lot of fun kidding him about it. If you listen to the record we made of "It's About Time," instead of singing, "Unless I draw a diagram," he says, "Unless I drawer a diagram."

On our first trip out for the Schribman circuit we played a place in Springfield, Massachusetts, called Cook's Butterfly Ballroom, the original home of one of the great New England bands, McEnelly's. In retrospect, I'm very happy we played the ballroom when we did because I must admit at the time I didn't have the faintest idea who McEnelly's band was and only later discovered the stature it rated in New England. I remember Mr. Cook, who still managed the place, proudly showing me all the pictures of McEnelly's in his office, and the fact they started in his place was probably the highlight of his life. He was always happy to show the pictures.

There were ballrooms all over New England, and they did good business. We played one in Orange, Massachusetts (where they had a factory that made minute tapioca), another at Revere Beach, and still another at Old Orchard Beach in Maine. The only thing I remember about the last one is going swimming because I have a lifetime memory of how damned cold the water was.

We went back to the Victor studios in Camden on June 7. Larry Murphy split the vocals with Jimmy Underwood. One of the titles assigned to Jimmy was "When I Put on My Long White Robe," an ironic twist in view of what happened only a short time later. We recorded again on June 14 in

New York, but Victor saw fit to release all the sides on the Electradisk label and under anybody's name except Joe's, thus making doubly sure that, if anybody ever succeeded in finding the records, Joe Haymes wouldn't get any of the credit. I never knew anybody who had any of these records—or even heard of anybody who had—until 1977 when they were reissued on the Bluebird two-record LP set of "Joe Haymes and His Orchestra 1932-1935" (AXM2-5552).

On June 23 we recorded for Victor again in New York, and on the next day we made half-a-dozen sides for the American Record Company. Changing recording companies didn't succeed in changing Joe's luck. He was still a victim of the name game and not one record was credited to "Joe Haymes and His Orchestra."

Some time that summer we got our first job at the Roseland Ballroom in New York. This proved to be Jimmy Underwood's last job. He had a tooth pulled and infection set in. It was giving him a lot of pain so he decided to go home until he felt better, and only a short time later we heard he had died. The news came as a great shock to the band because it was totally unexpected. None of us even suspected that having a tooth pulled could have such serious results.

John Riley Scott, Les Jenkins's old friend, came in to replace Jimmy, and we recorded with him on our next session for Victor in Camden on July 24. Afterwards we did a week at the famous Steel Pier in Atlantic City and then went back to New York for a recording date directed by Ben Selvin on the Columbia label.

I'm a bit hazy about the next few weeks, but I know we were up and down the Jersey coast and finally wound up in Wildwood. From there we made a jump to Fort Worth, Texas, and that's a long haul—at least two or three days of travel—to play Lake Worth. We may have gotten this connection through John Riley Scott, who was from Amarillo. I know he played the Fort Worth job with us, although he was already making plans to leave us afterwards.

Once we were in Texas somebody decided we should stay and work the area, so we went on the road, traveling by bus, for the Frederick Brothers. To this day musicians talk about the Frederick Brothers and their buses, and I have very vivid memories of them, particularly the buses. They looked like old schoolbuses and maybe they were, but by the time the Fredericks owned them they were ready for the junkyard. To begin with they had brakes that were not worth mentioning, and the driver couldn't slow down without shifting gears. When he came to a curve he'd yell, which was the signal for everybody on the bus to lean to the other side of the bus or, in some cases, to actually clamber over in a mad scramble in order to keep the bus from turning over.

I still get a chill at the recollection of an occasion in St. Joe, Missouri, which is a fairly hilly city. The bus started backing down a hill and the driver couldn't stop it. We zipped by one intersection and were lucky because nothing was coming the other way. Finally the driver had to back us into a

73

high curb to keep the thing from going all way down the hill and turning us into accident statistics.

We went to West Texas where it was as hot as blazes. In Vernon, where we played, they didn't have any water, not even for drinking. We toured the Panhandle, went on to Oklahoma City, played the Blue Moon in Wichita, Kansas, and finally Kansas City, where we picked up a black singer named Joe, who had been working with local bands. He toured with us for a while but it didn't work out very well. At night he wasn't allowed to stay in the hotels with the rest of the band and had to sleep in the bus. This was a constant source of embarrassment, both to him and to us.

Through September and October, still working for the Frederick Brothers, we did a series of one-nighters working our way back East. We picked up another vocalist, a gal with an established reputation as a singer around Kansas City. She was one of those buxom, heavy-voiced singers that were popular before the introduction of microphones. Her name was Emma Pritchard, and her favorite drink was ice cream with gin and coffee flavoring.

In the meantime we had a couple of other personnel changes. John Riley Scott had left, and another friend of Mike Doty's from the Dakotas or Minnesota territory came in to replace him, Ray Powell. I remember Powell particularly well because the guy was the spitting image of Stan Laurel. On the other hand, I don't remember if he was a good or a bad drummer, but I guess he sufficed for the time being.

Les Jenkins had also been making noises about leaving. One night we were playing an obscure ballroom in some little town when a nice-looking blond guy came up to me and introduced himself. He said his name was Ward Silloway, that he was a pretty good trombone player, and that he was playing in the territory with an outfit called Witt Toma's band. Since Jenkins was leaving, his timing was perfect. When we found out he played as good as he said he did, we took him on as Jenkins's replacement.

With these changes, we continued heading east to the Pennsylvania region, where by now we had a pretty fair following. We also made another trip into New England that winter, which included a date in Portland, Maine, where there was no place for us to stay. We had to ride 20 miles out of town until we found a farmhouse that took in roomers. On these trips I always rode in the car with Roy Wager, a quiet, serious guy not given to wasting words in a lot of idle chatter. We had become good friends and could ride hundreds of miles without saying anything. This suited us both, because by then I had taken pretty heavily to smoking pot and didn't want anybody talking to me. We kept a speedometer record on Roy's car for a period of five months, and during that time we traveled over 102,000 miles.

FOURTEEN

WE HIT NEW YORK in time for Christmas of 1932—at any rate, it was fairly close to New Year's Eve. On Seventh Ave. there were two places run by a Greenwich Village entrepreneur named Meyer Horowitz—the Village Barn, a very successful operation, and a smaller place called The Nut Club, which also did pretty well. We were booked into The Nut Club, probably through the efforts of our old friend Zugsmith, who by this time was second in command and well entrenched with the Columbia Artists Bureau, headed by Ralph Wonders.

We moved into the Chesterfield Hotel on 49th Street, another dollar-a-night place catering to musicians, but not the only one of its kind in New York. Musicians lived in the Van Cortlandt and the Plymouth across the street. Joe Venuti and Manny Klein were staying at the Plymouth, and that's where I first met Manny and Artie Shaw. Vic Engle was there, too, and also a heavy-drinking guitar player named Chick Reeves—but more about him later.

I roomed with Roy Wager, and Mike Doty was in with Ray Powell. The reason I remember this is because one night Powell got so stoned that he passed out in a chair, and when Doty tried to pick him up and put him to bed he slipped out of Mike's hands, fell to the floor in a heap, and broke a toe. Breaking a toe isn't a serious injury, but it is painful. Especially to a drummer. It put Powell out of action, so Charlie Bush came over to us from the Village Barn, where he'd been playing with Joe Furst's band. That was the end of Powell's career with Haymes.

I consider our period at The Nut Club the high point of my years with the Joe Haymes band for several reasons. The club had a radio wire and we were broadcasting five nights a week. This alone was a great help in establishing the band's reputation and popularity in the New York area and it also helped mine. There's no doubt in my mind that in the Thirties New York was the place for a musician to be. But it wasn't easy to get there, and it wasn't easy to get into Local 802. The Nut Club made both of these things possible for me. The Haymes band was a traveling group. Nobody had an 802 card when we went into The Nut Club. But it was common knowledge in the business that New York was where the big jobs and big money were, so all of us were very desirous of joining the New York local. On the other hand, union rules were strict. They stated that transferees into 802 couldn't work a steady engagement for three months, but could only take club dates. If a traveling band, such as ours, went in on a location job, it had to stay there at least six months before the men were eligible to join the local. Our uppermost thought was to remain at The Nut Club for six months, and our cards were deposited with that in mind. When the six months were up, we all went down and joined 802 in a body. To us it was a monumental event.

For that matter, we really hadn't been doing too badly and after the Greensboro incident nothing had approached panic proportions. We weren't getting rich, but we were working at a time when many people were without jobs. The evidence of that was before my eyes every night when I left the Chesterfield to go to work and saw the breadlines stretching four abreast from the soup kitchen at the World Theater all the way to Sixth Avenue. It was a very disheartening sight, but it made me appreciate what I had.

Working The Nut Club was quite an experience in itself, and I enjoyed it. We had five half-hour broadcasts over the CBS network, which in 1932 was pretty heavy air time. Once or twice a week the management brought in personalities like Hal LeRoy, Arthur Tracy, Uncle Don, and Nick Kenny, and it seemed to me the place was always full of comedians, guys like Milton Berle and Henny Youngman. They came in to hear a little guy named Lou Dolgov, a veritable Joe Miller's Joke Book on two legs. Lou was a tiny fellow, and he didn't have much floor personality, but he was very good on the radio and had been on the air once or twice over the New York station WINS. He could stand on the bandstand and rattle off jokes for a solid 15 minutes. The other comedians were sitting around jotting them down in shorthand. Lou was a tremendous storehouse of material, a human computer bank before the machines were ever dreamt of.

Our regular comedian was Jack White, who appeared in the Paul Whiteman movie "The King of Jazz," playing a drunk in several scenes. At The Nut Club he was the headliner and he had a group of stooges, Frank Hires, Jerry Bergen, and Henry Nemo. Nemo later wrote the hit songs "'Tis Autumn," and "Don't Take Your Love From Me," but he was a complete nut. They also had a woman stooge, Blanche Lebeau, who had a long, drawn, wrinkled face. She somewhat resembled the movie star Zasu Pitts. They always put on a good show. I remember one skit in particular that was a takeoff on the Paul Muni movie "Chain Gang." They came out in long underwear, chained together with links of frankfurters, and sang something like, "We ain't eatin' in weeks, we ain't eatin' in weeks . . . and if we don't eat soon we'll be driven to eatin' our chains." At which point they started gnawing on the hotdogs.

They did another thing that included seven-foot-tall John Langsford, four-foot-tall Jerry Bergen, and Henry Nemo—a routine about Washington, Lincoln, and Grant. You got a lot of entertainment for your money at The Nut Club. I don't imagine the cost for an evening was very high in those

Depression years. Prohibition had been repealed, and I remember buying my first case of 3.2 beer.

Haymes played until 4 a.m. at the club, and after the job I would go to visit Chick Reeves, who lived at the Plymouth. He was an orchestrator and at the time was arranging for Harry Reser's Cliquot Club Eskimos. He was always awake when I got there because he was one of those guys who always waited until the last minute before starting to work. He was also a heavy drinker. When I arrived he would get out the bottle and his guitar and we'd play the rest of the night. He introduced me to some of the men in the Reser band, including Bob Cusuomano (a fine trumpet player I later worked with quite a bit in the studios), and another arranger, Roy Chamberlain, who was, I think, the chief arranger for Reser. He's still going strong. I met him a few years ago in California, and he had a very successful career there.

I drank very little in those days, if at all, but I was smoking more and more weed and becoming more and more of an introvert. My prime interest in life was the band and playing good lead trumpet in it. Nothing else seemed important. I enjoyed myself immensely when I smoked, but I didn't enjoy drinking. To get bagged and then feel miserable was no fun, to my way of thinking, and I began to take a strong view against people who did drink. We had no heavy drinkers in the band, for that matter, with the exception of Ray Powell. I didn't start to do a lot of drinking until I went with Ray Noble. By then pot had been placed on the federal narcotics list.

In my opinion, I was better off on the weed. When I began drinking I went at it heavy, using alcohol as a crutch. It became a way of life. I wound up an alcoholic. Speaking from years of experience, I feel qualified to state that I frown on alcohol because it makes you into a slob; I don't care who you are. Some of my best friends have been wrecked by it, and I made a classic ass of myself on more than one occasion. I'm convinced that booze makes you hopeless, helpless, and numb-brained, and that's only part of it. I'm not promoting weed—latter-day research has uncovered some scary things about it, too—but I have never known anyone smoking pot to do the idiotic things drunks do.

While I was at The Nut Club the weed drove me further and further into my shell, and I spent a lot of time alone. Sometimes after the job I wouldn't feel sleepy, so I'd go for a ride on the Staten Island Ferry, or take long subway rides. I explored the whole city. I was quite interested in the way it seemed to be changing before my eyes. They were tearing down the 6th Avenue El, the metal from which supposedly was sold to Japan and later came back to us in the shape of bullets. And the Radio City complex opened, with the Music Hall, and the Center Theater. Horace Heidt played there, and the first movie I saw was "King Kong."

Whether or not it was the result of smoking so much weed I don't know, but my temperament was becoming less stable. One night while we were in the middle of a broadcast I hit a series of foul notes and lost my head. I literally tore the lead pipe off the trumpet, thereby putting the horn out of commission and depriving the band of a lead trumpet for the rest of the broadcast. Smoking weed has another dangerous tendency—the temptation to try something stronger. We had a Turk working in the men's room at The Nut Club who was able to bring in Eastern hashish which he sold to us at a dollar for a good-sized chunk. I tried it a couple of times and fancied that it helped my playing, so it's just as well that after we left the club I could no longer get it.

After Charlie Bush joined the band, he invited me to go along with him on visits to friends in New Jersey. One of them was a guitar player from Newark named Slim—I don't recall his full name—and we'd go to his home on Sunday. His mother would invite all the musicians in the Newark area— sometimes as many as ten or twelve—and she'd cook up a great washtub full of spaghetti. I got to know a lot of people in New Jersey, and I started going with Charlie to another place which was to become one of the most famous spots in the state, The Meadowbrook.

I don't remember if it was called The Meadowbrook then—it certainly wasn't as elaborate as it became later—but they had a band there, and it was a good band. I'm not sure that in April 1933 the band was Frank Dailey's, but it was his later on. In it were two very fine musicians, a bald-headed trumpet player named Phil Baird, and a whale of a tenor sax man, Charlie Frazier, who later went with Jimmy Dorsey. Those trips to New Jersey familiarized me with the place and this came in handy later. Some of the spots I visited, like the Chanticleer in Millburn, are still active.

About midway in our engagement at The Nut Club I found a furnished apartment in the Village. It was much more convenient to the job. I stocked up on 3.2 beer, more or less considered one of life's necessities then, and went shopping on Bleecker Street so I could have my meals at home. The apartment was on Jones Street, pretty close to the club, which was just south of Sheridan Square. I used to buy a lot of Italian food and cook in. I also got acquainted with a French family who ran a laundry across the street. A daughter was dating Andre' Baruch, the radio announcer. Across the street from The Nut Club on Seventh Avenue was an all-night cafeteria which was the hang-out for the Village people. It was a huge place, open 24 hours a day, and everybody went there. You met all the artists, musicians, and the gay people, at one time or another. I don't think the Village has changed very much.

The Joe Haymes band played The Nut Club for a full six months. At the end of that time we all went down to union headquarters and joined Local 802 in a body. I'm certain we finished the date by June 1, and this is borne out by the fact that we recorded for Columbia on that date. If we hadn't been members of Local 802 by that time we wouldn't have been allowed to record in the city.

78

FIFTEEN

AFTER WE LEFT The Nut Club we made a wide swing of one-nighters through our old stamping ground, the Lancaster-York area of Pennsylvania. We had decided (we were doing things by vote in the band by then) to add a girl singer as a way of making the band more commercial. Joe hired a young lady named Holt Paige, a lovely girl, rather tall, and a genuine southern belle from Richmond, Virginia. She rode with Charlie Bush and his wife, Ida, in their Chrysler convertible. As luck would have it, when we hit the Amish country we ran into the worst electrical storm in memory. The lightning was enough to scare anybody, but it scared this young lady so badly that I don't believe she stayed with us more than a week. She took off for home as soon as she could and that was the end of our girl singer.

After the Pennsylvania swing we went back to New England for a couple of weeks, a tour notable because we were booked for one of those "Battle of the Bands" that promoters were so fond of, opposite the great Ben Pollack band. The battle took place at the Claremont Ballroom in Claremont, New Hampshire, and it rained so hard we were lucky if 50 customers showed up. I think the combined bands outnumbered them. But this gave us the opportunity to get well acquainted, and I established friendships with the Pollack men, especially Charlie Spivak and Yank Lawson, which were important to me later.

We were back in New York on June 21, 1933 for another recording session for the American Record Company. I remember Roy Wager doing the vocal on "Lazybones" and Mike Doty singing "Gotta Go." The records were released on the Five-and-Ten labels: Melotone, Banner, Perfect, etc. At the same session we recorded two of Joe's originals, "Lost Motion," and "Not for Sale." The first title was a typical Haymes composition, noty and arranged for the saxes with some very difficult figures. I imagine we messed it up because the side was never issued. Nor was "Not for Sale," released. That was unfortunate for Joe had written it as the band's theme song. It had a very catchy melody. We used it on our radio broadcasts and it attracted quite a bit of favorable comment. Joe had showcased it in an outstanding arrangement. I have no idea why it was not released, but I certainly would like to hear it again.*

Next we went back to the Steel Pier in Atlantic City. We were there several times, but on this particular occasion Milton Berle was headlining in one of the theaters on the Pier. We had worked with him only a short time before at The Nut Club, so we all knew him. And he knew us well enough to come to see us, but it's a further indication of what a foggy guy Joe Haymes was that when Berle came into the ballroom where we were playing, walked up to stand in front of the bandstand and looked up at Joe, Joe did not even recognize him. After being ignored for several minutes, Berle finally said, "I'd like to have your autograph, Mr. Haymes." Joe nodded vaguely and started to say something about waiting until we were through playing, and Berle interrupted with, "I'd like to have your autograph on my navel."

Near the Steel Pier—about a half a block away—was a place called the Virginia Cafe, a hangout for all the musicians who were working in the bands in Atlantic City. The walls were covered with pictures of all the bands that played the Steel Pier, and the place specialized in the favorite dishes of musicians. Somebody in the Casa Loma bunch liked banana sandwiches with ketchup on them, for example, so these were a specialty of the house. Anyway, it was here I met and got pretty friendly with the guys who were playing with Isham Jones at the Ambassador Hotel—about a mile down the boardwalk from the Pier—especially the two trumpet players, Johnny Carlson and George Thow. They took me with them to make the rounds of the many after-hours clubs in the city. Both Carlson and Thow were well known to the black musicians. The following year I became better acquainted myself, because I spent the whole summer in Atlantic City playing with the Jones band.

After the Steel Pier engagement we went back once more to the old RCA church studios in Camden for a session that resulted in some of the best things the band ever put on wax. We cut eight sides and four of them are excellent examples of Joe's exceptional ability as an arranger: "Limehouse Blues," "Shine On Harvest Moon," "Modern Melody," and "I Never Knew I Could Love Anybody." As remastered and reissued on the Bluebird LPs many years later, they offer concrete evidence of his fresh and original approach to material that even then had been well worked over. It should be kept in mind that Swing was still several years in the future when these records were made, so it's obvious that Joe was ahead of his time.

Shortly after this, Walt Yoder joined us on bass, replacing Stanley Fletcher who went to join his brother Chris in New York, playing in Ernie Holst's society orchestra. I'm not sure, but I don't think Walt ever recorded with the Haymes band, even on the final date in New York in November, because I seem to recall Fletcher returned for a short time. After Yoder came

*Diligent research by the late Lt. Col. Bill Bryan of Salem, Oregon, a Joe Haymes collector, uncovered an excellent version of "Not for Sale," as recorded by the reorganized Joe Haymes band under the name of "Joe Hines," and released on a 12" Associated transcription, #A-50, dated 12/20/34. It has been reissued on IAJRC 46 "Joe Haymes & His Orchestra 1932-1937."

John Langsford, billed as the tallest saxophonist in the world, in a publicity pose with Pee Wee Erwin and Dick Clark.

with us, we took another trip out to the Midwest. We probably played our way out, but we did work a full week at Valley Dale in Columbus, Ohio. This was Yoder's hometown, so Roy Wager and I stayed with him at his parents' house. His mother was a marvelous cook and I ate myself into oblivion. This wasn't the smart thing to do, because for some time I'd been suffering from a condition that was probably chronic appendicitis. I didn't pay much attention to it—most likely I didn't realize what it was—but every so often there was a painful indication that something was wrong with my insides. It caught up with me a short time later.

Roy Wager and Stan Fletcher.   Mike Doty on a boardwalk stroll.

The Joe Haymes Orchestra in front of the Steel Pier in Atlantic City in July, 1932. Les Jenkins has replaced Joe Harris on trombone, and John Riley Scott is in for the ill-fated Jimmy Underwood. Roy Wager is in the band.

A rare and nostalgic photo from the personal collection of Pee Wee Erwin of the Joe Haymes band on the boardwalk in front of the Steel Pier in Atlantic City in 1932. Standing L to R: Dick Clark, tenor; Johnny Mince, alto & clarinet; Stan Fletcher, tuba; John Riley Scott, drums; John Langsford, "The World's Tallest Saxophone Player," baritone sax; Roy Wager, trumpet; Les Jenkins, trombone; Mike Doty, lead alto; Paul Mitchell, piano. Seated: Carl Snyder, guitar; leader Joe Haymes; and trumpeter Pee Wee Erwin.

Following the week at Valley Dale we played a three-day weekend at Coney Island Park in Cincinnati and then went on to another amusement park in Louisville, Kentucky, Fountain Ferry Park. By this time the appendicitis was giving me a lot of pain. I think I was only able to play a couple of nights at the park. As usual, I was rooming with Roy Wager. Things got so bad with me that he finally went to the corner drugstore and asked the man behind the counter, "Do you know a good surgeon? I think my friend has appendicitis."

The druggist recommended a doctor by the name of E.S. Allen, who turned out to be an excellent surgeon and a fine man. He did a blood count on me and determined that for certain my appendix was ready to come out, so I went to the Kentucky Baptist Hospital and he operated. Dr. Allen gave me the anesthetic himself—a spinal block—and I remained awake for the whole operation . . . saw the whole thing. Along with his expert attention, I'm pretty sure he saved me quite a bit of money by doing everything himself. The whole operation only cost me 100 bucks. I was in the hospital for ten days. I don't have any idea what the entire bill was, but I'm certain by today's standards it was pretty darn' cheap. In the bargain I found out I had quite a few relatives in the Louisville area. My grandfather Erwin had gone to medical school there, and my grandmother had come from there, so I had a number of uncles and cousins in the city. Some of them came to visit me in the hospital.

In those days they didn't get you out of bed the day after an operation, so I was still taped up ten days later when my mother and father came to get me. They loaded me into the back seat of the car, made me as comfortable as possible, and hauled me back to Kansas City, a long trip and a pretty painful one. To this day I don't know who replaced me in the band while I was laid up. Roy Wager was a swinging trumpet player, but I don't think he could handle the book alone. Bands on our level were not in a position where we could send to New York for musicians. Maybe the band took a vacation while I was out; I really don't know what happened.

I convalesced in Kansas City where there was a lot of musical action taking place. I couldn't go out and make the rounds, but the Ben Pollack band was playing at the Belreve Hotel with Jack Teagarden and Sterling Bose in the band and, I think, Al Harris on lead trumpet. Being able to hear their remote airshots every day made my stay in Kansas City worthwhile.

I spent about a month recuperating and then, around the beginning of September, I rejoined the band. They seemed to be in the area, which leads me to believe they took some time off while I was out. We headed back east and our first job was in Trenton, N.J., probably at the state fair near White Horse. We played there for a week as George Hall's Orchestra. Actually George Hall was based at the Hotel Taft in New York and was there for a long run, but he fronted our band at the fair. We worked opposite a very good outfit led by Snooks Friedman. I can't remember the guys in it, but they had a darn' good band.

Our next stop was in New York, where we began a rather lengthy engagement at a place on the west side of Broadway called The Empire Ballroom. It later became the Nola Studios. The place had a two-band policy, as many of the ballrooms did, and when we first got there we were working opposite Fletcher Henderson. We had heard this bunch several times; it was always a treat. It was particularly good this time because he had Coleman Hawkins on tenor, and I believe Henry "Red" Allen was just starting with him on trumpet. This was just before those really good records came out which featured him as soloist. The grand old man, Russell Smith, was still playing lead.

But within a week we were playing opposite a jumping outfit led by Rex Stewart. This was one of the greatest experiences of our lives. He had a fantastic group, and Rex himself was fabulous—a real cornet player's cornet player—with terrific technique and a tremendous register. I suspect that in later years he probably blew himself out from all the hard work he had done, but at that time he was hitting high G with ease. I established a friendship with him that lasted until he passed away.

At the Empire he had a great rhythm section, with Big Sid Catlett on drums and Roger "Ram" Ramirez on piano. His lead trumpet player was George Thigpen, a very nice man. Of course, all the soloists in the band were fantastic. Along with everything else this was our first exposure to Edgar Sampson's arrangements. He wrote quite a bit of material for Rex, and a lot of it was original. I was very impressed. Some time later, when I was with Benny Goodman, I suggested to Benny that he look into Sampson's material, especially some of the things that Rex had played. As a consequence, Benny began to use a lot of Sampson's original things. The most important was probably "Stompin' At the Savoy," one of Benny's biggest hits, which he recorded at least twice. Another thing we borrowed from Rex's band was the use of riffs to achieve a rhythmic lift, and we used almost their entire arrangement of "You Can Depend on Me," which they had turned into a riff tune that was very novel. The comradeship between our band and Rex's was very great; it was certainly a fine musical experience for all of us.

It was at the Empire too that we met two young ladies who were fine piano players, Babe Russin's sister Sunny, and Gladys Moser, both well known in the New York area. Three years later I saw a lot of these two girls when they were playing at the old Nick's on Seventh Avenue, many years before I played there.

I think we played the Empire at least six weeks. Although I don't recollect the session, we apparently recorded for Victor once more in New York, playing some doctored stock arrangements of rather commercial tunes, all of which were issued under Mike Doty's name. Then, around mid-November, we wound up once more in the La Casa Ballroom in North Philadelphia. We didn't realize it at the time, but this was to be our last stop and the end of Joe's original band.

Things weren't too good financially, which is probably why we holed up at the La Casa. It was from here that Joe began negotiating a deal with Buddy Rogers, the move actor. Rogers apparently already had an engagement booked at the Paradise Restaurant in New York, but he didn't have a band. So it was agreed (the whole situation was thoroughly discussed in the band) that we would play the Paradise under Rogers, who also assured us that he had an extended theater tour lined up afterwards.

SIXTEEN

IT WAS AS "Buddy Rogers' Orchestra" that we returned to New York, and if memory serves me right we started working at the Paradise in the early part of December. The band that preceded us had been Paul Whiteman's, a much larger organization than ours. Since we were going to use the same book to play the show this meant a considerable change in our format, which I'll explain shortly. But first let me offer a little background about the Paradise Restaurant, which was quite a place, as all of those Broadway theater-restaurants were.

They presented what amounted to miniature Broadway shows, complete with headline artists. The revue at the Paradise was produced by a fellow named Nils T. Grantlund, better known as NTG. He called it the "NTG Revue." It had also been the feature at another big club, The Hollywood Restaurant, where the Isham Jones band spent one full winter. Sally Rand and her much-publicized fan dance was our headline act for a short time (for at least a small part of her performance she was stark naked). She worked directly in front of the band and had a screen rigged in front of the sax section so they couldn't see too accurately. Actually, I don't think anybody in the band was overly interested in Miss Rand because she wasn't any novelty. There were a number of scantily clad beauties in the show, although still a far cry from things as they are today where it's nothing unusual for stage and screen actors to appear completely naked. A show girl in those days had nothing to do but wear some feathers and a headdress and walk around looking beautiful. But there were three girls in the revue who were outstanding. One of them, in particular, was one of the most beautiful women I have ever seen. She was the girlfriend of the notorious Lucky Luciano, who was still enjoying his heyday. Of course, in obedience to the unwritten laws of show business, although we worked with these people we never became familiar with them or got to know them very well.

As I mentioned earlier, we played from the same book the Whiteman band had used before us, so this necessitated some changes in our setup. First of all, we were immediately augmented by a string section. Then Rogers had to hire a lead trumpet player who could cut the show, because playing the

Whiteman book was far out of my realm. One of the violinists who came with us was Jerry Arlen, songwriter Harold Arlen's younger brother, who we first met when he was playing with Snooks Friedman at the White Horse Fair. The lead trumpet player turned out to be Bob Cusuomano, who made a career out of going from one theater-restaurant to another and playing the shows cold. He was a powerful player and one of the best in his field. I'd first met him when he was playing with Harry Reser's radio band, probably toward the end of the Cliquot Club Eskimos, when Chick Reeves was writing the arrangements. We used to get together in his room at the Hotel Chesterfield. To give you an idea of Cusuomano's ability, there was a period when he was working with us that he developed a terrific sore right in the middle of his embouchure. He'd come in, break open the sore, and proceed to play the show as though nothing bothered him.

I don't recall the exact length of our stay at the Paradise, but it was probably a month or six weeks. Roy Wager and I had a small apartment in the Whitby Hotel about seven or eight blocks away. I mention this because what sticks in my mind is that it was one of the coldest winters on record, at one point the temperature dropped to 14 below zero. If we had a rehearsal or a matinee, or anything else to do in the area of the Paradise, we wouldn't even walk the few blocks to the apartment to have dinner. We'd eat in the restaurant downstairs, a little place that didn't even have tables, just a counter, but served great home-cooked food. The meals in there were just superb, and it was very handy during the engagement.

Buddy Rogers, by the way, was a very nice guy. He and I had an affinity because he came from a town in Kansas just outside of Kansas City. I looked on him as something of a hometown boy who had made good. He had been a great success in the movies. His mother used to travel with him a lot (this was before he married Mary Pickford). He worked hard. I wasn't involved, but while we were at the Paradise he picked up another band someplace and was making personal appearances at various theaters in the New York area, commuting back and forth. Sometimes the severe cold and the snow made this pretty difficult and he would show up at the Paradise just in time or even a bit late.

Toward the end of the Paradise run he began putting the material together that we were going to use on the theater tour, and the band underwent some more changes. Cusuomano, who had only been hired for the Paradise, was out and the brass section reverted to Roy Wager, Ward Silloway, and me. We still had most of the original sax section but John Langsford left to take a job with Isham Jones rather than go on tour, so Toots Mondello came in to play lead alto. Mike Doty was still with us, but Rogers had used Toots before and liked him—as we all did—so the section evolved into Toots, Mike, Johnny Mince, and Dick Clark. Incidentally, something that isn't too well known about Toots is that he used to do a great imitation of Ted Lewis—hat, cane, everything—and even looked like him.

I believe Stanley Fletcher rejoined us for the tour, but I don't think Paul Mitchell made it. If he did we had two piano players, because another fellow who had been closely associated with Rogers, Dewey Bergman, played piano and came in to serve as musical director and liaison man between Rogers and the band.

Last, but not least by any means, Gene Krupa was with us on drums, the first extended run I played with him. I first met him in 1932 when he and Jimmy McPartland were rooming together at the Dixie Hotel in New York. At the time I didn't really appreciate his stature as a drummer even though I knew something of his history. However, I did hit it off pretty well with both Jimmy and Gene. As I seem to recall, Mal Hallett organized a marvelous band around 1933, and Gene was in it along with Jack Teagarden, Toots Mondello, and Frank Ryerson on lead trumpet. Also in the band was another good trumpet player, R.D. "Mickey" McMickle, who had Bell's palsy and was only able to play by holding a rubber shoe-heel against his sagging jaw muscles. He did this for two or three months. Mickey had played with the great Austin Wylie band from Cleveland, a great bunch of musicians which included Clarence Hutchenrider, Billy Butterfield, and Spud Murphy.

Carl Snyder, the guitarist, who had been our band manager under Joe Haymes, stayed in New York and eventually put his great talent for business to good use working for the Frederick Brothers booking office. He stayed with them for a good many years and was still in the Chicago office when they were booking my band in the early 1940s, although I haven't seen or heard from him since.

To the best of my recollection we broke in the Buddy Rogers tour in New Haven. Another stop was the Metropolitan Theater in Boston. From there we went on to play a huge auditorium in Montreal called the Mount Royal Arena. We did tremendous business everywhere we went, largely due, I suppose, to the fact that Buddy Rogers was still a big name, still well remembered for his years as a movie star, and an extremely good-looking guy. However, without any intention of putting him down, I must admit the show was probably as corny as anything you have ever seen.

We were touring around the end of the first administration of Franklin D. Roosevelt which had instituted the NRA (the National Recovery Act) designed to bring about the end of the Depression, and the CCC (the Civilian Conservation Corps) a nationwide effort to put the unemployed to work. Both were a big help to the country, but not to our show. We had a young man with us—a nice young guy—who had been with the CCC and was a singer. In the middle of the show we played a patriotic medley, with Rogers conducting wildly, and we all had square, black boxes with a red letter on the front and a flashlight inside. At one point during the medley we had to hold these up and flick on the flashlights, and the audience in the darkened theater would read "ROOSEVELT—NRA" in big block letters. Believe it or not. But that wasn't all. As part of the grand finale, a baby spot would hit an American flag on the stage fluttering in the breeze from an electric fan behind it, and our CCC boy would come on and sing "Home on the Range," a very popular song of the day.

For Rogers the highlight of the show was probably the gimmick he had used in a movie, playing all the instruments in the band. This was a number where he played the trombone for a few measures, the trumpet for a few more, jumped up on the piano with a clarinet for a few more bars, and wound up behind the drums. It was very commercial, naturally, but musically it was horrible. As you can guess I wasn't truly in love with the music we were playing. As a result, I was bombed a lot of the time. However, I kept up my end of the work.

From Montreal the tour took us to the Stanley Theater in Pittsburgh and the Palace in Cleveland. There we had a little excitement to break up the monotony. The dressing rooms were located on the first floor—incidentally, it was a beautiful theater—and Rogers had one with mirrors lining the walls. Somehow—and nobody was ever willing to admit they knew anything about it afterwards—a young lady managed to sneak into Buddy's dressing room and hide. When Rogers walked in, handsome devil that he was, and she saw his image reflected in all those mirrors, it was more than she could stand. She fainted. For awhile this created quite a big commotion backstage. But for Rogers this wasn't half as bad as what happened later when we played Columbus, Ohio. One day the poor guy walked out of the theater into a barrage of eggs thrown at him by a bunch of students, although I can't imagine what they had against him. He was really an awfully nice guy.

Around February 1934 we played the Palace Theater in Chicago, where there was still quite a bit of activity left over from the World's Fair of 1933. But for me the outstanding event of the period was meeting Zutty Singleton for the first time. He was playing with Carroll Dickerson's band at the Grand Terrace—they were the show band—and Zutty was doing a beautiful job backing the chorus line. In those days he was a very colorful show drummer. I got to meet him through a buddy of Roy Wager's, Ed Dingman. Ed had played trumpet with these guys in Minnesota when they were all just kids, and he was especially close to Zutty. We got to know them all quite well, but my friendship with Zutty lasted all through the years. I think this was my first real tour in Chicago—at least, it was the first time I had a chance to get acquainted around town so it served a good purpose. Especially in my association with Zutty.

Speaking of friendships, by this time I had established a close relationship with Gene Krupa, who had earned my admiration and respect. I don't think anybody ever worked harder at his chosen profession than he did. Once we were settled at a theater, he seldom left it, even to eat. His wife, Ethel, used to bring him his meals and between shows he did nothing but practice. In cities like Pittsburgh and Boston, where they had schools for symphony and parade drummers, he spent all the time he could spare learning anything and everything they could teach him about every aspect of drumming. He never stopped working and preparing himself. This showed up in later years when he decided to go out on his own and, for that matter, even while he was still with Benny Goodman. He practiced technique and showmanship constantly. As far as I'm concerned, the man was really and truly an artist. This isn't to say that I enjoyed playing with him as much as some other drummers I could name, because even by this time all his practicing had developed so much strength that he was getting awfully heavy. But at the same time I must admit that he tempered this with very good taste. When we played in small rooms he played the way things should be played—as Buddy Rich, in spite of all his pyrotechnics, is capable of doing when the situation calls for it. I'm ahead of myself, but one reason I enjoyed working with Benny's band at the Congress Hotel was because Krupa didn't play as heavy there as he usually did. In fact, the entire band wasn't playing as heavy as it was two years later when Harry James and Ziggy Elman came in and started to blow the roof off.

Getting back to the Rogers band, we were getting pretty close to the end of the tour and were due to wind up in a split week in Canton and Akron, Ohio, when Rogers announced he had arranged for us to go into the College Inn as the house band. The College Inn was quite a big room as far as reputations were concerned, but I was getting enough of the kind of things we were doing—obviously it was going to be a very commercial band—so I began making plans to return to New York.

What I had in mind was getting together again with Joe Haymes. He had visited us a couple of times and I'm sure he was getting income from Rogers while we were with the band, but I knew he had the bug to reorganize and I figured that if I went back to New York I could become part of his plans. I also liked Spud Murphy, the arranger, who was now a close associate of Joe's and had been for about a year. He used to hang around the band and we got well acquainted. In those days he was an awful drunk but I appreciated the fact that he got me interested in astronomy.

So I made up my mind to return to New York and find out what Haymes and Murphy were doing. Although I decided not to continue with Rogers, most of the guys in the band elected to stay and go into the College Inn. As far as I was concerned, this meant the end of the Haymes band—the original group, that is—and I didn't see where I had anything to lose by looking around for something I enjoyed doing. The idea even crossed my mind that if I rejoined Haymes I could become the band manager. Of course I wasn't qualified for anything of the kind, but I suspect that in those days I was an arrogant little idiot.

Although Gene Krupa was one of those who was going to play the College Inn, for some reason—maybe the band had some time off before they were due to start—when the tour ended in Canton he and his wife returned to New York with me. It was some trip! We came back by bus. I don't know how we ever came to do this, but it was the closest thing to traveling on the Toonerville Trolley I've ever experienced. The bus was one of those big-windowed, antique schoolbuses, even worse than the ones operated by the Frederick Brothers. The Krupas had a little Scotty dog they were very fond of, and the poor little thing caught pneumonia. For the entire trip to New York Gene and Ethel took turns holding the dog in their laps.

SEVENTEEN

BACK IN NEW YORK I took a room at the Knights of Columbus Hotel, later the Capitol. I liked to stay there because it had a swimming pool and I always pretended to myself that one day I would use it . . . but I never did.

As soon as I was settled in, I looked up Joe Haymes with the intention of picking up where we had left off on our discussions about his reorganizing. It turned out that Joe was very willing to build another band, but I wasn't the only one urging him to do it. In the forefront was our old friend Spud Murphy, who had contributed some arrangements to the old band, before Rogers entered the picture, and had even traveled with it for a few weeks. Charlie Bush had remained in New York, of course, since Gene Krupa had gone on the tour with Buddy Rogers. Charlie also urged Joe to return.

Spud Murphy was a very interesting and talented man. He used the first name of Lyle, but this, along with Murphy, wasn't his real name at all. He once told me he had been raised by Mormons somewhere around Salt Lake City. This was verified a couple of years later when I met his sister, a very dark and attractive lady. She told me Spud had been born in Serbia; during the upheaval of World War I he was sent over here by his aristocratic family to be raised by Mormons.

Spud was quite a drinker by the time I got to know him—a bouncin'-against-the-side-of-the-wall kind of drinker! But he got me interested in astronomy. He had a wide knowledge of the heavens, at least from an amateur's point of view, and in many ways he was a very bright man and obviously well educated. In spite of his drinking, I would classify him as brilliant. Later on we developed a very close friendship and I even moved out to Stewart Manor on Long Island, close to Spud, so we could set up a telescope and watch the stars. This was when he was Benny Goodman's first staff arranger. Of course, Fletcher Henderson's arrangements were becoming the identifying trademark of Benny's band, but Spud's were the backbone. The book needed padding, so to speak, and Fletcher couldn't do it all. It was very sensible on Benny's part to have another arranger anyway, because then when we played a Henderson arrangement it received more emphasis and focus.

Fletcher Henderson, pioneering arranger and bandleader.
Photo courtesy Columbia Records

As far as Haymes reorganizing was concerned, everything was still very much in the discussion stage, with no immediate prospect for a booking even if a band should materialize from all the talk. But there was lots of enthusiasm. I nursed a secret ambition to become more than just a trumpet player in the new outfit; I was seriously considering the idea of being the band manager. I don't think I ever confided this to anybody, and it was just as well, because Charlie Bush was eminently more qualified in this department than I was and I really didn't stand a chance. Time proved this to be in the best interest of the band, and Charlie turned out to be a very successful manager and booker.

Things in the Haymes camp were taking a long time to jell with no real prospects. Weeks went by, and I was getting impatient. I had to make some money some place so I started looking around.

The fine Ben Pollack band was working in a playhouse on 53rd Street off Broadway, now the Ed Sullivan Theater. At that time it was known as the Casino de Paris. (Benny's band later started in at another off-Broadway playhouse, Billy Rose's Music Hall, which is now the second CBS Playhouse on 53rd Street.) So I went over to see the Pollack band, which included my old friend Joe Harris on trombone, and Charlie Spivak and Yank Lawson on trumpets. It was a very good band, a whale of a band! I think Matty Matlock and Eddie Miller were in it, and I distinctly remember Gil Rodin. He was something of a power-behind-the-throne and I had a lot of dealings with him. Gil Bowers was the piano player, and I believe a fellow named Artie Foster, who lived at the Whitney Hotel (like a lot of other musicians), was also in the band. They were an awful nice bunch of guys—all of them.

I wound up playing with them for a brief period, two or three weeks, and Charlie, Yank, and Joe were after me to join them on a steady basis. I was tempted, but still reluctant to commit myself because as long as I can remember—and it is still true to this day—I have no inclination to play with a heavy band. That band was one of the heaviest I have ever heard! To give you some idea, they were working opposite Don Redman's band and there was a spot in the show where both bands played together. When this took place you really and truly could not hear the Redman group at all, and they were no creampuffs. This is just an indication of how hard the Pollack crew worked.

Even later when they became the Bob Crosby band they were still hard-blowing and hard-going. They got results, tremendous results, but the band always played too heavy for me. Maybe it's me and I'm just lazy, but I don't like to work that hard. Even later when I worked with Charlie Spivak in Ray Noble's band he was still a heavy trumpet player. I don't mean that as criticism. It's just that he was as strong as a bull, with a tremendous air column, otherwise he couldn't have played like that. Yank is a strong player too. They're both hard-playing guys. There is a lot to be said for this, because rhythmic players of this type have to be strong in order to endure.

I had another reservation about joining the Pollack band, rather ironic in the light of later developments in my career—it was basically a two-beat

93

band. It played with a two-to-the-bar dixieland feeling, and at that particular time I leaned more toward the four-four approach. Since then I have accomplished a complete about face, and I imagine the better part of my reputation has been established with essentially two-beat bands.

The point is I didn't remain with the Pollack band. For one reason or another Destiny didn't have it that way. But in the meantime I was not getting anywhere with Joe Haymes either. As those things sometimes happen—especially in the music business—I received a good offer. I don't recall just how the connection came about, but I did know quite a few of the men playing in the Isham Jones band—John Langsford, and Johnny Carlson, for example. So when George Thow, the second trumpet player, decided to leave in order to join the brand-new Dorsey Brothers band somebody recommended me for the job and I took it. (Jack Jenny also left Jones at that time to take over Tommy Dorsey's radio work. Tommy hand-picked him as the one to take his place.) Which, of course, meant I could no longer be part of the reorganized Joe Haymes orchestra. When I broke the news Spud Murphy, never one to mince words, told me, "All right, go to hell. We don't need you anyhow—I know a guy who can play rings around you!"

He was kidding, of course, but I found out what he was talking about when I visited the Haymes band after they went to work at the Hotel McAlpin and discovered Spud had gotten Andy Ferretti to play in my place. In many respects Murphy was right. Maybe Andy didn't have the flexibility or some of the speed I played with in those days, but as far as I'm concerned he was a helluva lot better lead trumpet player.

I joined the Isham Jones band in March 1934. I don't recall the exact date or the location, but it was probably on the road, although they were using New York as home base. The personnel at that time included Milt Yaner, Saxie Mansfield, Vic Hauprich, and John Langsford on saxes; Eddie Stone, Joe Martin, and Nick Hupfer, violins; George Wortner, guitar; Walt Yoder, string bass; Jiggs Noble, piano; Joe Bishop, tuba; and Wally Lageson, drums. I moved into a brass section with Johnny Carlson on lead trumpet, Clarence Willard on third (although he also played lead at times and had a fine high register), and Sonny Lee and Red Ballard on trombones. Joe Bishop arranged and contributed original material. Jiggs Noble arranged, along with the staff arranger, Gordon Jenkins. The band manager was Arnold Frank, a pretty nice guy.

The Isham Jones Orchestra was a good-sized outfit. Jones had a fleet of four Fords to transport the band. He traveled in one of those big Lincolns that you see in the old movies about the Chicago gangster days. In those days it was a great automobile, and he had a chauffeur named Scotty. Altogether, it was a great travel arrangement.

One of my earliest weeks with the band was spent at the Hippodrome Theater in Baltimore, memorable because on the same bill with us was a dancer named Ina Ray Hutton. She later became pretty famous, as a band leader rather than as a dancer.

94

We played our first record date in May 1934; afterwards we went on a college tour. We were booked to play at VMI in Plattsburg, Virginia, having spent the night in Roanoke, and were on our way to the job in one of the Fords when we had a head-on collision. It was one of those things that happen so quickly there's no chance to do anything about it. We were going down the road and another car was approaching us from the opposite direction. At the moment we got about even with it still another car suddenly pulled out from behind it and we met radiator to radiator. It was a pretty serious accident.

John Langsford was driving and Eddie Stone was in the front seat with him. Eddie went flying through the windshield and it took 12 or 15 stitches in his forehead to sew up the cuts from the glass. At that he was lucky. I was in the back seat with the other violinist, Nick Hupfer. I remember being thrown against the side of the car—I suppose we were knocked about in every direction—and then I came together with Nick, obviously a much stronger object that I was, because I broke a shoulder from the contact.

They shipped us to a hospital in Christiansberg and took X-rays of our injuries. For some reason—either the X-rays weren't dry in time, or we refused to wait—they just bandaged us up and we took off for the job. I didn't know I had a broken shoulder because nobody told me. I knew it was injured because they wrapped it up and it hurt, but that was it. Fortunately, it was my left shoulder so I was able to play the job one-handed.

On the job that night I established a lifelong friendship with a young student in the graduating class named Carter Burgess. He was chairman of the dance committee and since then has become a prominent businessman and the president of several large corporations. To this day he remembers the tunes and arrangements we played at the VMI prom and can sing them practically note-for-note. Through the years he has always amazed me with this tremendous ability of recall.

It wasn't until we were in Boston a week later that I found out my shoulder had been broken. A Boston doctor X-rayed the thing and found a crack in the clavicle and a dislocation. They built a cage-like affair to hold the shoulder with my arm in a V-shape, and I had to play with it that way for the better part of a month or six weeks. It was uncomfortable, of course, but it also had its commercial aspect—nobody is liable to forget you after they've seen you on the stand playing with one hand. Maybe that's one of the reasons for Wingy Manone's extreme popularity.

We toured New England, then opened at the Ritz Carlton Annex in Atlantic City. This was a separate building north of the Ritz Carlton Hotel, which was actually an elaborate wooden pavilion dining room, a very beautiful room; the band loved it. The bandstand was in the back of the building. The dining room had entrances right off the boardwalk; it was a beautiful place to play in the summer. In spite of the fact that we were back off the beach we always caught a nice breeze. It was a rather large room, seating 300 to 400 people, long and rectangular.

So began one of the most interesting and pleasant summers of my life. I

Mr. and Mrs. Walt Yoder

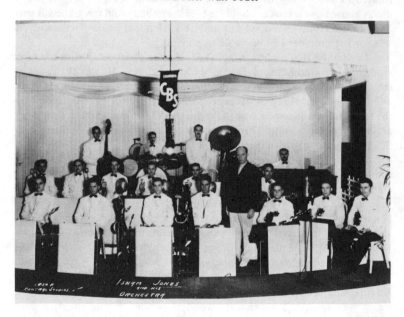

The Isham Jones Orchestra at the Ritz-Carlton Hotel in Atlantic City, July, 1934. Rear Row, L to R: Walt Yoder, string bass; Wally Lageson, drums; Joe Bishop, tuba; Jiggs Noble, piano. Second Row: Mark Bennett, Sonny Lee, trombones; Clarence Willard, Johnny Carlson, and Pee Wee Erwin, trumpets; Front Row: Vic Hauprich, Saxie Mansfield, Milt Yaner, and John Langsford, saxes; Isham Jones, leader; George Wortner, guitar; Joe Martin, Nick Hupfer, and Eddie Stone, violins. Martin and Stone were also the vocalists.

just had a ball for the entire season. To begin with, I liked the band and the material we played was interesting. Although it may not have been the greatest swinging band I have ever played in, it had a magnificent sound and beautiful arrangements; it was a treat to play in it. I played just enough of the lead book to keep a good embouchure all the time. It was also a very funny band; half of the members smoked weed and the other half were drunks (politely, of course). After the job you could see them all go off in different directions, the vipers one way and the drunks another.

For the summer Walt Yoder and I shared a room in an apartment taken by the other trumpet player, Clarence Willard, and his wife. It was about two blocks off the ocean, and half a block from another house where Sonny Lee and his wife were living. We were on the top floor of an old-fashioned house that gave us pretty good quarters. The Willards were a nice couple and we all got along very well together, although Walt Yoder and I were really nothing alike. He was a quiet guy who went his own way and so did I, so I guess that's why we got along so well.

At least three or four nights a week I'd go down to the black part of town and jam with the black bands—Atlantic City always had good ones. Charlie Johnson, who used to have the famous band at Small's Paradise in New York, had one of the show bands there. So I had a lot of opportunities to play, and that's where I first met Roy Eldridge.

Roy was playing with a drummer, Cuba Austin, who had been with McKinney's Cotton Pickers in his earlier time; I got an awful big kick out of Roy. He was blowing up a storm in those days—still is, for that matter—and he was a cute little guy. His identification was a fez cap he always wore and sometimes would stick over the end of his horn. He was a tremendous trumpet player even then; I learned a lot from him. The manager of the Kentucky Club was a lovable black man named Eef (the only name I ever knew him by). He used to take pretty good care of me, but I don't remember getting too bombed in those places anyway. I went there to play.

I also made friends with an old gentleman who set up an 8" refracting telescope on the beach and charged a fee to look at the moon and the planets, or whatever happened to be out. This was right up my alley, since I was interested in astronomy, so I hit up a rather close association with him and almost any night when I had the opportunity I would go looking through his telescope.

The Ritz Carlton was one block north of the Ambassador Hotel, where the Jones band had played the year before. Both were very high-class hotels, or, to state it more accurately, they were expensive. In between them was another hotel of the same type and in it a band led by Philadelphia bandleader Howard Lanin, with two guys I got to know very well and spent a lot of time with that summer of 1934; Art Barnett, a pretty fabulous man in many ways, and Jesse Berkman, who played tenor sax. Barnett was tremendous at imitating train and boat whistles. He is a train buff and has been all of his life. I still get Christmas cards from him with pictures of trains. He's an actor, too, and had a prominent role in the first Broadway production of "Oklahoma." I didn't see the show so I don't know what character he portrayed, but he has been quite successful as an actor since those days. I still occasionally play with Jesse Berkman, and we always reminisce a lot about that wonderful summer.

There was another band in the Ambassador Hotel, led by Little Jack Little, who had made quite a reputation for himself with his pianistic tricks and whispering vocals. He had picked up a set band for the season, made up mostly of guys from Brooklyn and actually under the leadership of Mitchell Ayres, later to become very successful with his own band, and still later to become a well-known conductor on TV, especially on the Perry Como Show. Even at that late date, he was still using some of the men from the band that played the Ambassador in 1934—a trumpet player, Jakie Koven, and a sax man, Harry Terrill. These guys were part of a great bunch of musicians, and I got to know them pretty well.

One of the greatest experiences of my life was brought about by Sonny Lee, who, I believe, was from Texas. He had been with the Jean Goldkette band in Detroit in the late Twenties, and was a far-better-than-average jazz trombonist. He can be heard soloing on quite a number of the records the Jones band made—notably the one I always identify with him, "Blue Room." (Incidentally, while I'm on the subject of trombone players, I think it was around this time our second trombonist, Red Ballard, left to join Benny Goodman. Benny was in the process of forming his first band, the one he had at Billy Rose's Music Hall. Red was replaced in the Jones band by a man from Newark, N.J., Mark Bennett, a good legitimate musician who had played in the Newark theaters. He probably started splitting the lead book with Sonny.) The important thing that Sonny contributed to me was an interest in flying. The year before he had taken some flying lessons at the Atlantic City airport, and he knew an instructor there, so he convinced me to take flying instructions with him.

Sonny was a long way ahead of me, of course. I believe he had already logged enough flying time to get his private pilot's license. But he was so enthusiastic about flying and described it in such glowing terms that I had to try it for myself. He drove me to Philadelphia for the necessary physical examination: standing on one foot, depth perception, etc. I passed it and started taking lessons at the Atlantic City airport.

I liked it and I was doing pretty well, but I still had only about four-and-a-half hours of instruction when one day my instructor looked at me sideways and said, "Tell you what—if you bring me a jug of booze I'll let you solo." The idea sounded great to me at the time so the next day I brought him the bottle, and he told me, "OK. Go get in the plane and take off."

The airplane was a Waco biplane with a Hispano-Suiza motor. I think it was held together with bailing wire—what they used to refer to as a "crate." Before I had any time to think about what I was about to do or realize I didn't have enough training to fly solo—especially since none of the planes in those days were spin-proof and they all had a lot of bugs—I got in the cockpit, gunned the damned thing, and I was in the air.

Violinist-vocalist Eddie Stone, 1937.

George Thow played second trumpet with Isham Jones, and left to join the brand-new Dorsey Brothers Orchestra at Glen Island Casino. Pee Wee Erwin replaced him with Jones.   Photo courtesy George Thow

Nowadays flying small planes isn't quite as complex as it was then. Looking back I can only excuse the whole thing on the basis that I was very young and stupid, or just plain nuts, to try it after so little instruction. After I was in the air I began to realize this with a sinking feeling in the pit of my stomach and knew that I hadn't had enough practice on the stablizer control. The plane required a different trim when only one man was flying instead of two. I was having trouble trying to keep it on an even keel. Of course, I could compensate for this somewhat with the stick. (Yes, it was still a stick in those days, not a wheel.)

In spite of everything, I made my solo flight without a hitch, and when I came down I managed to execute what was known in the flying vernacular of the day as "a perfect three-point landing." Beginner's luck. Then I taxied up to the apron with the plane. Everybody congratulated me, shaking my hand and slapping me on the back. It was almost like a birthday when you soloed. Just about the time I was beginning to feel very satisfied with myself the instructor poked a finger in my chest and said, "All right. Now take off and do it all over again."

So out I went to the middle of the field, feeling very confident now, and took off, flew around awhile . . . and then came in to land. Only this time I think I bounced as high as the hanger.

Nevertheless, from that point on I had a lot of fun with my flying. I not only flew the Waco, I was checked out in a cabin plane of the time called a Stinson R, a four-place plane. It was really a great thrill to fly around the area because we were right on the coast and there were lots of inlets to explore. You could fly out over the ocean and up the coast. The scenery was very colorful—rather spectacular, in fact—and there was a marvelous sense of exhilaration flying in those open cockpit planes.

One day my instructor told me to fly over to Brigantine Beach, which is north on the next island after Atlantic City. Across the inlet was another strip of sand designated on the maps as an emergency landing field where a plane could land in case something went wrong. This even applied to commerical planes. My instructions were to fly over and land, then take off and fly back.

Well, it really wasn't anybody's fault, but the instructor had forgotten to take into account that the night before there had been a tremendous downpour. With my minimum flying experience, I flew over, landed, rolled about four feet in the sodden sand, and wound up with the nose of the plane buried into the ground. It was very embarrassing.

I was rescued by the Coast Guard contingent which is based on the beach. They came over and simply threw a rope on the tail of the plane and then hauled in. To give my instructor full credit, he had always made a strong point of warning me that at any time I was caught in a situation like this the first thing to do was turn off the ignition. I had followed his instructions, so the plane wasn't damaged and I wasn't hurt. By the time they had the plane back into proper position my instructor had arrived on the scene. He got into it and taxied over the soft spot until he found some hard sand, then made me get in and go right back up again. I can see his reasoning. The idea is that you don't have time to think about what has happened and develop a fear of flying. I can readily understand how something like that could scare some people. In my case, I was too dumb to appreciate what I'd done and too busy to try to get out of it to think about being scared—that is, not until later.

Some time after our stint in Atlantic City, we had occasion to take a commercial airline flight during a tour of one-nighters in the Midwest; I think it was a trip from Louisville, Kentucky, to Cleveland. It was my only (thank goodness!) experience in one of those Ford tri-motored ancestors of today's airliners, which were still in use as late as 1934. Over Ohio we passed through a horrendous electrical storm. From the fright it gave me I have been forever grateful we never had to take another flight in that primitive airplane.

My flying career ended when we left Atlantic City, which probably was after Labor Day. Although I had every intention of continuing with more instruction in the New York area and may have continued to fly—at least for fun and pleasure—an insurance agent named Henry Nasburg changed my mind. In those days insurance companies took a very dim view of people who were flying. Although I was still single and had no dependents, Harry made me think better of it and I never took it up again.

I would like to mention one record date we did during that July, the session when we recorded "Blue Room," "Georgia Jubilee," and "I Found a New Baby." We drove to Camden during the day, and I rode with Sonny Lee. We had a bottle and a great drive, and by the time we got to the studio I was so bombed that when we made those recordings I had both feet firmly planted in mid-air. Yet—after listening many times since to my chorus on "Blue Room"—I really can't tell how drunk I was. I had the stamina of youth and could play come hell or high water. It's not a bad chorus, even if I say so myself. In fact, it's probably the best chorus I recorded with the Jones band.

After we returned to New York Isham Jones changed record companies and began recording for Decca, a brand-new company. We recorded a good portion of the library for them. Although the records are not as good technically as the Victors, Victor Young was associated with Decca and even then everybody was very much aware of his great ability.

EIGHTEEN

AFTER THE MARVELOUS SUMMER of 1934 in Atlantic City, the Isham Jones band made a swing out west. We returned to New York in time to play for a fall radio show sponsored, I believe, by Chevrolet. For this the band was augmented with a full string section, and in it was a violinist named Manny Green. I still work with him once in awhile, as recently as 1975. The Chevrolet show really brought Gordon Jenkins to the forefront and recognition for his ability as an orchestrator. The full string section enabled him to outdo himself in arranging for it. Unfortunately, the show was of short duration, only about six weeks. Afterwards the Jones crew was due to hit the road again, so I started doing a lot of free-lancing with an eye to remaining in New York. Jack Jenny was working the studios, as was Manny Klein. Manny began to work me in subbing for him. Through that contact I began to work on a three-a-week broadcast from the old CBS building at 485 Madison Avenue for Heinz Pickles.

I don't recall how early we started to rehearse for the show, but it was aired on Monday, Wednesday, and Friday at 11 in the morning. The repeat broadcast for the West Coast went on at 3 p.m., so it was definitely a daytime show. These details stick in my mind for a very good reason, because an incident took place that put me into one of the most embarrassing spots of my life. I was living at the Whitby apartment-hotel on 45th Street. One day I did the first show at 11 o'clock and then went back to my apartment to have a nap before the repeat session. I fell into a deep sleep and didn't wake up until about a quarter to three—just in time to be too late to make the repeat broadcast. What made it so bad was that the first arrangement was loaded with an effect called "pyramid trumpets," which was popular in those days. You know, each horn playing a note and building a pyramid—da-da-da, da-da-da; except that without me the two trumpets remaining could only play da-da, da-da. Leith Stevens was the conductor of the show (later he was very active in films) and such a nice guy that he never even mentioned I was late for the broadcast.

Leith, incidentally, is the only man I've ever seen pictured, as he once

102

was in *Down Beat*, with the baton behind his back. For some reason or other—he was reading a script, or something like that—he brought the baton down behind his back, and obediently the band started to play.

I began working for a lot of strange guys and doing a lot of recording, often subbing for Manny. I remember working for one named Ben Klatzkin, whom I had never heard of before—nor since. I was in on part of the Studebaker Show with Richard Himber, who was pretty successful as a radio conductor. Manny Klein and his brother Dave set me up with the Brunswick studios on 1776 Broadway, across from the General Motors building. The recording director (they weren't called A & R men in those days) was Harry Gray, who later moved to California. I did a lot of independent recording dates for them, especially when Bunny Berigan couldn't make them. After Harry Gray left, Russ Morgan took over as music supervisor. I always got along pretty well with Russ. When Bunny could not record, I continued to do a lot of the house dates, usually with the house singers, guys like Dick Robertson and Chick Bullock.

Harry Gray is distinctive in my mind for setting me up with a date to record with Henry "Red" Allen's band in order to work a gimmick that was Gray's idea. Every first chorus I imitated Henry Busse with a Harmon mute, and then Red took over. We did four sides like that—"Believe It Beloved," "Smooth Sailing," "It's Written All Over Your Face," and "Whose Honey Are You?" We had a lot of fun talking about these things years later, and only a short time back I found an album made in Europe that had these four sides on it. When we made the date I really had no idea who was playing on it, aside from Red, but according to Brian Rust the band was a reunion of all-star New Orleans musicians in New York. The piano player was Luis Russell, the clarinetist Buster Bailey, George Washington was on trombone, Danny Barker, guitar, Paul Barbarin, drums, and Pops Foster, bass. I was in very distinguished company. The records were fun things to do, and still fun things to listen to.

As a result of my Brunswick connection, other work began to develop. I was also doing a lot of recording with other outfits, just who and where I can't even remember. There was a lot of free-lance work around. Probably through my association with Russ Morgan and another trumpet player, Manny Weinstock, I began to make wider connections in the recording and radio studios. Weinstock, with whom I worked for many years, was quite a successful player at that time. He was an orphan who had been taught by Max Schlossburg, the great trumpet teacher, and like all of Schlossburg's pupils had great classical training.

Manny Klein sent me in his place on various shows, including my first date with Andre Kostelanetz. Playing in the Kostelanetz orchestra was always a great experience and very educational. Kostelanetz maintained great control over the orchestra; when you worked with him it soon became evident why this was possible. Under his leadership, the ensemble orchestra played softer than any other orchestra, which of course gave a lot of latitude for expression, and when the orchestra went to a forte from pianissimo it had some place to go. This soft ensemble playing has another great physical attribute, it allows for full vibration of the instruments resulting in eight times the resonance of a heavy orchestra.

This works so well in every kind of music that it is amazing to me that the average orchestra or band insists on playing so loud. (On the other hand I have often heard it said that an amateur can play loud, but it takes a real pro to play soft.) I had this proven to me conclusively in the Benny Goodman band when we were playing in the Congress Hotel in Chicago. We couldn't play loud without driving the customers out of the room. At this period the band had the best musical blend it ever had. The band played *under* the lead instruments instead of the lead instruments having to blow *over* the band. I'm secretly nauseated whenever someone says to me, "Listen to how powerful that trumpet player is—he's heavy enough to play heavier than any band." Ugh!

Don't get the idea this is confined to any one kind of music. I have had marvelous symphony players gripe to me about how heavy certain conductors insisted they play. The best example that comes to mind to prove how wrong this is is a recording date I was fortunate enough to play with the great circus-band conductor, Merle Evans, recording circus music. This huge band actually played softer than almost any dance band I ever played with. Yet when we listened to the play-back of the recording, due to the full resonance of the instruments the music came out like cannons roaring.

Some of the other guys in the Brunswick stable were Carl Kress and Dick McDonough, either one was almost always on a session —and Larry Binyon, who years before had played with Ben Pollack, and was a very active tenor player around New York. The trombonists were usually Miff Mole and Jack Lacey, although sometimes Russ Morgan would play. Through Brunswick I got to meet Freddy Martin, who was then playing at the St. Regis Hotel. Martin's was practically the house band at Brunswick. I used to do two or three record dates a week with him. Sometimes we used two trumpets, the other one being Manny Weinstock, who preceded me with Martin.

I started working with the Martin band at the St. Regis, although I can't remember just when. There were some interesting points about the Martin band of that period. Jack Lacey was on trombone, a very nice guy, and Elmer Feldkamp, the featured vocalist, played sax. We also had a violinist, Benny Eaton, who went back to the early days of the Scranton Sirens and knew the Dorseys, Russ Morgan, and many of the others who had worked with Billy Lustig. (In 1976 I received a letter from Benny, who now lives in Florida, asking me to get a trumpet for his grandson.) Another fine man was the lead violinist, Sid Harris, whom I worked with off and on for forty years until he passed away a few years ago.

One of the most interesting features of Martin's group, though, was the two pianos he featured at the St. Regis. One was played by songwriter Terry Shand, who wrote the hit, "My Extraordinary Gal," and the other by Claude Thornhill. Of all the bands I have ever played in, this was the drinkingest. I wasn't included, because I wasn't much of a drinker at that time, but I think the other guys were perpetually stoned.

We had a drummer named Ernie Schaff, a real nice guy from Fort Lee, N.J. Once the band was booked to make a movie short for Warner Brothers at their studio in Brooklyn. Claude Thornhill used to double on vibraphone once in awhile, hit last chords and such. But Ernie decided that it would be nice if it was made to look on the screen as though he were the one playing vibes. Well, in those days you made the soundtrack one day and the next you did the posing. Thornhill had played a beautiful passage at the end of one number and Schaff asked him to let him hit the vibraphone for the camera as though he had played it. Thornhill agreed readily enough, but then some jokester hid the mallets. While the sound of the passage was being heard on the soundtrack, the movie showed Ernie looking for the mallets. A few years ago I took my kids to Palisades Amusement Park, and the guy manning the roller coaster was Ernie Schaff.

The Martin band at the St. Regis was a society-styled group, but it was one of the best and it certainly had good men in it. We always had talented people working in the room with us as part of the floor show which was a feature of all good supper clubs of the period. This always included a dance team, and in particular I remember a hoarse-voiced gal named Sheila Barrett, a typical supper-club chanteuse and entertainer, who sang risque songs. Her act, included a few quiet spots so the people could hear all the words of her songs. Thornhill and Shand played twin grand pianos with the tops removed and placed on opposite sides of the bandstand; alongside the pianos were potted trees or plants with red berries on them. When the quiet spots came along while Sheila was singing, either Claude or Terry would pick off a berry and toss it across the stand at the other's piano. In the hush there would suddenly be heard a sharp "ping." Then a short time later, whenever the next quiet spot came along, another berry would fly in the opposite direction and there would be another "ping." Shand and Thornhill were great drinking buddies and always clowning around together. (The bass player with Martin was Barney Pottle and another of the violinists was Ross Dickson, who died only recently.)

While I was with this band, my father had been hanging around the East, although my mother and my brother were still living in the Midwest. At his instigation I rented a house in Stewart Manor, one block away from Spud Murphy's house, and brought my mother and brother East. At the same time, I bought a big telescope for the backyard so Spud and I could look at the stars. The only trouble with this was that I was so darn' busy all the time that I was seldom home.

Things were getting pretty lucrative, so I might as well mention here the kind of money it was possible to make in those days. Around this time I was probably averaging $1,000 a week, which for 1934 and 1935 was pretty good cabbage. But as an indication of how much work was involved, in order to average that amount, consider that record dates only paid $30. I don't remember what they paid for overtime—or if there was overtime pay— because usually the bands were so damn' good I don't recall that they needed overtime. I believe my salary with Isham Jones was $125 a week. It was probably about the same with Buddy Rogers, because this figure seems to stick in my mind as the going rate with the top-flight bands of the time. Record dates and such were extra, so it was possible to come up with $200 or $250 a week. I'm sure I had weeks like that with Jones; as band salaries went, this was about average.

While I was still working with Freddy Martin, Bunny Berigan started at the Music Hall with Benny Goodman and also played on the first "Let's Dance" radio program with him. After the first or the second show he was unable to continue. Since Benny's book was set up so that Bunny played about 70 percent of the lead in addition to all of the jazz, they needed somebody to replace him that could do the same thing.

I had never worked with Benny before, but he called and made an appointment to meet me between sets at the St. Regis. I went downstairs at the appointed time; and Benny had John Hammond with him. I think Hammond did as much talking as Benny, but between them they convinced me to join his band immediately for the "Let's Dance" program. Mind you, Benny didn't say, "Come join the band." It was the radio program they wanted me for. I don't think at that time Benny felt as though his band had a great future even though it was a set band and it was working.

Benny's personnel included Toots Mondello on lead alto; Dick Clark on tenor; Hymie Schertzer, third alto; and Arthur Rollini on tenor. The trombones were Red Ballard and Jack Lacey, who played lead. The rhythm section consisted of Frank Froeba on piano, Gene Krupa, drums, George Van Eps, guitar, and Harry Goodman on bass. The vocalist was Helen Ward.

The trumpet team included Sammy Shapiro (later to become well known as Sammy Spear, musical conductor of the Jackie Gleason TV show) and Jerry Neary. Jerry played third and was a pretty darned good trumpet man. I took over Bunny's chair. I was always trying to get Jerry to play some of the jazz because he was good at it. But the only thing we ever could get him to play was those "answers" to Benny's clarinet on "Good-bye," the tune Gordon Jenkins wrote for our closing theme.

The "Let's Dance" program was sponsored by the National Biscuit Company and was aired across the country. It came from Studio 8H in the NBC building, the largest studio NBC had, and was always performed before a live audience. The studio could hold up to 400 people and they were always walking in and out. They came in shifts. A lot of musicians came to hear the band after work.

Those were the golden years of radio. But when I started on the "Let's Dance" program—which included a couple of hours' rehearsal on a Tuesday, a couple more on Thursday, and a final rehearsal of two or three hours before the actual broadcast—the salary for the entire package was $125. I was doing two shows, that one and another on Saturday for RCA. My recollection is that I made $185 for the second show. You have to remember, though, that this meant additional rehearsals on other days.

106

By then, however, Benny had quite a set library from which to work because the band was playing regularly at Billy Rose's Music Hall. His rehearsals mainly consisted of running over new things he planned to use on the broadcast. It should be obvious that in order to average the money I was making I had to work my tail off. I can't be exact about the hours we worked, maybe 9 to 4 or 10 to 4, but I do know that refreshments were set up for us in a side room during the show, which was in three parts, with three bands alternating. First you would hear a set by Benny, then one by Kel Murray's Orchestra, and finally one by Xavier Cugat. This meant you could have just about any kind of dance music you wanted in your home for three or four hours. It was a pretty good idea, and a very successful one.

Kel Murray, whose real name was Murray Kellner, was an NBC violinist. He directed a large studio-type orchestra which included some rather illustrious musicians. I'm pretty sure that Arthur Schutt played piano, and the drummer was Harry Stittman, who later worked for Toscanini. The xylophonist was one of the foremost hammer men of the time, Harry Brewer. The brass section included Sammy Lewis, who later played with the NBC symphony, Charlie Margulis, and Manny Klein, and a very fine trumpet player, Hymie Farberman. In the sax section was Arnold Brilhart, well known for his work with the California Ramblers, Alfie Evans, and another excellent studio man named Henry Adler. The concertmaster of the violins was Louis Raderman, a marvelous violinist. On some occasions they added another trumpet, Benny Baker, who was an excellent symphony player. One of the male singers with Murray was Frank Luther. Years later we made an album for children called "Songs of Safety," written by Irving Caesar.

Xavier Cugat's band made its reputation on the show. As far as Benny's band was concerned too, there's no doubt the "Let's Dance" program was mainly instrumental in establishing the jump-off point for his future popularity. As everyone knows, the Fletcher Henderson arrangements were the backbone of the style he was trying to develop. But Spud Murphy was the staff arranger and did the bulk of the work. I also recall at least one arrangement by Ben Ludlow (who used to hang around the band and later became fairly successful with his own) of "On the Alamo." I don't think it was ever recorded. Fred Norman and Brick Fleagle also contributed things. I used to see these guys at rehearsals.

My first record date with Goodman was also the first for Helen Ward. She sang a vocal on "I'm a Hundred Per Cent for You," and we also made "Music Hall Rag," "Cokey," and a tune called "Like a Bolt from the Blue." Then a couple of months later we played another session when we recorded "The Dixieland Band," which was written by Bernie Hanighen and Johnny Mercer, and "Down Home Rag." These sides were all for Columbia and were issued on blue shellac. I think we had one more session for Columbia, and then from there on everything was recorded for Victor.

Incidently, for those who are interested in discographical information, Ralph Muzillo is listed on some of these early sessions, but I'm pretty sure he didn't join the band until we were at the Roosevelt Hotel in June. Then Joe

Harris is listed as replacing Jack Lacey. This didn't happen until the end of the summer of 1935, after the California trip. Muzillo, Lacey, and Berigan were with the band on the road. Finally, the reason Jack Teagarden is listed by Rust for the April date is because he played the release on one of the tunes we recorded. I remember the release as one of the usual Teagarden masterpieces.

Shortly after we finished the "Let's Dance" series, we went into the Victor studios on 24th Street for one of the strangest recording sessions of all time. I may be wrong, but to my knowledge it may still stand as the longest record date in terms of number of tunes recorded at one sitting because in one afternoon we recorded the whole "Let's Dance" library, or 54 tunes for the NBC Thesaurus transcription company. (In later years these were reissued on three commercial LPs on the Sunbeam label.) We just set the library up and played it as though we were on the air, rather than making separate masters of each tune as in normal recording procedure. I have recently heard quite a few of these numbers and I'm really surprised at the few mistakes to be heard because there was a lot of blowing involved. For my own part I would have played the bulk of all the lead parts and probably all of the jazz choruses. As it is, I'm convinced that Nate Kazebier worked on this date. Nate was a much better trumpet player than anyone gave him credit for, a truly great jazz player with good taste and lots of talent to back it up.

NINETEEN

ON OCCASION Benny would book the band out. We played Nutting-On-the-Charles in the Boston area and worked at the County Center in White Plains. I rode up on the train with Jack Lacey, and when the train pulled into the station he was so stoned that he fell out of the door. Then there was another date in Binghamton, and one in Scranton, where we played in the Masonic Temple. After the job Frankie Froeba, Harry Goodman, another guy, and I went to an after-hours place to try the house specialty, boiled chitlins. All I had to do was take one look at the plate and smell the odor, which was bad enough to stop a freight train, and I couldn't eat a thing. Neither could Froeba or the other guy, but Harry Goodman sat there and ate all *four* orders. He just loved it.

While we were waiting for Harry to polish off the food, Frankie started playing an old upright piano, but by the time Goodman finally finished eating, it was well into the wee hours of the morning and we wanted to leave. We yelled, "Hey, Frank! Come on, let's go!" But instead of getting up he waved a hand at us and called back, "You guys go ahead without me. I'll see you later."

So we left, and we didn't find out until the next day that some guy was holding a knife on Frank to keep him playing. Actually, we left the poor guy in an awful situation, but we had no idea what was going on.

I enjoyed playing with Benny's band. It was working on a musical concept that just about anybody in 1935 would have been happy to be part of. But on the other hand, and to be absolutely honest, I can never remember being carried away by it. Why, I really don't know. I wasn't blase' about it, or feeling too big for my breeches, but it just didn't impress me the way it did some people. Of course, anybody in his right mind couldn't help but admire Benny's playing—the early records are enough proof of that—and I was no exception. The band was good, it was interesting, and, as the records indicate again, it was a perfect setting for Benny's playing, as all his bands have been. But still, I wasn't carried away, and maybe this was simply because I was so busy doing other things. Toots Mondello, George Van Eps, and I were involved in so many things on the outside that possibly playing with Benny was just another part of the week's work.

I brought my mother and brother East around the end of 1934. At first I had taken an apartment in Woodside, Queens, and after the Buddy Rogers thing finished up in Chicago, Roy Wager returned to New York and stayed at the apartment for awhile. I believe he went to work with Joe Haymes at Roseland. Paul Mitchell was probably still with Haymes too, but I doubt if many others of the old band were left.

Anyway, I don't recall exactly when I rented the house in Stewart Manor, but I do know that Johnny Mince was back in New York. Being the friendly guy he is and fond of family life (and now I had a family) he moved into the house with us and lived there for quite awhile, in fact, the whole time we were together in the Ray Noble band, which was about to be organized. Actually my recollections of this period are understandably jumbled because I was involved in so many things. My date book was so crammed with dates that the pages were black. I was doing an awful lot of radio and recording work, of all kinds, and working morning, noon, and night. I was pretty young then, or I couldn't have kept up the pace. I recollect one time Roy Wager drove me up to Binghamton for a date with Benny. I guess I had worked too late to take a bus, so Roy drove me up and back so I could make my schedule. I was very close to Roy and all the other Haymes guys. Mike Doty was on the scene again too.

I find it rather difficult to explain the situation at that time because while I was working with Benny Goodman I was also playing with Ray Noble. To try to simplify things and put them in some form of logical order I'll finish up with the Goodman band and then go on to the organization of the Ray Noble group which was being put together by Glenn Miller.

Toward the end of the thirteenth week of the "Let's Dance" program, it became pretty obvious that Benny intended to keep his band together. He booked three weeks at the Roosevelt Hotel and I played most of it, but I'm sure I had to take off on occasion. This probably didn't sit too well with Benny, but I don't recall getting any flak. I mention this because he has always had a reputation for being a tough guy, yet I never had any personal experiences of this kind. During the entire "Let's Dance" program I can't remember any flak at all from Benny. However, as I look back I probably didn't care if I played in his band or not, in spite of the fact that I liked to play with it, and this may have had something to do with it. The Roosevelt date probably started at the beginning of June. We played in the Grille, but I don't remember much else about the job except that as far as the public was concerned it was a dismal failure. Nate Kazebier and Jack Lacey were regulars with the band, and the sax section remained intact—although I'm not too sure of Toots Mondello because he was also pretty busy on the outside.

It became common knowledge that Benny intended taking the band on the road, because George Van Eps began grooming his pupil, Allan Reuss, to join the band (which he did, staying for a long time), and Bunny Berigan planned to rejoin if the projected road tour materialized. It did, and I can talk with some certainty about this because I was on the scene.

The trumpet section that went on tour included Ralph Muzillo, (a very strong lead man and a lot of fun), Nate Kazebier, and Bunny Berigan. The trombones were Red Ballard and Jack Lacey. Toots Mondello, George Van Eps, and I were working with Ray Noble, so Toots was replaced by a guy from Pittsburgh, Bill DePew, and Allan Reuss went in for George. The shift in the reed section was accomplished very smoothly because Hymie Schertzer, a great saxophonist who knew the entire library, simply moved over to play lead alto and Bill DePew took over the third alto book. As for the trumpet section, you couldn't lose with Muzillo and Kazebier backing up Bunny Berigan. According to the stories I used to hear, Muzillo, Lacey, and Berigan took every opportunity to play golf, leaving a trail of half-pint bottles of rot-guy behind in every sand trap on the course.

I don't recall the exact date I was approached to go with the Ray Noble band, but it had to be while I was playing with Goodman. Ray Noble had been a big success in England, and his records were very much admired in the States. There's no doubt that, from the sound standpoint alone, the English recordings of the time were far superior technically to anything being made over here. The word was that Ray Noble was coming to this country with his very popular vocalist Al Bowlly, and his drummer and manager, Bill Harty. This was done under the auspices of the William Morris Agency, which was a bit strange because this agency only booked theatrical attractions, and I don't think they had a band listed among those attractions at that time. Nevertheless, they arranged to bring Noble over, and, to handle the bookings for his prospective American band, they contacted the Rockwell-0'Keefe office, which was very big in the band field. In turn, Rockwell-O'Keefe hired Glenn Miller to organize a band for Noble. Miller had established quite a reputation as an arranger and organizer from his work with the Dorsey Brothers Orchestra, which had been handled by Rockwell-O'Keefe.

Naturally, Glenn approached the people he liked and respected musically, and he did it all on an individual basis. He told us about Noble's coming over and that he was authorized to build a band for him, which would rehearse at RCA-Victor and do a lot of the arrangements that Noble was noted for. We were all aware of Noble's recordings, of course.

The strangest thing about Miller's approach was that he told us money was no object! We could name our own salaries, within reason. After all these years, I can't recall the exact amount that I named, but it was probably somewhere between $200 and $300 a week; I never did know what the other men in the band received. We each made our own deal. But I imagine Charley Spivak, for instance, who was a really extraordinary lead trumpet player, made out pretty well, as he should have. But in my entire career I have never again been approached on such a basis, which leads me to guess that this was the only band in history to start at the top and work down, financially, that is. Certainly Ray Noble, Bill Harty, and Al Bowlly had all been guaranteed good salaries, so more than likely quite a number of people benefited from Ray's trip to America.

I don't mean to sound presumptuous or egotistical, but I was working with so many bands and so many people that at the time all this happened, I can honestly say that my attitude toward it all was simply to regard it as just another job with just another band. I never did get into the spirit that prevailed among some of the guys that this was the greatest thing that had ever happened. It just didn't strike me that way. I don't mean to imply that I wasn't cordial and I tried my best to get into the spirit of things, musically, but even though it may seem a bit ambiguous, I wasn't overly impressed by the orchestrations that Glenn Miller brought in nor those that Ray Noble brought with him from England. This was mostly due to my personal taste in music at that time. For one thing, you should remember that I was playing with Benny Goodman's band with Fletcher Henderson's arrangements. For another, I was strongly influenced by my associations with Roy Eldridge and Red Allen, and the black bands. Red Allen was my favorite trumpet player, and I much preferred the four-beat feel of the black bands. Glenn Miller, of course, was a two-beat player, and everything he did was in the dixieland vein. Noble's scores were legitimately correct and in excellent taste, but I didn't find them particularly inspiring. Nevertheless, as I see it now, all of this was merely an indication that I had not yet matured musically. I still hadn't grown up to the extent of having a broad concept of the various musical forms so I could accept and appreciate what a guy was trying to say.

Mind you, I didn't exactly assume a lackadaisical attitude toward the band, but I must admit that throughout I had a reserved outlook about it, partly conditioned by my concern for my embouchure. If I had to work too hard in any given situation, or if anything interfered with the flexibility of my embouchure, which I had taken such great care to develop, I took a dim view of it. So I wasn't too fond of Miller's phrasing, because playing the two-beat arrangements taxed my flexibility too much. Since then I've completely reversed my attitude. I've had to pound under any and all circumstances and it has been good for me.

In any case, I joined the band and started rehearsing at the Victor studio at 24th Street. It was just another gig. Brian Rust lists the first recording date as February 9th, and the tunes as "Soon," "Clouds," and "Down By the River." I can recall those tunes and that session easier than I can remember the first rehearsals. Nevertheless, the actual beginning of the band would have been two or three weeks earlier, so I must have joined Benny's band on the "Let's Dance" program and the Ray Noble set-up almost simultaneously, at least within two or three weeks.

As I recall the Noble group in the beginning, it included Toots Mondello on lead alto, Johnny Mince on third alto, Bud Freeman, tenor, and Jim Cannon on baritone. Jim, I believe, was tubercular and he didn't stay with us very long. I have no idea what became of him. Charley Spivak, Will Bradley, Glenn Miller, and I made up the brass section, two trumpets and two trombones. We had two violinists, Nick Pisano, concertmaster and lead, and

Ray Noble and Ted McMichael, of The Merry Macs vocal group.

Fritz Prospero contemplates disaster for his Stradivarius.

Ray Noble, late 1936.

Fritz Prospero, a little guy from Philadelphia with a terrific sense of humor who was also a talented cartoonist. Dan D'Andrea, who played both violin and sax in the band, came in later. I don't remember his being there at the beginning. George Van Eps was on guitar, Claude Thornhill played piano, and Delmar Kaplan was on bass. Bill Harty, Ray Noble's manager, played drums, and Al Bowlly was the vocalist.

Once in awhile Andy Russo came in to sub for somebody. He's even in one of the band pictures. He played once or twice with Freddy Martin's band, which is where I probably met him for the first time, but in later years we worked together quite often. Another trombonist, Phil Giardina, also subbed with both bands and has remained a friend of mine all these years.

My foremost recollection of the early Noble band was its very social atmosphere. Ray Noble was a wonderful gentleman and an extremely genteel man. He typified the American idea of an English gentleman, as seen in the movies. Perhaps that's why he did so well later when he played the part on the Edgar Bergen radio show. However, there it was done for laughs, and he was pictured as rather foggy when actually he was a brilliant man. He set the tone for the band, and it was a genteel group. You might say the social activities stemmed from the top, because if you met Ray, or Bill Harty, who had a tremendous sense of Irish humor, or Al Bowlly off the bandstand, the first suggestion would be, "Let's go have a spot!" As a result, I made my first attempt at genteel drinking, and there were some pretty genteel, or otherwise, drinkers in the band. Van Eps drank a lot, and Claude Thornhill already had a well-established reputation.

Al Bowlly was the only South African I had ever met. He was born in Johannesburg, of a Greek family, and he eventually migrated to England where he became quite a big name (I was told he was the Bing Crosby of England, which was probably true). He drank a bottle of scotch every day because he had been told this would keep his malaria in check,, and I suppose it did, as he never gave any indication of having malaria symptoms.

All three Englishmen were very interesting and talented. I became very close to Bill Harty because I sat beside him in the band. His sense of humor never stopped. Incidentally, I worked with Noble and Harty long after the dissolution of this band. They used to do the Edgar Bergen show, the first two weeks of which were always done in New York, after which it would move to California until the final two weeks, finishing up in New York. I worked on these broadcasts and also did some record dates with Noble, including some with Buddy Clark. I remember one in particular, because Buddy Morrow took a beautiful trombone solo on "Full Moon and Empty Arms."

Anyway, to get back to the beginning, RCA-Victor was very interested in the band and in trying to recapture the exceptional sound of Ray's English recordings. Our second recording date was in Camden, and in an attempt to achieve the sound they were after, Victor built a rectangular box in the old church studio, just big enough to hold the entire band. It was constructed of hardwood and designed in the shape of the old phonograph horns—very wide at the front and tapering to a small section at the back. I suppose they were hoping to get a form of natural reverb or to enhance the sound in some way. It must have been quite costly, and it was not a successful experiment. We did just that one date in the box and that was the end of it. In fact, Victor never did succeed in capturing the "live" quality of the English records, but years later, when some of the sides were reissued on a Vintage LP, the sound was excellent. I don't know what they did, but I really believe the sound is better than on the originals.

The Brian Rust listings of the personnel for these records include a few understandable errors. I started with the band in 1935 and remained with it through Christmas and into January 1936. I played on all the records, with the exception of one session, and I don't think that was even released under Ray Noble's name. Glenn Miller used the band on a date where they played an arrangement of "In A Little Spanish Town." The other men in the band played it, but Bunny Berigan took my place. That's the only date between February 1935 and January 1936 that I didn't do.

I don't recall much conflict being created by my working with Benny's band and Ray Noble at the same time. I guess the reason there was so little interference was that for a month or two we were just rehearsing with Noble. The first public engagement was a commercial radio program broadcast from Studio 8G, just down the hall from 8H, the big studio Benny was using. There was a lot of preparation for the show. We rehearsed and rehearsed and rehearsed. The one thing that has always stuck in my mind is the memory of playing an original tune by Claude Thornhill, which he tagged "8G," after the studio. I have since heard an air check of the Coty program and they gave the tune a title for the broadcast, "A Fountain In Havana," but we only knew it as "Opus 8G." It was a beautiful thing, and later it became the theme song of Claude Thornhill's band under the much more descriptive name of "Snow Fall."

The Coty program was aired on a Wednesday night, so it didn't conflict at all with my work with Benny. As a matter of fact, I was taking Benny's band a little more seriously than Noble's, at least in the early stages, and I continued to work with Benny through June. The Coty program, which probably started in March or April, was the introduction of Ray's American band.

We had a vocal trio with us called The Freshmen. It included a singer named Andy Love (who later became very successful singing jingles), a big guy named Ryan, and Jack Lambert, who later sang with Glenn Miller. Ray Noble, as did Benny, took the band on outside dates. We made a trip to New England for a string of one-nighters and we played just about the same spots that I had played with Benny. One time we left New York by bus for a date in Binghamton, on the morning that Charley Spivak's first son was born. He got on the bus carrying a market basket full of booze, and by the time we got to Binghamton, the brass section was so damn drunk it was a wonder we were able to play. But we did get through the night, and the fact that I can recall the incident indicates that I couldn't have been completely bombed.

The Ray Noble Orchestra in Studio 8G at NBC, February, 1935, on the air for the Coty Perfume program. L to R: Claude Thornhill, pno; Al Bowlly, vcl; Jim Cannon, Johnny Mince, Toots Mondello, Bud Freeman, saxes; Nick Pisano, vln; George Van Eps, gtr; Bill Harty, drms; Fritz Prospero, vln; Ray Noble, conductor; Andy Russo, and Glenn Miller, trbs; Delmar Kaplan, bass; Pee Wee Erwin and Charlie Spivak, tpts.

Musically, however, it must have been pretty bad, because the whole brass section (Spivak, Miller, Bradley, and I) was completely ossified.

In fact, it was after this job that the booze brought out a streak in Glenn Miller's character nobody ever realized existed. Glenn, like the rest of us, had a bit of an alcohol problem. He had a wonderful position with Noble, they were paying him a lot of money for his orchestrations, and he had organized the band, so he was probably being well compensated. Furthermore, Ray Noble and Bill Harty were great people. Ray always gave me the impression that he was awe-struck by Glenn and forever grateful to him for organizing the band. He had been familiar with the work of most of us and he felt he had the best band in the world. You got the idea he felt we were doing him a big favor by playing for him—you would have to go a long way to find a nicer guy. All of which made what happened seem all the more embarrassing. I'll never forget it. We finished the date at the George F. Pavilion in Binghamton and were starting to get back on the bus for the home trip. Miller cornered Noble and, in a voice loud enough for everybody to hear what was going on, proceeded to rip him up one side and down the other, raising pure hell with him.

"You limeys are all the same! You come over here and you're gonna make a great deal of American money, and then you'll haul it back to England and give it to the King's realm . . . " and on he went, telling him off without mercy in a way that was simply terrible. Noble, in his genteel fashion, took it all and never said a word. He wasn't intimidated by the abuse; he was just too much of a gentleman to reply in kind.

Miller, of course, was loaded and it was the booze that was talking. He was saying things he would never dream of saying while sober. After we got back, somebody told him what he had done and he felt terrible—so bad, in fact, that I don't recall seeing him take another drink for the duration of his time with Noble. I think he swore off for the entire stint.

I have heard some talk that when Miller and Spivak left the band about a year later they were rather unkind in their remarks about Noble. It may be that they asked for more money than was feasible but, in any case, I understand some hard feelings resulted and possibly these were instrumental in hardening Ray's attitude, making him more realistic and businesslike. Because from then on money *did* become the object. On my second tour of duty with Noble, it was a different band and a different attitude. I don't mean that Ray was any less the gentleman, but by this time things were being conducted on a more businesslike basis. Bill Harty had taken over the distribution of salaries, and now they would negotiate with you. Maybe the band had not attained the heights that had been expected of it, so money was a bit tighter, but, whatever the reason, they no longer asked you how much you wanted and then agreed to it without question as they had in the beginning. I wasn't working cheap the second time around, or anything like that, but they had definitely wised up.

TWENTY

WHEN BENNY took his band on the road in June of 1935, my tightrope act of playing with two bands at once ended. I elected to stay in New York about the same time that Ray Noble's band was booked into the swank Rainbow Room of the RCA building in Rockefeller Center. This was the top room of the world, a truly beautiful room. We started there around the end of June or the beginning of July, and I worked there with the band as long as I remained with it, until January 1936.

Once again no horses were spared in making things comfortable for the Ray Noble band. The bandstand was beautiful, and I have fond recollections of the room itself. It's the only place I have ever worked where there was a "color organ," a dome in the center of the room that was sensitive to sound and volume. If the band played a little louder the intensity of the color brightened and increased; if we played softer the light diminished. The colors were also sensitive to frequencies, with one color for high frequencies and other shades for medium and low frequencies. It was a pleasure to play in the room and watch the color organ work. The clientele came from very polite society. I recall seeing William Randolph Hearst and his girlfriend, Marion Davies, and, of course, there were many other notables.

The Rainbow Room was an ideal place to work. It was on the 65th floor, and the band's room was on the 67th floor, between the Rainbow Room and the observation roof. It was complete with dressing facilities, a ping-pong table, and all other comforts. We spent a lot of time there.

Our bandboy was a guy named Josh Billings, who had played suitcase with the Mound City Blue Blowers. I imagine Glenn Miller was responsible for getting him the job. Josh didn't have to play with the band, so he had a lot of free time, and one evening he brought a couple of lady guests to the 67th floor. They were having quite a social time of it when one of the Rockefellers walked in. The resulting big stink lost Josh his job. He was a very nice guy and we all hated to see him lose his job. Since then I've seen Josh many times, the last time in Chicago. But I think it's more interesting that his replacement was a young man named Jack Gilman, who had been a doorman at the Center Theater in the Radio City complex. Jack was a young, amiable guy, and after he came with the band we began learning more about him. He was quite a remarkable character. For one thing he had more money than any of us; he worked as a bandboy or doorman as a lark. He was also a philatelist with a fabulous stamp collection that was worth all kinds of money. His specialty was first-day covers. He also had another hobby, collecting debris from dirigibles which crashed, including the *Macon*, the *Shenandoah*, and the *Hindenburg*. He sold some of these items to other collectors for considerable amounts of money, as much as four or five thousand dollars. With us, he was probably getting forty or fifty a week—a mere trifle. He came from a wealthy family and on his eighteenth birthday inherited about a quarter of a million dollars, with another quarter million due when he turned thirty-one.

Those bandboys have always been a marvel to me. After all, when you came right down to it, they were actually only hangers-on around bands, yet in many cases they became more successful than the musicians. I remember when Bullets Durgam started—and he went on to become a millionaire. Richie Lasella was the bandboy with Tommy Dorsey's band when I joined it. One of his relatives married Tommy's sister, and he became Teresa Brewer's manager.

By this time I was well settled in at the house in Stewart Manor. I had established my family in residence there, and Johnny Mince was living with us. At this point I must mention certain incidents that probably had a lot to do with the deviations in my character which took place shortly after this. For one thing, I had a pretty unhappy home life. My mother was always a very nice, middle-of-the-road lady, able to go along with any situation, but my father had reverted to his ambition to become the world's classic drunk. He would go off on binges once a week, usually on weekends, and his drunks created one traumatic experience after another for the family. I don't mean that every moment of our home life was unreasonable or uncomfortable, but one session of my father's drunks was enough to last for six years. If you never had to experience it again, it would be too soon. I realize now that the poor guy probably couldn't help himself, but he certainly made life miserable for everybody else. He would berate everybody in sight, set himself up as far better than anyone else, and, altogether, create one helluva scene.

My brother was about ten years old, and he and Johnny Mince had a wonderful time together, so it wasn't all bad at home. The trouble was that Johnny and I were often away and the boy and my mother had to contend with my father alone. So here I had rented this ten-room house, had furnished it beautifully—although I was beginning to wonder what I was trying to prove—and although I was making a lot of money, I was also spending it. I even had a shop in the basement that was so complete that if I added a forge I could have built an automobile.

My father's drinking habits were really starting to upset me in a serious way. I gave him an allowence of $100 a week, and all he had to do, really, was enjoy himself. In all fairness, when he was "right" he would take my mother and brother out for dinner, or to the beach, and all the other things a normal family would do. But every week or two he would wind up drunk and then there would be hell to pay! He would literally become a raving maniac, threatening the family with physical harm, threatening to kill somebody, ridiculing my mother, my brother, and me. And sometimes this would last for two days for a full 24-hours a day.

One night I came home from work at 4 a.m. and found him screaming obscenities at everyone, and naturally he started on me. I was dead tired, had worked all day and night, and I felt I had been more than fair with him, so I came to the end of my patience. I hauled off and hit him on the chin hard enough to knock him completely across the room. This did far more damage to me than it did to him. If you have even the slightest sensitivity to such things you can't help understanding how this affected me mentally. After this I was almost frantic. I was willing to try almost any way in the world short of killing him to get rid of him, and the only way I could think of was to break up our home and send the family away.

I speak of my father's drinking and what it was doing to me, and yet when I would go to work in the Rainbow Room, we probably started around seven in the evening, the first thing I'd do was visit Hurley's Bar, where a bottle of scotch was sitting with my name on it, and have a couple of drinks. In addition to this, our playing schedule gave us extended intermissions. The job went from 7 p.m. to 3 a.m., but we had an hour off from 9 to 10 because the evening was split into two segments—a dinner session from 7 to 9 and the supper session from 10 to 1. We also alternated with a Latin band. This gave us plenty of time to drink, and daily I was drinking a bottle of scotch, although I don't recall getting stoned. But in light of all this, I suppose I shouldn't pass to many reflections on my old man, as obnoxious as he was when he was drunk. I don't know why I drank so much either. You'd think that I'd be so disgusted and fed up with my father's example that I wouldn't have any desire to touch the stuff.

To return to the Rainbow Room, I should mention that when we started to play there Toots Mondello didn't go with us. Mike Doty continued to play baritone sax, bass clarinet, and flute, but Milt Yaner, who had been with Isham Jones, came in on lead alto. All of us were still doing whatever outside work we wanted to and could handle. I don't remember worrying about business or money, so I must have been doing well financially, though I can't recall how much I was making at the Rainbow Room.

Sometimes I'd stay over in New York so I could drop in at Small's Paradise where Frankie Newton was playing. I liked the band there, and Frankie and I had become good friends. After hours, about three in the morning, I'd sit in with them sometimes. I guess I had Sundays off, because I also used to go to a jam session at a place called The Hay Loft, somewhere around Hempstead. I did this almost every Sunday for a long period. I met a couple of drummers there, and I helped one of them, Maurice Purtill, get his first job, with Red Norvo. Red and Mildred Bailey were working at a place on 52nd Street, and Red had asked me to locate a drummer for him so I recommended Purtill. The other drummer, Charlie Carroll, is now with

Conn Instruments. There were also a couple of trumpet players at these sessions—Joe Bogart, one of two guys haphazardly studying with me (I say haphazardly because I didn't have too much time to devote to teaching), and the other a big fellow named Walter Hughes.

I also met a family in Hempstead named Lianzo. They ran a restaurant in Stewart Manor. The oldest son was John, who later ran the business, and the younger brother was Phil, a very good trumpet player. I used to jam with them at their restaurant. They had a little drummer named Pompeo, and a clarinetist, Louis Catropa. I remained friends with these people for a great number of years, and Louis used to write to me from the South Pacific during World War II. A wonderful group of people.

I was also close to George Van Eps, who lived in Oceanside. He used to sit in on the Sunday sessions too, once in awhile. We got stoned, played the night out, and the people loved it. George came from a very talented family. His father, the elder Fred Van Eps, had been a banjo player, going back almost to the turn of the century, and had manufactured banjos at one time. George's mother's father had been a successful inventor, and George inherited his mechanical gift. Working alone with his own hands he built one of the most beautiful seaplanes I have ever seen, but his mother would never allow him to test-fly it. So George kept it in a boathouse at their place on Long Island. I don't know if he ever had it tested or not, but it was a beautiful job and a fine example of his mechanical ability. In later years, as any guitarist can tell you, he invented the seven-string guitar. He's also a great musician. But shortly after this he moved to the West Coast, and I haven't seen him in over forty years. I knew the whole family, though, including Fred Jr., a trumpet player better known for his arrangements—it seems to me he wrote some for the Noble band. Another brother, Bobby, was with Jimmy Dorsey's band on the Coast, and the youngest, John, later played tenor sax with Ray Noble and was with the band when I joined it for the second time. They were all excellent musicians and very talented people. Unfortunately, young John was killed in an automobile accident.

Another close neighbor was Milt Yaner, who had married a young lady named Bunny when we were with Isham Jones in Atlantic City. Another girl, Virginia, was going with Vic Hauprich at that time, and later Johnny Mince dated her while she was living with the Yaners. She eventually married Wendell DeLory, the trombone player. Mike Doty and his wife used to visit us often on Sundays. On the subject of social activities, once Ray Noble rented a pretty good-sized boat on the Hudson to take the band out for a Sunday outing. We sailed up to Indian Point, or one of those places up the Hudson. In the party were all the wives and children of those associated with the band, except Charley Spivak didn't have his wife with him, and I was single, so the main thing I remember about the day was Spivak and I standing beside a barrel filled with four or five cases of beer on ice and drinking one after another all day and all night until the boat docked back in New York. I don't know how Spivak made out, but I had to be rolled back to Stewart Manor by Johnny Mince and Mike Doty.

121

A favorite hangout for musicians in New York was Hurley's Bar. We always used to collect there—the NBC musicians and all the others working the area. Sooner or later you met all your friends there. Bunny Berigan, for instance, always came in when he was in New York. But a fixture in the place (he was *always* there) was an orchestrator named Phil Wall. He wrote for radio shows like "The Manhattan Merry-Go-Round," and for Gustave Henschen's musical group, and stories about him are almost legendary. He'd be sitting in Hurley's and suddenly remember that he had three arrangements that were due the next day. Then he'd drink right up to the last minute before going into production on what amounted to a system of prefabricated arrangements. He maintained a file on arrangement parts—an introduction going into the key of F, an interlude modulating from F into B♭—so whenever he needed an arrangement he'd go to the filing cabinet and pull out the parts he needed. He also carried a briefcase which I was given to understand was crammed with introductions, interludes, first choruses, and such. This allowed him to hang out just awhile longer at Hurley's and still have an arrangement ready for the "Manhattan Merry-Go-Round" on Sunday night.

Around this time I also worked on a radio show put together by an English friend of Ray Noble's. His full name was Austin Croomb Johnston, but it had been shortened to Ginger Johnston, a very nice guy. With the backing of NBC he put on a rather unusual program called "Soft Lights and Sweet Music," which was unusual in another way too. Both Artie Shaw and Benny Goodman were on it together.

George Simon has already recorded for posterity the night Claude Thornhill came down to play the last set at the Rainbow Room without his pants. This could easily happen because we used to dress and undress on the 67th floor. I imagine Claude thought the night was over and then somebody yelled, "Hey, we've got another set to play!" and in his hurry he forgot to put his pants back on. But the most humorous incident in the Rainbow Room—at least the band thought so—took place on our first New Year's Eve. And for all his polish, Ray Noble had a whale of a sense of humor.

It's a safe bet that since it was New Year's Eve the band was pretty well stoned. I know for certain the customers were. It all started innocently enough while the band was playing and Al Bowlly was out front singing. I think a dancer passed by too close and accidentally kicked a microphone which was in front of Noble's piano and projected well onto the dance floor. Anyway the mike the customer kicked hit Al Bowlly, who took a pretty dim view of the idea, and he threw something at the customer—a tom-tom, or something else at hand. The customer went back to his table, picked up a couple of hard rolls, and fired them at the band, and the band fielded them and fired them right back.

The next thing we knew all kinds of things were flying through the air of the very sedate Rainbow Room. Some people were even throwing ice-cream balls and the band was returning them. It got to be bedlam—like a pie-throwing scene in a Mack Sennett comedy. One of the trombone players used a plunger mute that had a hole cut out in the middle of it, and Ray Noble retreated to the brass section, picked up a horn, inverted the plunger over the mouthpiece, and then held it in front of his face for protection. You couldn't see him, only the plunger. After awhile things settled down, but the next day we received a lot of adverse criticism in the press. Reading the stories I got the general idea that, aside from being rather shocked at such undignified behavior in the Rainbow Room, most people objected to the spectacle because they had paid the lavish price of $15 per plate for their dinner, and I suppose they lost most of it to the need for ammunition. Today $15 would barely pay for the appetizers.

The band had a spot in a movie, "The Big Broadcast of 1935." We filmed it at the Paramount Studios on Long Island. Ray Noble wrote a beautiful song called "Why Stars Come Out At Night" that was featured in the picture as part of the small segment we played, with a vocal by Al Bowlly. I never did see the picture, so I don't know much about it except Paramount went to great pains to duplicate the bandstand at the Rainbow Room, even to the balcony behind it. We also recorded "Why Stars Come Out At Night" for Victor.

Our drummer, Bill Harty, was a big fan of network radio and he spent a lot of time at the NBC studios. He used to listen to the Rudy Vallee show, and on one broadcast he saw and heard a ventriloquist named Edgar Bergen and was very impressed. Of course, everybody knows who Edgar Bergen is now, but at that time he was still an unknown. At the instigation of Harty he was hired to work on the floor with the band in the Rainbow Room. This was great for us because we loved Bergen and his two dummies, Charlie McCarthy and Elmer Snurd, and we got to see and enjoy them every night. They were fantastic. I have no doubt that this is where the long association between Edgar Bergen and Ray Noble was established. When Bergen became the star of the Chase & Sanborn Hour, Noble became musical director. He also had a speaking part on the show as a foil for Charlie McCarthy.

I doubt that Bill Harty ever received any financial reward for his talent hunts, but he seemed to enjoy it anyway. Another guy he discovered was Jerry Colonna. We all knew Jerry, a doggone good trombone player with the morning band on CBS, but it remained for Bill Harty to get him started as a comedian by getting him booked into various places.

It was while I was with Noble that I attended my first jam session, at least, the first one I can recall. Eddie Condon promoted it and it was held at a recording studio in mid-town. Dave Tough was there. We had met once before under rather amusing circumstances. One day at Hurley's Bar this little guy came up to me and started a conversation. We talked for awhile and he finally left without even once having mentioned his name. Bud Freeman came over and asked, "Do you know who that guy was you were talking to?" and I had to admit I didn't. "That was Dave Tough," Freeman told me, "the world's greatest drummer." Well, I'd heard such extravagant claims before, so I didn't pay too much attention, until I worked with Davey in Tommy Dorsey's band.

Jack Teagarden was around New York in those days too, probably working with Paul Whiteman. He and my father hit it off pretty well, and one time my father took him out to the house for a few days and they spent time fooling around with my telescope. Jack had quite a mechanical bent and he was interested in such things. Besides, the two of them had a grand time getting stoned in the daytime and looking through the telescope at night. We all loved Teagarden.

TWENTY-ONE

IN THE FALL of 1936, probably October, we started a show on CBS sponsored by Coca Cola. Featured with us on the weekly broadcast was the singing star Connee Boswell and a vocal group called Babs and Her Brothers. The program followed the usual format of an overture followed by featured numbers. For me it is memorable as the first time I ever played that deathless musical classic, "The Music Goes Round and Round." I think it was also about this time that the Noble band recorded "Dinah," and "China Town."

I was always a nut about astronomy, although I never had enough time to devote to it. Working at the Rainbow Room proved to be the ideal place to combine business with the pursuit of my hobby because there was a telescope on the Observation Deck of the building. When we left the bandstand we had to come out through the kitchen. This led to a hall that took us to the elevators for the Observation Deck, where a young lady was taking tickets. A young man was taking tickets at the main entrance. Since I spent so much time in the hall I got to know them both quite well. Her name was Louisa Brooks, his was Pat Asta, and they later married.

Louisa learned about my interest in astronomy and kept telling me that she had a place in Arizona that would be the ideal place for me to retire and set up my telescope. I agreed with her, though I didn't know anything about Arizona, except the air out there was supposed to be clear and the skies bright for viewing—it seemed only logical. She told me her uncle had gone to Arizona and homesteaded 160 acres in Cochise County, but later he shot somebody in a fight and was sent to the penitentiary, so he deeded the property over to her. She had no use for the property, and since I was so interested in astronomy she said she would give the property to me. Why on earth she decided to do this, I'll never know, but sure enough, we went to a lawyer and for the sum of one dollar she deeded the property over to me. So I became a landowner in eastern Arizona near a town called San Simone. Actually I didn't get a chance to look at it until a considerable time later, but as a token of my appreciation I made Louisa a piece of furniture in my shop.

The story has a footnote. At some time after we left the Rainbow Room,

Louisa and Pat got married. About thirty years later I received a letter from a lawyer—a very nice letter—in which he said, "My client, Louisa Asta, who is the wife of Pat Asta, many years ago gave you some property in Arizona. At that time she had no dependents, but since then she and Pat have been married and have children, and they would like to know what steps would be necessary to redeem this property so as to leave an estate for their children."

I wrote back to the lawyer explaining that Louisa had sold me the land for $1 when she was single, retaining 1/3 of the mineral rights, and I was perfectly willing to do the same thing in reverse. Actually, I doubt if the property was ever worth very much, but for a time I was a landowner— probably acres of sagebrush and rattlesnakes. Louisa gave the property to me in 1936, and I gave it back to her in 1965.

All through this period my home life was getting more and more unpleasant. Inwardly I was already beginning to look for ways to break up the situation. It all stemmed back to the same old source—my father, who had reappeared on the scene while I was still working with Isham Jones. I couldn't get rid of him and, looking back, it's easy to understand why. No doubt I spoiled the guy, because for quite some time I gave him a hundred bucks a week spending money, so he didn't even bother to work. I think he made a couple of half-hearted pretexts at getting a job, but nothing serious— nothing, for sure, that was going to interfere with the lifestyle to which he'd grown accustomed.

I had spent quite a bit of money on the house in Stewart Manor, renting it and refurnishing it. I should have bought the house. I could have had that ten-room house for $8,500, but I wasn't the kind to make wise investments. I felt that the least he could do was behave himself, since all he had to do was live and spend money on himself while I paid all the household expenses. All he had to do was eat, sleep, and enjoy himself—not a bad existence—but he wouldn't behave himself and he was giving me a lot of trouble.

I'm not the type that could simply tell my old man I'd had enough and he had to get out, so I gave it a lot of thought and finally came up with what I considered the only way out of the situation—giving up my job at the Rainbow Room. I had received an offer to rejoin Benny Goodman's band at the Congress Hotel in Chicago, and I decided to take it. This meant quitting Noble but it gave me a good reason for telling my family I could no longer keep the house in Stewart Manor. I arranged to ship all of the furniture, even the basement workshop, to Kansas City, and set up my mother, father and brother in a comfortable house out there. I did everything I could to make the transition as easy as possible and I wasn't concerned about the cost. Still I did nurture fond hopes that my father would go back to making a living in Kansas City, where he had always done so well. He was a terrific salesman. To give him benefit of the doubt, maybe he would have except that I made a couple of critical mistakes—I gave him a sizeable lump of cash to tide him over until he got a job and I bought him a car.

I sent my mother and brother ahead to Kansas City by train and then prepared to make the jump to Chicago. Roy Wager had been working in

Chicago, leaving his car stored in my garage. Now that I no longer had a garage it seemed a good idea to drive his car to Chicago and deliver it to him in person. However, it was mid-Winter and driving was treacherous. The logical step was for my father to follow me in his car, as the first leg of his journey back to Kansas City, and in that way we could help each other in case of any difficulty. This would prove to be the fatal mistake.

We set out for Chicago, and one hour out of New York we hit ice, and we drove on ice until we reached Gary, Indiana. We wouldn't have made it to Chicago except that at a diner my father hit it off with the crew of a snowplow. We followed the plow into Chicago all the way from Gary—even trains were not getting into Chicago that night. It was well below zero and there was a tremendous amount of snow. But we made it and checked into a northside hotel, where we stayed a couple of weeks.

I joined Benny's band, and for awhile deluded myself into believing my father would take the money and the car I had given him and drive on to Kansas City. But things were so comfortable for him in Chicago he decided to hang around. Since the whole idea had been aimed at getting rid of him, I was fuming that after all my trouble the plan hadn't worked. And I was stymied—I didn't know what else to do.

Things went along that way for a couple of weeks, and then destiny stepped into the picture. I met a girl, I had known briefly when I was playing at Wildwood Lakes. She was the only girl I knew in Chicago, Roberta Greding, and, after a couple of dates, the bright idea hit me that if I married her my old man would surely have to move out. So I asked her, and she said okay. I don't recall that her parents were too enthusiastic about it, and when I told my old man he was pretty upset, to put it mildly. He said I was marrying the first girl to come along, that I didn't know anything about her, and so on—fighting like mad to keep his happy home and hunting ground. He went so far as to tell me I was marrying an alcoholic harlot, and that the marriage was doomed to be a disaster—even though he didn't know Roberta and had never heard of her before this. When this didn't work he went to Roberta and told her I was loaded with venereal disease, and she was destined for a horrible existence of pain, disease, and disgrace if she married me.

I must admit the old man was pretty resourceful when driven to the wall and fighting to hang on to his breadwinner. Nevertheless, he lost out. He was practically in tears at the ceremony, which was performed by a judge at the Harrison Hotel where we were living.

I suppose it must appear pretty drastic and a foolish reason for getting married, wanting to get rid of my father so badly, but actually Roberta was a pretty nice girl and we were married for fifteen years. Furthermore, looking at it from her standpoint, it was probably the roughest fifteen years of her life, so I have small cause for complaint. After the ceremony a couple of her cousins, who happened to be in Chicago, and the guys from Benny's band gave us a party at the hotel in one of the reception rooms. They put on quite a spread with plenty to eat and drink, and I think it was the only time in his life that Hymie Schertzer ever got loaded.

Hymie and I were pretty close buddies in Chicago. He liked to eat like I did and we used to go around after the job looking for good places. One of our favorite spots was a delicatessen on Randolph Street called the W & R. Anyway, Hymie chose my wedding as one of his rare times for having a few drinks, in spite of the fact that after the party we had to go to work. We started at 7:00 o'clock at the Congress, and, wedding or no wedding, party or no party, we had to be there. (Frankly, I don't remember what happened to my brand-new wife.) We started the evening session with a radio broadcast. I never did know why, but about fifteen minutes before we were to go on the air Hymie decided he wasn't going to play the broadcast. With great injured dignity, he started to remove himself, his saxophone, and his sax stand from the bandstand. It took a heap of doing on Benny's part to convince him to come back. This was all totally out of character for Hymie, a very straight-living, amiable, and happy guy who before this most likely had never defied anybody in his life.

The wedding accomplished what I was after, and my old man was left with no alternative but to go to Kansas City. So, at least temporarily, I got rid of him. I gave him another stake of a couple of thousand dollars. Since I had already given him the car, which would now leave me without one, I had to buy another. I took an apartment in the New Lawrence Hotel, which was way out on the north side of town. It had a swimming pool, and Roberta was quite a swimmer. Arthur Rollini and his wife also lived at the hotel, which was close to the Aragon Ballroom.

Roberta Erwin

128

I didn't mind being married. I'll admit that I was selfish and only thinking of myself when I decided to do it just to get rid of my old man. Without any question you're right in thinking it was a helluva reason to get married, but once it was an accomplished fact I accepted it and that's all there was to it. In fact, I had a rather nice time with my wife's Chicago relatives—and she had quite a few. One rather elderly couple belonged to a group of ten or twelve people who got together every Sunday night to try a different restaurant. They made a family affair out of it, and I was accepted into the family after I married their cousin. It got to be a nice ritual, because there are some marvelous eating places in Chicago and they seemed to know all of them. Besides eating well, we had a lot of fun. They were all nice people.

Benny's band was playing in the Joseph Urban Room of the Congress Hotel. Some Chicago people—I remember especially Helen Oakley and a gentleman named Squirrel Ashcraft—had a jazz club. (There were others in the club too, but these are the people I recall as the most active.) Benny's band was jazz oriented, so they got behind it and started having jazz sessions in the Joseph Urban Room every Sunday afternoon. Like the jazz clubs of today, they invited guest artists. One of these, brought in from New York, was Teddy Wilson, and although I understand Benny, Gene Krupa, and Teddy had made trio records earlier than this, I believe this is when the trio numbers became a feature of the band and Teddy became a regular member.

Our regular band pianist was Jess Stacy, a great drinking buddy of mine. We split a fifth every night, which isn't as bad as it might sound, because a fifth between two people over an evening wasn't enough to make either of us drunk, and I don't recall ever being stoned while I was in Benny's band. At that time I could hold my liquor fairly well anyway—much better than I could later. And Jess was a great guy.

Joe Harris was playing trombone with us, but Joe wasn't much of a drinker. He was more of a "crier," a sad guy in many respects. On the other hand, Red Ballard was a drinker of the strong, silent type, who could put away quite a bit without anybody being the wiser. Nate Kazebier was a quiet drinker too.

I've always laughed at the stories about Gene Krupa being a dope addict as simply ridiculous. The only thing I ever knew to cause Gene any trouble was alcohol—he simply could not drink under any circumstances. If he took a drink he practically lost his mind immediately. He was incapable of drinking.

The jazz club put 100% effort behind the band and began to stir up a lot of interest around Chicago. We were on the air five nights a week over WGN, which didn't hurt us at all locally, and some of the broadcasts may have gone over the network too. The jazz concerts went on every afternoon. I remember Buck and Bubbles, Mildred Bailey, among many others, and the sessions became a huge success. In addition to all this, *Down Beat* (in its infancy at the time under the management of a man named Glenn Burrs) latched on to the Goodman band and began to promote it on a national basis.

Up until this time Benny's band had met with only moderate success.

The first road trip to the Coast hadn't done too well. In fact, the Ilitch's Gardens date had been a disaster. It wasn't until they got to the Palomar Ballroom in California, and the people there accepted the band, that it got off the ground. Even then it wasn't until the engagement at the Congress that it really became established. All of a sudden a national reputation began to develop, and it was obvious from all of the activities that were going on it was getting to be a whale of a popular band, not only with jazz fans but the general public too.

In addition to our job at the Congress (and don't forget I had given up all that money in New York to join the band at $125 a week), I was happy when Benny started a commercial radio program in Chicago for the Elgin Watch Company, emanating from the Merchandise Mart. Eddie Dowling, a very popular Broadway performer, was the star and master of ceremonies. The standby studio orchestra was directed by Caesar Petrillo, and in it were two fine musicians—a trumpet player from Kansas City, Frank Anglin, and a tuba player who was part Indian, John Coon, an artist on his horn, who had played with the original Isham Jones Orchestra in the Twenties.

The Goodman band was pretty busy, I guess, because although there were plenty of other bands in Chicago at the time, I don't remember getting involved with them. I remember seeing Zutty on occasion, and Joe Thomas, the trumpet player, both working with Carroll Dickerson's band at the Grand Terrace. I became very friendly with Joe. Also Chu Berry was around, and the Dodds brothers were probably at the Three Deuces. We were usually working the same hours as the other bands and my after-hour activities had been somewhat curtailed now that I had a wife, so I wasn't able to get around the way I used to.

Actually, I don't think any of us at the time were aware of how fantastically popular Benny's band was getting to be. We just did what we were supposed to do, and it seemed to happen all of a sudden. The first time anybody began to appreciate what was happening was after we left the Congress. Our first trip out took in the closest territory—Niles, Michigan, South Bend, Indiana, the Indiana Roof in Indianapolis—and the attending crowds were absolutely phenomenal. I had never seen such crowds before. Benny, I'm sure was being booked by MCA on the usual percentage basis, and he began to make so much money that handling it became a problem. Since we were always on the move it wasn't always possible to get to a bank, and I know of at least one instance where Eugene, Benny's younger brother, who drove the instrument truck wearing coveralls, had $70,000 concealed under them. It wasn't likely anybody would bother holding up a panel truck, so it was probably a pretty smart trick, but I imagine Eugene did a lot of sweating. As it was, Benny had his entire family involved by then. Our salary checks were paid to us by Harry Goodman, and he in turn got them from his sister Ethel, who handled the band's business affairs.

By this time, the band at the Congress had jelled into a unit which was much better than the band that had played for the "Let's Dance" program, where essentially it had been a studio group. I had replaced Ralph Muzillo, so most of the time I was playing lead because Ralph wasn't much of a jazz player. I doubt if I had more than two jazz choruses in my book. Nate Kazebier, a musician I admired very much, handled the jazz. I consider him a very underrated player, and he was ideal for this kind of band. Then, too, at the Congress we were working in a hotel room so the band wasn't constantly blasting away. As a consequence it devloped a great blend and was an extremely interesting band to play with. I enjoyed it. We were still playing the standard library contributed by Fletcher Henderson and Spud Murphy, but while we were in Chicago a young fellow named David Rose wrote some things for us. I don't recall exactly what they were (possibly "Goody Goody," and the other tunes featuring vocals by Helen Ward) but I know he did some writing for us.

Then another great new arranger started bringing in things, some of which we recorded while we were at the Congress; this was Jimmy Mundy, and his arrangements really suited the band. "Swingtime In the Rockies," was one of his charts and one of Benny's all-time standards. He also brought around a typical three-minute arrangement of a tune called, "Sing Sing Sing," which was a great riff tune, but we didn't record it, although we played it every night on the job and started adding new riffs to the end of the arrangement. If a guy came up with an idea we liked, we tacked it on the end of "Sing Sing Sing," and the arrangement kept growing longer and longer. Some of the added riffs came from classics, like Holst's "Planet Suite," and others were the Rex Stewart riffs which Chris Griffin and I borrowed from Rex, whom we both admired. So "Sing Sing Sing" gradually developed into masterful treatment and it became a classic.

Incidentally, at the end of the Congress run there were some personnel changes. While we were at the hotel the trumpet section consisted of Nate Kazebier, Harry Geller (a fellow from California) and me. Geller, I believe, had been brought in to replace Bunny Berigan. He wasn't a great jazz artist, but he was an excellent trumpet player. After the Congress date he left us, and Chris Griffin came out from New York to join the band on tour. He had recently been married too, so we hit it off pretty well. On the road we traveled in private cars, and since I was now the proud owner of a new Oldsmobile, Chris and his wife rode with Roberta and me, and this arrangement lasted for the entire tour.

There has always been a lot of controversy, pro and con, in the music business on the subject of the appropriateness of taking your wife to work with you. After many years of observation I have formed very definite ideas about it. These ideas are my own and in no way intended as criticism of the views held by my fellow musicians, which may be completely contrary to mine, but I feel pretty strongly about them. A musician's married life is understandably different from the average guy's. For one thing, he's almost always working on holidays and weekends and other times when most people are looking for entertainment, and this makes it pretty rough for the musician's wife who enjoys social activity and wants to be with her husband. Unless she can adapt herself to these conditions, she has little chance to succeed as a musician's wife.

On the other hand, music is a profession, and I look at it as requiring the same dedication a doctor, or a lawyer, or a mechanic, must bring to his work, which means I don't like to take my wife to work. It distracts me. I'm concerned with things I shouldn't be concerned with—whether my wife is being properly tended to; how she is enjoying herself. These things shouldn't be allowed to interfere with my paying proper attention to the customers, and generally taking away from my full concentration toward doing my best for the patrons. Besides, there's always the chance an incident may take place to cause animosity, such as someone being discourteous to my wife, a chance that is completely eliminated if she isn't there. Furthermore, when you are employed to entertain, the employer is not obligated to hire your family. Some are very nice, and will attempt to do their best to please, but it is not technically a part of the business.

Nevertheless, when I was first married Roberta traveled with me on the road. I had no home, and other wives traveled with the band. We were like one big family. I must admit we had lots of pleasure and fun. Yet, in the long run, it eventually created a rift between my wife and me. Roberta liked to dance. (Actually she would have been much better off if she had married someone who liked the same things she did.) When we played one-nighters she would dance with the customers. She was nice looking and friendly, so she never lacked partners. But I wasn't keen about the idea, and I found it distracting and worrisome—especially when one night she left the hall (quite innocently, I'm sure) with someone she had been dancing with to go a short distance up the road and then return. They had simply gone out for some air, but I missed her and it bothered me. I never made much of a scene, but I guess subconsciously my respect for her was badly dented. It took a long time to fester, but I believe this incident resulted in my loss of interest in her. We both would have been smart to get a divorce right then.

To get back to the band, while we were at the Congress Joe Harris had been receiving offers from Hollywood from people like Georgie Stoll and Ray Heindorf, presenting opportunities for him to get into the studios, something he always wanted to do. A young guy, Murray MacEachern, came down from Toronto to take his place. But after he arrived he had to wait around for about six weeks before the immigration work permit allowed him to play. Murray, as everyone knows, is an excellent trombonist, but when he later joined the Casa Loma band he played as much saxophone as he did trombone, which amazed me, because the whole time he was with us I never knew he could play sax.

After we left the Congress Hotel, Chris and Murray were in the band. We made the very successful tour around the region bordering Chicago and then came East. We took another tour out of New York, down into the Virginia-North Carolina school circuit, and I remember playing the University of North Carolina and a swing into Virginia. By then Teddy Wilson was a regular with the band, and I believe we were the first to travel the area with a mixed group, but I don't recall any incidents. Teddy was, and still is, such a gentleman that I can't imagine anybody creating an embarrassing situation because of him. But I do recall that Benny and Nate Kazebier got into a pretty heated argument in Raleigh, N. C., and Benny's brother had to get into the middle and break it up before it went beyond mere words. But this didn't change anything; Nate was still with us when we went to California.

After the southern swing we went back to New York, and then worked our way out to Detroit where we played one week at one of the ballrooms. By this time we had the word that Benny was booked to make a movie. The year before I had played with Ray Noble in "The Big Broadcast of 1935," and now Benny's band was set to do one called "The Big Broadcast of 1937," even though it was still 1936. This meant a trip to California.

TWENTY-TWO

WE WERE at Westwood Gardens in Detroit when Benny got the movie offer. By then it was obvious the band was close to being number one in the country, but this didn't alter any of our decisions, opinions, or playing. It was a good band, no two ways about it, but when we got the word about California we all started making our own plans and things got hectic.

To start off with we were instantly faced with a deadline. I forget just when we were supposed to start the picture, but a definite date had been set for our opening at the Palomar Ballroom, where we would be working while the picture was being made. This date didn't leave enough time for such pleasures as a leisurely drive to California by private car. We all had cars, so arrangements were made in Detroit, about a week before we were to take off for California, to drive our cars to Chicago and put them on a boxcar—more likely a half dozen boxcars—to be shipped to California, while we boarded the *Santa Fe Chief* for the two-and-a-half day trip.

The *Santa Fe Chief* was the Ritz of railroad trains, and our trip was made in style. We all had private staterooms complete with showers, and the accommodations aboard the train were quite lavish, almost like the European trains of today. There was even a barbershop and a beauty parlor. It was the fanciest train ride I've ever taken in my life. All the guys and their wives had a lot of fun. I don't think we could buy booze on board, but we played cards and had a wonderful time all the way to California.

We opened at the Palomar as scheduled. It was just off Wilshire Boulevard, and Chris and I were very lucky because we each found an apartment in a building directly behind the Palomar called the Rayfield Apartments. For sheer convenience this was ideal. During intermissions or after the job Chris and I could leave the ballroom through a door behind the bandstand and just walk across the street to our apartments. If we had fifteen or twenty minutes off we could go home and have a snack. By this time Benny had made the trio with Gene Krupa and Teddy Wilson a regular feature with the band, which gave the rest of us at least a twenty-minute break. When they performed, the people would be stacked in front of the bandstand. We made it up though; we were required to play some waltz sets,

Chris Griffin

the usual thing in all ballrooms, and since this wasn't exactly what Benny was noted for, he would leave the stand while we played for the dancers.

This was my first trip to California, also the first for several of the other guys, I'm sure, and to me it was a big event. Everything seemed to be going so well for us I don't think we could be blamed for feeling on top of the world. The Palomar was a beautiful ballroom, we were in a great band with a big following, and we were doing business on a grand scale. Furthermore, Los Angeles was a beautiful city, more on the tropical side then than it is today since it has been built up to such an extent. There were a lot of things to see, especially for those of us there for the first time. So we visited Griffith's Park and other points of interest.

In addition, my Aunt Hazel and Uncle Harry Bivens were now living in Pasadena, which turned out to be something of a fun-type situation. We'd visit them and they'd entertain Roberta while I made a quick trip to the observatory at near-by Mt. Wilson, where they had the largest telescope in the world with a 100″ reflector. To me that was a fantastic attraction. At other times we would drive out Wilshire Boulevard to Santa Monica and have early morning swimming parties, although the Pacific was always too cold for me.

This is as good a place as any to tell about Aunt Hazel and Uncle Harry and their amazing success story. You recall they had owned a chicken farm outside of Kansas City where I lived with them for awhile. Much of the equipment Uncle Harry used to raise chickens was manufactured by a company named Jamesway. They did fairly well for a time, but then Uncle Harry came down with a severe case of pneumonia that left him in very poor health, and on his doctor's advice they sold the chicken farm and moved to California. He took a job selling Jamesway poultry equipment, traveling Southern California and Arizona, and this is what he was doing when we visited them in Pasadena.

Judged by the standards of the time, Uncle Harry did pretty well, because he managed to save $8,000. About a year later he bought a piece of property he had spotted in downtown Phoenix and, practically single-handed, built a motel which he and Aunt Hazel operated for several years. Shortly after the war began, around 1942, he sold the motel—for almost a million dollars.

As for the Pasadena set-up, it included a surprising development I hadn't counted on—my father and mother were there too. Instead of trying to reestablish himself in Kansas City with the money I gave him, my father had convinced my mother that California was the land of opportunity for him. After the money ran out he sponged off Aunt Hazel and Uncle Harry. He was a good salesman, but if he had put as much effort into selling other people as he did into selling my mother a bill of goods most of our problems would have disappeared. It seemed to me I would never get him out of my hair.

I think our engagement at the Palomar was for eight weeks. This gave us lots of opportunity to get acquainted, or reacquainted, with the West Coast musicians. There were some very busy and prominent ones in the studios that we hooked up with. In particular, I recall a clarinetist, Archie Rosoatta, who was probably number one in the studios, a trumpet player named Martin Peppy—originally an easterner who had played with many of the early bands—and a trombonist, Randall Miller. By this time Joe Harris was also well established in the studios.

Jimmy Dorsey's band was stationed in the Los Angeles area too. They were doing the Kraft Music Hall show with Bing Crosby and were his set band in the way Les Brown's became Bob Hope's through the years. They had already been in California for a year when we came in. George Thow, the trumpet player I had replaced with Isham Jones, and Andy Russo were in the Dorsey band and, of course, it was a very good one. By then these guys were men-about-town. All they had to do was play one show a week and maybe work weekends. They led the life-of-Riley for an awful long time. I used to meet Jimmy and George Thow quite often in an after-hours place, and we'd jam the rest of the night.

On the subject of jam sessions, I still have a letter from Al Jarvis, then the West Coast's foremost disc jockey, inviting me to a Sunday session at his studio. My invitation came to me by way of Gene Krupa who was also invited. This was something of an upper-crust super-session because of the illustrious names included, and I felt very flattered and honored to be part of it. Benny and Jimmy Dorsey were both there, and Joe Sullivan, and Bobby Van Eps, and I met bandleader, Jimmy Grier, who was doubling as bartender for the occasion. Bing Crosby and his wife, Dixie Lee, were present too. Bing didn't drink at these things, but his wife was quite a two-fisted drinker.

The Palomar Ballroom was the showplace of the area, as far as ballrooms were concerned. We played for a chorus line, I guess it was part of a show, and at one point they used wooden horses in a mock horse race. To back it up Chris and I rigged up a thing on "Pony Boy," the greatest cornball thing for a horse race you've ever heard. We still remember it, and once in awhile we rip into it. Toots Camarata, who was playing and arranging with Jimmy Dorsey, married one of the girls in the Palomar chorus while we were there. This was my first meeting with Tootie, although Chris had known him back East when they both played with a New Jersey band, Scott Fisher.

We were at the Palomar a couple of weeks before we started work on the movie, and I don't remember much about the picture except that it involved a lot of time and work. I won't say Benny was greedy, but I know he got fifty grand for the picture and the rest of us worked for studio scale. Chris and I have often talked about the little we made in proportion to the amount of work we did, because in addition to playing at the Palomar and working on the picture, Benny began to book outside dates on Sundays. We played in Bakersfield, and I remember one particular job in San Diego that gave Chris, Helen, Roberta, and me a chance to run over to Tiajuana. We came back with a couple of bottles of tequila and some Mexican weed, and we were smoking the pot when we came to a roadblock. Lights were flashing and cars

The Benny Goodman Orchestra poses for a publicity still on the Paramount set in Hollywood, August, 1936. Front Row, L to R: Pee Wee Erwin, tpt; Gene Krupa, drms; Bill DePew, sax; Murray McEachern, trb; Second Row: Hymie Schertzer, sax; Red Ballard, trb; Benny Goodman; Allen Ruess, gtr; Arthur Rollini, sax. Rear Row: Dick Clark, sax; Jess Stacy, pno; Nate Kazebier, trpt; Chris Griffin, tpt; Harry Goodman, string bass.

were backed up, and we didn't know what it was all about, but you never saw four car windows roll down so fast. We went through without any trouble.

Just to give you an idea of how hard we were working and how much we needed those outside dates on Sunday nights, let me run down our routine. To begin with we were playing at the Palomar every night except Sunday from 9 p.m. until 2 a.m. Then when we began work on the picture we had to get up early enough to be in the make-up room at the studio at 8 a.m., and on the set by 9, where we put in a full day until 5 p.m.

In the beginning we didn't mind too much, but in the first two days we made all of the sound tracks that Benny had anything to do with, and then part of the sound track consisted of Benny's band augmented by a string section conducted by Victor Young. We were paid for this, roughly somewhere around $20 an hour. We made maybe a couple of hundred dollars for the music we played in the picture, but beyond this point and for the balance of the three weeks on the picture we put in most of the time just sitting around the set. We still had to be in the make-up room at 8 each morning, five days a week, and then we sat around posing for background scenes, and the like. They called it side-lining, and we got a hundred bucks a week. This was our first experience with one of the big studios and it was

extremely interesting to everybody, but for the amount of time involved—
and especially in view of the average man's idea of the big money to be made
in movies—this wasn't much. We were all pretty tired, and I could fall asleep
sitting upright in a chair.

Burns and Allen were in the picture. They played a radio team who had
hired a juggler to appear on their shows—a great attraction on radio. In our
segment of the picture we worked with the Broadway comedian Benny
Fields. He wasn't my kind of comedian but he was a loveable guy, and years
later I got to know him very well in New York when he lived near me on Sixth
Avenue. He and his wife, Blossom Seeley, were wonderful people. While
Benny Fields was doing his part in the movie something happened I'll never
be able to understand. Benny lost his pivot tooth somehow, and they scoured
the lot looking for it. When they couldn't find it they suspended production
on his segment for three days until a new pivot tooth could be flown in from
New York. Why a California dentist or somebody local couldn't have done
it, or why a big studio like Paramount couldn't rig up a replacement, is
something I have never been able to figure out.

Once in awhile to relieve our boredom from just sitting around we'd
start a jam session, entertaining the stagehands and electricians. But not too
often. This was the month of August and it was hotter than blazes, in
addition to which the studio lights put out heat that was almost unbearable.
I've always been able to stand heat pretty well, so it didn't bother me as much
as it did some of the others.

Leopold Stokowski had a segment in the picture, and he was fascinated
by Gene Krupa. He was absolutely carried away, and I think he would have
stolen Gene for his symphonic orchestra if he had any kind of an
opportunity. Jazz just cracked him up. He was in seventh heaven listening to
it, especially if he could watch Krupa.

W. C. Fields was working on a picture on the next sound stage to ours,
and since we all ate in the central cafeteria we got to hear all the Fields stories
being told by the technicians working with him. They said he would never get
in front of a camera unless his glass, which held exactly one bottle of beer,
was just out of camera range but handy. You could never get him in front of a
camera at all unless his booze was available.

We posed for a lot of still publicity shots which were to be used in
advertising the picture, and during these sequences I got to see a number of
the stars who were working around the lot. I remember Martha Raye, quite
young and very well put together, and Fred McMurray, who had once been a
sax player himself and liked to hang around the band. In fact, he had worked
in a band with Earl Hagen. I got to know Earl quite well later with Tommy
Dorsey. Another gal working on the set was Mary Martin, and Ray Milland
was also in the picture. It was quite an experience for us, seeing the inner
operations and going through the sound stages and looking at the sets they
built. Paramount at that time, was located in Culver City, a small suburb of
Los Angeles. It would have been a lot more fun if we hadn't been so tired.

Another interesting aspect of this California trip was the number of people I met from back home. One night at the Palomar a young man came up to the bandstand and introduced himself to me as Burl Uban. I had known him as a boy in Falls City, but aside from the surprise of meeting him in Los Angeles, the thing that amazed me was that when I had known him he had been wearing leg braces as the result of polio and now he was walking perfectly straight without any sign of it. This was a remarkable accomplishment for the time. Another guy I met and was associated with for awhile was Tommy Whitwer, who also came from Falls City.

Still another guy from back home was a bandleader, named Giannina, in the Majestic Ballroom in Long Beach. I hadn't known him in Falls City, but his family had known mine for years, so I went down to Long Beach to visit him. This in turn led to my getting familiar with Long Beach, and the discovery that the municipal band which played at the Long Beach horseshoe pier was conducted by the famous cornet virtuoso Herbert L. Clarke. He was in his seventies by then, but it was still a thrilling experience to see him as a conductor.

Long Beach was quite an interesting place. They had a big horseshoe pier that jutted well out into the water and was always crowded with fishermen. But the ocean, from all the reports I ever heard, was loaded with barracuda and stingrays, and as far as I was concerned was to be avoided like the plague.

Another unusual sidelight of our California stay was provided when Bill DePew, our third alto player, decided to get married. In the middle of the Forest Lawn complex, besides the cemetery there's a gorgeous church surrounded by a greenhouse. It's called the "Wee Kirk of the Heather," and this is where Bill got married. The ceremony was early in the morning and all those bleary-eyed musicians must have presented quite a sight. Maybe it was the beauty of the setting, or self-pity induced by hangovers, but I know we were all sitting around bawling like babies during the ceremony.

Hymie Schertzer and I continued the routine we had instituted in Chicago of looking for good places to eat after the job. In the process we also discovered some all-night movie theaters we could attend. This led to our stumbling onto a place that catered to naval personnel—the joint was always packed with sailors. They had a terrific band and a show-stopping musician-entertainer named Lionel Hampton. After one visit Hymie and I kept going back, and we talked about the place so much that other musicians began to hang out there too. Finally all the chatter must have gotten to Benny and he decided to check it out for himself. He was immediately so impressed by Lionel that he hired him to join the trio with Wilson and Krupa, and it became a quartet.

Another guy who appeared on the scene was Vido Musso. He sat in with the band a few times, obviously a great tenor player, and this paved the way for his joining us a short time later. This had its humorous angle for everybody except Benny's younger brother, Eugene. Two thirds of Benny's family were in California. Benny and Eugene were living somewhere on the outskirts of town, almost in Santa Monica, and after the job they would drive home together. Vido's sitting in with the band had created a lot of talk among the guys. He couldn't read music, but he was a tremendous musician with a fantastic ear. He could sit in a sax section and once over he'd have the arrangement memorized. All of this must have impressed Benny, so riding home with Eugene one night he asked, "What do you think of Vido Musso? I'm thinking of adding him to the band." Eugene wasn't a musician, but he did his best to answer the question logically and honestly. "Well, Benny he can't read music. And if he can't read, what good will he be to the band?" Well, whatever answer Benny wanted to his question, this wasn't it. He got so sore he put Eugene out of the car and made him walk the rest of the way home.

Benny's older brother, Charlie, was also around, and spent a lot of time fishing. He kept us all in fresh fish, being very generous with his catches.

While still at the Palomar we started a radio program that was to add a lot of prestige to Benny's name, "The Camel Caravan." It began in California—probably after we finished work on the picture. In the beginning there were two bands on the program, Benny's and a studio orchestra led by Nat Shilkret. By the time Goodman was back in New York at the Pennsylvania Hotel in the fall of '36, however, he had the program alone. The show format included guest stars, and since we were in California where many of them lived it wasn't too difficult to line up guests for a variety radio program like "The Camel Caravan." I distinctly recall John Barrymore as one. He showed up with a four-day beard and so stoned that nobody was likely to forget it, and to add icing to the cake he was rather insulting to the young lady who was working with him. At other times we had Martha Raye, Mary Martin, Fred McMurray, and George Jessel.

Chris Griffin and I have often talked about the salaries we were paid in those days, and by today's standards they sound pretty small. Our base pay was $125 a week, and if we did a record date (which we often did) it paid $30 for a three-hour session. Then we might make another $40 if we played an extra date on our night off, and, of course, a radio show like "The Camel Caravan" paid extra, probably another $40 or $50 per show. Add the $100 per week we were paid for our work at Paramount, and we still rarely averaged over $250 a week for being soloists and members of the number-one band in the country. No vast fortune.

The Isham Jones band hit California while we were still there, and by this time Woody Herman was the featured singer and assistant conductor. I visited with all of my old friends, of course. Back in New York the previous fall I had been best man at the wedding of one of the trombone players, Wendell DeLory. He married Virginia Walker, who used to go with one of the sax players. I had gotten to know her very well, from the time we first met while I was still with Jones, and later when she was living with the Yaners at Stewart Manor and dating Johnny Mince.

TWENTY-THREE

WHEN THE GOODMAN BAND was due to leave California I gave Benny my notice. Why? Well, looking back over the long span of years I'm not sure just why. I know I liked California, and there seemed to be a lot of opportunities for a musician, and I guess I wanted to stay. I had been getting messages from Tommy Dorsey about joining his band—mainly made up of my old buddies from the Joe Haymes outfit—but for some reason even this didn't interest me.

There's no doubt about it; California is a very attractive place to live. It's tropical without the humidity of most tropic places, and the scenery is often spectacular. It's no wonder that the movie industry concentrated there, because the great percentage of sunny days (before smog) permitted more outdoor shooting in the proximity of Southern California than anywhere else.

However, the rules for joining a local of the American Federation of Musicians were the same no matter where you were. You had to deposit your card and then live in the area for six months before you were eligible for membership. During the first three months of your transfer period you were only permitted to work casual engagements—parties, banquets, etc. During the second three months you could work a steady job. When the six months were up you could join the local for a fee and have no further restrictions. The hitch was getting through those first six months. During this time you were not permitted to record, do any movie or radio work, and there were not many of those "casual" jobs. As a result, you had to live for six months with almost no income.

As much as I liked California, I had to give this a lot of consideration. And I wasn't the only one to think about it. Dick Clark also left Benny and stayed in California and eventually wound up in Phil Harris's band. He knew a lot of the guys with Phil, especially Roy Wager and Stan Fletcher, who had joined earlier.

Meanwhile, another development may have influenced me into changing my mind. For no particular reason my father had brought my mother and brother to California. By now the money I had given him had run out,

Roy Wager

although he still had the car. From my point of view his reappearance was just one more indication that he intended to keep sponging off me as long as he could. When he approached me for money at the Palomar I refused to give it to him. This was a pretty difficult thing for me to do because he was an expert at twisting my arm and playing on my emotions. But the final straw to break the camel's back was when he came around trying to sell me the automobile I had given him six months before. When I wanted no part of that, he tried to sell me a radio, which I had also given to him.

We had reached the ridiculous stage and the time had come for me to make a stand. It wasn't an easy thing for me to do, but I knew that if I didn't I would have him on my back for the rest of my life. So I simply refused to give him any money. I later learned that eventually my mother had to return to Falls City where she stayed with my grandparents. Frankly, I don't know what happened to my old man at that point, but he did wind up back in Kansas City so no great damage was done to him. He was entirely capable of earning a living if he had to, and the stand I took did accomplish making him earn his own way.

The most impressive trip anyone can take is driving through our great western country. The mountains, canyons, and deserts present a fantastic panorama and are good for the ego—they certainly acquaint you with the insignificance of man. So when I decided to leave California, I suggested, and Roberta agreed, that we take the opportunity to view some of the wide open spaces and drive back across the country. We drove east on the old Route 66, then the main highway, across the Mojave Desert, through the Petrified Forest, and along northern Arizona past the Painted Desert and Navajo territory. After crossing New Mexico I turned north at Albuquerque, and we went through Sante Fe into Colorado, through Raton Pass to Denver, and across Nebraska to Omaha. At this point we detoured 100 miles south to Falls City for a visit with my folks, then continued south to Kansas City for a visit with Roberta's parents, Mr. and Mrs. Sidney Greding, and her sister and her husband, Mr. and Mrs. Phil Katz. All in all it was a nice trip because we were in no hurry. I had no job to rush to, so we could take time to enjoy the scenery and local color.

The trip across country held two memorable experiences for me. When we were in Flagstaff, Arizona, we stopped for dinner, and afterwards I couldn't resist the temptation, though it was quite late, to at least drive around the grounds of the famous Lowell Observatory. It was just about dusk when we got there, and I noticed one building was still brightly lit. It proved to be a library, and when I knocked at the door a pleasant young man answered. I told him I was interested in astronomy and asked if it would be possible to visit the observatory.

"Tell you what," he said, "I'll take you to see our large telescope, which is the 26″ refractor that enabled Professor Lowell to discover the two moons of Mars, and if it is not in use you can look through it." This was more than I had hoped for and I was really thrilled, but when we got to the telescope house the instrument was in use photographing the heavens. Nevertheless, I was happy just to see it.

The next incident happened only a few hundred miles further east. When we got to Gallup, N.M., I noticed a number of street posters advertising a dance that was being held to honor an Indian princess. Roberta suggested, "Why don't you go and sit in and play a set to help keep your lip up." It sounded like a good idea, so I paid admission and entered the dancehall with my horn under my arm. I didn't recognize any faces in the band, but I finally worked up enough nerve to approach them and ask if I could sit in—only to be quite shocked when I was told they couldn't allow any such thing. My modesty wouldn't allow me to tell them that I had been playing with a pretty good danceband, so I left the dancehall with my tail between my legs. I never knew who they were, nor did they know who I was.

I had given all the furniture from the house in Stewart Manor to my mother and father, so when Roberta and I got back to New York we took an apartment at the Whitby Hotel, and for the first time since we had been married I bought new furniture. I didn't have anything definite in mind as far as working was concerned, but I didn't expect getting a job to present any great problem. There was too much going on.

I started off by doing some studio work, took a few free-lance dates, and then began to get offers. Artie Shaw was organizing a band to go into the

Hotel Lexington, where the Crosby band with Ward Silloway and Artie Foster had been working. It was a pretty-sounding unit, utilizing a string section, and I recall being very impressed by the unusual bass line that ran through the arrangements, an approach I had never heard before. But when Artie approached me about playing with him I hesitated about committing myself.

The Isham Jones band was back in town and I was seeing quite a bit of Walt Yoder and my other friends. Jones had decided to retire, and they were involved with reforming a cooperative unit. They elected Woody Herman as leader, and for a time I was seriously considering going with them. In fact, I played the first date under Woody's name in the Brooklyn Roseland. It was an excellent band and they had good material, playing a lot of blues and specialties by Joe Bishop.

But I didn't go with either Shaw or Herman. Instead, I rejoined Ray Noble at the Rainbow Room. By this time the Noble band had undergone quite a few changes. Johnny Mince, Mike Doty, and Dan D'Andrea were still in it, but Glenn Miller had left. Johnny Van Eps had taken over for Bud Freeman on tenor, Claude Thornhill's piano spot was filled by Frankie Vino. On trombone we had Byron Caron, and, from time to time Frank D'Anolfo (who was later in Glenn Miller's band) and Alex Palocsay. I probably replaced Charlie Spivak because I came in on lead trumpet. Sterling Bose was playing with me, which was a fun thing. He was drunk most of the time, but he was a lovable drunk, a great guy, and a pretty darn good cornet player in his Chicago dancehall style. For a good part of this stint with Noble I put in a lot of time covering up for him. Every so often he was too stoned to play, and I'd try to keep Ray Noble from finding it out. Of course, I couldn't play two parts at once, and with only two trumpets it's not easy to cover, so although Bose quite often made a spectacle of himself Noble very graciously never fired him.

We were playing in the Rainbow Room, but the Rainbow Grill also had a band—both rooms were going full blast in those days—Ruby Newman had come in from Boston. Playing trombone with him was Roland Dupont, who later joined Noble, and a saxophonist, Floyd Tottle, who doubled on practically all of the reed instruments and became very active in the studios. My old friend Bob Nevins was playing trumpet. This was my first meeting with him, but to this day we still work together on occasion. Another brilliant musician, Tom Parsly, played sax with Newman. My association with these fine musicians developed considerably in later years. I worked with Roland Dupont for years at CBS, and with Floyd Tottle in varius Ray Bloch groups during the Forties. However, I don't know what became of Alex Palocsay or Byron Caron.

I judge I rejoined Ray Noble around the beginning of October 1936, and the band remained in the Rainbow Room until early in 1937, thus including another New Year's Eve, this one made memorable by Sterling Bose. We'd been on the job for two or three hours already, but it was still before midnight when Bose, who had been making repeated trips down to Hurley's Bar,

Mr. & Mrs. Sterling Bose

started to walk to the bandstand and got just about body-length from making it when he fell flat on his face. So we finished the night without him.

After the first of the year Noble took the band on a theater tour. We played the Paramount, I remember, because I was trying out a large-bore Besson trumpet and my lips were all swollen. We were joined on the tour by The Merry Macs—my old friends the McMichael brothers. By then they were a quartet, and had added a girl named Lynn Martin to the group. The band personnel included Van Eps, D'Andrea, Mince, and Doty on saxes; Roland Dupont and Alex Palocsay, trombones; Bob Norris and Fritzie Prospero, violins; and Bose and myself on trumpets. On piano was Frank Vino, the guitarist was Ned Cosmo, Sam Fidel on bass, and Bill Harty was both drummer and band manager. Al Bowlly had returned to England, and our new vocalist was Howard Phillips.

I had a ball during this period. We played the Metropolitan Theater in Boston, a nice engagement, and some of us used to go roller-skating between shows. There are a lot of marvelous restaurants in Boston, like the Union Oyster House, Jake Worth's (a German house) and an Irish place where they had clay pipes hanging all over the ceiling. Another was Durgen's Park, in the market district, world-famous for steaks.

We stayed at the Turaine Hotel, a rather elegant old place, but our stay was marred because somebody decided to commit suicide by jumping from one of the windows. It was just my luck to come along while the body was still lying covered on the street, and for a moment I panicked because the open window was on the same floor of the hotel as our room and I was hit by the terrible thought that Roberta may have fallen out of the window.

From Boston we went to Montreal. Another fun place with great restaurants. It was winter and they were using sleighs instead of taxis. It was the height of the ski season, so I made a trip to Mt. Royal to watch the action, or more accurately, the carnage. They even had a couple of ambulances stationed at the ready at the bottom of the mountain to pick up the skiers who hit trees on the way down. I'm certain there were serious accidents daily because the trees were a hazard on the entire run.

We played Loew's Theater and I got acquainted with the trumpet players in the pit orchestra. One of them, Tommy Tomasso, in addition to playing excellent lead horn in the pit, owned an Italian restaurant. I kept this association going for a number of years, and Tommy even came to visit me in New York. I recall in particular—I was working with Bose, remember—that we had to stock up on Black Horse Ale for the weekend because there were no alcohol sales in Montreal on Sunday. Toronto was our next stop, and there we got a beer named Old Dominion Number One, which was very potent stuff. Even a whiskey drinker couldn't handle any more than a couple of bottles without getting loaded.

It was during this week in Toronto that we learned Ray Noble intended to disband. He had met a trumpet player there named Trump Davidson, and shortly after disbanding the American group he took Davidson and a Canadian unit on a tour of England. This probably had great appeal to the English audiences, hearing a Canadian band, and Trump Davidson was quite a trumpet player. He always had fine groups on the Canadian networks, so it was a wise musical venture for Noble.

I had dinner with Trump at his home in 1978, a short time before he passed away. It was pleasant to reminisce with him about our early years. He told me about the successes of his trip with Noble to England, and we also talked about our mutual friend Phil Napoleon. It's too bad that Canadian and American broadcast facilities don't have closer liaison. Trump is a typical example of a talented man who was a huge success in Canada, yet practically unknown in the States. And this between two friendly countries that are a stone's throw apart.

I don't recall exactly how long the Noble tour lasted, but when it was over I returned to New York, living again at the Whitby on 45th Street, at that time a very pleasant and sociable place. Toots Mondello has always lived there. My namesake, Pee Wee Hunt, was another resident. We had a running gag we loved to pull; people used to think we were crazy. We'd meet on the crowded elevator, and he'd say very politely, "Hello, Pee Wee," and of course I'd answer, "Hello, Pee Wee." This never failed to make the other people on the elevator take a quick assessment of the vast difference in our sizes and then look at each other with skeptical expressions.

The Whitby apartments were not only very well located in relation to New York playing jobs, they also provided an excellent opportunity for our wives to enjoy a nice social life. Roberta had the company of a lot of friends and the convenience of a great food-shopping center only ½-block away, at 45th Street and 9th Avenue. Chris and Helen Griffin, Ethel and Gene Krupa,

147

Mr. and Mrs. Gene Prendergast—we were all good friends. Roberta and I had picked out nice furniture and our apartment was very attractive.

It was during this period, too, that the great Benny Goodman band was making musical history at the Pennsylvania Hotel and on "The Camel Caravan." Harry James was now an important feature in the band, but at this point he still didn't have a card in Local 802, so if the band worked out of the hotel on its night off, I would substitute for Harry.

Tommy Dorsey's band was playing in the Palm Room of the Commodore Hotel around the end of February 1937. I don't recall the negotiations with Tommy, but the result was that Johnny Mince, Mike Doty, and I, all from the Noble band, joined Tommy's band at the same time. The band also included Andy Ferretti, Joe Bauer, trumpets; Red Bone and Les Jenkins on trombones, plus Tommy, of course, and the sax section became Mike Doty on lead alto; Johnny Mince, Freddie Stultz, third alto; and Bud Freeman on tenor. Dick Jones was on piano, Gene Traxler, bass, and Carmen Mastren, guitar. The drummer was the great Dave Tough. Edyth Wright, of course, was the female vocalist, and Jack Leonard was the "boy." He had been part of a vocal trio with Joe Bauer and Alex Stordahl, the arranger, when Tommy hired them away from Bert Block's band, but with Tommy he performed as a single.

The head band manager was Johnny Gluskin, brother of bandleader Lud Gluskin. Arthur Mitchaud was an assistant manager, and the road manager was Bobby Burns, one of Cork O'Keefe's associates. We had first met him in New England working for the Shribman brothers. The bandboy was a kid named Bobby. We called him "Gate," and he was a nice kid and a lot of fun. He even had an associate we called "Little Gate." Once "Gate" fell asleep in a recording studio during a date and his snoring ruined the master.

The band worked in the center of the room at the Commodore and did good business because it was becoming very popular. Sometimes we played for breakfast dances up in Harlem after we finished at the Commodore, and at least once we played the Savoy Ballroom. This was a real baptism of fire because you knew right away if you had it or not—the dancers had a way of letting you know.

The first record date I did with Tommy was with the small group called "The Clambake 7." We played "Twilight In Turkey," and "You're A Sweetheart," and we worked these out at a rehearsal at the Commodore. Shortly after this Howard Smith came in for Dick Jones on piano because Dick wanted to devote more time to his orchestrating.

Only a little while after I joined the band, Tommy took a week's vacation in Bermuda. We were broadcasting from the Commodore all during the time he was away, however, so they had to bring in somebody to play his parts. Will Bradley came in part of the time, but we also used a young guy named Earl Hagen, a trombonist from California who was in town for awhile after coming in with a stage group. And Earl Hagen was some trombone player! He did such a good job of playing Tommy's parts on the air that after hearing a broadcast Tommy couldn't wait to get back to find out who was playing them. Since then Earl has become a very successful TV writer, and I often see his name listed with the credits for a TV show. He continued with Tommy's band for awhile though, and it presented a funny situation. Earl was just a kid and Tommy the old pro kept trying to give him pointers on playing the trombone, but Earl wasn't having any. He'd look up at Tommy and say, "You know, I had a teacher in California named Spike Wallace. This is the way he taught me to play the trombone, this is the way he taught me to hold it—and this is the way I'm gonna do it!"

As you can imagine, this was pretty frustrating for Tommy.

TWENTY-FOUR

AFTER I was in the Tommy Dorsey band for awhile I became very friendly with Davie Tough and started to hang out with him a lot. He was a literate man and an interesting companion, probably the greatest drummer I have ever worked with, although I can't possible tell you why. I only know he was able to work some strange magic that could make you play over and beyond yourself—play things you were really incapable of playing or so it seemed. Up to that time I think the best things I'd ever done in my life, as far as solos were concerned, were with Tommy's band. I must give Davie credit for this because the feel of the band was so great. He wasn't drinking at all then, and it was a sad day for music when he started on the booze. He lived with his wife, a black girl named Casey, just above the Park around 117th and Lenox, and I used to spend a lot of after-hours there.

Actually, I found working with the Dorsey band to be a great experience. He was the greatest leader I ever worked for because his musical taste was broader than most, and he believed in diversification. So we did things like "Nola," adaptations of the classics, and arrangements of Willie "the Lion" Smith's pieces. The dinner sessions we played were completely different from the things we would do later in the evening. In other words, there was a much broader musical scope to everything we did although it was all in the Dorsey style.

Working in Tommy's brass section was almost like going back to school, because he was not only a great teacher but also a perfectionist. Which is not to belittle his ability as a jazzman; he was a legitimate trombone player who knew his instrument and still worked like a horse—and you had to work like a horse trying to keep up with him, because he wasn't asking you to do anything he wasn't doing right along with you. I don't recall my salary, but it was probably the usual $125 a week, with an additional 50 or 60 bucks for the Raleigh-Kool radio show we did each week. Besides this, Tommy did an awful lot of recording, far more than I'd ever done with any other band.

It was around this time that Glenn Miller, a very good friend of Tommy's—of all of us, for that matter—decided to form his own band. He

Dave Tough in Studio 8G NBC, 1937.

talked to me about it, and he talked to Johnny Mince. But in those days somebody was always thinking and talking about starting another band and most of them never got beyond the talking stage because of the money involved. So we listened with interest but not too seriously. Then one day Johnny and I received calls from Glenn asking us to meet him in Hurley's— the usual place of business. When we got there he said, "Let's go upstairs and talk. I've got a great proposition for you."

It turned out he had two seven-year contracts already drawn up by a lawyer, one for me and one for Johnny, offering us positions with his band on the basis that in addition to our usual salaries we would be partners with 20 percent interests. That was a total of 40 percent of his band he was willing to give away to get Johnny and me to play with his band, although I suppose we would have had other duties based on whatever we could offer. And we turned him down!

In light of the way things developed, although I don't exactly regret my decision I must admit I've had a lot of second thoughts about it. I imagine that a 20 percent interest in the Miller band during its second year of organization could easily have amounted to something like $80,000. On the other hand, I know very few musicians who have made decisions strictly on the basis of money, and I would have needed a crystal ball to see what was to happen that far ahead. You could never tell who would or who wouldn't make it, and for that matter I had already turned down Artie Shaw and Woody Herman, certainly similar situations, although without the percentage.

Mainly I was enjoying playing with Tommy's band and I didn't want to give up what I had to start all over again. I didn't want to go on the road with a new band, and I didn't want to go through the formation of one either. I figured that Glenn planned to take his new band into the Glen Island Casino for thirty-six bucks a week until it started taking off—if and when it ever did.

At any rate, we turned the proposition down and I've often wondered how it would have been if we had accepted. Two years later Johnny and I would have been wealthy, yet I doubt if I would have been able to stick it out for the full seven years, contract or no contract, because I don't think that Glenn and I were musically compatible. Frankly, while I liked and admired him, I wasn't too crazy about his arrangements. They were hard work to play.

Yet, knowing Glenn as I did, I know I overlooked a few important things in his makeup which I should have taken ito consideration, especially his great organizational ability. Without any doubt he was one of the greatest organizers of all time, and I had already seen evidence of this with the first Ray Noble band. Another indication was that almost the first thing he did was hire two of the best orchestrators in the business to write for his new band, Billy Finnegan and Jerry Gray. Finnegan was recommended to him by Tommy Dorsey. As I recall, somebody had told Tommy about Finnegan, and Dorsey suggested that Billy write an audition arrangement for the band. This turned out to be "Lonesome Road," which we recorded for Victor. Anyway, Tommy suggested Finnegan to Glenn as a staff arranger, and Miller recruited Jerry Gray on his own. Of course, I'm sure that Glenn had a lot to do with advising his arrangers as to what he wanted and in getting what he wanted.

Incidentally, it was Glenn who took me to Shillinger and we both studied with him. The Shillinger system is a mathematical music method that places at your disposal something like 1,540 scales in one octave. This was a pretty revolutionary idea then, and it still is. One of the Arabic scales included is Zerafkin, which literally translated means "String of Pearls," and it became the foundation for the hit tune of the same name in the Miller library.

While he was organizing Glenn spent a lot of time hanging around Tommy's band, and there was no question that Tommy was helping him to get started. I'm quite sure that he set Glenn up with the Schribman brothers, because both Charlie and Sy fared quite well with the Miller band, and Sy figured high in the band's management. It's possible he helped finance some of the considerable amount it took to launch a band—although to be completely honest, I really don't know where the money came from to get Glenn started. Maybe a good portion of it was his own. Glenn himself told me that Tommy called him in one day and said, "Look, you're starting your own band and I know it takes a lot of cabbage—cabbage which you don't have—so I'll help. I'll give you a hundred bucks a week for Helen to live on while you're out fronting the band."

Which was a nice, friendly gesture on Tommy's part, but I have often wondered what he thought a couple of years later when Glenn's band was number one in the country and whether he regretted having any part in

The Tommy Dorsey Orchestra in NBC Studio 8G for the Raleigh-Kool Radio Show, 1937.

getting it started. But that's how Tommy was—impulsively generous to his friends.

Tommy's other side, though, is illustrated by a story that became a classic within the band. Andy Ferretti and I were preceded on the Raleigh-Kool show by a trumpet player named Stevie Lipkin. Stevie and Tommy weren't getting along, so Tommy, in his own inimitable manner, was making things as rough as possible. One day during rehearsal he backed Stevie into a wall and proceeded to chew him out. "You're so damn' dumb," he yelled, "you don't even know what *D.S.* means!" Stevie glared back and retorted, "Oh, yes I do! It means *Dorsey Stinks!*"

Working the Raleigh-Kool show was one of the nicer aspects of playing with Tommy's band. I think it had started as a comic show but was revamped by the agency so that it featured the band with Edyth Wright and Jack Leonard. Herb Sanford, who years later would write the book *Tommy and Jimmy: The Dorsey Years*, directed the program, and one of the announcers, Paul Stewart, is now a movie actor. He's a nice-looking guy but they usually cast him in gangster parts. He married Peg LaCentra, who sang with Artie Shaw's band. She was also very active in the studios, and I remember making some records with her.

Joe Dixon was in Tommy's band before Johnny Mince. Tommy liked

153

Joe, so his reasons for leaving had nothing to do with friction between them. Tommy also was fond of Joe's mother and father who lived in the Boston area. In the years I was with Tommy, he didn't drink, but Joe's mother got him used to the Italian bitters called Fernet-Branca. I guess she told him it was good for his stomach after overeating—and Tommy was always overeating. He was one of the biggest eaters I've ever known, and he loved Italian food. From all reports it was eating that finally killed him.*

Tommy Dorsey in Victor's 24th Street Studio, Summer of 1937.

While we were at the Commodore Andy Ferretti and I became close friends, real drinking buddies, although I soon found out I could never keep up with him. He could drink a barrel and never show it, and he remained that way all his life. We used to hang out in Kelly's, the bar across the street, with another good friend, Deke Magaziner, an insurance broker. To this day, I still get my insurance from him. Another guy who used to hang around the band a lot was Jack Egan, a writer who went back to an early association with the Rockwell-O'Keefe office and the original Dorsey Brothers band. He

*On November 26, 1956, after eating and drinking heavily, Tommy fell into a deep sleep. While still asleep he regurgitated and choked to death on food particles lodged in his windpipe.

was later responsible for Alvino Rey's publicity, and he and Gene Krupa were lifelong friends.

We made a lot of friends during the Commodore stay. The headwaiter in the Palm Room was "Leon," who always welcomed friends of the band and made them feel at home. One of them, a trumpet-playing friend of our arranger (Paul Weston) was Hal Marley. To this day he still keeps in touch, and at one time was "Air Attache'" at our embassy in Poland. I used to send him dance orchestrations, unattainable where he was, which made him very welcome in the local music circles.

About a year before I joined the band, it had played a place in Georgia called Tiby Beach and then gone on a Texas tour. Max Kaminsky was with the band, and a lead trumpet player named Sammy Skolnik from Boston. Maxie made the first of the "Clambake 7" records. One was "Royal Garden Blues," and another title was "At the Codfish Ball." He probably made at least four sides before either Bunny Berigan or I were in the picture.

The Commodore period lasted until the first of April, 1937, and then we started a series of one-nighters in the southern territory around Virginia, West Virginia, and Maryland as usual. Red Bone was still playing trombone, although a short time later he gave it up to concentrate on arranging, and he and Les Jenkins rode with me on several of these jaunts, along with Howard Smith. I was still driving the Olds I'd bought in Chicago when I was with Goodman.

Coming back from one of these trips we had to pass through Lakehurst, N.J. It was the morning after the dirigible *Hindenburg* had crashed and burned (May 6, 1937), and as we went by some of the wreckage was still burning. It was a pretty gruesome sight even though little remained.

Vocalist Edyth Wright, 1937.

155

But the *Hindenburg* fire wasn't the only disaster of the previous night. We had one of our own. We had stopped for gas at a little place out in the country, and experience had taught us to visit the restrooms on all such remote stops. I recall talking to the station attendant, when Roberta broke in to ask where the restrooms were located. He pointed to the back and told her, "Well, we have outhouses. They're around to the right behind the station." It was still dark, but Roberta stumbled her way along the path to the outhouse according to the attendant's directions, and suddenly we heard her scream. She had fallen into an open pit—a gaping hole where the outhouse used to be. It seems that only the day before they had moved it, and had just left the hole unprotected and uncovered.

Needless to say, poor Roberta was in a terrible state. We had to fish her out of the open latrine, and she was covered with—well, you can imagine. She was wearing a red coat and it was plastered with you-know-what, and she smelled to high heaven. She had to change all her clothes, and the best we could do was give her some gasoline to wash with. Altogether it was pretty horrible. I'll never forget the idiot who ran the place; he was beside himself, but at the same time he didn't hesitate to tell us he'd had a bad heart condition the week before and was just about ready to go into another. In the course of conversation while my wife was trying to clean up, he said, "I meant to put boards over that hole and cover it up yesterday, but a dog came along and fell in there." Red Bone asked, "Well, what did you do with the dog?" "Oh," the big brain answered, "I just shooed him off the lot."

We played quite a few one-nighters. I recall a ferry ride across the Chesapeake and taking Tommy's picture while he relaxed on deck. Wherever we went we had to make sure we were back in New York on Wednesday in order to play the Raleigh-Kool program, a very important part of the band's activities. I have a picture of Glenn Miller doing one of the shows with us, and I also have a keen recollection of one where he had a very embarrassing moment. We were right in the middle of the broadcast at an extremely quiet spot when Glenn accidentally kicked over one of those metal-hat-and-mute stands. It had about three trumpet mutes on it and each rolled in a different direction, setting up a terrific clatter.

It was during this early period with Tommy that we did a re-creation of the Jean Goldkette recording sessions—that is, of the tunes they played. One in particular was "Clementine," and we played an arrangement that duplicated the original note-for-note. Herb Sanford mentions this in his book about the Dorseys.

TWENTY-FIVE

DURING THE SUMMER of 1937 we opened at the Hotel Pennsylvania Roof for an extended engagement. It ran through the summer, and it was a pretty good summer for me. For one thing I hit it off with Edyth Wright pretty well—I'd even go so far as to say I got along with her better than anybody else in the band. Edyth became almost like my brother—and I use the term "brother," because it pretty well describes our relationship. We were great drinking buddies and just good pals.

Around June of that year Roberta and I made frequent visits to Edyth's mother's house. Her family lived in Highland Park, N.J., and we became very friendly with her mother, Mrs. Bradshaw, and her two brothers and several sisters. We began to spend every weekend there. Her younger brother, Jack Bradshaw, had a buddy named Jack Honeywell, a well-known trumpet player around New Jersey. They were kids then, around fourteen. Since it was a very large family, there was also a great assortment of cousins, nephews, and nieces.

At the time Edyth was going with a real-estate dealer from Sea Girt, and on at least a couple of occasions we spent a few days there at the shore in houses he donated for our use. We'd buy a couple of jugs on the way down, maybe do a couple of one-nighters in the area, and then spend a few days at the beach. Edyth and I were great drinking buddies, and I don't know many men who could drink as much as she did without showing it, but we had a lot of fun. Sometimes the three of us would go to a local gin mill, one of those where the people throw peanut shells on the floor as part of the atmosphere. It was a very pleasant summer and the weekends were especially enjoyable.

I made a lot of friends from among Edyth's friends. I'll never forget a great big guy named Jack Halthusan. One day while they were out fishing, he decided he'd had enough so he jumped off the boat with a twenty- or thirty-pound tuna tucked under one arm and swam the mile or so to shore. Another I still see now and then is Joe Garrigan, always a close friend of the band. I became acquainted with these people during our frequent visits to Point Pleasant, where Edyth's family rented a beach house for two or three seasons. It was also the first time I heard about the big local attraction,

Tommy Dorsey

Jenkinson's Pavilion. It was probably the same year we were at the Penn Roof that they put a radio wire into Jenkinson's, WOR, I believe it was, and it became very instrumental in building up the bands that played there. This was the valid formula of the time. All the bandleaders figured, and they were right, that if they could get a location spot with a lot of sustaining time on the air people would soon learn who they were.

The formula certainly worked well for the band at Jenkinson's, which happened to be Sammy Kaye's. I doubt if many people had ever heard of him before this—although supposedly he had been very successful around the Cleveland area where the band originated—but the summer at the Pavilion with that sustaining radio wire launched Sammy well on his way, nationally. With the strong commercial aspect of the band, he made it big.

My meeting with Sammy was unusual, to say the least. One night we stumbled into the Pavilion to hear the band, which I admit was not my style, to put it politely. It was a commercial sweet band. Sammy talked Edyth into a date for an off-night. Then Edyth proceeded to forget all about it. I was holding down the fort all by myself at the house when Sammy and his trumpet player showed up. I haven't any idea why he thought he needed a second to go along on a date with Edyth, but it didn't make any difference because she wasn't home. I ended up entertaining these two guys because Edyth stood Sammy up. The trumpet player was a nice guy, but I can't say that I was impressed by Sammy Kaye as an individual or as a bandleader. For one thing, he didn't play anything and, obviously, if I were going to be impressed by somebody in the music business he had to play something. Even though I didn't give him much credit for anything, I'm sure he became a very rich man. Years later I heard him on a radio broadcast, and the guy was very good at reading poetry.

Getting back to the Pennsylvania Roof, in Herb Sanford's book he mentions the band table where Edyth used to hold court. She used to make wonderful green salads with great dressings. And the place was always packed with song-pluggers. Tommy was the fair-haired boy with a lot of the music publishers, and they were always trying to get Tommy to play their latest tunes because we had so much air time. In addition to the sustaining wire at the hotel our sponsored program was very unusual in that it ran all year. Most sponsored programs started around September and were terminiated in 26 weeks.

Howard Phillips and Robert Doty Jr., 1936

This constant air time was very important to the band. The sponsored show was on a Wednesday or Thursday night, and when we took off to do the broadcast we had a stand-by band take over on the Roof. It was led by a trumpet player named Lew Sherwood, who built a nice reputation as a vocalist and sideman with Eddy Duchin's band. He was being groomed by

MCA to lead one of their road bands. The clarinet player was a fellow I'm still friendly with, Artie Baker, but I don't recall ever hearing the band because we weren't around when it played.

Some strange things happened at the Penn Roof. On at least two or three occasions Tommy was out in front of the band playing his trombone when he lost the slide, and the thing would travel the entire distance of the dance floor, propelled by the terrific momentum he had going. The King Instrument Company was kept busy replacing Tommy's trombone or having him test new ones. He played either a King 2B or a King 3B, I'm not sure which, and he had a gold horn that he used as long as I was with him. Nevertheless, King kept sending him instruments. One night he brought one along to try out, blew about twelve notes on the thing, then put it on the floor and stepped on it. This was all part of his personality—he was saving anybody else from the ordeal of playing that particular trombone.

The band underwent a few personnel changes before we started at the Pennsylvania Roof. For some reason Tommy and Mike Doty didn't hit it off. Mike was an excellent sax player, but he and Tommy had a personality conflict, so Skeets Herfurt came in to take his place. This worked out to Tommy's satisfaction, but Red Bone's replacement in the trombone section was Walter Mercurio, who turned out to be something of a cut-up and an irritation to Tommy. Les Jenkins could do no wrong in Tommy's estimation, but Mercurio was another ball game.

It was the usual thing for us to make a fast trip between sets—down the elevator, through the lobby, and across the street to Kelly's. Somehow we always gravitated to places named Kelly's. There was one across from the Commodore and another across from the Pennsylvania. The trick was to get off the bandstand as quickly as possible and make it to Kelly's in time for two or three quick belts before going back for the next set. Like the rest of us Walt Mercurio was quite a drinker, but he had the added facility that after a few snorts nothing bothered him. He played a good trombone too, but Tommy, always the perfectionist, kept trying to improve the trombone section and insisted on giving pointers to Mercurio. Tommy would make a suggestion, and Walt would look up at him innocently and then flick his thumb and index finger in a gesture of nonchalant unconcern. Tommy would burn with frustration because talking to Mercurio was like talking to the wall, but he put up with the aggravation and never fired him.

Some big-name sports figures made a habit of hanging around Tommy's band. A lot of them came to visit Edyth, who was a pretty darn good public relations promoter and made friends easily. In particular I remember the tennis players Don Budge and Gene Mako were around a lot, and so was Tommy Heinrich of the New York Yankees. It's my opinion, based on observation, that a lot of baseball players are frustrated musicians—at any rate, they seem to like jazz.

Another big fan who became good friends with Edyth and spent a lot of time around the band was F.D.R. Jr., the president's son. Several months after we left the Penn Roof we played a date at the University of Virginia. He was there, and afterwards some of us were invited to his house. He was married to a very nice gal named Ethel Dupont, of the Delaware Duponts. She was a pretty fair cook, and she cooked up a storm for us of crepe suzettes until the wee hours of the morning. We were traveling the area by train at the time, and F.D.R. Jr. went out of his way to drive us to the station. He even shoved a fifth in my hand. All of which was great and much appreciated— except he put me on the wrong train. Fortunately, I found out in time to get off and take the right one.

While the band was at the Pennsylvania, Tommy started to rake in considerable amounts of money. I think it's an interesting sidelight into his personality that he never hesitated to spend it—in sizeable amounts. He was a great eater, but he never liked to eat alone and was always surrounded by an entourage whenever he decided it was time for a real meal. He loved Italian food, and very often he would invite almost anybody he could trap, and it wasn't difficult to be trapped, and take along half-a-dozen to a dozen people to his favorite restaurant, the Grotto Azura, at Mulberry and Broome Streets. He'd call ahead while we were still at work and give them forewarning that he was bringing a party. If necessary, they'd stay open after hours because when Tommy threw a banquet it was really a banquet, everything from lobster Italian-style to all of the delicacies. The sky was the limit. Tommy always footed the bill; there was never any question about it.

Tommy was capable of making a lot of money, and so was the band. I'm sure that, at that point, we were grossing a million dollars a year. "Marie," of course, was a fabulous hit, and the band was so popular we were in and out of the New York Paramount so often it was almost like a second home. Tommy, making all this cabbage, decided it was about time he bought an estate and became a country gentleman.

I don't know how he figured he'd have the time to enjoy it, but he bought a place anyway, near Bernardsville, N.J. It was a great, rambling colonial house on the top of a hill, with a lot of land around it. I haven't any idea how many acres were involved, but there had to be a lot of them because there was a pair of gates, electrically controlled from the house, that were about a quarter of a mile away. That should give you some idea of the size of the place. It was a three-story mansion, and Tommy converted the top floor into a playroom, with the most elaborate set of electric trains I've ever seen.

Tommy was still married to his first wife, Toots, and they had two children—a daughter, Patsy, and a son, Tom Jr. Tommy called the boy Skipper. We still see Tom Jr. once in awhile. He's married, has three children of his own, and lives in Colorado. He's very much like his father in looks and in some of his mannerisms, especially when you're sitting around with him in the relaxed atmosphere of his home. This is odd, because he really wasn't exposed to his father that much. Tommy was always on the road or away from home somewhere. Tom Jr. wasn't more than ten years old when his father bought the estate, and it was quite a number of years before we saw him again in Colorado. Johnny Mince was with me, and his comment after our visit was, "How on earth could such an evil kid grow up into such a nice man?"

Almost immediately after Tommy bought the estate he decided to build a swimming pool, and for some time this was the main topic of conversation on and off the bandstand as we got reports on the various accoutrements he was adding to the installation. He built a beautiful pool on the lawn, complete with "His" and "Her" bathhouses, and all the necessary heating elements and pre-cleaning processes before you got into the pool.

There wasn't any question about it, it was a gorgeous estate, and Tommy had the whole corps there on free weekends. In fact, it was damn near a command performance to appear at Bernardsville every Sunday. Tommy never made any bones about wanting company. He more or less took it for granted that the band would be there, and it certainly wasn't any hardship to be invited to Bernardsville every weekend. Besides, we were a pretty close-knit group and everybody got along. As far as the entertainment was concerned, there was no limit—plenty to eat, plenty to drink, and everything that goes along with it.

Dick Jones

In addition to the band there were always other guests, always a batch of song-pluggers, for instance. On one occasion at least, Hal Kemp was there with his manager Alex Holden. We got pretty well acquainted with those guys. Which reminds me of something which amazed me when I first heard it and still strikes me as something rather remarkable. This was an acetate record that Alex Holden played for me in New York which the Kemp band had recorded that day. As was easily recognized then, the characteristic sound of the Kemp band was the clipped, triple-tonguing brass section, and somebody had the bright idea of utilizing this in a musical arrangement that was actually a message in Morse code to Admiral Byrd in Little America. The record was sent to him, I understand. This was only a short time before Hal Kemp, a very nice guy, met his tragic death.

Anyway, Tommy's command performances lasted most of the summer.

TWENTY-SIX

I CAN'T SAY just when we left the Pennsylvania Roof, but it was probably around Labor Day, the usual thing in those days, and I don't remember another steady job until the following summer. The central focus was still on the weekly broadcast, but I believe extended road trips took up most of the fall of 1938.

I picked up an infection on my hands that I tried to cure with zinc oxide, only to discover I was allergic to this medicine. All I succeeded in doing was burning my hands so badly that all of the skin peeled off. I had to wear white gloves at all times because my hands looked so terrible. Without realizing it, I had happened on the most commercial thing I could have dreamed up. I still meet people, more than forty years later, who remember my playing with white gloves.

At the time, however, I didn't particularly enjoy the problem and it led to another incident that was costly, even though it now seems funny. We played a job in Easton, Pennsylvania, one night and were scheduled to travel by bus to Pittsburgh for another date on the following night. After the Easton job, I was in my room medicating my hands, and the bus left without me. The band was 200 miles away before my absence was discovered. Since I didn't have anything else to do I went to bed, and I had logged eight hours of sleep by the time Tommy called from Pittsburgh.

He said, "Look, you have to make the job tonight, so go out to the airport and wait for the airplane I'm sending for you." Following his instructions and disregarding the rain that was coming down in buckets, Roberta and I went out to the airport and waited. Finally, during a brief let-up in the storm, a Beechcraft came out of the clouds and landed. The pilot taxied up to the apron and motioned us aboard. We climbed in, and he immediately took off into the storm again, headed for Pittsburgh. He told us he had flown over from Floyd Bennett Field and the storm was everywhere.

We made it to Pittsburgh all right. The only trouble was that when we got there everything was completely closed in and we couldn't land. The pilot decided to try Ohio, but conditions there weren't any better. "I'll turn around and head back to Pennsylvania," the pilot told us finally, "and see if we can set down any place."

Luckily, on the way back conditions around Harrisburg improved enough for us to land, so we got off the plane and caught a train for Pittsburgh, arriving around 12:30 a.m.—or just about a half-hour before Tommy's job finished. He told me later that the plane and pilot had cost him $400, and I still never made the job.

When we were playing one-nighters we often preferred to drive on to the next town right after a performance. This allowed us to sleep late in the morning instead of getting up early to drive a long, grueling hop and then work the same night. It was during such a drive, around 6:30 or 7:00 a.m. in North Carolina, when we were moving along at a pretty good speed, that I passed a hitchhiker. As we went by I couldn't help but wonder why a guy was out so early in the morning trying to hitch rides. My wife and the other people were all sound asleep in the car, so nobody else saw the man. After we had gone another mile or two, the thought suddenly struck me that he had looked very familiar— in fact, he looked like my father. I dismissed the idea as far-fetched and entirely unlikely, but when I saw him a couple of months later he told me he had been visiting relatives in South Carolina at just about that time. I never did tell him I probably passed him by on the road.

After awhile it became pretty obvious that we were destined to be on the road for a long time, so we gave up our apartment at the Whitby and put our furniture into storage.

We played in a great many theaters. One, in particular, the Earle in Philadelphia, we worked several times, and we began to do our commercial broadcasts from the various theater locations. We played the Paramount more times than I can recall, and in the process we all became very well acquainted

Bud Freeman

165

with Bob Weitman, the manager.

The Paramount was the scene of one incident that almost wrecked the show, although what took place was fairly common in band theater appearances. A lot of kids used to play hookey from school and go to the early shows during the day, and they liked to throw things. I always sat next to the drums, either on the right or the left, depending on the stage set-up, and this time I was watching Tommy play a profile solo under the microphone in front when suddenly from the balcony an egg came flying through the air. I don't think it missed Tommy's nose by more than two inches, but luckily it did. It came on back through the band and hit one of the cymbals near me, broke, and splashed all over the bandstand. Without my realizing it, most of it wound up on my plunger mute; I found this out when I went to use the mute and came up with a handful of raw egg.

Things were thrown at the bands in the Paramount pretty frequently, and some of them were dangerous. Benny's band was once bombarded with staples, which can be pretty nasty.

In addition to playing theaters in Philadelphia and Washington, we often played the Stanley in Pittsburgh. This had an excellent orchestra in the pit, and we got well acquainted with the musicians in it, especially two fine brassmen. Johnny Marino played first trumpet in the theater orchestra, and second and third French horns in the Pittsburgh Symphony. The other, Matty Shiner, was one of Tommy Dorsey's favorite trombonists, which automatically meant he was a tremendous player.

We went on to play other theaters, the Metropolitan in Boston, and a little later those in cities like Cleveland and Chicago. Somewhere along the line we went south for a date. This sticks in my mind because we were ready to leave New York and Davy Tough hadn't showed up. Somebody went to check and discovered that Davy, after many years on the wagon, had decided to get stoned. Davy was one of those guys (as I became later) who couldn't work when drunk, so we had to pick up a substitute drummer in a hurry.

I don't remember the exact location of this job but it was somewhere around Baltimore, and it was the first time I met the legendary trumpet player Leo McConville. Leo had been very well known and successful in New York until he developed a phobia about heights. His fear grew steadily worse until he couldn't bear to make the trip across the Queensboro Bridge, not to mention looking out the windows of tall buildings, so he decided to give up the music business to buy a chicken farm on the outskirts of Baltimore. When I met him that's what he was doing—raising chickens. But he sat in with the band and he was a tremendous trumpet player.

Tommy was always looking for ways to further the band's reputation, to improve its quality, and to promote the business end. He enlisted the services of public relations man Jack Egan, who began publishing a Dorsey-financed newspaper of several pages called "*Bandstand*." I guess it was a give-away, handed out on locations and possibly also mailed. I'm not sure how it was distributed. Nevertheless, it came out periodically and each guy in the band,

and others associated with it, would write a column for each issue. The idea was to write for people interested in your particular instrument, along with incidents and anecdotes about the band. There was also a question-and-answer feature. A fan would write in from Albany, for instance, asking Andy Ferretti a question about the trumpet, and Andy would answer in the paper. It was well handled and done in a professional way.

Another thing that Tommy (in collaboration with some of the writers for the Raleigh-Kool show, I imagine) came up with was an amateur contest for swing musicians. This grew into quite a big thing and had some amazing results. In the New York area, the advertising agency handling the Raleigh-Kool account BBDO (Barton, Barton, Dursten, and Osborne) even set up an audition room in their office on Madison Avenue where they tried out potential contestants. The contestants were limited to jazz musicians, or at least to those who could point their solos toward swing.

I believe the first contest was held in Studio 8H at NBC. The format included asking the contestants a few questions—who they were, where they came from, what their training had been—and then, in turn, each would play a solo. Four amateurs competed on each program, and on the first show there was an excellent trumpet player, Murray Rothstein, who is still active. One year he ran for the presidency of Local 802. His solo, as I recall, was Bunny's chorus on "Marie," which called for quite a bit of flexibility on the horn.

When we were touring the theaters during this period we usually started on a Monday and did four or five shows a day. We'd have one amateur come out on each show and audition for the amateur program. By Thursday, when the show actually went on the air, we had plenty of opportunity to choose the most talented. I must say, in all fairness, that musical ability really determined the outcome. As anyone knows who has ever seen many amateur contests, an accordian player can whiz through "Flight of the Bumble Bee," or a banjo player hammer out "The World Is Waiting for the Sunrise," and walk away with the contest under any and all circumstances. In this case we were looking for genuine musicianship in these young performers. In the first place, the musicians in the band conducted the auditions and we had charge of them. Although the applause from the audience had some effect on the final decision, it was mainly our judgment of the contestant's musicianship that counted— and a number of the contestants we picked went on to professional careers.

At the Earle Theater in Philadelphia one young man who won, about sixteen years old at the time, was Buddy DeFranco, an indication of the caliber of musicianship we were seeking. In Pittsburgh, we had two excellent contestants who have since done very well. One was a trumpet player named Carl Poole from a small town north of Pittsburgh. He was so good that I invited him to visit me between shows and we would play duets together. I followed his career afterwards, too. He later went to a music school in northern Missouri, and after that he came to New York where I introduced him to Will Bradley. He worked with Will's band for awhile and then wound up as a marvelous lead trumpet player working for NBC, appearing on the "Show of Shows" for many years. The other Pittsburgher was a clarinetist by the name of

Pee Wee cleverly characterized by English artist Peter Manders in 1980.

Ernie Morrow. He followed music as a profession and has done very well at it, becoming an excellent oboe player working in Broadway theaters. He is still active.

But the amateur who went on to make the biggest name for himself was auditioned in a Chicago theater and came from Chicago Heights, Johnny Mince's hometown. He was a young guitarist named George Barnes. He auditioned for us early in the week, and he was so outstanding, even at the age of sixteen, that we made him a regular on every show.

Early in the tour we played the Fox Theater in Detroit, and while we were in the Motor City I shopped around and traded in the Oldsmobile for a LaSalle sedan, a car I liked very much. It had a gear ratio that made it quite a fast car, it was heavier than the Olds, and it was very comfortable.

While we were in Chicago we all spent a lot of time listening to the Bob Crosby Orchestra, which was playing at the Black Hawk Cafe. It was a truly great band with a tremendous trumpet section—Charlie Spivak, Billy Butterfield, and Yank Lawson—not to belittle the other great stars in the band like Fazola on clarinet, Zurke on piano, and Miller on tenor sax.

Tommy's band was scheduled to open at the Palomar in Los Angeles that June, but since we were still broadcasting weekly on the Raleigh-Kool program the long jump presented a problem. It was decided that to attempt the long drive to Los Angeles without a break was too risky, so a show was scheduled to be broadcast from Denver, to give us driving time before and after as we made our way to California. En route to Denver we stopped at my hometown, Falls City, and visited with my grandparents, my mother, father, and brother. Although there was no way I could know it then, the next time I would see my father, the circumstances would be very different.

Roberta and I continued on to Denver to do the show. Tommy's brass section was in for an experience there. We ran head on into difficulty with Denver's high altitude and rarified atmosphere as soon as we started to blow. We were used to playing in long phrases, but now we found we were simply running out of steam. Even Tommy had trouble because he was accustomed to playing a lot of measures before taking a breath. All of us had to make some quick breathing adjustments.

The day after the show we took off for California, making a stop in Colorado Springs to visit briefly with my old friends Matt and Frank Betton, who had the house band at the Broadmoor Hotel. They were originally from the Kansas City area and I had worked with the band a few times. We also visited the world-famous "Garden of the Gods," and took pictures. We still had 2,000 miles to go, so again I took the scenic route—Pueblo, through the Raton Pass, Gallup, Flagstaff, Wickenburg—and across the Mojave Desert in the middle of the night to beat the heat. When we got to Los Angeles, we were lucky enough to get an apartment again in the Rayfield Apartments, directly behind the Palomar, so we looked forward to a pleasant engagement.

The amateur segment of the Raleigh-Kool program was phasing out, and the producers came up with a novel idea to bring it to a big finish. They brought in a group of Hollywood stars to perform as amateurs, and the results proved to be a big success. We had Bing Crosby playing drums, Jack Benny on violin, of course, Ken Murray on clarinet, Shirley Ross on piano, and Dick Powell blowing trumpet. They sounded pretty darn good, but the dialogue introducing them as amateurs was very funny.

The Palomar engagement went well too. One of the continual sources of amusement to the guys in the band was watching the girls who would line up just to observe Lee Costaldo (now bandleader Lee Castle), who had the end seat in the trumpet section. He was a very handsome guy and even attracted the attention of some movie stars.

Just as on my previous visit to California with the Goodman band, our stay this time proved very interesting and pleasurable. Johnny Mince had brought along members of his family for the summer, his mother and sisters, and they added a lot to the fun. Then Roberta and I took up fishing. We would take a small boat out to the bait barge anchored off Redondo Beach, where the fishing was good, and they would supply us with tackle and bait. In short order, we would have all the mackerel and barracuda we could carry home.

I also enjoyed a "busman's holiday" on one night off, running down to Balboa Beach to hear the house band there. This band had a great reputation in California. It had been together a long time and many people were of the opinion it was the best band in the state. It was, of course, the Stan Kenton outfit. I got acquainted with the guys and had a great evening. It was a good band.

While we were in California, Morton Downey introduced Tommy to a wildcat oilman. Tommy wanted to invest in the man's oil drilling project, but didn't have enough cash on hand so he offered a proposition to anyone in the band who would help him invest in the venture. "Whatever amount you want to invest you will collect in proportion to the amount you invest, if the well comes in. If it proves to be a dry hole and nothing happens I'll give you back your investment."

Some of us invested, but we took with a grain of salt Tommy's promise to give back the money if the well was a bust. We looked at it as a gambling proposition, and as such we didn't expect any refunds. Well, as time went on we got daily reports of the well's progress—most of which none of us understood. We were told that at 2,000 feet they struck oil sand, and after another 1,000 feet they reached something else, all this with pictures of the drilling rig, and the like. Finally they were down almost to China and decided the well was a turkey. Everyone shrugged off the loss and forgot about it, but about six months later Bobby Burns, the band manager, came around with checks for the full amount each guy had invested.

Tommy could really be thoughtful. One evening in the middle of our session at the Palomar, Bobby Burns came up to the stand and told me Tommy wanted to see me in the Palomar office. I went to the office and when I walked in Tommy handed me an envelope and said, "Pee Wee, we've just received word that your father has been seriously injured. Here's two airline tickets, one for you and one for Roberta, and you're booked on a flight leaving from Glendale in about an hour-and-a-half. I'll see you when you get back."

Not many people would be that considerate—to say nothing of the generosity and efficiency. Roberta and I rode a TWA DC3 to Kansas City, and in 1938 that was still a pretty long flight. We went immediately to the hospital to see my father.

The story of what had happened to him is not one I am apt to forget. He had been drinking with a close friend and they got into an argument in front of the hotel where my father was staying. The argument developed into a fistfight. The other man hit him and he fell backward, hitting his head on the curb of the sidewalk. They picked him up and carried him to his room, thinking he was only drunk and would sleep it off. It wasn't until a day or two later that someone looked in on him and discovered he was hurt. He was taken to the hospital, where it was determined that he had a fractured skull, complicated by the fact that the drinking had caused his brain to swell. Then he contracted pneumonia. He lived for just one hour after we got to the hospital—almost as though he had been waiting to see us.

Naturally, we felt bitter about the situation because he was only 48 years old, and except for his drinking problem he had been in good health. The police asked if I wanted to prefer charges, but I didn't think the fight with his friend could be classified as foul play, so I told them to forget it. Later on I had reason to be glad of this decision because I heard that his friend felt so terrible about the accident that he died a short time later. As for my father, his tragic ending may have been for the best. I can't help but think his life would always have been unhappy as a result of his problem with alcohol.

We had his body sent to Falls City for the funeral, and he was buried in the family plot. At the funeral our old friend and associate Elmer Herling sang beautifully, which would have made my father happy. Unfortunately my brother James, only twelve years old, was in the hospital having his appendix removed and couldn't attend the funeral.

TWENTY-SEVEN

ON OUR RETURN to California I once again fell under the spell of the place and suggested to Tommy I wanted to remain behind when the band left the Palomar. It wasn't just a whim. I really thought I'd like to spend some time there. But Tommy had other ideas. He told me that Andy Ferretti and Lee Castle were both staying in Californa and he had hired Yank Lawson and Charlie Spivak to take their places, so he wanted me to travel east with the band to Detroit and break Yank and Charlie in on the book before I left. Tommy was always pretty hard to say no to, so I agreed.

We got one unexpected break before going back East. Tommy, who was living at the Beverly Hills Hotel, was quarantined with the measles for three weeks and although he had our sympathy, his misfortune made it possible for us to enjoy a nice California vacation. I rented a cottage near Mt. Wilson and had a wonderful time resting, feeding the deer, and looking at Jupiter through the marvelous 60" telescope.

With me in the car on the drive back to Detroit were my wife, Dick Clark's wife, Rhea, and Estelle Wright, Edyth's sister. I joined the band at the Eastwood Gardens and for a week played the book with Charlie and Yank. Then, having lived up to my promise to Tommy, I left the band and went back to New York, once more changing my mind about settling in California. As for Tommy's band, to be quite honest about it, I left because I was tired of it. I wanted a change.

That September I rented a furnished apartment at the Whitby, wanting to be a bit more certain of my future before leasing a permanent set-up, and went back to free-lancing. I was happy and doing pretty well, but Tommy and Edyth Wright—especially Edyth, my old drinking buddy, who was very friendly with Roberta—kept making offers for me to rejoin the band. Tommy had Edyth work on Roberta, and Roberta worked on me. I believe Tommy's idea was that the contrast in styles between Yank Lawson and me would give him more tonal color in the trumpet section. I had no intention of rejoining the band and kept telling him so, but he kept insisting and finally invited me down to the Pennsylvania to talk it over. He was hard to say no to, so I agreed to meet him, figuring there was one sure way to make him change his mind—I'd ask for

Cape Charles Ferry, 1937.

Red Bone and Gene Traxler

A wind-blown Pee Wee.

Gene Traxler, Carmen Mastren, Les Jenkins

Edyth Wright

Alex Stordahl

Les Jenkins

Howard Smith

Dave Tough

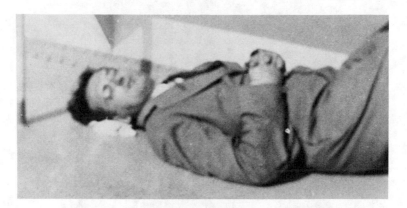

T. D. napping.

Pee Wee in repose.

more money per week than he would be able or willing to pay. I never got the opportunity. Before I could say anything, he offered me more money than I was going to ask for.

I rejoined Tommy in February and in March we were back on the road, once more starting off by playing the New York Paramount. In the meantime we had made more records and I recall some interesting sides. One of these was "Marcheta," on which Yank plays half a chorus and I play the release. It was a nice format, and I wish we'd done more of it. Another great recording, in my opinion, was "Lonesome Road," which was such a long arrangement it had to be done in two parts, in those days before tape.

On this tour the band traveled by Greyhound bus, so I hired a driver to drive my car and transport Roberta, Muriel Ferretti, and Dorothy Herfurt, so our wives could be with us on the week-long theater engagements. We played the more popular theaters—the Earle in Washington, D.C., the Earle in Philadelphia, the Stanley in Pittsburgh—and then we took a swing south and played a broadcast for the Raleigh-Kool show from a tobacco warehouse. I believe this was in Asheville, N.C. After that we made another swing that was so tough we had to travel by train. For two weeks we had our own private Pullman car which would be switched to the various rail lines taking us to the different cities where we were playing. Deane Kincaide was a railroad buff, and he really enjoyed this trip. We traveled in the same car for the entire two weeks and by the time it was over the car smelled like an active gymnasium.

The trumpet section was made up of heavy drinkers, but Andy Ferretti and Yank Lawson could hold their booze better than I could. The drinking was beginning to affect my physical well-being. On the train trip I kept a wooden candy bucket filled with beer and ice under my berth, and in Nashville I had to be thrown into the shower to sober me up so I could make the show. A very unhappy situation was beginning to develop.

There was one outstanding highlight of this tour—a week at the Lyric Theater in Indianapolis, where Hoagy Carmichael was our guest on the radio show. This was natural since he was a native of Indiana. But the big surprise was Hoagy's mother, who accompanied him and really broke things up by playing terrific ragtime piano.

Around May I started giving Tommy my notice. Finally, perhaps due to my drinking, I made it stick. I think I played my last date with the band at a pavilion in the Allentown, Pa., area, in June 1939.

I don't recall the preliminaries, but I had been hired to join the Raymond Scott Quintet before I left Tommy. I was scheduled to start in September when the Quintet returned to New York after fulfilling an extended contract in Hollywood. Then we were all slated to join the staff at CBS. Scott would become a staff conductor, and we would work away from our base job at CBS as a unit. This gave me at least two months for vacation or to do anything I pleased. I planned to take a short vacation and then do something I had always wanted to do—extend my daily practice sessions to improve my playing. Or so I hoped.

I rented a small house on the Intercoastal Waterway in Fort Lauderdale, within two blocks of the ocean. With my base established I was ready for my vacation. We started things off in a big way by flying over to Havana on one of those old Pan American flying boats they used on the South American run in those days, and we had a great time living it up in the land of Batista. I smoked great cigars, drank rum at 5¢ a shot, Fundador brandy at 15¢, and we took in the jai alai games, the cockfights, Moro Castle, drank the delicious espresso coffee, and altogether enjoyed ourselves. I remember being pleasantly surprised at the comfortable temperature in Cuba for the summer season, but I also noticed that most of the rooms had high ceilings, which undoubtedly helped.

At one point I struck up an acquaintance with an ex-burlesque queen named Trixie, who operated a small off-the-street saloon. She is the only person I have ever met who succeeded in training cockroaches. Trixie would whistle and out from behind the bottles would come a pair of cockroaches as big as field mice to run up and down in front of the bottles. Then Trixie would whistle again and the bugs would vanish behind the bottles as quickly as they had appeared. I never learned her secret, but I witnessed the exhibition several times.

During our tour of Morro Castle we had a guide who showed us the torture chambers. He told us he had been tortured himself during one of the Cuban political upheavals. His hands were deformed and mutilated, the result of every finger being broken.

Back in Fort Lauderdale I settled down to a daily session of from four to six hours of practice, fully confident that concentrated effort would improve my playing—only to become quite discouraged after awhile when I discovered that practice alone, without actual performance, didn't do the trick. Instead I became the frog on the wall and started developing mental hazards that had never entered my thoughts before. But I must say that Florida at that time was an ideal vacation place. Renting the house off-season was only $40 a month, good oranges for juice were only a penny apiece, and my wife and I had two months of ease, eating, and sleeping well for less than $500. We experienced one hurricane warning, but the biggest storm was brewing in Europe with Hitler's invasion of Poland.

We returned to New York in September. I joined CBS as a staff musician, and started to learn the library of the Raymond Scott Quintet, none of which was on paper. I had no idea what a chore this was going to be until rehearsals started. For that matter, I was due to be confronted by a number of situations that would be new to me.

I rented an apartment at 63-50 Wetherole Street in Rego Park, Queens. It was quite a nice place, and we had enough furniture in storage to furnish it well, but settling in led to an unfortunate incident. Roberta decided to clean the rugs with a solution that contained camphor crystals. When she was finished, she unthinkingly threw the waste into the incinerator. The resulting fire and explosion hospitalized her with very serious burns. While she was recuperating in the hospital, the New York area was hit by a hurricane and heavy rains which caused considerable damage throughout the metropolitan district.

TWENTY-EIGHT

AS A CBS STAFF MEMBER I played in one of the two dance bands they maintained. They also had a small concert or symphony orchestra. The union contract required a fixed number as staff musicians, but they were not permitted to do commercial programs; as a consequence all staff shows were sustaining airshots. The band I played in was known as the "Morning Band," and only a short time before Bunny Berigan, Babe Russin, and Jerry Colonna had been regular members. Most of the programs we did in the morning were aired over what was called the "Dixie Network." One was called "Al Bernard's Minstrels," and featured the singer who had recorded with the Original Dixieland Jazz Band back in 1917 or '18. Essentially the band was made up of the members of the Raymond Scott Quintet—Pete Pumiglio, clarinet; Dave Harris, tenor; Lou Shoobe, bass; and Johnny Williams, drums. These men were augmented by Artie Manners on sax; Mike Miola, lead trumpet; Vincent Maffe, guitar; and Roland Dupont on trombone. Either Raymond Scott or one of the regular staff members would play piano.

There was another complete dance band on staff, with an equal number of musicians, and there were still other musicians working in various groups. At times they would combine us for special shows. Some of the others included Nat Natoli, Harry Johnson and Willie Kelly, trumpets; Reggie Merrill, sax; Harry Ross, tenor; Milton Schlesinger, percussion; Johnny Blowers, drums; the symphony players, Harry Friestadt and Frank Venezzio, trumpets; Mitch Miller, oboe, and many excellent string players. One of the first shows I did at CBS was with a large symphonic group under the direction of Mark Warnow, accompanying the "Mercury Theater" players. The dramatic portion of the program was directed by William N. Robison, and the Mercury Theater group was made up of the finest actors and actresses in radio. Some of them had taken part in the famous Orson Welles dramatization of H. G. Wells's "The War of the Worlds," which was done so well and seemed so real that it fooled a lot of people into believing we were being attacked by Martians. I also remember Joseph Cotton and Agnes Morehead taking part in some of the Mercury presentations.

One show, entitled "He Doubled In Pipes," was built around a marvelous theme composed by Raymond Scott called "Dead End Blues." I don't recall who wrote the orchestration, but it was the first time I had ever played a solo with a symphonic background. The story was about a mysterious trumpet player who appeared out of nowhere and astounded everybody with his great playing in the Paris bistros. Finally somebody followed him out of the club one night, and somewhere on the banks of the Seine he disappeared into thin air right in front of their eyes. All they could find were traces of cloven hooves in the mud, implying that the trumpet player was the reincarnation of the god Pan.

I have heard that recordings of these Mercury Theater shows still exist, and I have asked people to look for this particular one but to no avail. It was aired on CBS in September 1939 and, incidentally, was performed without an audience in the old Leiderkrantz Hall on 58th Street between Park and Lexington. At one time (before they made the mistake of remodeling it) this was considered the finest recording studio in the country.

Besides Mark Warnow, other CBS conductors included Lynn Murray, Ray Bloch, and Leith Stevens. Stevens conducted the "Saturday Night Swing Session," a broadcast which featured jazz stars like Bunny Berigan and Ella Fitzgerald. The staff pianists were very good too, and I worked with a number of them—Vera and Irving Brodsky, Walter Gross, who later conducted shows himself, and Sammy Liner.

I started rehearsals with the Raymond Scott Quintet which had a repertoire of about twenty-five numbers—all to be committed to memory. I have always had a good musical memory, but I must admit that this was a pretty tall order. In addition, most of the routines were played with a Harmon mute which I have always managed to hate. The combination was pretty hard to take, but I did my best.

If you've ever heard the Quintet you know it played some very unusual music, most of it composed by Raymond Scott. It was highly descriptive of situations and experiences, or fantasies, and really did project musical pictures. The proof of this is that the bulk of it was sold to a film company as background for animated cartoons. Typical titles included: "Powerhouse," sounds made to represent a power plant or generators; "The Toy Trumpet," a rhythmic impression of a Christmas toy; "Bumpy Weather over Newark," a rough airplane ride; "Dinner Music for a Pack of Hungry Cannibals," a tone poem filled for some reason with duck quacks; and "The Happy Farmer," a rural travesty.

Obviously, Raymond Scott was loaded with imagination. His original recordings by the Quintet won a year's contract with a Hollywood movie studio. Still, the entire concept took some getting used to. One day I ran into Scott in the hall at CBS and he said, "I'd like to have a quack rehearsal this afternoon." I didn't know if he meant we were going to a convention of bad doctors or if we'd be working with a choir of ducks. Of course, he was referring to "Dinner Music for a Pack of Hungry Cannibals," where the trumpet has the wonderful part of making all those quacking noises.

As it turned out, my first big public performance with the Quintet, a guest shot on the Chesterfield program, conducted by Paul Whiteman, proved to be a personal disaster. For the first time in my life I got buck fever—stage fright—and began shaking so badly that I couldn't blow a note. I experienced absolute terror and broke down.

I suppose there are many ways to look at this experience. For one thing, maybe if I had taken a drink *before* going on it would have never happened. But I went on cold sober, and for at least ten years afterwards the memory of what took place that terrible day was such that I never attempted a solo performance under any circumstances in a studio without drinking first. A great many kind friends were always on hand to offer remedies and, since I played a lot of performances with the Quintet like a two-week engagement at an East Side club called Le Mirage, and another week at the Paramount Theater, always with some alcohol in my system, I obviously had a new and very serious problem on my hands. When I knew I had a solo performance upcoming the anticipatory anxiety was absolutely overwhelming. Then, too, while we were at the Paramount I committed a serious error in public relationis. Mark Warnow was the brother of Raymond Scott, whose real name was Harry Warnow. I met Mark off-stage one day and he asked, "Why do you drink so much?" Maybe it was the tone of his voice, or simply a combination of all the tensions that were building up inside me, but I couldn't resist telling him, "Come on downstairs with me and I'll introduce you to your brother." I'm afraid Mark never forgave me.

The members of the Quintet were extremely proficient musicians. Pete Pumiglio, the clarinetist, had been in some great musical groups dating back to 1927 when he was with Red Nichols in the Cass-Hagen Orchestra. Dave Harris, the tenorman, was one of the greatest technicians I have ever heard on the instrument. The drummer, Johnny Williams, aside from being a fine dance-band drummer, was a tremendous percussionist with a wide experience in all kinds of music. Our bass player was Lou Shoobe, later to become the most successful music contractor of all time. He was responsible for keeping me busy in the studios until very recent times when he retired.

I decided to seek professional help for my problems. Psychoanalysis was the usual course of action in such circumstances, so I enrolled with Dr. Daniel Schneider, an ex-musician and a cousin of Sanford Gold, the pianist. Although it proved to be quite expensive, I found analysis to be a very valuable and worthwhile experience. It's also a long-drawn-out process, too long and too slow to help much with my immediate needs. I was very busy as a staff musician, besides doing a lot of recording work. In addition, I was doing a lot of free-lance, out-of-state radio shows. On all of these I was always a soloist. I had a big reputation as a soloist, so I was hired as a soloist—yet I was scared to death of solo performances, a helluva state!

Knowing what I went through and how common this happens to performers, I'm fully convinced that a great number of them, like John Barrymore, Judy Garland, and countless others, become alcoholics and addicts because of fear. Barrymore always admitted fear of an audience, and

181

many movie people have been unable to perform on a stage before a live audience. I don't want to expand on this, but I think it should be plain that this overwhelming problem was the primary cause for my developing alcoholism, and it affected my behavior pattern for many years.

My fears finally forced me to give up working with the Quintet when it became part of the Chesterfield Show as a regular attraction, but I remained on staff and actually played on the first recording Raymond Scott made with a big band. The tune was "Just A Gigolo," and I played a brief solo of 8 or 16 bars.

One of the more pleasant aspects of my term at CBS started during the early days, with a radio series for Philip Morris cigarets conducted by Johnny Green, who was the composer of "Out of Nowhere," "Body and Soul," "Coquette," and a number of other beautiful songs. He did four commercial shows a week for them, and collectively they were very lucrative. I also did quite a bit of recording with Johnny, including some novelty records with comedian Danny Kaye and with Fred Astaire. I was very fond of Johnny Green as a man, as a composer, and as a conductor. Besides leading a fine orchestra with such excellent musicians as Joel Herron, Murray Cohen, Leo Kahn, Mac Ceppos, Jimmy Lytell, Jimmy Roselli, Dude Skiles, Bernie Kaufman, Buddy Morrow, and Chauncey Morehouse, he used choral groups with marvelous singers—Audrey Marsh, Elizabeth Newberger, Beverly and Judy Marr, and Margie Miller, all under the direction of Ray Block. This was a most interesting period because Johnny Green was interesting as a person and as a musician. My first daughter, Suzanne, was born during this sojourn, on June 19, 1940.

It was also during the Johnny Green period that I began working a lot with Joel Herron, and we have since been closely associated both musically and socially. Dude Skiles, the other trumpet player in Johnny's band, was not only a good jazz cornet player but an excellent vibraphone player. We had some good small-band sessions on the shows, with Dude on vibes, Jimmy Lytell on clarinet, Chauncey Morehouse on drums, Wes Hines (our jazz trombonist) and me on trumpet. Toward the end of my work with Johnny, Dude Skiles left the band and Charlie Teagarden replaced him. That was the only time I ever had the chance to play with Charlie, one of my favorite trumpet players.

As for Dude, he involved me in a small tragedy, or so it seemed at the time. Johnny's band played a party at Doris Duke's town house one night, and in one of the pantries I spotted a large number of wooden tubs filled with huge bottles of champagne being iced for the guests. After the job, I talked one of the house guards into giving me a double magnum of Mumms champagne to take home to my wife. Dude Skiles, who lived near me, rode the subway home with me and all the way kept pretending to grab my champagne away from me. Finally we came to my stop and I started to get off the train, and Dude—who still had one more stop to go—made a final grab for the bottle and knocked it out of my hand. It broke on the platform, and that, I'm sure, was one of the most expensive moppings any subway station ever got.

On the whole I was doing very well at this time, but I wasn't completely satisfield. I was making a lot of money. I had just purchased a beautiful Cadillac, and yet in the back of my mind I was toying with an idea I'd had since the Dorsey days—having my own band. There was a lot to be said for fronting a band and only having to play solos instead of the much harder job of playing all the parts and the solos too, as I was doing. What's more, certain people had expressed confidence that I would be successful with my own band. Bunny Berigan hadn't done badly, in spite of his alcoholism, and the people who were encouraging me didn't seem to consider my drinking any great drawback, so I was giving it a lot of thought. But it's possible they didn't realize how much the booze was affecting me.

Before going into my plans for a band, it might be a good idea to mention some details of my personal life. We lived in a nice apartment, and there was a little club next door that was convenient for a fast beer. I became very friendly with Dr. Murray Hanigsberg and his family, who lived in our building, and he became my personal physician. I also established a lifelong friendship with George Kraner and his wife, Sylvia, and he has been my accountant all these years. In addition, a number of good friends lived in nearby Jackson Heights—Bobby Hackett, Les Paul, Walt Yoder, and Johnny Blowers, among others, and I also met a group who knew Bunny Berigan. One of them, Rollo Laylan, later became well known in dixieland circles as Preacher Rollo. The others were Elmer Gottschalk, Ray Ekstrand, and Gene Schroeder, all musicians I would later work with extensively.

By this time Chris Griffin had left the Goodman band and was frequently working with me at CBS. I was also doing a lot of playing with my old friend Charlie Margulis, who had been largely responsible for my joining Johnny Green. But all the while, drinking and psychoanalysis figured in my schedule—not enough to stop me, but very much a part of my life.

TWENTY-NINE

IN THE SPRING of 1941 I began talking seriously to Tommy Dorsey's ex-manager, Bobby Burns, and to Cork O'Keefe, formerly of Rockwell-O'Keefe, about what it would take to get me started in the band business. I already had some ideas about the men I would like to have with me, and one of them was a marvelous piano player in Kansas City named Dave McClain, who played great blues.

So I decided to make a trip to the middle west to scout around and see who might be interested or available. This included a side trip to Des Moines to hear a good commercial band, Ozzie Clark's, with the idea that I might take the entire band back East with me. Nothing resulted from the trip, however, and when I got back to New York I met an old friend, Jack Maisel, the drummer, who offered me Bunny Berigan's old band intact, complete with Bunny's library. I immediately accepted the offer. The personnel, as I recall, included Jack Thompson, Charles Mitchell, and Charles Tessar, trumpets; Johnny Castaldi, Andy Fitzgerald, and another sax player on reeds; Mort Stuhlmacher, bass; and Buddy Koss, piano. Danny Richards and Katy Little were the vocalists.

The bookings started out very well, and my good friend George T. Simon gave us a nice send-off in *Metronome*. Our first engagement was a break-in week at a pavilion near Albany, and then we did a week at the Stanley in Pittsburgh, farmed out as Pinky Tomlin's band on a bill with John Boles, the movie actor. Next we opened at the State Ballroom in Boston, and after some minor changes in the band, made a sweep of one-nighters in Michigan and then did two weeks at the Trianon Ballroom in Cleveland. For the western trip I had hired Dave McClain, the Kansas City piano player, Chick Reeves and his wife, Blue Drake, who was our girl singer, a new male vocalist, Bill Usher, and Herb Winfield Jr., as trombonist and arranger. I should also mention that Red Bone, the arranger from Tommy's band, had been writing for me from the start. We had an agreement of some sort, but I'm no longer sure what it was. I believe he arranged for us on a percentage basis, and I'm pretty sure he got the short end of the stick. In later years we had a discussion about it, but I can't remember if we ever reached a decision.

Suffice to say, he wrote some very good arrangements for the band.

After our return from Michigan, there were more changes in the band's personnel, and the bookings were switched to my old friends the Frederick Brothers, whose main base of operations was Chicago. There were probably several reasons for the change, but the important ones were probably that Carl Snyder, who managed the Joe Haymes band, and Freddie Williamson, a friend from Nebraska days, were in the office. Of course, I was well acquainted with Bill and L. A. Frederick. As a result of this change, we were booked into the Rainbow Rendezvous in Salt Lake City. It was a long trip from New York City, so the long jump was broken by an engagement at Creighton University in Omaha, The Turnpike in Lincoln, and the Elks Club in Scotts Bluff, all in Nebraska. We planned to follow the Salt Lake City booking with an extended engagement in San Diego.

We were all set to go, but just before we were due to take off along came December 7th and Pearl Harbor. Overnight the country was at war. Nevertheless, we started on our safari. Beforehand I had made some very necessary economical moves. I traded my Cadillac for a new 9-passengar station wagon, with a two-wheel trailer for hauling luggage. In addition to this, the road manager, John Oberon, drove a 9-passenger limousine, also towing a two-wheel trailer. These two vehicles provided ample transportation for our road tour at relatively low cost.

To the best of my recollection the band I took west included: brass— Jack Thompson, Don MacDonald, Phil Belzar (later Allen Klaus), Joe Harris, Herb Winfield, and Greg Phillips; reeds—Jess Marino, Barney Marino (no relation to Jess), Harry Poole, and Willard Greenawald; rhythm—Dave McClain (later Larry Pryor), Mort Stuhlmacher, and Cody Sandifer, and vocals—Billy Usher and Peggy Stevens.

I remember little about our leaving, other than getting a phone call the night before from Peggy Stevens's mother asking me to protect her daughter. Although the request was reasonable, honesty forced me to tell her that her daughter would have to take care of herself because I had enough responsibility to start with. Our first engagement, the Military Ball for Creighton University held at Peony Park in Omaha, was a lovely affair, and following this we played two nights at The Turnpike in Lincoln, and another night in Scotts Bluff. These all went well, although on the way out we ran into a blizzard in Wyoming, which made the going pretty rough. We fought through and made our way down out of the Wasatch range into Salt Lake City.

The Rainbow Rendezvous proved to be a delightful two-month engagement. We worked for a nice guy named Jerry Johnson who had two places in Salt Lake City. The band sounded good, and almost nightly we were aired on the Don Lee radio network which covered the West Coast. A nice feature about this was that we could go home after work and at 1:30 a.m. listen to a replay of the broadcast we had done at 11:30 p.m.

For the first month in Salt Lake I lived at the Majestic Hotel. Then I took an apartment and Roberta and Suzanne, who was a little over one year old, joined me. It wasn't long before poor Suzanne developed a terrible cold, possibly due to the change of climate and the high altitude. We put in a lot of worry before she got better.

Salt Lake City is a fascinating place. Deer used to come right into our back yard to forage for food. The Mormons have set a great example of how much can be accomplished by concentrated effort. When you fly over the area it's a thrill just to see the agricultural achievements of little over a hundred years. It's easy to believe their reputation for being the most self-sufficient people in the country.

The Mormon Tabernacle in Salt Lake City, aside from its architectural beauty, must have just about the most astounding acoustics anywhere. A pin dropped at one end can be heard at the other end. They say it was constructed from lumber which was hauled a great distance over the mountains and is held together by leather thongs and wooden pegs. No nails were used in the entire structure.

Following the Salt Lake booking, our itinerary called for an extended run at a San Diego ballroom, but now the war was really becoming a grim reality. While we were still in Salt Lake a Japanese submarine managed to penetrate the coastal waters near Santa Barbara. They lobbed only one shell into an on-shore oil tank, but this was enough to scare the entire West Coast into a complete blackout, and our booking was cancelled. This was a disappointment, but since we were being handled by a midwest agency they were able to place us at the Music Box in Omaha which salvaged the immediate situation, but our troubles were far from over. In fact, they were just beginning, because now the draft began to whittle away our personnel. The first to go was our lead alto player, Jess Marino, who was called up from Salt Lake City, and the next was our wonderful pianist, Dave McClain.

I replaced Dave with a young fellow from Salt Lake named Larry Pryor, a nice guy and a good piano player. He was a Mormon and when the customers found this out they'd ask him how many wives he had. He'd tell them he still had only one but he was working hard to find another. While I was making changes, I decided to let one of our trumpet players, Phil Belzar, go, replacing him and the lead alto spot with two friends of Cody Sandifer's. They were from Fort Worth, Texas, and as physically unfit as I was, which meant they weren't apt to go to war unless the manpower situation grew desperate. The sax player was Jerry Albright, and the trumpet player was Allen "Snuffy" Klaus—both terrific musicians. Snuffy had a great jazz ability reminiscent of Charlie Teagarden.

Before we were due to open at the Music Box we had a few days off, so I decided to make a quick trip home to Falls City to visit my folks. Besides my wife and daughter, I took along a couple of band members, making a brief stop in Omaha to leave them off. I drove the 1,100 miles to Falls City without staying over any place. I kept awake with the help of benzedrine tablets, and they worked fine on the drive, but when we finally got to Falls City and I had a chance to rest, my heart was pounding so hard I couldn't sleep.

The engagement at the Music Box, a very lovely supper club, went well and we had a pleasant stay in Omaha. Our vocalist Billy Usher was also a native of Nebraska, his family living in Omaha. We spent a lot of time with other local musicians. One of these, an extremely talented pianist and arranger, Marvin Wright, wrote a great arrangement for our band, a dance-band version of "Afternoon of a Faun." I also saw my old friend, Omaha-bandleader-turned-radio-executive, Fred Ebner, and met a trumpet-playing bandleader, Mort Wells, with whom I am still in contact.

Omaha was eventful too in that we discovered a truly great restaurant, "Jeff's Barbecue." Jeff specialized in barbecued meat of all kinds that would melt in your mouth, but that wasn't all. Without any doubt, he made the greatest pies in the world. He had once worked for the Harvey system as a chef for the dining cars of the Union Pacific Railroad, traveling between Omaha and Salt Lake City. In the process of trying to bake pies on board a moving train he discovered that altitude was very important in the way the dough would rise. He made an exact study of this and finally worked out a formula for the proper measurement of ingredients required at any given altitude, from the highest point in the Rockies to sea level and, as a consequence, he became the greatest authority on pie crust and baking pies you could ever hope to meet.

We were followed in Salt Lake City by the Stan Kenton band, fresh out of Balboa Beach, and that band as a unit and in material and precision was too good to be for real. After we left Omaha and moved on to Columbus, Ohio, to open at the "Ionian Room" of the Deschler-Wallach Hotel, we were again followed by the Kenton crew when they opened at Valley Dale. This created a rather ridiculous situation. There we were playing commercial hotel music to packed houses every night—mainly because we were in a big hotel in the center of a city teeming with war contractors and clients, and within easy access of everything. While the Kenton band, one of the all-time best, was doing no business because they were on the outskirts of town. By then the public had become very distance-conscious, because of gas rationing, and it was also too preoccupied with the war to really listen to music.

For a bandleader traveling with a family, I consider the Deschler-Wallach Hotel the best job I ever had. As part of my contract, I was provided with a fine suite to live in, plus an allowance for meals in any one of the three excellent dining rooms, and this was enough to feed us very adequately. All in all, we had a very successful two-month engagement. While we were at the Deschler I hired a new girl singer, Roslyn Dean. We went on to play two weeks at a nice pavilion in Chippewa Lake, Ohio, another week at Walled Lake in Michigan (where Tommy Dorsey broke in his Joe Haymes band), and then moved in for an indefinite run at the famous Trianon Ballroom in Chicago. I don't remember just how long we were there, but it was probably about a month. By then our automobiles, especially the tires (now rationed), were in sad shape. Road travel seemed out of the question, so unless we could come up with an alternative it looked like the band was finished.

Somewhere we had heard that Eddie Peabody had been able to keep the Clyde McCoy band together by enlisting them as a unit in the service. This seemed like a pretty good idea—at least it was a way to go—so we went down to the Navy Pier in Chicago, which was the enlistment center, to check out our chances of going into the service collectively. Although they were very nice to us, they said they couldn't give us any assurance that we would remain a unit. However, if we signed up, they promised to try. Since this seemed to be the best we could get, we signed up. They took eight men and unceremoniously rejected four, including me, because of a mastoid injury dating back to my childhood. So I was left with no band, no tires, no gasoline, and no prospects.

I finally received an offer from Irv Brabech (who later wound up in a torpedo-boat squadron) to take a booking in Kalamazoo, Michigan, at a place called Shenzil's. But I needed a band. I scrounged around and found a sax section that had been left high and dry by another defunct band, led by a good sax player named Bill Hitz, with a good tenorman from Pittsburgh, a guy nicknamed "The Mole." So I wound up with a pretty fair band for my last stand.

There were some humorous as well as sad aspects to the Kalamazoo job. Our drummer, Keating Chase, drank a lot, and we had to play for a show which included a nervous juggler. The juggler would get so upset because our drinking drummer would miss cueing his tricks that he was constantly dropping his dumbbells and plates, or whatever else he was using in his act. It wasn't only the drummer who drank. I used to take a bottle of Canadian Club to work every night and hide the empties in a drum case. Finally I had collected too many empties, so I carried them out and dumped them into an ashcan behind the place. The next night the owner raised hell with the band and told us that if he ever found out who drank all that booze he'd fire him. Neither he nor the band knew the bottles were all mine.

Kalamazoo was also memorable to me and my family because the apartment we had in a motel was alive with cockroaches. The dresser drawers were full of them, and when you opened a closet they jumped out on you. We were never lonely.

The union local helped me to fill vacancies in the line-up as they kept occurring. Once I had to replace a trombone player, and they sent me a pretty fair replacement, but I found out he was an out-patient from a mental hospital. Then a few days later I called the union for a bass player and they sent me a male nurse from the same institution. They must have had a good band at that hospital.

We managed to hold on for two or three weeks to wind everything up, but in September 1942 I returned to New York—out of the band business. I really believe that if the war hadn't come along I would have enjoyed reasonable success in the business, leading a good, middle-of-the-road, and always working dance band.

THIRTY

WHEN WE RETURNED to New York in 1942, World War II was well under way and most of my friends were in the armed forces, although many were stationed in the New York area. We took a studio apartment at 1393 Sixth Ave. (57th Street), and this is where we were to remain for almost 20 years. It had an 18-foot-high north-light ceiling designed for an artist and was located in a building of only 12 apartments. These were tenanted mainly by musical or professional people, and most of them were gone during the day, which allowed me to practice as many hours as I wanted without interference.

It was pretty obvious that I wouldn't be doing much traveling for the duration of the war, so I sold all of my automotive rolling stock. In addition to the cars, I still owned a lot of power tools, stored in Nebraska, which could be used to manufacture war material, so my mother gave these to a plant near Falls City which manufactured small parts for an aircraft factory.

Our apartment enjoyed a great central location, so we soon established a social center for a lot of friends. We were within walking distance of almost every recording and broadcasting studio in use at that time, and friends were always dropping in. I recall entertaining Jean Goldkette, Willard Robison, Ralph Douglas, Charlie Margulis, Billy Usher, Rudy Puletz, Buck and Bubbles, and others too numerous to mention. On our same floor lived a vocal coach, a Russian concert pianist, and our next-door neighbors were Jean and Charles Sanders. Jean, for most of her life, was a professional dancer and had worked with Ted Lewis. Charles was a salesman for the Benson & Hedges Tobacco Company, but at one time he had managed the legendary Cinderella Ballroom where Bix, Phil Napoleon, and the Original Dixieland Jazz Band had played. So we were surrounded by professional people from my own field.

I was lucky, too, that I was able to go back to work in the studios, which was to be my way of life for the next eight years. I worked on several of the "script shows," those with continuing story lines which kept them running for many years. They provided a marvelous base to lean on and at the same time gave me plenty of leeway to take on free-lance work. The first show in my grouping was "Mr. and Mrs. North," which ran for 12 years on NBC. It was a husband-and-wife detective story performed without an audience in Studio 3C, and the principal actors and actresses were well known in their field. Some, Frank Lovejoy, for instance, went on to become movie stars; another was Ted DeCorsia.

For a few months the studio opposite 3C was used to rehearse and broadcast an Air Force band that was being groomed for overseas duty. It was a marvelous 30-piece orchestra under the direction of my old friend Harry Bluestone. My main reason for mentioning it is a young fellow playing lead trumpet who was so outstanding that we tried to hear the band as much as possible. His name was Dick Cathcart, and years later he became well known for his work with Jack Webb on the "Pete Kelly's Blues" series on radio, records, the movies, and TV.

The "Mr. and Mrs. North" program used a 12-piece orchestra directed by a very capable composer-conductor named Charles Paul, which supplied thematic material for each segment of the play, punctuating accents in the script, and supplying background music for the various scenes. This was the established format for all theaters and movies, and the writers and conductors who handled this work were well equipped to take care of it. The musicianship was therefore of a very high caliber; these conductors set very high and exacting standards. As a further result, a relatively small number of musicians did the bulk of the work because the conductors preferred men and women who were experienced in this type of work and they were reluctant to try new people.

The orchestra that did the "Mr. and Mrs. North" show was typical. Our lead trumpet player was Charlie Margulis, whose wide experience was well known. The trombonists were Jack Satterfield, from the New York Philharmonic, and Al Godlis, from the Philadelphia Orchestra. The lead reedman was Al Howard, who was remarkably equipped, with a wide experience in radio orchestras on flute, clarinet, and all the other reed instruments. The solo flute and double reeds were handled by Sal Amato and Ted Gompers. The viola player was Harold Colletta, one of Stokowski's favorite musicians. The Concert Master was Jacques Gaslin, who later went on to fill the same spot with the Los Angeles Symphony.

Shows like "Mr. and Mrs. North" could be pretty lucrative, real "plums" for the studio musicians. The conductors had very little trouble in attracting the best people available. Each show would be performed twice, maybe 8 p.m. for the East Coast and Midwest, and again at 11 p.m. for the West Coast, so it paid very well. In addition, rehearsals would generally start around 4 or 5 p.m., and this left the rest of the day open for recording dates or anything else that might come along. For a period of two years, I had four of these shows the year round, providing a good base income and permitting me to sandwich other major shows in between. Again, the location of my apartment proved a tremendous advantage. I was only seven blocks north of the NBC studios, five blocks from the major CBS studios, and right next door to "Fine Sound Studios," where we did many sessions. I was one long block away from the MGM studios, and a scant half-block from the Decca recording studios. I could always have my meals at home and spend time there between shows and when I had repeat broadcasts. The unbelievable part of all this was that we were in a rent-controlled building, so the rent was only $70 a month. Even after ten years, when a raise was permitted, it was only $80 a month. Pretty hard to beat.

Early in 1943 I started work on a CBS show called "The Gay Nineties Revue," under the direction of one of radio's most successful conductors, Ray Bloch. This ran for years on Monday nights and was an entirely musical program featuring the music of the Nineties. It starred singer Beatrice Kay and the Master of Ceremonies was Joe Howard, the very prolific composer and singer of songs of the era, who, I believe, was already in his eighties but turned in a superb job.

Later in the year I started two more shows, both of which ran more than two seasons. One on CBS was "Stage Door Canteen," under the direction of colorful California conductor Raymond Paige. This was a musical program in a patriotic vein, following the format established at the numerous canteens around the country which had been set up for the entertainment of servicemen. One of the directors was actress Helen Menkin, daughter of the famous H. L. Menkin. In keeping with the Paige tradition, we had a large orchestra with a full string section, and we played the stage-production type of arrangements that he had used so successfully in the West Coast theaters. The trumpet section included names that will be very familiar to many record collectors—Nat Natoli (formerly with Jean Goldkette and Paul Whiteman), Russ Case (an established orchestrator, well known as an A & R man for RCA-Victor), and Billy Butterfield.

Keep these names in mind as I tell you about one of those happenings that are funny in retrospect but not funny at all when they take place. Russ Case wrote an arrangement for the "Stage Door Canteen" show that was dedicated to the armed forces and included just about every bugle call ever written. As these things often go, if one instrumentalist misses a note, it seems to be catching and the next guy will also miss. Well, when we aired this particular arrangement the first guy loused up his bugle call, followed by the next guy who messed up his. Each bugle call went awry until the very last one, which, of course, was taps, the hardest of all. It was left to Russ Case himself to do a flawless performance on taps—but nothing could vindicate the rest of us.

The second show, also directed by Raymond Paige, was aired by NBC as "The American Youth Program" every week. At first Paige had tried to employ the best young musicians he could find to make up the orchestra, but being an NBC network show, it was felt that the music had to maintain a high standard, and as a result certain members of the ensemble scarcely qualified as youths. In the brass section, for example, I was teamed with Andy Ferretti, Billy Butterfield, and Will Bradley. Dave Bowman was on piano. Even so, we did have some fine young musicians. Two were drummers, a girl named Rose and a boy named Walter Rosenblum, who later joined the New York Philharmonic. Mainly the youngsters made up the string section, and the most prominent was the Concert Master, Arnold Eidus, a Juilliard graduate who became a very successful studio musician. We also had a very beautiful young harpist, Elaine Vito, daughter of Toscanini's harpist, Ed Vito.

Another one of those unexplainable faux pas took place on this show. We had a lovely arrangement of the old standard "Dinah," which, like most of the Paige presentations, was switched around from one section to another for different tonal colors. Andy Ferretti had a release in the middle of the arrangement, which he was to play as a cup-mute solo close to the microphone, a very intimate and beautiful tone color. For some reason, Andy miscounted his entrance and came in wrong—about two beats late—on his solo, which made it sound completely out of rhythm with the rest of the orchestra. Although it probably wasn't that noticeable to the listening audience, it was the subject of a lot of laughs and comments at Hurley's Bar between shows—but what capped the climax was the repeat show, when Andy did exactly the same thing.

One of the radio conductors I often worked with over a span of years was Al Goodman, who had been a Broadway theater conductor of some note. He was a very nice guy as well as an excellent conductor, but much of his reputation with musicians was based on his dry sense of humor and his way of twisting words. Billy Gussak, who played drums with him for an extended period, actually compiled a collection of Goodman's sayings. I played the fabulous "Fred Allen Show" for some time with Goodman, then he went away to California for a year or so. When he came back he greeted the orchestra with the words, "Well, we've passed a lot of water under the bridge since the last session, haven't we?"

During rehearsal, if a musician said, "I think I have a wrong note in bar 12," Goodman would tell him, "Make an X around it." Then if questioned as to what the note should be he'd squint at the score awhile and then answer, "Oh, I'd say that's about a C7th." One of the funniest stories about him took place during a broadcast Goodman was conducting called "The Million Dollar Band." Billy Butterfield had an 8-bar jazz solo in the middle of an arrangement of "Bugle Call Rag," and, as can happen to any trumpet player, he missed every note in the solo. Not one note was in the chord pattern of the tune. As tragic as this seems to the performer, it still comes out funny to everybody else, and after the show Goodman went up to Billy and innocently inquired, "Why did you change your solo? I liked what you played at dress rehearsal much better."

Of course, the humorous aspect was the spice of life in the studios. It helped everybody keep going. One of the classic stories concerned a very fine symphony drummer who was being heckled by his peers who wanted to know why he couldn't play like Gene Krupa. They kept needling him until he finally lost his temper and yelled, "The only thing Krupa can do that I can't is keep time!"

The camaraderie between studio musicians during the peak years of radio was really wonderful; pranks, gags, and laughs galore were a way of life. Richard Himber, who was an amateur magician of considerable talent, was also a great prankster. He enjoyed pulling practical jokes on members of his orchestra on the "Studebaker Hour." This included a number of the really great studio men, like Arnold Brilhart, Manny Klein, and Charlie Margulis. After putting up with Himber's gags for some time, the musicians cooked up one of their own to get even, and it was a beauty. With the cooperation of the studio engineers and personnel every clock in the broadcasting studio was set ten minutes ahead. Then they all sat back to wait for Himber.

He showed up a few minutes before air time and, when the hands of the clock reached the hour and the red light signified they were on the air, he gave the band the down beat—and nothing happened. Nobody blew a note, they all just stared back at him. A little flustered and unbelieving, Himber gave the down beat a second time, with the same result. Then, red in the face and furious, he tried one more time and almost collapsed when the orchestra still refused to start. At that point, he was greeted by a gale of laughter and he realized that, for a change, he was the victim of a gag.

Charlie Margulis had a farm and every now and then he'd collect some fresh eggs and bring them in to sell to the guys. One day he had a dozen eggs stashed under his chair, and Artie Foster sneaked them away, had them all hard-boiled except one, and put them back. Whoever wound up with those eggs is probably still trying to figure it out. Then there was a sax player who left home for work one day and on the way to the subway stopped to light his pipe. He was headed into the wind, so he turned around to shield his match. When the pipe was lit he forgot he had turned around and walked back to his house.

The professional versatility of the studio musicians of that period was awesome; they were the most talented people imaginable. Many would do shows with a popular or jazz flavor and two hours later be playing classics or semi-classics with equal proficiency. In between you could usually find them at one of the favorite hang-outs that catered to the broadcasting people. For those at NBC it was Hurley's Bar on the corner of 49th and Sixth Avenue. The CBS people congregated at Colby's Restaurant in the CBS building at 485 Madison. The lesser lights and the musicians with more of the dance-band and jazz flavor went to Charley's Tavern on 7th Avenue between 51st and 52nd. These places served as a sort of headquarters—they were food stops and drinking places, and offered such services as cashing checks and running charge accounts (tabs). Charley's was also a mail drop, with messages tacked to the wall.

By far the busiest, though, was Hurley's. In Hurley's on any given evening it wouldn't be unusual to run into Carl Kress, Dick McDonough, Claude Thornhill, Andy Ferretti, Sylvester Ahola, Glenn Miller, Charlie Spivak, George Van Eps, Artie Schutt, Jack Jenny, Jack Lacey, or Bunny Berigan, among many others, as well as scriptwriters, announcers, and all the others who made up the broadcasting business. Hurley's was run by two brothers, a brother-in-law, and a partner, Paddy Daley. The story goes that one night one of the brothers came out from behind the bar with the avowed intention of evicting a drunk from the premises and was so stoned himself that he fell down before he reached the drunk.

My daughter, Suzanne, was two years old when we moved to 6th Avenue, and my wife took her to Central Park every day for her outings. This also gave Roberta a chance to make friends in the new neighborhood. Because of our central location, we were never at a loss for social life. We had very nice people living in our building and the general atmosphere of the neighborhood was especially pleasant. Then, too, we often visited friends on Long Island, like Chris and Helen Griffin and Joan and Johnny Blowers.

Suzanne was a very attractive child, even if I do say so, and even before my second daughter, Merrily, was born, Roberta became interested in submitting pictures of Suzanne to various agency people, notably Pat Allen, to see if she could be placed for some modeling assignments. Roberta finally succeeded and when she was four years old, Suzanne was photographed as a sailor's child for the cover of "Parade" magazine.

THIRTY-ONE

IN 1943 AND INTO 1944 I was playing service dances at the old Ritz Carlton ballroom every Saturday night with a good friend, Dick Raymond. The dances were held for servicemen stationed around New York or visiting the city. Dick was a trumpet player who always managed to surround himself with first-rate players. For many years he was the musical director for the Astor Hotel, and he always came up with club dates for his friends. He contracted for Van Alexander, had standby bands for Vaughn Monroe, and supplied bands for a lot of affairs in the various ballrooms and hotels.

There were a number of notable musicians playing these jobs because, among other things, it was a chance to play dance music with a good band, have a few laughs, and to *drink*. These dates also started me on a practice that has come in handy ever since—working free-lance club dates, at least on weekends. Through the ensuing years, this has proved to be a big help in making a living. There is certainly more than one facet to the music business, and, as I look back how, I can readily appreciate how valuable the club-date side has been to me financially.

New York is unique in the club-date field. It is the only city I know where club dates are so plentiful, and there are many reasons for this. Until very recently, it had a constantly growing population, and wherever you have a lot of people you have a lot of social functions. Also, it is the business hub of the country, home base for countless businesses and groups having conventions or sales meetings, the center for most music-publishers, the heart of live-performance theater, and the site for many of the social functions of the rich as well as a variety of ethnic groups. Thus New York has been a haven for many who have survived for long years in the music field, simply by providing work in so many facets of the business that when one branch was slow the others provided income, particularly to those lucky enough to maintain connections in more than one branch. I have experienced such periods, and I'm properly grateful for the associations I've maintained in diversified areas. The hey-day of radio was great, but I distinctly recall when 30 major radio shows decided to migrate to California, leaving a mighty big hole in the New York studio work. Club dates filled the breach until most of the shows returned to New York.

In 1979, on a visit to Cape Cod, I was invited to a film showing at the home of Jack Bradley, Louis Armstrong's official photographer. Jack showed a movie short taken when I was in a group put together by Dick Raymond for Will Bradley. There were a number of well-known jazz musicians in the short, including Johnny Pepper, the clarinetist, and Billy Butterfield. In addition to the service dance with Dick Raymond (later to continue under the direction of another successful club date leader, Jimmie Lanin) I started working for society bandleader Meyer Davis, probably the most successful of them all. This was an association that lasted more than 20 years. In addition to playing in his bands, I orchestrated half of the music on his first two phonograph albums.

Meyer had booking offices in New York City, Philadelphia, and Washington. Quite often a large number of orchestras were working under his banner in several cities on the same nights, as well as on the ships operated by the United States Lines. Of course, if Meyer Davis himself was engaged to lead the orchestra at a party, the price was much higher than for a Meyer Davis orchestra under the leadership of somebody else. In order to capitalize on this, there were times when Meyer was sold on two jobs running simultaneously, and he had a unique system perfected allowing him to be "in two places at once." If the jobs were within a radius of 20 miles, he would show up at the start of one, conduct for an hour or so, then turn the job over to an assistant and make a fast trip by *private ambulance* to finish the other date.

Over the years Meyer often hired me as a jazz player, and I would travel with him to Washington, Wilmington, Baltimore, Philadelphia, or Chicago, to augment the local bands he fronted in those cities. During the August season of society parties, I would join a New York band working in Newport, Rhode Island. At the time I seldom knew who we were playing for, but later I would find out we had been at Jackie Bouvier's coming-out party or had played at the wedding reception of John F. Kennedy. We were at the Rockefeller estate in Pocantico Hills quite often, or at Lake Forest, Illinois, for Marshall Fields. We played the Annual Hunt Club Ball in Baltimore and the April-in-Paris Ball in New York. The latter function was notable because they would import the entire company of the Folies Bergere, and guests would include people like the Duke and Duchess of Windsor, or Queen Juliana and Prince Bernhard of The Netherlands.

Some interesting experiences came my way as a result of some of Meyer's dates. For instance, it was at a luncheon for newspaper publishers that I was given the chance to hear Babe Ruth's last public speech. At another, I heard Jimmy Walker and George Jessel. I never appreciated Jessel as a performer, but as a toastmaster he was probably the greatest that ever lived.

There have been quite a few club-date orchestra leaders who have made fortunes catering to the single-engagement business, and most of them followed the Meyer Davis format. However, the ethnic population of New York created a demand for live music far beyond anything possible in other localities, and musicians and leaders willing to specialize in these fields made out very well. Greek work has always been lucrative and plentiful, but, above all, the Jewish dates proved to be the most tremendous field. For quite awhile I

Billy Butterfield

worked for another leader, Joe Mass, who had started with Meyer Davis and then decided to concentrate on Jewish work rather than the society parties, and he built a business that made him a wealthy man.

I was frequently amused by these bands from the musical standpoint. To my ears a job played by twenty-five men sounded just the same as one played by five—only louder. Nevertheless, there are some interesting and exacting requirements of the business. To begin with, very rarely do members of a club-date band read music, so to be successful the club-date musician has to develop the ability to play an "ad lib" repertoire of great variety. The party orchestras follow set patterns and the emphasis is always placed on the customers having a good time so the music is secondary, but there has to be a lot of it. Therefore, another qualification is that the musicians must have great stamina. So-called "continuous" music is more costly but it is more lucrative to both the leader and the musicians, so the better club-date men never accept a noncontinuous job.

A continuous job means just that! Once the music starts, it never stops. Union regulations demand that a musician get five minutes' rest in each hour, but in practice the leaders will stagger the breaks for the men so the music keeps going, or others will play with the entire band for three hours and then take a fifteen-minute intermission. I have played coutless six-hour continuous jobs and on occasion even seven-hour ones. The only way I can describe it is to call it brutal punishment, especially for the lead trumpet player.

Meyer Davis used a trumpet player named Don Miles in his Philadelphia orchestras, and he was the most indestructible trumpeter I have ever known. He wasn't the best player I've ever heard, but it seemed he could play the lead forever, without stopping or tiring.

A lot of emphasis has been placed on the importance of large orchestras, like those of Jean Goldkette and Paul Whiteman, as breeding ground for jazz musicians, who in turn made small-band records with groups drawn from these orchestras, all of which provided steady income for the jazz players. Although this may be true, a lot of credit is also due many of the club-date leaders for providing a source of income for a great many free-lance musicians who were capable of fitting into the style of these bands. Over the years they employed a lot of musicians who have become part of jazz history.

As for me, in 1943 I had a lot of things going for me. I was still young (only 30 years old), strong in many ways (necessary for physical survival), very much in demand (thanks to many friends in all facets of the music business), and musically capable of holding down my chair, whether it was playing in a jazz band, a dance band, semi-symphony, or club-date group—and today I wonder how I was able to keep up the pace. In addition to playing many hours, every day I practiced almost as many, and, although I wasn't yet aware of it, I was well on the way to becoming an alcoholic.

The schedules we worked tended to encourage drinking. Sometimes we would record from 9 a.m. to noon, have an hour off, record from 1 p.m. to 5 p.m., then go to a script show from 6 p.m. to 8 p.m., and repeat it at 11 p.m. or 11:30 p.m. This presented quite a few opportunities during the long day to spend the off periods in one of the favorite saloons, and one could consume a tremendous volume of booze between jobs, if so inclined, which many of us were. But becoming a heavy drinker has a way of sneaking up on you. You can walk around and function without being aware of how hooked you are or what a great dependency on alcohol you've developed. You consider it normal to drink great amounts, day and night, and then to have several heavy belts on getting up in the morning, to fortify you just in case you decide to eat breakfast instead of drinking it. I was definitely becoming an alcoholic, yet for a long time I was always able to play well enough, drunk or sober, to hold my jobs—although I did lose a few before I finally overcame the problem.

The thing is, whether or not the drinker realizes he is becoming more and more dependent on booze, it is both obvious and disheartening to his family and those around him. Watching this happen to any member of the family is heartbreaking but when it is the breadwinner who is involved, it becomes a serious situation. Sooner or later the alcoholic becomes a worry, a burden, and a constant source of anguish. There is a point in the drinker's career at which it is possible to become saturated short of the point of falling flat or staggering into a corner, but the brain gradually loses its capacity to think rationally and the drunk can delude himself into some strange ideas. In my case, this happened in a way that eventually worked out to my benefit, but it illustrates the irrationality of the situation at the time. I was doing a single NBC show, the name of which escapes me, but it was a program of partially classical music under the direction of Lou Bring, conducting an orchestra that included quite a few people from the Philharmonic, along with Charlie Margulis and me. The principal performer was Metropolitan star Leonard Warren, who, to say the least, was a meticulous artist, and much of the music was not only difficult it was intricate.

We rehearsed the show, probably for a few hours, and when it came time for us to go on the air I left my music closed on the stand and announced to Margulis that I knew all the parts by heart and was going to challenge myself by playing it all from memory. Obviously I was so damned drunk I had no idea what I was doing. Fortunately, Charlie came to my rescue and opened the book so all the parts were correctly played, and since the scene had taken place quietly no one was the wiser. However, Rudolph Pulitz, the great French horn player from the Philharmonic, had been close enough to overhear our conversation and observe what was going on, and, since he was also an alcoholic, he understood the situation. After the show was over, he made it his business to get better acquainted with me, using a subtle pretense, but intending to help me face my alcoholic pattern.

Most people today are aware of the patterns of addicts, whether alcohol, drugs, or tobacco. Those addicted have regular sources for getting whatever they're hooked on, and a confirmed addict will make sure he prepares ahead to supply his habit. The alcoholic not only has his favorite watering holes, he makes certain he has a regular home supply of booze and a home base where he is known and where his credit is good, in case he is temporarily short of funds. I was no different. I ran tabs in all my regular bars, two of which were within one block of our apartment, and usually when I drank in these places the bartenders wouldn't even bother with a shot glass. When I ordered a drink, it was a short, four-ounce highball glass full of whatever I happened to be drinking. This served several purposes—I didn't have to bother bending my elbow so many times (one drink would be four ounces instead of the usual one-and-a-half), and if I happened to be drinking with a well-meaning friend (which often happened) and he insisted I limit my intake to two drinks, I would agree. Unless he was aware of the capacity of shot glasses, my two drinks would be the equivalent of eight. Such deception is common to addicts.

Shortly after the Lou Bring episode I started a five-per-week program with popular artist cartoonist Robert Ripley, of "Believe It Or Not" fame. This meant playing a show every evening from Monday through Friday, and, despite the fact that my new associate Rudy Pulitz was in the band, I'm convinced it was a collection of the heaviest drinkers to be found in one group. We had five brass, four saxes, and the usual rhythm section, and the show was under the direction of Frank Novak, who had been an active radio conductor for some time. I'd rather not mention names but the band was loaded with classic drunks like me.

So Rudy Pulitz, aware of my heavy drinking pattern, began talking to me in a humorous fashion about some of his own drinking experiences, an approach I now realize is often used by members of Alcoholics Anonymous in their initial attempts to help other alcoholics. His tragically funny story concerned a time when the great Toscanini had selected four key men to accompany him to Buenos Aires to play with the orchestra in the beautiful opera house there. Rudy Pulitz, in spite of the honor of being one of those selected and traveling 9,000 miles to perform, wound up on the roof of his hotel—stark naked and stoned out of his mind, playing the Seigfried Horn Call. He never made the concert.

Such stories fit the classic behavior of far-gone alcoholics, and relating tales like this helps kindred souls to feel comfortable, knowing they are in the company of someone who has gone through the ridiculous patterns of addicts and understands. I have my own collection of personal boo-boos—and I will relate them from time to time—but the important thing is that Rudy inspired in me enough trust that I agreed to attend a meeting of Alcoholics Anonymous.

For those not familiar with AA, let me explain briefly that it is a voluntary organization of reformed alcoholics loosely banded together by a twelve-step program designed to help themselves and others with an alcohol problem. These people have had wonderful success. The twelfth step in the program is very important, because it means going out into the world to aid other alcoholics. It's a critical stage and it has one great advantage—if you are aiding other alcoholics to stay "dry," the term usually used, you are less apt to slip and have a drink yourself.

I agreed to attend a meeting with Rudy Pulitz because, believe me, if you are an alcoholic you are seeking a way out. But regretfully I must admit that at the first meeting I was still pretty saturated—not enough that I didn't know what was going on, but fortified well enough to overcome any apprehensions I may have had about attending a meeting of drunks. It was held at the Capitol Hotel at 50th and 8th Avenue, and the first thing I noticed was that everybody was without drinks, a most unusual situation for me at the time. Nevertheless, they all seemed to be enjoying themselves, and, as I listened and learned more about the program, I began to appreciate the opportunities it offered.

The principal speaker was a man named Bill Wilson, one of the two founders of AA, and the other was a woman, Marty Mann, who devoted most of her life to the organization. At the time I had no idea who these people were, but I'll never forget meeting Bill Wilson. It must have been obvious to him that I was loaded when we were introduced, but he very jovially acknowledged our introduction, smiled, and said, "Just stay around here and listen for a few days or weeks and your problems will end."

It was the custom at the meetings to take an intermission after a couple of alcoholics had spoken, relating their experiences with alcohol, during which people would visit and get acquainted, or use the bathroom or whatever. Then the meeting would continue with two more speakers before coming to a close. At this first meeting, I excused myself on the pretext of going to the men's room, ran downstairs, and took a cab to my bar on 56th and 6th Avenue. After four fast straight belts, I grabbed another cab back to the meeting. Rudy never knew this until I told him later.

This was in 1944. I attended AA meetings whenever I could, usually two or three times a week, some at the Capitol Hotel and others at the Seaman's Institute on 23rd Street, and listened to some of the most interesting speakers I have ever heard. These were real people who often had hair-raising and almost unbelievable experiences to tell. In many cases they had gone from the top of the ladder in their professions to winding up in a doorway on the Bowery, and they truthfully related their miseries in the hope that others would learn and benefit from them. At the very least it established a brotherhood among those with alcoholic problems and, by the way, those are the only problems dealt with at AA meetings. The reason a person goes to AA is because he has finally admitted to himself that he is having a problem with alcohol. One of the primary rules of the group is to maintain a strict "hands-off" policy toward any other problems in his life.

Around this time I began doing a radio show with Harry Sosnik which featured vocal stylist Hildegarde. Working with me was a friend from the Raymond Scott Quintet, Johnny Williams. I knew that he had an alcohol problem, and I had recently heard a story that the weekend before Johnny and Yank Lawson were working on the Kate Smith Show while roaring drunk. What I didn't know was that Johnny's wife and family were beside themselves with worry and anxiety about him and at a loss as to what they could do to help him.

I didn't say anything to John about his drinking, but I invited him to my apartment for dinner during our break, and, while we were waiting for Roberta to put it on the table, I simply handed him the book on Alcoholics Anonymous. The more he read, the more he kept telling me, "This sounds like me." Finally, at his request, I took him to an AA meeting. He took to the program whole-heartedly and it completely changed his life. He hasn't had a drink since. Later he moved his family to California. His son is the John Williams who has won so many awards for movie writing and is now the conductor of the Bosten Pops Orchestra.

Perhaps this is a good time to take a look at why so many performers—musicians, actors, newspaper people, writers, and almost anybody working under pressure—become alcoholics. As psychological as most of these pressures are, they are very real to the person enduring them, and performing very often becomes a traumatic experience, in spite of all the good wishes of the audience. After all, the listener hearing a musician or an actor is only looking for entertainment and is seldom as critical as the performer imagines. But, truthfully, the performer is really not thinking about the person or persons listening to him, nor is he particularly interested in them or their opinions, what he is mainly concerned with is pleasing himself—and I know of very few performers who are able to do this. It probaby all stems back to the performer's attempts, by practice and study, to attain perfection—a process of mental aggravation stimulated by the fact that we are our own worst critics. But there are other factors too. The person sensitive enough to be creative is also super-sensitive to extreme anxieties and often resorts to alcohol or drugs for help in enduring these anxieties, with the result that he eventually becomes addicted to whatever crutch he is using. A great number of superb performers have rendered themselves helpless and mentally ill or have even killed themselves with these stimulants. There's no doubt that this is part of life for many performers and it presents a terrible problem. Which is not to say that performers are the only ones or that the entertainment field stands alone in this regard. My problem, as with many of my contemporaries, was the bottle, but among present-day performers it appears that drugs have replaced alcohol, and the result is often disastrous. But frankly, I have never known a jazz trumpeter worth listening to who has not, at one time or another had a problem with alcohol.

During my dry period of over two years I deliberately looked for work that would not create any real anxiety and give me a reason to drink. In retrospect, I find it really remarkable that I was able to do this because I had established quite a reputation as a soloist, and to play for two years without playing solos was quite an accomplishment.

THIRTY-TWO

DURING 1945 AND 1946 I worked on two radio shows with Broadway theater conductor Jay Blackton. One was sponsored by Ballantine Beer and the other by RCA-Victor. They were special Sunday-afternoon shows which featured great concert artists—not only those who recorded for RCA-Victor but many of the foremost instrumentalists and singing stars of the day, like Kirsten Flagstad, Lauritz Melchior, Erica Marini, and Josef Hoffman. Jay Blackton was an excellent conductor and the orchestras were relatively large concert groups. I found the work of great interest because of the challenge presented by the transpositions and the good taste of the musical accompaniment involved. It was the most extended period of my career where I had the opportunity to play classical music. Toward the latter portion of the RCA Sunday show, Tommy Dorsey came in as the regular Master of Ceremonies and each week he would play one or two of the classic trombone solos he recorded for Victor, utilizing the fine arrangements made for him by Hugo Winterhalter on such numbers as "Estralita," and "Smoke Gets in Your Eyes."

I also had two shows on station WOR with my regular conductor Charles Paul, a truly thorough musician. One of these was with Gabriel Heater, a well-known news commentator. The brass sections were comprised of symphony musicians and this served as great training for me. My fellow trumpet player was Murray Karpilovsky, and on trombones were Neal DiBiasi, and Abe Perlstein, all top symphony players. I gained more knowledge of the proper way to approach my instrument from Murray Karpilovsky than from any other man I ever worked with. I not only played with him and could follow his approach and learn from his playing, I tried (unsuccessfully) to match his broad, lovely sound and to balance the section in my own way. It was like going to a conservatory.

In addition to working with him, I studied with Murray. He called the Bach Company and gave them a design for the mouthpiece I still use to this day, and trained me in the classical repertoire by taking me into the French school of Etudes.

Aside from the professional advantages of working with these symphonic players, I made friendships which have endured and been most pleasant through the years. One of these was trombonist Ralph Leise, who has since become the manager of the Houston Symphony. When I was working with him, he had a milk business as a sideline and kept cows. Ralph was a fine musician, but I think his way of handling the dairy business may have been unique. As I understand it, cows have to be milked twice daily in order to keep them functioning properly, but since Ralph worked rather unusual hours for a dairy farmer, he trained his cows to be milked at 2 p.m., before he went to work, and again at 3 a.m., when he was sure to be home.

In spite of my drinking problem, this was a time of great personal productiveness and interest in music for me. I had access to lucrative work, ample opportunities to learn from some of the best equipped musicians in the country, and lots of time to practice. I was both associating with classical musicians and playing and rehearsing with a big band under unique musician, writer, guitar player—and good friend—J. Roger (Brick) Fleagle. Fleagle was forever experimenting in interesting fashion with big bands. We rehearsed weekly and recorded at the Nola Studios, and I also played in small groups under his supervision, recording for the Hot Record Society (HRS). In these little bands were great players like Rex Stewart, Sandy Williams, Tab Smith, and Cecil Scott, but I can't vouch for the quality of some of the dates because we always started them by sharing several bottles of booze.

It was during this flurry of studio activity that my second daughter, Merrily, was born on July 10, 1944, at Flower Fifth Avenue Hospital. It was a very hot evening, and she came close to being born in a taxicab on the way to the hospital. As it was, she entered the world less than an hour later, with a Dr. Spielman attending. I saw her immediately after delivery and I'll never forget her eyes—they were brown to begin with, but I guess they had been dabbed with argarol and the dark brown medicine accentuated them to such an extent they looked like goggles on a bicycle rider.

Living with two children in the heart of Manhattan entails such obligations as assisting in the children's outings, so for some time it became the custom for us to push a baby carriage with one hand while holding four-year-old Suzanne by the other for the walk to the playground in Central Park. Between the playground, the lake, and the zoo a beautiful outdoor area was available to the residents of the neighborhood, and we soon became acquainted with many people who worked in the park, as well as the parents of other children taking advantage of the wonderful facilities near home.

The playground, in particular, became as much of a kibitzing place as any village square in a small town. Of course, many mothers—and fathers—would gather for the children's outings, and living in any area of New York for a length of time establishes acquaintances and friendships just the same as living anywhere else. You meet and visit with your neighbors in the same way, and naturally you meet people who follow a similar pattern of daily activities.

Since I was in the entertainment business, it also followed that we would make friends in related fields, and in Central Park we had many such friends. Oscar Levant, the pianist, was often there with his daughter, as were Rodney McClennon and his wife—singers and entertainers of note from the Broadway theater. Fred Allen's wife, Portland Hoffa, often came with her niece, her sister's daughter. Her sister's name was Laston Herskowitz, and the story circulated was that she had acquired the very unusual name of Laston by being the *last one* born in the family.

We also made friends in Central Park with Audrey Christie, who visited the playground with her daughter Chris. Audrey was married to movie actor Donald Briggs, who at the time was devoting most of his time to radio. He was the announcer for a program called "Death Valley Days," which started with a magnificent trumpet call, played by America's foremost classical trumpeter, Harry Glantz. Briggs had also been associated with Glenn Miller in the air force so we had mutual friends to talk about.

Our immediate neighbors with children were Mimi and Tony Pastusak, and Ed and Malvina Bush, all of whom became our very good friends. I have always been interested in woodworking, and Tony made it possible for me to enjoy this hobby whenever I could spare the time. He was the manager of a huge building, directly across the street from our apartment, which had a large subterranean basement where he maintained a workshop. He made this available to me during the years we lived there, and I could work on furniture and run power tools 24 hours a day without the noise bothering anybody. I could build things to my heart's content, and it was there I made the built-ins and furnishings for our apartment.

There were a lot of other friends too, like those who lived in the building next to ours—a Mrs. Hickey, her brother-in-law, a man named Arthur, and Tom MacGuffin and his family, with brother-in-law Cliff. And, some time during 1944, I helped Moe Zudicoff (known professionally as Buddy Morrow) get an apartment in our building, with the aid of a couple who lived two floors below us, Ann and Bob Klein. The building was operated through the office of Bob's father.

We lived in this area for about twenty years. One of the favorite meeting places was an automat around the corner on 57th Street, which was not only convenient for coffee klatch sessions, it came in handy for a fast dinner if you were not inclined to cook. My personal hangout was the Park Circle Bar, between 55th and 56th on Sixth Avenue. I became quite friendly with the owners, Max and Joe, and most of the people working there. Like many similar neighborhood places it did a big business for lunch. I ran a tab that usually totalled around $100 a week and I was a pretty steady bar customer. They were nice people and concerned about their customers. Once Joe even asked me to stop drinking so much in his place, especially during hot weather, because he was afraid I would keel over dead.

About the same time I started attending AA meetings, I was working a lot with Charlie Margulis, and Charlie began trying to interest me in Christian Science, giving me a lot of literature to read. Since he performed in much the same way as I did on the trumpet, I was interested in finding out how he managed to perform with such great confidence in the pinches. He went to great lengths, trying to explain and show me how he relied on and followed Christian Science reasoning, which had become his philosophy. Coincidentally I learned that my friends in AA, Rudy Pulitz and Florence Larsen, were also very interested in the Unity Movement. It was becoming pretty obvious that I had to develop some means of gaining confidence without resorting to alcohol. The spiritual aspect of AA is considered an important one of the twelve steps but AA doesn't suggest or care how, or in what manner, you find a power greater than yourself, merely that you seek some form of spiritual experience. I remember a man at an AA meeting saying he had been dry for eight months, but since he was an atheist he wasn't interested in seeking religion. Someone responded by pointing out that his eight months of sobriety was a spiritual experience in itself.

Now, I've never been the kind to run to the first church where I found a door open, and, in spite of my fairly regular attendance as a child in various Christian churches, I can't be classed as a follower of religion or of spiritual enlightenment. However, Florence gave me a small book written by a man named Emmett Fox, and even though I distinctly remember thinking, "Some other concepts for me to argue with," I found little room for argument in his writings and instead found myself attending his Sunday morning lectures at Manhattan Center. I always found these to be extremely worthwhile not only logical but, just as important to me, entertaining.

As a result of all this — the time devoted to the Unity Studies, the reading, and listening to Emmett Fox—I gradually started doing the daily lessons laid out by the Christian Science Quarterly. Now, I am not a Christian Scientist, nor am I a particularly religious person; I have too materialistic a character. I have smoked for many years, imbibed more than my share of alcohol, and, during a period of five years or more, I smoked pot morning, noon, and night. Still when I consistently read the science lessons nothing but good ever happened to me. In fact, on many occasions some really remarkable surprises came my way. It may be voodoo, it may be accidental, or it may be that the lessons tune one's actions, but whatever the case may be in all honesty I can say I have never seen it fail.

So why haven't I kept it up? Well, I guess the only reason I still don't is because I'm a lazy, head-strong idiot. Although it may also be that I felt a bit of a hypocrite, reading Christian Science lessons and then going out to have a drink, and consistently smoking tobacco, although I never found anything in the lessons that specifically said anything about not drinking or not smoking. Still it bothered me.

Then I met a wonderful lady, Ida Parr Oberhuber, who was a very good friend of Charlie Margulis's and a Christian Science practitioner. I met with her for quite a few years and found she had an unusually interesting approach to life. She was highly intelligent and viewed her studies with a broad perspective. I found that I could level with her and always get honest opinions and answers, so one day I inquired bluntly, "How can I do Christian Science lessons when half the time I reach for the bottle, I'm always smoking, and being loose in society may even shack up with a young lady on occasion?"

Her answer was in two parts, both of which seemed to fit the situation. First she suggested I continue to read the Bible on the one hand while balancing the jug with the other and see which won out in the long run; and then she said,

"If you were a saint, you wouldn't need any of it."

Needless to say, I had a great deal of respect for Charlie Margulis, but at the same time I was a bit envious of his ability to rely so much on his faith and beliefs. I really feel this is what gave him such a positive approach, not only in his daily life, but in his capacity to play confidently without aid of alcohol or other stimulants. He used his Christian Science to govern his life, even to the extent of not turning to doctors when he was ill but using his religion to overcome everything. In later years he became a reader in his church, and I'm convinced he took more pride in that than in any of his musical accomplishments.

A month or so before Charlie died, it became obvious that he was very ill, and some of his close friends suggested he seek medical help. But his answer was that he had lived his life by Christian Science beliefs, and if he were to go to doctors now and they decided to give him Materia Medica methods of treatment—shoot him full of medicine and confine him to a hospital—he would be denying everything he believed in. This would be so distasteful to him that it would be worse than passing on still keeping to those beliefs. You can't help but admire a man of such steadfast faith and sincerity—not to mention his great musical ability.

I was passing through a personal period of seeking help from anything that would give me more confidence as a performer and help me to conduct my life in a more orderly fashion, but I really can't say my life was all that black. It really wasn't. Living in a relatively small neighborhood, we were practically surrounded by nice, well-meaning people, and we enjoyed lots of social activities, expanding these further when pyramid clubs became popular and when the kids started school. Of course, this automatically involved us in a whole new sphere of living.

Our children went to P.S. 69, an elementary school on 54th between 6th and 7th Avenues (noted for having once been attended by Bernard Baruch), and Roberta became very active in the PTA. The president was Frederick Fox, the noted Broadway theatrical designer. He was a great guy and he gave me constructive tips and ideas about the hobbies I liked to mess around with—like using very thin mahogany plywood sheets for curved furniture and decorations, or utilizing a substance composed of whiting, plaster of paris, and glue over canvas which, when hardened, could create unusual shapes for building. I used to enlist some of my friends to play for the PTA bazaars and other affairs, and, much to the glee of all, we used the name "Pee Wee Erwin and the 69ers."

Malvina Carlin, one of our friends from the automat, married an ex-Marine named Ed Bush, who became a buddy of mine. Besides being a nice guy, Ed was one of the most creative and talented men I've ever known. During World War II, he had been a fighter pilot for a Marine wing stationed in the South Pacific. When he was off duty he collected rare and unusually colored woods. From these he hand-carved a number of extremely fine artistic creations that won numerous awards from museums after the War. One of these was an ebony pelican mounted on silver legs. Another was a figurine which utilized the natural contrast in the colors of the wood to accentuate the prominent parts of the female anatomy almost as though they were painted. Still another, in lignum vitae, was a rose bud of lifelike realism. Ed taught me lots of tricks in woodworking and finishing, for which I have been very grateful.

The Bush family also gave me one of the frights of my life. Ed was still in the Marine reserve, so sometimes he was required to be away for a week or two at a time, attending sessions at various Marine bases. Since we were good friends, I agreed to stay close at hand in case I had to drive his wife to the hospital when their baby was due. So naturally it was during one of these absent periods that I got a call from Malvina asking me to please pick her up quickly because she was afraid the baby was going to be born any minute. I rushed to the Bush apartment in a near panic for fear her estimate of the situation might be right, but we made the hospital in ample time. Nevertheless, I've always felt I played a vital role in the delivery.

THIRTY-THREE

WORLD WAR II ENDED in 1945, and it seemed to me like a good time to try my hand once more at leading a big band. Why the rush? Well, maybe I had some idea that if I could put a band together quickly and before all the other leaders reorganized, we had that much less competition on the road to success. I've never had much foresight, obviously, so I didn't realize that never again would there be such a thing as "business as usual" in the band business, that the day of the big bands was over. Yet I should have been able to read the handwriting on the wall because it was being scrawled in big red letters. MCA, for example, at one time the largest agency in the band-booking business, was quietly but quickly spreading out into other facets of the entertainment world. They were booking radio and screen stars and laying the groundwork for the next giant of the industry—television. Less and less of their work effort was being devoted to booking bands. Willard Alexander and Joe Glaser (Consolidated Booking) were still active, but they had the only really big names left in the field. Realistically, it was a lousy time to attempt organization of a band.

Nevertheless, I went ahead. I was in contact with several people who were interested in the formation of a band, who still had faith in the band business, and—I'm happy and grateful to say—faith in me. One was my very good friend Bernie Hanighen, who had helped me with my first big band and wanted to contribute now. Another very special friend, Lou Wagner, from Peoria, Ill., was the owner of several jewelry stores. He came to New York on business several times a year, had a strong interest in the entertainment business, and wanted to get into it as an investment, so with the provided funds I started the preliminaries of building a band.

I was using a saxophone player named Bill Hitz in my first band when it broke up in Kalamazoo. In 1946 he was in New York, so he became our lead alto man. Next I added two exceptional tenormen, Frank Socolow, and Al Epstein, as part of a six-man reed section—one chair for flute and clarinet only. Jessie Berkman played these utility parts, and the other reeds were Bill Vitale, alto, and Dave Kurtzer, baritone. In addition we had four trumpets, four trombones, one French horn, and three rhythm. Tiny Kahn, the drummer, also orchestrated special material for us, and so did Tony Aless, our pianist, and George Sirola, the bass player. We had a girl vocalist, Patti Cameron, sometimes joined by another marvelous singer, Phyllis Wood. Our male singer was again Billy Usher, who had been with my first band; he was a great vocalist and we were good friends. We also had a vocal quartet, organized and coached by the very talented Dave Lambert, and our chief arranger was Manny Albam, who wrote some very unusual charts for the band.

We started rehearsing two days a week at the Nola Studios at 51st and Broadway, and in a very short time we had a good library and a truly fine sounding band. It had a different feel and approach, though, than those I had worked with through the earlier decades. Rather than feeling it was necessary to remain on top of the beat in order to swing, as in the better of the block-chord bands, here there was a greater sense of relaxation which gave a freer form to the linear style of improvisation, which in 1946 was just becoming the vogue, as exemplified by the small bands in the Bop trend. For its time, the band had a very modern concept, and I found myself surrounded by ideas that were new to me and by young men who were creative and good players. The arrangers took good care of me by writing lines for me to play that fit the pattern of the band.

In a short time we were creating quite a bit of interest in musical circles. Manny Albam orchestrated his "Suite of Jazztone Poems," also called, "Nicotine Nocturnes," and these were equal to, or even ahead of, other contemporary music. They had titles like "Oom Paul," and "Flame Grain," and he incorporated mixed time values, such as 5/4, 6/4, and 3/2. In due time, of course, such things were to become accepted practice in the postwar bands of Woody Herman and Stan Kenton, but in 1946 they were great innovations.

There was plenty of interest on the part of the various booking agencies. Irv Brabech came over from MCA to hear us, and so did Cork O'Keefe. Plans were discussed, but the agencies were up in the air themselves and in a state of confusion regarding the future of the business. Most of the ballrooms, the backbone of the band bookings, were closed, theaters were no longer interested in bands and, as always, the financial commitment would have to be considerable. The latter was always a problem, even in the old days when the bands were riding high, but postwar costs were higher than ever and the risk was much greater.

On top of everything else I was trying to promote an 18-piece band, not to mention the vocal group. The cost was prohibitive from the start—so much so, that I couldn't interest any of the recording companies. I approached all of the major companies and then tried the minor ones. Although they concurred that the band had a lot of merit, and they all claimed they would have liked to have it on their label, they weren't willing to pay for it. Still, I'm convinced that the records would have sold well. Many of the people involved in writing material or performing as soloists went on to make excellent reputations—Dave Lambert and Manny Albam, for example. Their material was fresh, original, and in tune with the times and therefore salable, especially since these styles were coming into public favor, stimulated by people like Woody Herman and Dave Brubeck.

We used quite a bit of such original material, including vocals that used rhythmic phonetic singing. I recall one arrangement, in particular, by Dave Lambert, that was based on "How High the Moon," and used the then-current style of modern linear patterns. Tiny Kahn, our extremely talented drummer, wrote half-a-dozen originals, and so did Al Epstein and Tony Aless. Jack End, another great musician from the Eastman School of Music in Rochester, made two arrangements for us. One, a fine piece of music called "The Grass Is Greener," featured his coauthor and a most unique singer, Phyllis Wood, and the other was a piano solo with a Latin flavor, "Cloth of Gold."

All during the tenure of the band's existence, about a year, it was necessary for me to earn a living, which I was doing very nicely by working in the studios. But now, with the vast wisdom provided by hindsight, I see that the demands of my studio activities probably prevented me from devoting as much time as necessary to sell the band. Although this may have contributed to the ultimate decision to disband without ever getting off the ground, I honestly feel that we did give it an all-out effort, but circumstances beyond our control were too much to surmount. As I said earlier, it was a lousy time to start a band.

Our New York apartment, in those days when air-conditioning was still largely in the future, would get pretty uncomfortable in the summer, so Roberta looked around for a place to spend part of the summer where she and the children could escape the heat. She found a small apartment for rent near 115th Street in Rockaway Beach, and this worked out very well, because that summer after giving up the big band I had an easy schedule and was able to spend a lot of time at the beach with the family. I had four script shows which ran right through the summer months, but the earliest rehearsal started at 5 p.m. After the repeat broadcasts, which were over by 11:30, I could still catch a train to Rockaway. I remember the names of two of the shows, "Mr. and Mrs. North," and "Topper."

I began to play quite a bit with the Vincent Lopez orchestra, which played for many years at the Taft Hotel. This most likely evolved from the simple fact that our apartment was close by. Then, too, because I lived so close by and because the band had a Saturday broadcast at noon, very often a music publisher who had a tune he wanted introduced on the show would have Lopez call me to pick up the tune on Friday afternoon, then commission me to make a vocal-instrumental orchestration of it—literally score and copy all the parts overnight. Since the first rundown of the arrangement would be the actual broadcast, it made writing with accuracy a necessity, which was quite a challenge for a guy who was not essentially an orchestrator.

Nevertheless, Lopez seemed to like some of the orchestrations, because he asked me to arrange some Latin-flavored piano solos for him which he later recorded. One of them, I remember, was Victor Herbert's "Pan Americana."

It seemed a natural sequence that I began playing with the band on a regular basis in the spring of 1947 and worked with it for a few months—until alcohol got in the way of my reliability. It was quite a flexible band with good players—Irving Berger on lead trumpet, Tony Martell on fine jazz clarinet (one of the famous Martell brothers associated for many years with the Roseland and Arcadia ballrooms), and Joe Ortolano, a fine trombone soloist I knew from the early days when he worked with the Hank Biagini band.

Vincent Lopez was one of the pioneer big-band leaders, and even before Paul Whiteman's sensational rise to popularity, was considered one of the two or three most popular band leaders in America. I have heard that when Lopez was at the top Paul Whiteman hired away his manager, a man named Gillespie, who then became one of the powers behind Whiteman's meteoric rise to success.

L to R: Jack Fay, bass; Billy Maxted, piano; Cliff Leeman, drums; Andy Russo, trombone; Al Failla, clarinet; Pee Wee Erwin.

Personally, I found Vincent Lopez to be an extremely interesting man in many ways. For one thing, he was a numerologist, always making predictions for the future; for another, in spite of his age he had a very optimistic outlook on the future. He was instrumental in launching the careers of several stars and musical personalities, including that of Betty Hutton, who sang with the band and then went on to a very successful movie career. One of my lifelong friends, Bob Effros, was the lead trumpet player in the band when Lopez was at his peak in the Twenties, and the band manager of my day, Manny Hecklin, a man of splendid character, went on to a great career in the sports entertainment field. One Lopez saxophonist, Johnny Messner, has done very well in the TV radio jingle business.

The vocalists with Lopez were Chris Weston and Patti Dugan, both good friends of mine. Patti recorded two vocals with my jazz band in the early Fifties. It's my opinion that the most interesting arrangements in the Lopez library were written by pianist, Joe Cohen. As for Tony Martell, without any doubt he was one of the most sincere men I've ever known, and he spent a lot of his valuable time trying to convince me to stop my heavy drinking. Even in my soggy state, I was always very grateful for his interest and friendship.

THIRTY-FOUR

IN THE FALL of 1947 I resumed my full schedule in the studios. The "North" show was still running year around, without a seasonal break, and the Hildegarde show had resumed. In addition I started another program which proved to be very popular, "Duffy's Tavern," under the direction of Peter Van Steeden. I continued to work with Harry Sosnik on the transcription series he had had for many years, the "Treasury Bond Show," and to play on countless programmed music transcriptions made for radio stations under the direction of D'Artega.

I was pretty busy most of the time, but not too busy to squeeze in some very interesting single engagements. Among these was an occasional guest shot with the house band at Nick's, the famous jazz spot in Greenwich Village. At that time the band included Muggsy Spanier, Pee Wee Russell, Miff Mole, Al Casey, Gene Schroeder, and Joe Grauso—a great group that was fun to play with. I enjoyed these outings, but I have to admit that when the night was over I had usually consumed enough at the bar to offset whatever I was paid.

On the other hand, for me it was exposure in a new field of music that would eventually lead to a full-time small-band career—so it was great training! And I was pretty green, especially in the matter of the jazz repertoire; I was still heavily in the big-band and studio syndrome of playing, which means I had the mistaken concept that the higher I played the more I was saying. I only learned how wrong this idea was in later years, after I really got involved in the music. Another fault I had to fight in this context was utilizing too much technique, or, as it works out in practice, playing too many notes instead of a clean-cut lead, which leaves very litte room for fills by the clarinet or trombone. I still have to fight this tendency, I'm afraid, and it has led to some funny comments. My good friend Kenny Davern, for instance, has many times told me, "You're a frustrated clarinet player!" Andy Russo used to growl, "Get off my notes, you S.O.B. Why didn't you take up trombone?"

During this period traditional jazz was picking up in popularity. Besides Nick's, Eddie Condon had opened his own club on Third Street and was

214

doing very well with groups that included Wild Bill Davison and George Brunis. The Stuyvesant Casino had been going strong since the previous year and had revived New Orleans music by importing Bunk Johnson, George Lewis, Jim Robinson, and other early jazz masters. Eddie Condon's Town Hall concerts were beginning to draw well too.

Another unusual experience came my way at this point. Walter Smith, the second trumpet player with the Guy Lombardo band, became ill in the middle of a record date, and since I lived only a half block away from the Decca studios, they called me to fill in for him. It turned out to be a rather pleasant and interesting date. It was worthwhile to me just to watch the mechanics involved in the operation of this musical institution. My job was to follow Leibert Lombardo, who played lead trumpet, and the overall band direction was in the obviously capable hands of Carmen Lombardo. I was very impressed by the cooperative attitude of the musicians and their serious approach to the recording. I was well treated, both musically and financially, by Guy Lombardo, who paid me in person. I look back at it as a marvelous opportunity to meet and play with the most popular stylized band of all time and a group of very nice gentlemen.

All in all, it was a year of very interesting recordings. With Russ Case as the musical director, I played for Perry Como's recording of "If I Loved You," which was, I believe, his first really big record hit. I also recall a date with the McGuire Sisters, and I think it was their first recording.

I was still good friends with Billy Usher, who had been the featured vocalist in both of my big-band ventures. We had a number of interesting experiences together, but one episode was far from pleasant. One evening we decided it would be nice to visit the famous McSorley's Old Ale House, located on 7th Street between Second and Third Avenues. We were standing quietly at the bar, and next to me were two policemen in uniform having a glass or two of the splendid ale served there. It never occurred to me that cops were not supposed to be drinking on duty and I thought nothing of it. Some time later, with all the innocence of a friendly drunk, I asked one of them if I could hitch a ride uptown with them.

He gave me a hard look, but nodded his head and said, "All right, sure. Come on out with us." I followed him out of the door and had no sooner reached the sidewalk than he turned on me and threw a punch that hit me a glancing blow on the side of the face, knocking me flat. Like an idiot then, I raised my head to see what had happened, just in time for the cop to kick me square in the forehead with the toe of his boot. Then he took off down the street with his partner.

I was still conscious, and when I saw them leave I managed to get to my feet just as a huge man came out of McSorley's and stopped still to stare at me in surprise. He was perfectly innocent, of course, but at that moment, my friend Billy came out and saw him standing there, took in the spectacle of me bleeding from cuts on my head, and jumped to the wrong conclusion. Billy, who isn't a big man, glared at the man and hauled back his fist. "You can't do that to my friend!" he yelled—but before he could throw the punch the big man retaliated with a fast left hook. If the blow had really connected Billy would have gone down like a bowling pin, but instead the fist just grazed the side of Billy's face, and the big man was caught off balance and fell down. Then he made the same mistake I had made earlier. Instead of staying down, he started to get up. He was on his knees, almost in a praying position, with his face looking up, when Billy parted his hair with a beer bottle. The man's scalp was cut and he started to bleed, but he went out like a light. Billy and I took off like a pair of scared rabbits, only to have Billy spend the rest of the night calling Bellevue Hospital every fifteen minutes to find out if the man had been brought in.

That year brought other experiences—of a more pleasant nature, fortunately. Through my good friend Bernie Hanighen, the songwriter ("The Dixieland Band," "Lute Song"), I was introduced to a group of people from the theater. I met Michael Meyerberg and his wife, Adrienne. Mike had taken an American youth orchestra, under the direction of Leopold Stokowski, on a tour of South America, and he had also produced a number of Broadway shows and reviews. Adrienne was a very good singer who was interested in working in supper clubs, and her mother was famous Metropolitan Opera contralto Madame Metzenhauer, a very charming lady who favored us on a couple of occasions with some songs. Adrienne wanted me to put together a suitable musical group for her accompaniment.

So I had some arrangements made of the standard material she wanted to do, things like "Alone Together," and "You Go To My Head," plus a few instrumental selections, for a rather unusual chamber music group. The combination included two violins, one viola, a cello, string bass, one French horn, an oboe, piano, and drums, and it turned out to be a very nice background unit for vocals. But all it generated was a lot of social fun for my wife and me at various parties where we met some interesting people; we certainly didn't make any musical history.

With the advent of 1948, the first real action began in the new entertainment medium of television, though only a few of the studios were equipped for it. The third floor at NBC had a few, plus a couple on the sixth floor, and CBS was starting to use the playhouse they had on 54th Street and the big studio facing Broadway, between 53rd and 54th.

My first involvement was with Joel Herron at NBC. Those were the days when all of the white shirts had to be blue, because blue photographed white on camera. We were made up with blue make-up, and every show had a variety show format because situation shows were still to come. Dumont Broadcasting was probably the most active at the time since they were the ones most interested in selling TV sets. I think it was then or a little later they launched the first Jackie Gleason shows. The first show I remember doing was in the NBC studios in Radio City and, shortly after that, I played another at the Pathe' studios at 106th and Park Ave. These were with Joel Herron and the first times I played with my good friend Bobby Rosengarden, who was doubling at the Copacabana, the big Broadway nightclub. Off the air at 9 p.m., we would ride down Park Ave. with Bobby so he could make his

216

first show at the Copa at 10 p.m.

That same year the Meyer Davis office came up with an unusual job at the Avila Hotel in Caracas, Venezuela, to run for eight days, Christmas Eve through New Year's Eve. A few of us decided to take the gig for the fun and adventure of it. Since we were going out of the country to South America, we had to undergo all of the preliminaries—passports, visas, smallpox shots, and attendance at a couple of briefing sessions at the Venezuelan consulate— before we could get started. The group was under the capable but serious-minded direction of a young conductor named Tony Cabot. We had four saxes (including Tony), one trumpet (me), and four rhythm (George Hines, a great singer-entertainer-guitarist, Al Seidel on drums, Tommy Abruzzo on bass, and Lester Sims, a very bright imp, played piano). Danny Lapidos, a great guy who was always good for a lot of laughs, was also in the company.

We took off from Idlewild Airport (now Kennedy) on December 23rd with the temperature down around zero. The plane was one of those old reliable Costellations, with a scheduled stop in Puerto Rico where we landed about 3 a.m., with just enough time to buy a fifth of rum. The booze was especially welcome because we had been flying through a snowstorm for most of the trip from New York. By contrast, Puerto Rico's warm climate and rum were a delight. After Puerto Rico we were on the way to La Guaira, the port for Caracas (with a short stop in Aruba), so the natural step for a bunch of musicians was to break out instruments and have a jam session. We had a group of pipefitters on board who immediately joined the session by beating time on the sides of the plane and whatever else was handy, so the Christmas celebration got off to an early start.

But when we arrived in La Guaira around 8 a.m., we were promptly told that a revolution was in progress in Venezuela, and we were detained in customs for an extra long time while the authorities went through our belongings with a fine-tooth comb. We never were told what they expected to find. Adding to the discomfort of the situation was the presence of numerous soldiers armed with old Springfield rifles who gave the impression they didn't know what to do with them.

At first we didn't realize the full import of the situation or how it would affect us so we weren't very worried. We were happy in the false security of numbers, enjoying the spirit of adventure, and generally having a lot of laughs and a good time. Finally we were allowed to board cars for the 27-mile drive to Caracas—over the most dangerous highway I have ever had the misfortune to be on anywhere. From La Guaira you immediately start climbing into the northern Andes Mountains, over winding roads with sheer drops on either side that I estimated to be at least a few thousand feet. It's very rugged country, and the drivers, instead of slowing down for curves or for passing another car, just honk the horn more often and louder and pass on hills at breakneck speeds. It soon becomes obvious that the best driver is the one with the loudest horn who blows it most often. On the other hand, to be fair and make certain we were relieved from fear and worry, our driver told us that if a car went off the road and fell the one or two thousand feet, it was next to impossible to do anything about it and it would simply remain at the bottom of the valley. Verifying this information, about half way to Caracas we passed a stone monument with an auto which had gone over mounted on the top. This pinpointed quite vividly the fact that there was no sense in worrying about a car that went off the road or about being rescued afterwards—there wasn't enough left to save. It was most reassuring.

We arrived at our hotel, "The Avila," at about 4 p.m., and the management informed us that we would be able to play a full night only on Christmas Eve and on New Year's Eve, because of the revolution. For the rest of our week's engagement we were scheduled to play in the dining room from 7 to 9 p.m. Only the people checked into the hotel would be there as patrons and, again due to the revolution, there weren't many of these. Anyway, since a 6 p.m. curfew was in effect, except for Christmas Eve and New Year's Eve, nobody except the hotel guests would be able to attend our scheduled nightly performances.

The 7 to 9 set-up was fine with us, except for one thing. The hotel management insisted we have dinner before performing, and we didn't mind that either. The problem was that dinner was usually about six courses long and wasn't served until 7 p.m.—so if we hurried up to finish dinner, there might even be a few minutes left to play a little music.

Before I tell you how things worked out, I should describe the hotel. We were given to understand it had been built as a vacation spot catering mainly to Americans employed by various companies in Venezuela. It was located about half way up the side of a rather high mountain. The front of the hotel, mostly glass and mahogany, overlooked the city of Caracas, a beautiful panorama at night. The rooms were spacious and luxurious, and each one had a wall made up entirely of sliding glass doors that opened on a grass-covered patio that ran the entire length of the hotel. Each room presented a magnificent view of the mountains. Add to all this an average year-round temperature of 70° F. and you have the makings of Paradise.

Our only full performances were to be on Christmas Eve and New Year's Eve, from approximately 7 p.m. until 3 a.m., and we would be playing in an outdoor dining room that was illuminated by beautiful varicolored lights. Since we had arrived around 4 p.m. on December 24th, we had only three hours to check in, unpack, and dress for our formal opening—the Christmas Eve performance—so we didn't waste any time getting to it. I had unpacked, showered, and was in the process of assembling my formal attire when I heard a knock at the door. My roommate, Lester Sims, was still in the shower so I answered. When I opened the door I found a very handsome gentleman in full dress who immediately smiled broadly, bowed deeply, and addressed me in Spanish.

I didn't understand a word he said, so I ushered him into the room and to a chair, excused myself in sign language, and made my way out through the sliding glass doors and down the patio to the next room which was occupied by Tony Cabot and George Hines—the one member of the band who spoke Spanish. I told them about my visitor, and they returned with me and introduced themselves to my Spanish-speaking friend. Tony told

George to ask him what we could do for him, and George put the question to the man in Spanish. The answer caught us all by surprise.

"He says he is our radio announcer, and since we go on the air at 7 p.m., he would like to talk over the program."

Tony was horrified. This was the first he had heard of any radio show. "Here we are in a new country," he moaned to me, "with a band that has never played together, and now they expect us to make up a radio show!" He thought for a minute and then said, "Well, we'll just have to make the best of it. We'll work up about a half hour of standards we can probably sound pretty decent on, and we can routine it on the air." Then he told George Hines, "Ask the man how long we're on the air."

The handsome gentleman, still all smiles, answered George promptly, and George just as promptly relayed the startling news to Tony that the program would last five hours.

"*Five* hours!"

Cabot really went into shock, because if he's nothing else he's a perfectionist, and here he had a collection of musical strangers in an even stranger country facing a five-hour broadcast which would surely have a lot of listeners because it was Christmas Eve. We feverishly went about trying to line up five hours of music that might sound passable, while Tony sweated in a near-panic. It wasn't until we were actually on the bandstand that we discovered we could get by with playing a normal dance set and the station would fill time with records until the next regular set. The language barrier sure played havoc with understanding.

After this rough start, it turned out that the engagement proved to be a first-class party for the band. On the two full nights we played, Christmas Eve and New Year's Eve, the biggest table in the dining room, fully stocked with food and drink, was reserved for the band. Our regular meals were also an experience to remember. We usually had to have George Hines or Tommy Abruzzo (who understood Italian so he handled Spanish fairly well) read the menu for us. It's the only one I have ever seen where at least seven entrees were listed for breakfast, and a lot more for lunch or dinner. Due to the curfew and the revolution—which didn't seem to interfere with us any—the hotel had very few guests, so the band received VIP treatment at all times. On Christmas Day they had a punch bowl that was at least three feet in diameter and full of the best brandy eggnog I've ever tasted—and practically nobody to drink it.

We were free to roam the city during the day time, and most of us had some nice experiences as well as a few rather unusual ones. One day I was stood up against a wall by a soldier in officers' uniform while he carefully examined my passport. He let me go after a few minutes. My most novel experience came about when I was sitting in a downtown Caracas bar trying a few of the local libations. I was joined by a young man who spoke some English and was in the process of trying to drown his sorrows. After we had shared a few drinks, he got the message across to me that he had just lost his wife and was about to go to her funeral. He showed me his wife's picture and those of his three children, and, after I expressed the appropriate sympathy, he invited me to attend the funeral. So I marched behind the hearse with the mourners and was well on the way to the cemetery when Tony Cabot came along and pulled me out of line.

Revolution or no revolution, the trip turned out to be a lot of fun and we thoroughly enjoyed ourselves. On the way home on January 2nd our plane again stopped in Puerto Rico. We had a couple of hours before take-off, so Danny Lapidos and I decided to take a cab into San Juan to see the sights. We visited an amusement park and had a look at the capitol building—and on our return to the airport we were no end surprised to see our plane at the end of the runway, about to take off without us. After much arm waving, screaming, and contacting the control tower, we finally succeeded in getting the plane to turn around and come back for us—otherwise we might still be waving our arms on the runway. Still, when we got back to New York, gripped solidly in ice and snow, that 90° runway didn't seem so bad after all.

Shortly after my South American adventure, I began doing a considerable amount of transcription work for a relatively small advertising agency from Schenectady, N.Y., called "Nelson Ideas." It was run by a very successful salesman, George Nelson, and he lined up such extremely lucrative accounts as Sealtest, St. Joseph's Aspirin, O'Cedar Products, General Electric. We made an extended series of advertising transcriptions for them, and I made a great deal of money working for this agency. George and I became personal friends. Later on, he handled the Mohawk Rug account when I was fronting the jazz band at Nick's, and he placed me in some very good TV shows.

THIRTY-FIVE

IN 1949 ROBERTA and her friends began visiting the studio of Charles Melohs, an artist, whose place at 56th between Madison and Park was about three long blocks from our apartment. She and her friends were interested in the modern works of this painter, and she insisted I go along on a visit to one of his informal showings. She pushed me into it, with the result that I became very friendly with Melohs and he offered to teach me to paint. He gave me a list of materials to acquire, and I began regular visits to his studio where he introduced me to this beautiful form of self expression. Right from the start, it was no secret that I would never become an artist, but from that point forward and for several years I enjoyed Melohs's company, his instruction, and his relaxed philosophy toward life.

Action in the TV studios began to pick up around then, and my old friend Lou Shoobe was able to place me with the orchestras working several of the early CBS shows. For a time I worked a TV version of Ken Murray's "Blackouts," and also a program called "The 54th Street Revue," with an orchestra conducted by Harry Sosnik. This was a variety show, MC'd at first by comedian Jack Carter, then Al Bernie, and Jack Sterling, who was new in New York. On these shows I worked with my old friends Bob Cusumano and Charley Butterfield, as well as other brass players I felt comfortable with.

I was also involved in a couple of unusual recording sessions. One, for Decca with Frank Luther, resulted in an album for children called "Songs of Safety." These were cute little tunes composed by Irving Caesar, with lyrics warning children not to chase a ball into the street, not to play with matches, and advising against other dangers common to young children. I understand the album was used by every elementary school in New York State to help teach safety to children. Another album for youngsters featured "Tubby the Tuba," by composer George Kleinsinger. There were also a couple of dates with my old buddies Yank Lawson and Bob Haggart for Decca Records, and a TV show featuring Kate Smith and directed by Ray Block which gave me a chance to play again with Andy Ferretti.

Professionally I had little cause for complaint. I was making the transition from radio to TV without a hitch, still active in the recording studios, and working as much as I was able. But domestically I was in trouble, and my marriage to Roberta was sagging badly.

Without any question, Roberta had put up with a great deal. She had tolerated my self-centered alcoholic life to the breaking point, not to mention that the normal requirements of a musician's life left her pretty much on her own for entertainment and social contacts. She loved to dance and, with my approval, she and a number of friends—very nice people with a mutual interest in dancing—often went to Roseland Ballroom. Roberta had even entered some dance contests there and taken some lessons in ballroom dancing.

I saw nothing wrong in her going to Roseland. On the other hand, I expected her to pay her own way in, confine her socializing and dancing to the dance floor, and then come home alone. This was probably expecting too much, now that I think back about it. She had a couple of near-romances, probably the logical result of my lack of interest in her affairs, and I'll admit I may even had considered she was entitled to them. Of course, you may say that's no way to run a railroad, but then you have to keep in mind that she had stuck by me through some very tough psychological crises. In all fairness, I couldn't bring myself to be too critical of her when the shoe was on the other foot. Still it is inevitable that children suffer some neglect in these situations, and in spite of the fact that we always had baby sitters, I couldn't feel comfortable about a mother sleeping very late, leaving two small children to keep quiet in order not to disturb her and to entertain themselves in a small apartment. I hope that doesn't sound like harsh criticism; it is a statement of a not-too-happy situation.

With the arrival of summer, we again took an apartment at Rockaway and for awhile this alleviated the situation. I did my usual commuting during the lighter summer schedule at the studios, and we were able to spend time at the beach, eat clams on the half-shell, drink beer, and enjoy the Irish dancing, which is one of the attractions at Rockaway. Then, for some reason, I went into one of my classic drunks. Afterwards, while trying to sober up, I started to suffer through one of those terrible nervous sweats. I was lying on a bed with a cool ocean breeze blowing over me while perspiration oozed from every pore as my body tried to throw off the alcoholic poison, and I came up with a severe bronchial infection and completely lost my voice. For a long period after the summer was over I was still barely able to whisper.

Naturally, I was worried. Roberta was worried. For awhile, it seemed nothing could help. The fall came and we were into November and I still had no voice. Then my mother called from Nebraska and spoke to me through Roberta. She said she had heard about my condition, that my Aunt Hazel and Uncle Harry were visiting in Falls City so why didn't I come out and drive back with them to their home in Arizona to see if the climate change would help my problem.

It seemed like a good suggestion, so I took a plane to Kansas City. With characteristic forethought, I figured that since I was going to Arizona I wouldn't need any warm clothes. The temperature in Kansas City was 3°

below zero when I got there, and all I had was light summer clothes, so I froze all the way to Falls City. The next day we left for Arizona—not only my aunt and uncle, but my grandparents.

Uncle Harry owned and operated a very beautiful motel in the country club district of Phoenix, and in the winter months the area was mainly populated by retired people who were escaping to the warm climate. It worked magic for me. In about three days my voice completely returned, and from there on I had a great time playing canasta every night for three weeks with some of the fine people who were staying at my uncle's motel, even being invited on several desert safaris by my uncle's friends. When I returned to New York I felt like a new man.

As 1949 eased into 1950 I was doing rather well in the studios. I still had all my regular shows, and had just started a Saturday night TV program called "The Show of Shows," which starred Sid Caesar and Imogene Coca, under the direction of Charles Sanford. I was well acquainted with the contractor for the show, Aaron Levine, and had worked some dates with him where he played guitar and banjo. This was a highly rated show and the general opinion was that it would run for some time. Nevertheless, it's a standard pattern in our business, sort of an unwritten rule, that if you are busy someone else is sure to call, and now some circumstances were taking shape that would have a long-term influence on my career.

Phil Napoleon had been playing at Nick's, the famous landmark for jazz in Greenwich Village, for a very long run and he decided he wanted some time off. The management had to find a replacement. I knew very little about the club's operation or the kind of music required, except that over a period of years I had occasionally appeared as a guest soloist there and at Eddie Condon's place on W. 3rd Street. I had also performed as a guest at the Stuyvesant Casino—home of the Bunk Johnson-George Lewis Band— which was operated by an impresario named Bob Maltz. In addition, once in awhile I played at the Central Plaza (under the aegis of Jack Crystal and Bernie Burns), something of a unique experience in itself. Every Friday and Saturday night at least 800 young people would gather there for a jam session. The most popular attractions were trombonist Conrad Janis and pianist Willie "the Lion" Smith, and Jack Crystal—one of the best friends jazz musicians ever had—would make up bands to back his stars. Over a period of time he probably managed to use every musician ever associated with jazz, and I believe he often went out of his way to find musicians who needed the jobs for subsistence, filling in his bands with those who financially needed help. (The Central Plaza and Stuyvesant Casino were the only places where I ever had the opportunity to play on the same program as the George Lewis Band.)

Still, it must have been as a result of these guest appearances that the management of Nick's decided to see if I would be interested in taking over for Phil Napoleon on a regular basis. And I must admit I liked the idea, especially since it would involve very little interference with my studio work. The music didn't start at Nick's until 9:30 p.m., so I could continue to do almost everything I was doing in the studios—with one exception. I would have to give up "The Show of Shows." I didn't see this as any great sacrifice. Without a crystal ball, how was I to know this show would become so successful or that it would result in most of the members of the orchestra going on NBC staff, some of them doing the early versions of "The Tonight Show?" However, let me add immediately that I have never for a second regretted my move.

Stepping into Phil Napoleon's shoes wasn't all that simple though. His background went back to The Memphis Five and other early jazz bands, and to me he has always been one of the great authorities on the music and tunes generally tagged "dixieland," for want of a better name. And I was expected to front his band, work in the formula he had developed, and do all this in a club known across the country as the "Eastern Home of Dixieland Jazz." To be honest, I didn't know more than a half dozen of the tunes in the dixieland idiom, which is nothing unusual for big-band and studio musicians. Furthermore, Pete Grant, who had been selected by Mrs. Rongetti to manage Nick's, was a jazz fan who really knew the music, so I couldn't go in as the leader of a dixieland band and play "Back Home Again In Indiana" all night.

My savior and musical mentor was my good friend Billy Maxted, who played piano in the band. The band, of course, didn't use charts—it would have ruined the illusion of an improvising jazz band, but I had to have some kind of guide in the beginning, so Billy wrote out the leads for about 30 of the most-often played tunes. We placed them behind the intermission piano in front of the bandstand, where I could read them but the audience couldn't see them. In short order I had them memorized and from there on it was easy sailing, so thanks to Billy Maxted I became a dixieland trumpet player.

Nick Rongetti had founded the club and given it his name. At this time it was run by his widow, Grace, one of the nicest ladies anyone ever met. Under no circumstances would she allow anything out of line to take place in the club, and as a result it became one of the most respected jazz clubs of all time. Nothing suggestive or crude was tolerated, and parents, knowing this, allowed their youngsters to patronize the place. It was always a nice feeling to have a parent call the club and ask for his or her son or daughter. People were made to feel at home and they became a part of the family at Nick's. I never ceased to marvel at the diversity of our audiences; we would have longshoremen sitting next to members of the United Nations, with every strata of society in between. All were treated equally well; nobody rated special favors. I remember one night when Milton Berle was turned away because no table was available.

The maitre d' in charge of all operations was Jack Russell. Jack was born in Greenwich Village and went to work for Nick Rongetti when Nick opened his first club. Jack had literally thousands of friends, and Grace Rongetti was very fortunate to have a trusted lieutenant who was also extremely efficient at running the place. I still meet people who ask about him.

224

The management insisted the music follow the dixieland pattern for each of the seven sets we played each night. A typical set might include such tunes as, "Original Dixieland One-Step," "I Wish I Could Shimmy Like My Sister Kate," "Satanic Blues," "If I Had You," and Runnin' Wild." We played requests as long as they fit into the format—which they usually did—and avoided as long as possible playing the overworked "Muskrat Ramble," and "When the Saints Go Marching In." "Saints" in particular was a problem because for some reason after it was played, the clients decided they had heard all they came to hear and the club would empty out.

As most jazz fans know, Nick's enjoyed a wide reputation and was part of a jazz tradition, so it was quite an honor for me to follow the jazz greats who had graced the bandstand there over the years. The club first opened in the Thirties, across the street from the final location (7th Avenue and Bleecker Street). The first band I ever heard there was that of the legendary Sharkey Bonano from New Orleans. Sharkey always had a good band and he was a great entertainer. I also remember Sunny Russin—Babe and Jack's sister—playing intermission piano, usually joined by Gladys Moser, another good pianist and a very nice person.

When Nick's moved across the street into the spanking new building that was Nick's pride and joy, Bobby Hackett's fine little band was the first to play there. Eddie Condon's groups were frequently on the bandstand before he opened his own place. He was always surrounded by great jazzmen—Pee Wee Russell, Wild Bill Davison, George Brunis, Rod Cless, Chelsea Quealey, Miff Mole, Muggsy Spanier.... The list is illustrious but too long to review in entirety except to mention that among the great piano players were Dave Bowman, Joe Sullivan, and Gene Schroeder.

Part of the tradition were the many stories associated with the place. It was said that the angle-iron railing was built around the bandstand to keep Pee Wee Russell from sitting on the rail, and a customer once described the front line of Muggsy, Pee Wee, and Miff Mole, as a cocker spaniel, a tired Mack Sennett comedian, and a retired dentist. Who knows how many of the stories are true, or how much they came to be expanded with the telling, but true or false they're interesting. For example, there's the one about Nick and the animal trophies. Nick was understandably proud of his club and its decor. One day he was offered a bargain in stuffed animal heads which he immediately decided would make striking wall decorations for the club. It wasn't until after he had bought them that he found out the trophies were packed with cement and so heavy he had to have the walls reinforced to hold them.

But Nick was a shrewd businessman too. At the outbreak of World War II it didn't take long for such niceties of life as good scotch to grow scarce, and in no time at all liquor distributors were demanding that buyers purchase two cases of rum in order to get one of scotch. Anticipating something of the kind, Nick is reputed to have laid in $250,000 worth of scotch in his storeroom.

Pee Wee Russell played at Nick's for so long and in so many bands he

225

was almost a fixture. He is reported to have shown up for work one night in an attitude of extreme dejection, announcing that his mother had passed away. Everybody loved Pee Wee and felt sorry for him, so they took up a collection and by the end of the night there was quite a sizable sum to give him as token of their respects. However, several months later Pee Wee showed up very dejected with the announcement that his mother had passed away. Obviously, it didn't work the second time!

Another story goes that one night a frustrated and rejected girlfriend climbed up on the bandstand and stuck a knife into Miff Mole's back, which must have been very disconcerting, to say the least.

In any case, Nick was a real friend to jazz musicians, keeping plenty of them going when things were rough. He also helped establish many big reputations. At one time he hired the great boogie woogie piano team of Meade Lux Lewis and Albert Ammons—then moved in a third piano so he could play along with them. Reports on his artistry at the keyboard were never very impressive, but nobody could fault the big grin that he always wore when he was playing, positive indication he was having a great time.

The King Cole Trio was another intermission group, and Sidney Bechet fronted still another. Guest nights were Tuesdays in the early Forties, and the guests always ran a tab at the bar. I can remember playing with Muggsy and the boys and drinking away my night's salary on the tab.

It was a sad day for music when Nick passed away in 1946, but Grace Rongetti continued to run the club for many years and she always maintained to the letter the format that Nick had laid out.

THIRTY-SIX

THE BAND I LED at Nick's in 1950 was quite good in its style, which was mainly patterned on the work of Billy Maxted. Billy and I are really very different in personality. He's exuberant, full of steam, and a hard worker on the bandstand, while I'm a take-it-easy guy. But the band had been going along well under Phil Napoleon, utilizing the routines and arrangements (head) laid out by Billy, so even if I had the know-how to make changes (which I didn't), it only made sense to continue with the successful format. Anyway, it was Billy who acquainted me with the library necessary to carry the job, and he was the one who kept adding new material in order to maintain interest. By following Maxted's format, it was only necessary for the two new members of the band to learn the parts. (The other new member was Cliff Leeman, to my mind, one of the greatest time-keepers of all time.)

All of the guys in the band were seasoned and experienced musicians. Billy Maxted, from Racine, Wisconsin, had been a navy fighter pilot during the war and a flight instructor at Pensacola. In his formative years he had idolized Bob Zurke, the pianist with the Bob Crosby band, at one time rooming with him—so it wasn't surprising that some of the Crosby Bobcats styling showed up in Billy's work. I once asked him how he had developed his piano style, which is a fast-moving series of phrases, and he answered, "Look how short my fingers are. I can't play wide-stretching chords, so I had to pattern my style to suit my physical make-up." This also made him a master of such piano styles as boogie woogie, and tunes like "Gin Mill Special," and "Little Rock Getaway." Before coming to Nick's, he had worked and arranged for Red Nichols and also scored for Benny Goodman and Claude Thornhill.

After Billy and I had been together a few years we happened to be in Columbus, Ohio, where we made some good friends at North American Aviation. Billy expressed interest in flying a jet plane—still relatively new at the time—so these friends accommodated him. They gave him a briefing and then turned him loose in a jet. Afterwards, he told me how scared he was, afraid that because of the great speed of the plane he would go too far too soon and get lost. Then, when he solved that problem and landed back at the

227

field, he opened the side panels too quickly with the chance of filling them with dust, an unacceptable procedure.

Cliff Leeman, essentially a big-band drummer with the fantastic ability to impart a big-band feel to a small jazz band, which adds a lot of fullness to the sound, came from Portland, Maine. He first left there to go on the road with Danny Murphy's Musical Skippers, a band that played the circuits of the early 1930s. Later he was with the classic Artie Shaw band of 1938, put in considerable time with Charlie Barnet, and worked with me in the Tommy Dorsey band. He is a rock-steady swing drummer, and has that faculty I always found so outstanding with Dave Tough and Jo Jones of making a band soloist play better than his capabilities seem to be.

Our clarinetist was Phil Olivella. He had a magnificent sound and never lost that quality in any register, was an excellent jazz player, and knew our repertoire perfectly.

Andy Russo, the trombonist, had the most full-bodied sound in the low register (important in the dixieland pattern) I have ever heard in a jazz band. His sound retained the quality and roundness of a true trombone tone at all times, was never raucous or raspy, and added a lot to the musical quality of the ensemble. Will Bradley, something of a virtuoso on the instrument in his own right, once remarked that if Andy had chosen to play bass trombone he could have been accepted into any symphony orchestra in the country. Andy was born in Brooklyn, N.Y., and had received excellent classical training in the music departments of the parochial schools, something he shared in common with quite a few of the early jazz band musicians like Phil Napoleon, Frank Signorelli, Jimmy Lytell (originally Sarapede), and Miff

Bobby Hackett

Mole. Andy had his own jazz band during the Twenties, contemporary with Phil Napoleon's Memphis Five and The Indiana Five. He played in the Balconades Ballroom and the Cinderella Ballroom before joining Mal Hallet's band to tour the New England circuit. I first worked with him in the studios and for short periods with Freddy Martin and Ray Noble.

Andy loved to drink and could hold it well, but his trademark on the bandstand was his cockeyed sense of humor. If the mood struck, he would march up and down wearing a funny hat and, when the audience laughed, tell them, "You're only jealous because you are not a bum." Or during a period of comparative quiet would abruptly announce: "The band drinks!—Anything!"

Jack Fay, our bass player, was a quiet man from Boston who had spent several years with the very successful Vaughn Monroe Orchestra. During the war, he was in the infantry, and afterwards he freelanced around New York until joining Phil Napoleon. He was an excellent and powerful bass player who supported the band very well, and, in spite of his reserve, he had a great sense of humor. His forte was a gift for understatement that could break me up. In the middle of a radio broadcast, playing one of our hell-bent-for-election ride-out choruses, Jack would look up at me and with a deadpan expression inquire, "Interesting, isn't it?"

I must mention at this point that Hank Duncan, the man who played intermission piano between the band sets at Nick's, was not only a fine pianist but a great man with an illustrious career both as a soloist and with bands. He made some of those great records with Sidney Bechet in the early Thirties. And we always had fun with Hank. When the crowd was large enough to warrant it, we had a number called "Railroad Man," which Hank did with us. The ensemble would start things, and then, after a couple of choruses, the rhythm section would take over in backing Maxted and Duncan as they built chorus after chorus on the tune to a climax where the band would again come in for the grand finale. This always brought cheers and yells from the audience and was a great flag-waving end for a set when the club was full.

I have never been able to understand why, with all the publicity and exposure our band received, we were not more sought after by outside people. We had five remote broadcasts a week on the Mutual Network (a half hour each), and also made several Armed Forces Radio broadcasts for listening all over the world. At that time the Mutual Network included 544 radio stations and was the world's largest. Then another big break came our way that should have brought about greater results than it did.

George Nelson, my advertising friend, for whom I had made the transcriptions for Sealtest, O'Cedar, and others, came up with the Mohawk Carpet account and a show headed by singer Roberta Quinlan, which followed the very popular "Kukla, Fran, and Ollie," on the full NBC television network at 7:15 p.m. Due to an illness or some other misfortune in Miss Quinlan's affairs, George arranged for our band to fill in on three different occasions. There we were, on a full network show, in the most prime-time slot anybody could ask for and following one of the most popular shows on TV, and we had very little response to what we had reason to believe were pretty good shows. I've never been able to figure it out—except that maybe not many people were interested in jazz bands in 1950-51. Oh, yes! We also made six records that were released on the King label—standards like "Wolverine Blues," "Tiger Rag," and "The Saints."

In addition to working at Nick's I was still active in studio work which, in spite of the fact that Nick's paid me a very good salary, I wanted to keep. I imagine we all have a tendency to push for a higher gross income, particularly when we have families to support. Anyway, I was still doing some script shows. "Mr. & Mrs. North" ran for twelve years—quite a respectable track record—and I was also working the Hildegarde show under Harry Sosnik, with whom I also made a number of transcriptions. Record dates were plentiful, and on Saturdays, for quite an extended period, I played on a show called "The Four Star Review," which used a new comedian each week. Danny Thomas and Jimmy Durante were regulars.

Putting all this activity together made for long working hours. The night's work at Nick's ran from 9:30 p.m. to 4 a.m. on Tuesdays through Fridays, and from 9:30 p.m. to 3 a.m. on Saturdays. On Sundays, there was an afternoon session from 4 p.m. to 8 p.m., and then the regular stint from 9:30 p.m. to 4 a.m.— altogether, a pretty long time to be standing up and playing. I used to estimate my week as having two 15-hour days, four 11-hour days, and one day (Monday) to recuperate. I considered myself strong enough to weather the storm, but there were times when benzedrine played a big part in helping me get through the week.

Needless to say, except to sleep I wasn't home very much. By the time I started at Nick's, in fact, my marriage to Roberta had deteriorated considerably, and to a large extent we were living our lives apart. There wasn't a great deal of animosity between us, but we were a long way from having a close-knit family life. We were people of vastly different likes and dislikes, and there's no question but what I was very hard to live with because of my singular concentration on music and my own interests to the neglect of ordinary domestic duties.

With my blessings Roberta started doing more of the things she liked to do. In the main, she loved to dance. This in itself is fine, except it isn't something that is likely to bring a musician and his wife closer together for the simple reason that most musicians I know can't dance at all, or if they do they're pretty bad at it. That is how things stood when, in the fall of 1950, I met a very unusual young lady at Nick's and became more than just casually interested. It's pretty difficult to explain why one person is attracted to another, but I began to invite this girl to dinner and we quickly developed a close relationship. Her name was Jean Tracey, and she became my most important activity at Nick's to the extent that the only thing left to do was introduce her to Roberta and explain that I was serious about the young lady. However, there was another obstacle to be overcome—a slight drawback I chose to ignore for awhile—she was 19 and I was 37. Her family took an understandably dim view of this.

As far as Roberta was concerned, there was no problem. She admitted she was interested in a man named William Gavin and was quite willing to call it quits. So it was decided that the best resolution to the situation was for her to take up residence in Florida for six months, the time necessary to establish residency and obtain a Florida divorce, since the only grounds for divorce in New York was adultery.

We obtained a New York separation agreement, split our worldly possessions down the middle, and Roberta moved to Florida with our two children, Suzanne and Merrily. My romance with Jean lasted only until the fall of 1951, though, and then we decided to break up. I really believe it was too soon for me to consider going from one marriage to another, and the split was logical. Nevertheless, when my divorce came through that December I must admit I felt pretty good about it.

Roberta married Bill Gavin, and then they decided they wanted to move back to New York. While they made the necessary arrangements, Suzanne and Merrily came ahead to stay with me. I was all excited at the prospect, and I'll always remember the rainy night they flew up from Florida. My friend Bill Wolff was a control-tower operator at the airport and he kept calling me at Nick's with reports of their flight through the rain to Newark. They stayed with me until Roberta and Bill Gavin found a permanent residence.

Once I was well settled in at Nick's, a group of friends became regulars at the club, sometimes coming twice a week, and in return I took to visiting them in the day time at their public relations office on 53rd Street. As a result, Harold Meyers and his associates, Albert Sussman, Jess Wolff, and Bob Greene, put their heads together and came up with a TV package for our dixieland band. In my opinion, they invented a whale of an adventure series depicting the trials and tribulations of a Lilliputian-sized jazz band. The idea was novel, to say the least. The main character was to be a southern Kentucky colonel-type resembling Colonel Sanders (who wasn't yet introduced on a national basis). He kept a tiny jazz band in places like a dresser drawer or a suitcase and would travel around the country getting into all kinds of humorous situations—such as losing the band in a taxi, or startling people by taking them out of his pocket to perform on a counter top, and other situations along these lines. It was to be done by using over-size sets, trick camera shots, etc., and really should have had a wide appeal to audiences, jazz fans or otherwise.

For six months afterwards, they tried every avenue of approach to sell the show to one of the TV networks, but to no avail. I doubt if any more effort was put into "Gunsmoke" than went into "The Colonel's Dixieland Band," and whether I did the show, or Spike Jones, or Phil Spitalny, it was a great idea and deserved a chance. However, I suppose this sort of disappointment is common in the TV business.

One of the happy aspects of working at Nick's was the opportunity it afforded to make new friends. People liked the music, and I have always had the lucky facility of being able to remember names and faces, so it wasn't long before I had lots of friends—not only new ones, but renewing acquaintances with people I hadn't seen in years, like my old high-school buddies Bill Muchnic from Atchison, and Henry McNary. New friends included the British musicians working on the liner *Queen Mary* and the famous English bandleader Ted Heath. We became especially well acquainted with a family living in Greenwich Village, Mr. and Mrs. Ted Sprague and their son, Jeremy. They were artistic people and they entertained us at their home which was nearby to Nick's. They liked our music, and Jerry and I became good friends.

I also spent many a pleasant intermission talking to two gentlemen from Michigan, William MacQueen and his brother-in-law, Robert Lindell. Mr. MacQueen, a lawyer, had known Bix and Charlie Margulis when they were working in the Goldkette and Whiteman organizations in the Twenties, and he could tell very interesting stories about the glory days of the Graystone Ballroom in Detroit and the Whiteman years. On one of their trips to New York, these gentlemen brought along famous bandleader and clarinetist of the Twenties Boyd Senter, to visit us at Nick's. Boyd Senter and his "Senterpedes" had been a premier vaudeville attraction, and many of his records are collector's items because he used musicians like Tommy and Jimmy Dorsey, Eddie Lang, Phil Napoleon, and other top jazz men.

Other regular visitors included three great songwriters, Harry Woods, Willard Robison, and Jack Palmer, and very often those two joyous and illustrious Princetonians, Randy Hall and Herb Sanford. Herb, you will remember, had produced the Raleigh-Kool radio program for Tommy Dorsey; now he was producing the Garry Moore daytime radio show. Randy Hall has the unique distinction of being the only person I have ever tried to paint a portrait of. He opened a restaurant in Florida, so I did a 28" by 46" oil painting of Randy playing his famous tin whistle for him to hang in the restaurant. It was quite an undertaking. In fact, it took at least three months and a lot of coaching and encouragement from my friend Charles Melohs. I'll never attempt another portrait.

An artist I will never be, but I enjoyed painting and spent a lot of time observing Charles in his studio where he often worked late hours. I was once invited to exhibit some of my paintings on a TV talk show, and afterwards one of the viewers suggested they should be shown *only* on TV, because on camera they seemed to make sense.

In addition to painting, I pursued two other interests. I bought a bicycle and quite often rode it to work at Nick's, and sometimes I rode for recreation in Central Park. I also went back to my favorite hobby of woodworking and cabinet making, using the shop made available to me by my friend Tony Pastusak. Eventually, I built all the furniture for my 6th Avenue apartment.

There was a group of young musicians from Bayonne who used to cross the river and visit the club at least once a week. The first thing we knew, they had memorized our entire library. They would get on the bandstand and play a whole set that sounded like the same band. In the group were Ben Ventura, trumpet; Marv Ross, clarinet; Joe Acito, piano; and Charley Acito, trombone.

While we were at Nick's, Cliff Leeman met a lovely young lady from New Brunswick, N.J., and fell in love. One Tuesday night he failed to show up for work; instead we were handed a wire which read: "Won't be in tonight—I just married Irene."

THIRTY-SEVEN

I LEFT NICK'S in February 1952, after two years and two months, going back to free-lancing around New York. I'm very grateful for the fact that I've never had to worry about getting work whenever I needed it. Even more important, very often it was the kind to maintain my musical interest. The perfect illustration of this is that March brought one of the genuine highlights of my career.

I had always been close friends with Bobby Hackett, who at that time had a very fine band working at Lou Terassi's Club on W. 47th Street. He also free-lanced a lot, and, because of his commitments at the WABC studios, he was unable to work every night at the club. He arranged with the club to front his band with three leaders: On Monday night it was Billy Butterfield, on Sunday, Wednesday, and Thursday it was me, and on Friday and Saturday it was Bobby Hackett.

Bobby was a great creative cornetist, but he also had another talent in common with Tommy Dorsey and Phil Napoleon—he knew how to put together a good band. And the band at Lou Terassi's was *very* good. Gene Sedric was on clarinet, Vic Dickenson, on trombone, Teddy Roy, piano, Morey Feld, drums, and John Giuffrida, bass. Frankly, it was the most relaxed and fun-to-play-with band I ever worked with.

Gene Sedric was from St. Louis and had been a mainstay in Fats Waller's great groups. He was a marvelous and imaginative clarinetist and one of the nicest guys I've ever met. It hardly seems necessary to mention the great talents of Vic Dickenson, who played with many great bands and for many years was a very close musical associate of Bobby's. As for the rhythm section—well, Bobby put it together, and it was great. It was an inspiring group and, like icing on the cake, the intermission piano was played by the great Cliff Jackson. Cliff was full of fun and a master of the keyboard, with many years as a soloist to his credit.

Lou Terassi, a most amiable man, owned the club. He gave the musicians a completely free hand to play as they pleased, and once in awhile would even sit in on jazz fiddle when the mood struck him. I really enjoyed playing with the band and working in such a pleasant atmosphere. The band

A night at "Nick's." Helen Griffin, Pee Wee, Sal Pace, Ethel and Bernie Privin, and Chris Griffin.   Photo courtesy of Chris Griffin.

was perfect to play with—something that happens very seldom in this business—and the tapes I still have of some of our radio broadcasts prove it. Listening to them now only convinces me more that this was one of the finest musical experiences I've ever had. And just think—in addition to all the fun and enjoyment I got from playing this job, there was a great chili parlor on the corner of 47th and Eighth which we visited almost every night.

As I mentioned earlier, my two kids were living with me until Roberta and her new husband got settled. They were attending the elementary school on 54th Street. My daughter Suzanne had become very efficient as my acting secretary. She was a bright girl and almost like an adult in the way she handled my phone calls and appointments. In May word arrived that Roberta and her husband had purchased a home in West Islip, Long Island, and, as agreed, the girls would be going there to live. I was going to miss them, but common sense told me they'd be better off in a household that ran on normal hours and under their mother's supervision. Suzanne's twelfth birthday wasn't until June 19th, but I decided to give her a birthday party anyway and invited all the kids from the elementary school. I had the affair catered by my old friend Irving Cohen, who owned the Park-Chambers deli across the street from my apartment. Those thirty-odd twelve-year-olds did everything but plow up my living room.

I had no way of knowing it, thank goodness, but the party was the last and the best thing I could do for my child. On the following weekend my youngest, Merrily, was invited by her friend, the daughter of comedienne Jean Carol, to visit at her home in Wurtzboro, N.Y., so Suzanne went to Long Island to spend the weekend with her mother. About ten o'clock that Sunday night I received a phone call from the Long Island police, and an official-sounding voice wanted to know if I was the father of Suzanne Erwin. She had been in an automobile accident in Copiague, Long Island, was very seriously hurt, and I had better get to the Copiague Hospital as quickly as possible.

I rushed to the hospital, and there I learned just how serious the accident had been. Roberta's husband had been driving the car and had hit a concrete stanchion at a railroad crossing. He suffered head injuries that required surgery, but eventually he recovered completely. Roberta and Suzanne were so badly injured that the doctors had difficulty telling which was the mother and which the daughter.

They were under the care of a Dr. Lurie, who was on duty in the emergency room, and he had called in a neurosurgeon because of their serious head injuries. After talking with him I was satisfied that the best medical procedure was being followed, but to make sure that the best care possible was available, I called Mt. Sinai Hospital the next day and was fortunate in persuading a fine neurosurgeon, Dr. Gross, to make the trip to Long Island. He told me that Suzanne needed another operation to relieve cranial pressure, but there was less than a fifty-fifty chance she would survive. She died on the operating table.

This was, of course, the most heartbreaking experience of my life. And since Roberta's condition was still touch-and-go, there was no telling if she would live or die, I had the further agonizing chore of telling Merrily the terrible news. She was almost eight years old, and it was a very heavy blow. I will be forever grateful for the support of Harold Meyers, who stepped in to take care of the myriad details that demand attention at such times, and to Joel Herron for opening his home to Merrily and me.

Under the circumstances I thought it best to take Merrily to stay with my mother in Nebraska. I arranged to have Suzanne buried in the family plot in Falls City, and I left a request to be called whenever Roberta regained consciousness.

I took Merrily and my mother to visit my brother in St. Paul, and from there went on to Rhinelander, Wisconsin, to see my cousins Dr. and Mrs. Chet Goosin. Somewhere around the first of August a call came from Roberta, who had finally regained consciousness a month after the accident. I felt obligated to take Merrily home to see her mother, but when we visited her in West Islip we were both shocked to find Roberta changed beyond recognition.

I returned to free-lancing and also went back to work at Lou Terassi's, but by this time the band had undergone a few changes. Gene Sedric had left, and Cecil Scott, the great tenorman from the Savoy Sultans, now held the reed chair. Morey Feld had also departed, replaced by Gary Chester, who in turn was followed by George Wettling. Nevertheless, I have fond memories of Terassi's. The music was always interesting, and a great bunch of guys make for a great job. I recall that at one point Cecil Scott and I decided to make a batch of good old homebrew in the Terassi basement; we went so far as obtaining a 20-gallon crock before we woke up to the fact that a regular liquor license didn't authorize such activity.

The bandstand was heavily carpeted and my foot couldn't be heard when I kicked off the tempo, so somebody came up with the idea of an inverted tin plate on the floor for me to tap on. I was still riding my bike to work now and then, and I'd park it in the vestibule of the club. One night somebody came in to tell me Cliff Jackson, who wasn't exactly a kid any more, was riding my bicycle up and down Eighth Avenue. When I asked him how come, he told me his first job had been delivering Special Delivery letters on a bicycle in his hometown of Washington, D.C.—he just wanted to see if he could still do it.

That October of 1952 my friend Joel Herron found himself without an apartment so he moved into mine. Joel was about the only guy I could room with because we both followed the principle of live and let alone. He was usually involved in show work of some kind, and at this time he was working with Jill Allen, a young lady of considerable vocal talent. He wanted to record her in a format that would be unusual enough to attract attention, and he thought it would be interesting to make a record utilizing a voice-and-trumpet duet-and-answer arrangement.

Joel had a couple of original tunes, and he dusted one off called "Hold Me Closer." We wound up using it along with a couple of standards for the recording date he set up—a very interesting experiment. He started off by recording the girl's voice in the flat, but adding some reverb to the sound of the trumpet. When this was played back, it sounded as though she was singing to her lover and the trumpet was the voice of her lover. The same idea was used for the standard "Melancholy Baby."

This was the first record I had ever made in which I felt satisfied with my own performance—a statement that may require explanation for those who have never made a recording. On most record dates you have about three or four hours to do four tunes, and if you have a hangover or an acid stomach—or any other problem—you simply do the best you can under the circumstances. Then when the record is released, if you're lucky a reasonable or fair performance is all you can hope for. Unfortunately I've had records released that had clinkers on them or I considered just plain bad. On the whole, it's a rare thing when the result is a performance you can be proud of. For this reason, I have always questioned whether or not Bix, or Bunny, or any other of the great performers were ever captured on records at their best. As far as Bunny is concerned, I knew him well and was directly associated with him for a long time, and I distinctly remember him playing far greater things in person than ever showed up on records. One thing is certain—no record ever fully reproduced the quality of his tone.

In this instance, when Joel and I went into the recording studio there was absolutely no time pressure on us, so we recorded our tunes until we were completely satisfied with the results, although the masters, or the pressings, were rather unsatisfactory. Anyway, we wound up with four sides we liked and then had to decide what to do with them. I don't remember if we tried to sell the masters, but if we did we weren't successful. We finally went ahead with production on our own, and this meant paying for the records to be pressed and afterwards trying for distribution.

I don't recall our exact investment figure—most likely, one or two thousand dollars—and we probably had a stock of a couple of thousand records. In the process, I learned many things about the record business—having the labels printed (we used the label owned by a friend, Bill Bird, "Avalon Records"), and visiting the pressing plant, which was in a warehouse on the corner of Broadway and Lafayette. Here I witnessed the wonder of evolution, from master to mother to stamper, and the final marvel of watching a chunk of vinyl go into a press and in one stroke emerge as a finished record.

Joel took charge of distribution and promotion, making trips to visit distributors in Baltimore, Philadelphia, and Boston, plus making contacts in Memphis and Nashville for western distribution. He also arranged for the record to be plugged by disc jockeys on radio stations. I still recall one reaction it got after "Hold Me Closer" was played on a Boston station. The disc jockey asked for opinions—and got a letter from a lady who indignantly declared that the record was positively lewd.

By the time we tired of these activities, we had realized most of our investment, so Joel took the records to Bob Thiele (at that time director of

Coral Records) and Bob was supposed to place them for distribution by Coral. I guess they went on the shelf never to be heard of again. I recall this as the first time I played a solo with an echo chamber enhancing the illusion of the tone soaring to vast heights, and I believe Joel originated this idea which, of course, has since become standard procedure.

THIRTY-EIGHT

AROUND THE BEGINNING of 1953 I was again asked to spell Phil Napoleon at Nick's, so I found myself back on the bandstand with some of my old buddies. As is more often the rule than the exception in the music business, however, there were some changes. Sal Pace, the veteran dixieland clarinetist, had replaced Phil Olivella, and his playing was a new experience for me. Sal has a strong, throaty sound which blends beautifully with the trumpet and trombone in the traditional three-man front line, and his tone has always impressed me with its fullness, resembling the sound of the New Orleans clarinetists who use the Albert system instruments.

Cliff Leeman had returned to the studios to play for Raymond Scott on "The Hit Parade." In his place was a young and very impressive drummer named Kenny John. Kenny was very talented, but it was his physical appearance that attracted most attention. He was fair complected, with long blond hair that he combed in a fashion almost like a clown's wig, and when he played hair was flying in all directions. It was a big commercial gimmick, but to some it probably was construed as the look of a wild man, and the conservative atmosphere at Nick's made it all the more obvious. The result was that a number of people suggested to the management they were certain our drummer was a dope fiend. The management felt obligated to check him out, so they hired a couple of plain-clothes detectives, a man and a woman, to observe the drummer for two evenings and determine the reason for his unconventional appearance. At the end of the second night they turned in their report: "The drummer is O.K., but some of your customers ought to be examined."

The rest of the band remained as it had been on my first go around— Andy Russo, Jack Fay and, of course, the guiding light, Billy Maxted. Billy never stood still musically. He was always thinking up new material and ways to improve the band and keep it on its toes. This went a long way toward preventing the lethargy that often pervades a group of musicians on the same job for an extended period. One of the things he turned in at this time was a special feature for Kenny John called "The Big Crash from China," which gave Kenny a good chance to show off his technique and amazing speed. Billy also created arrangements on such unusual material as "Peter and the Wolf," and "American Patrol," adding a wider dimension to our musical presentation. (Coincidentally, around this time I recorded a cute version of "Peter and the Wolf," narrated by the distinguished actor Hans Conreid, and produced by Joel Herron.) Of course, there might be some question as to what these things had to do with jazz, but they did have merit. They were novelties, and therefore entertaining, but we also played them in a rhythmic fashion and improvised on the themes, so to that extent, at least, they qualified as jazz. And it broke up the monotony of always playing the same tunes night after night.

A change of pace was very important in a club like Nick's, where we were playing strictly to a listening audience. There was no dancing or other form of entertainment, so it was up to the band and very necessary to keep the music novel and interesting. This was especially true because we always had a number of friends and regulars in attendance and we had to keep our approach fresh and appealing.

Over the years we had a lot of fun on the radio broadcasts, which must have numbered in the hundreds. We were in something of the same position as the hotel bands of the Twenties and Thirties—this is, we were a house band that was readily available for remote hook-ups—on the bandstand six nights a week for an extended period each evening, and to be depended upon whenever a program of live music was needed. When you're doing so many shows, a slip now and then is bound to happen. For instance, in the middle of a broadcast, I suddenly lost the melody of the verse to "I Wish I Could Shimmy Like My Sister Kate"—a tune I had played several times a week for years. I simply went blank. These things just happen—and at least they become funny in retrospect.

It was only natural that we became friends with the announcers assigned to us, especially John St. Leger, a guy with a terrific sense of humor. It was always necessary to clear in advance with the network the tunes to be broadcast. This was done in order to prevent too much repetition and to give proper credit in the logs to ASCAP or BMI, the composer organizations, who received a fee for the use of their music. Generally the announcers would show up just before broadcast time and I would hand them a list of the tunes to be announced. One night I handed the list to John St. Leger and before he realized it, he had said, "And now the band will play the old dixieland favorite, 'Mahoney's Eleven Arms.'" We still wonder if the network executives scurried to see if the tune had been given proper clearance.

It was customary for the announcer to acquaint the radio audience with the members of the band by mentioning their names and instruments. One night it came out this way: ". . . Pee Wee Erwin on trumpet, Andy Russo on trombone—and Kenny Drums on the john."

The most traumatic broadcast of all occurred on a show called "Bandstand," a weekend program with a roving format where odds and ends of entertainment were picked up from almost any place on the NBC network. Naturally, it was tough to be precise about the time a particular segment would be aired, but they tried to give some forewarning or an approximate time, but at best this was only a close guess. One night we were taking a break and I was sitting alongside the bandstand, when without any warning the announcer gave me the cue that we were on the air. It was a shock—because not only was the bandstand empty, I knew that most of the band members were in Julius's bar around the corner. I sent someone to alert them and then climbed on the bandstand just as the announcer was saying, "And now from Nick's in Greenwich Village, Pee Wee Erwin and his band."

Under such duress, I'm not very quick on the draw, so I looked at him and asked (on the air), "What do you suggest?"

He looked right back at me and said, "It's your show. What can you do?"

"How about a few bugle calls?"

He shook his head. "That's hardly dixieland. What else do you offer?"

Just then I saw Billy Maxted scrambling through the door and knew the situation was in hand, so I told him with more confidence than I felt, "Well, I'll start the theme song and we'll see if we can build a band over the air waves." I went into "Tin Roof Blues," the house theme, and by the end of the verse and the first chorus we had the full band, winded and flushed but complete, back on the stand.

In the spring there was another change in the band. Kenny John left, replaced by Tony Spargo, who not only played drums but was a virtuoso of that rare and exotic instrument, the kazoo. Those of you familiar with early jazz history know that Tony was the drummer with the Original Dixieland Jazz Band when it opened at Schiller's Cafe in Chicago in 1916, and going on to create a sensation at Reisenweber's on Columbus Circle in New York. They made the first jazz record of all time in January 1917, and three members of the band—Tony Spargo, Larry Shields, the clarinetist, and Eddie Edwards, the trombonist—wound up owning the copyrights on several of the tunes they recorded, which set them up very well financially. "Tiger Rag" alone was enough to provide a good lifetime income.

Tony added a lot of color to our band, and we had a lot of fun with him and his kazoo. I used to tease him by introducing him as "our drummer, Alfred Hitchcock," because he bore a remarkable resemblance to the famous movie director. As for his drumming, the best beat he ever played was with the one brush he used to accompany himself on the snare behind his kazoo.

That kazoo was actually a little tin horn made to resemble a cornet, and it had been manufactured by a toy maker during World War I. It had a special cup mouthpiece to hold the vibrating material, and instead of using paper, Tony had acquired a special fish-skin material which, unlike paper, would not absorb moisture and didn't have to be constantly replaced during a job. For years Tony tried without success to have this horn duplicated by a number of instrument manufacturers. As a consequence he took great care of it, carrying it in a little black bag every place he went. He took better care of his tin horn than he did his drums.

I'll never forget the expression on Charlie Parker's face the night he walked into the Metropole in the middle of one of Tony's kazoo choruses. His eyes almost jumped out of his head, and he strode back and forth screaming, "What *is* that! What *is* that!" I never did find out if anybody told him what it was, or his opinion of it.

That spring the band at Nick's started talking about a vacation. Pace, Russo, Fay, and Maxted had put in close to three years without any time off. We approached the management with the idea and they agreed, so we started looking for a replacement band to take over for us during vacation. We tried several people, including Doc Evans, the Minneapolis trumpeter, and Sharkey Bonano in New Orleans, but finally succeeded in getting Muggsy Spanier, who was touring the East with a good band. We lined him up for an eight-week period starting on July 15th. With him were the great clarinetist Darnell Howard, a very fine trombonist named Ralph Hutchinson, and the veteran bass player Truck Parham. We were certain the change would be good for Nick's as well as giving us a chance to enjoy a change of scene. We decided to take a month off and then play a brief booking at the Colonial Tavern in Toronto before returning to Nick's.

My grandmother Josephine had passed away in June, and I had been unable to attend her funeral because of work commitments, so now I wanted to spend part of my time off visiting in Falls City. This I did, and then after two weeks I returned to New York to pick up Merrily and take her with me to Miami Beach for the rest of my vacation. As it turned out, Florida was a good choice because playing in the Poinciana Hotel in Miami Beach was a great jazz band, Preacher Rollo and His Band, with Tony Parenti on clarinet, Marie Marcus on piano, a good trumpet player, Tommy Justice, and of course, Rollo "Preacher" Laylan on drums. This made for an ideal situation. Merrily, then nine years old, had the beach and swimming all day long, and at night I had a jazz band to help keep my lip in shape.

With vacation over we reassembled our well-rested band and headed for the Colonial Tavern in Toronto, one of the best towns on the continent for jazz. Almost all forms of entertainment are popular in Toronto. Canadian audiences are very friendly and receptive to music, and the Colonial Tavern was already a well-established jazz spot where we had been preceded by such great groups as those of Bobby Hackett, Muggsy, and Jack Teagarden. We had a successful and enjoyable engagement, and, while we were there, we became friendly with famous sports figure and columnist Ted Reeves, which resulted, as far as I know, in the only time a jazz band got a write-up in a sports column.

At that time Toronto closed all places of entertainment on Sunday, so to us it was like a continuation of our vacation because our work hours were only about half of what we were used to at Nick's. The Toronto date also gave me the opportunity to renew acquaintanceship with an old friend, Trump Davidson.

We returned to Nick's in September, to stay until January 1954. The idea of having a trade-off in the bands at Nick's had proved to be so successful that it was decided we would do it again in 1954. Since this was to be the new pattern, I began laying the groundwork for another road trip after New Year's Eve, to begin on January 15th. I contacted the Associated Booking Company, headed by Joe Glaser, the famous manager of Louis Armstrong, who was ably assisted by two very proficient road bookers, Bert Block (the former bandleader) and Larry Bennett. They proceeded to set up a very good nine-month tour for our group. This time several bands replaced us at Nick's. Muggsy Spanier came in again for a run, followed by a very fine New Orleans group headed by ace trumpeter Roy Liberto.

THIRTY-NINE

PRIOR TO OPENING at the Colonial Tavern on February 1, 1954, we were booked to play a private three-day affair at the famous Meadowbrook, in Cedar Grove, N.J. Three days before the opening at the Meadowbrook, I slipped on some ice about eight feet away from my front door and broke the small bone in my leg just above the ankle. I must have looked like a total wreck when I hobbled into the Meadowbrook on crutches, my leg in a cast up to the knee. I sat on a stool in front of the band with the leg hanging out prominently. I figured if people didn't like my playing, they could at least feel sorry for me.

I couldn't help but think back to the time when I was with Tommy Dorsey and burned my hands with too much zinc oxide so I had to wear white gloves for several weeks. After all these years I still meet people who remember the white gloves—mainly because it was thought to be an affectation or a trademark. On the other hand, I haven't had too many recall when my shoulder was broken in an auto accident while I was with Isham Jones, having to play one-handed for several weeks.

Anyway, as if a broken leg weren't enough, two nights before our Toronto opening Jack Fay decided he didn't want to go on the road. Naturally, this resulted in a frenzied scramble, but we turned lucky when a good bass player, Billy Goodall, agreed to go with us.

I had to make the trip to Toronto by Air Canada in a wheelchair. When we got there, we found more good news waiting—the town was buried in snow and ice. Getting around on crutches in this stuff was no fun, but to add insult to injury, it turned out that I had to negotiate two flights of stairs at the Colonial Inn in order to get to work and, believe me, that was no mean accomplishment. Nevertheless, the cast on my leg proved to have unexpected commercial value on the bandstand as just about everybody in Canada automatically assumed I had broken my leg skiing in the Laurentian Mountains and wanted to autograph my cast. The cast was on for 13 weeks, like it or not, so there was nothing to do but go straight ahead. My band buddies took good care of me in the meantime, and I wasn't in a lot of pain.

There are almost always some bright spots in times like these to add a little light and humor to life. Our good friend Ted Reeves always invited a group of close friends to his house on the otherwise quiet Sundays, and on one occasion he included Billy Maxted and me. The rap session proved highly enjoyable with a very pleasant gathering of people, and all went fine until I needed to use the bathroom. It turned out to be on the second floor—and there I was with my unwieldy cast. When Ted learned of my predicament, he obliged by bringing forth a positively wonderful, hand-painted chamber pot, which prompted a lot of interest and conversation. Needless to say, I managed to maneuver the stairs. The pot was too beautiful.

The Colonial Tavern was an ideal stop for a jazz band, and in spite of the cold weather and my cast we enjoyed a second successful engagement in Canada. On leaving Toronto, we moved on to another club that we eventually came to consider our home away from home.

Columbus, Ohio, along with Cleveland, Toledo, Youngstown, Dayton, and Cincinnati, has always been a haven for good music. I really believe that Columbus had more fans of dixieland jazz than any other city its size in the country. I had a taste of this back in 1942 when we were playing in the Ionian room of the Deschler-Wallack Hotel, and still earlier in 1934 when I played a theater with Buddy Rogers. But now we went into the Grandview Inn, a lovely restaurant owned by a highly competent man named Mike Flesch. Mike not only featured a great cuisine, he had good taste in music. As a result, he enjoyed an excellent reputation with his clientele for presenting the best in food and entertainment, including bands led by Muggsy Spanier and Eddie Condon, and a group of young musicians from New Orleans who called themselves the Dukes of Dixieland.

We had the advantage of having already a good many friends in Columbus, who knew us from visiting Nick's. Now we also met some close friends of our pal Bobby Hackett, who was a particular favorite in Columbus. These people, along with Mike Flesch's popularity, got us press and radio coverage the likes of which we had never seen. Bobby got us acquainted with two brothers who loved jazz, Ed and Dick Wolfe, whose family owned a string of newspapers and entertainment media in Ohio. We also became friends with Bob Thomas, who ran the local TV station, and Dick Borell (another of Bobby's friends and a cornet player), who ran the local radio station, not to mention countless members of the medical fraternity who, for some reason (I'm happy to say), seem to be staunch supporters of our style of music.

Putting all this together, we had a one-month engagement (March) unequalled by any I ever experienced, before or since. It even included the presentation of a formal citation to the band by the mayor of Columbus, Mr. Maynard E. Sensenbrenner. In an atmosphere of such conviviality, every night of the week was like a New Year's Eve celebration, so you can readily understand why we were only too happy to adopt Columbus as our home away from home. But the music business is a fickle mistress, and we were shortly due to have this brought home to us.

246

Our next stop on the tour was a club in Chester, Pennsylvania, called El Rancho. Flushed with victory and our great success in Columbus, we anticipated no problems. Besides, it has always been my firm conviction that first-night impressions set the pace for an entire engagement, so I have always tried to make sure the first number played is one of the best in the band's repertoire, and sets a happy mood. Following this formula, we opened at El Rancho, and when we finished our first number—one I would have sworn was a guarantee of an enthusiastic reception—about two people were moved to feeble applause. The rest of them simply sat, drinks in hand, and stared at us with expressions that seemed to say, "Big deal! Now what do you do for an encore?"

More than a little surprised—we weren't used to this kind of reception—but undaunted, we reloaded and played another barn-burner (to borrow a term coined by our friend Bill Bacin). With the same result. So we accepted the challenge and gave it all we had for the rest of the set—and the reaction to our all-out efforts was one of complete indifference. We were stunned.

I went looking for the management, feeling like a beaten dog with his tail between his legs, but when I started to apologize I was quickly informed I needn't be concerned. The establishment was a private club, essentially licensed to serve drinks at off hours and on Sundays, so the clientele came to drink. The music was strictly secondary, serving only as a background for the really important business of drinking.

Our next location was the Rendezvous, a club in the Senator Hotel in Philadelphia, owned by Lee Guber, the impresario who has become extremely successful as one of the creators of the summer-stock circuit and theater-in-the-round. In view of his reputation, I had a lot of respect for Lee's knowledge of the entertainment field and his judgment and, since I had a few doubts in my mind concerning how much money we could get for our band in comparison to the high prices I knew some other outfits were getting, I asked his advice and opinion on the subject. He gave me an honest answer—one that bore out an earlier assessment I had gotten from Mike Flesch: "I can pay Muggsy Spanier $2500 a week and you only $1250 a week, but I'll make more money when Muggsy is here because that week I'll sell more whisky. Don't ask me why."

Mike Flesch had given me essentially the same answer when he compared our engagement at the Grandview Inn to that of the Dukes of Dixieland. These opinions were important to me because I was thinking in terms of a full-time road band, and the gross amount of the contract was of prime importance to support such an undertaking. Unfortunately, neither Guber nor Flesch were able to explain why some bands attracted heavier spenders than others, but what they were saying boiled down to one hard fact: Your value to a promoter was in direct proportion to the amount of money you put in his cash register. He didn't care how you did it, but survival depended on it.

The two biggest attractions on the circuit we were trying to break into were the Dukes of Dixieland and Pee Wee Hunt, and I think their success could be attributed mainly to their records. Both the Dukes and the Pee Wee group (which could only loosely be termed a jazz band) were very successful on records, and they were entertaining units, offering vocals and showmanship that appealed to a wide segment of customers who were not particularly interested in jazz played by short, fat, middle-aged men. For that matter, it has never been a secret that jazz alone is difficult to sell to the public at large. If I needed any further proof of this I had only to recall the couple of times we followed Jack Teagarden into locations. Beyond any doubt, Jack was one of the all-time jazz giants, and as such he commanded big salaries, but he lost money for many promoters in the Fifties. I think it might be different today, with a worldwide market now available.

While we were at the Rendezvous, I was exposed for the first time to rock'n'roll amplified instruments. My room at the Senator was directly over the Rendezvous, and whenever I was home, all I could hear above everything else was the bass guitar downstairs. Not only did the sound blanket out any other, the vibration bordered on a minor earthquake. I have detested the electric bass and all other contrived electronic noises ever since—an opinion obviously not shared by the general public.

From the Rendezvous we were booked into one of the great phenomena of the music world of its time, the Metropole, located on Broadway between 48th and 49th in New York City. The original location had been a block south on Broadway, and at that time the place had a big-band policy. After the move was made to the new spot, it switched to the New Orleans format of the band playing on a stage behind the bar. The bar at the Metropole was one of the longest I've ever seen, so the band looked out over a sea of faces—not only those of the people seated at the bar but more who were seated at tables on the far side of the room. We were there during June and July so the glass doors facing Broadway were left wide open, and the music could be heard up and down the street for quite a distance, acting as a natural ballyhoo.

We were well received on that first engagement, both by the management and the public, and we alternated on the stand with a very fine quintet under the leadership of clarinetist Sol Yaged. Actually we were filling in for the man who, in my opinion, more than anybody else was responsible for the Metropole's huge success, Henry "Red" Allen, fabulous trumpet player and entertainer.

The Metropole's business had been built on a policy of volume and quick turnover, a format it was able to follow easily because of its location in what may very well be the center of the world's greatest entertainment area. It grew rapidly into a great showcase for many of our most prominent jazzmen, and I'll have more to say about this unique establishment later.

Our bass player, Billy Goodall, left the band at this point, and we replaced him with a young fellow who had already made himself a reputation as a member of the famed "Scarsdale Gang," Charlie Traeger. Charlie was one of the youngsters from Scarsdale High School who created quite a musical sensation—Bob Wilber, clarinet and soprano saxophone; Eddie Hubble, trombone; Johnny Glasel, trumpet; Dick Wellstood, piano; Eddie Phyfe, drums; and Charlie on bass. I first heard this band filling in one night at Jimmy Ryan's on 52nd Street, and it was easy to tell that, despite the youth of the musicians, they were destined to become musical giants of the future. Most of them are still active and have fulfilled this judgment. Charlie Traeger certainly became a very valuable asset to our band.

We opened in mid-August of 1954, in the famous Savoy CLub in Boston, which at the time was really a swinging town. Besides the Savoy, George Wein operated two busy clubs in the same hotel (the Copley Plaza) Storyville and Mahogany Hall, where he employed top jazz musicians. Only a half block away from the Savoy, on Massachusetts Avenue, was another place, the Hi-Hat Club.

Like Nick's in New York, the Savoy was operated by a lady, Mrs. Donahugh, and like Grace Rongetti, she was a gracious person and easy to work for. She had a nice clientele, largely made up of students from the many schools and universities in the area, and she hired some of the best bands in jazz for extended runs, such as those of Wilbur DeParis and his great Riverboat Jazz Band, and the Jimmy Archey band. Jack Teagarden, Muggsy Spanier, and other top groups had also played the room, so we were following in a fine tradition. We made a lot of new friends, and I was especially lucky to have personal friends in the area, such as Barbara Tolman and Bob Wild, who went out of their way to escort me around town and show me the sights. This made the days very pleasant and our new friends did a lot to bring listeners in to hear our nightly offerings.

I never gave any particular thought as to why the Savoy was such a peacefully run club until many years later I read the autobiography of Malcolm X. In it, he refers to a black detective whose very presence commanded full respect from good and bad alike, and then I recalled that this detective had been a regular at the Savoy every night, and very amiable to all.

On August 30th, New England was hit by a major hurricane, carrying the name of "Carol." Activity around Boston, including ours, was curtailed for two days. The storm was really a full-fledged blow, and citizens were warned to stay off the streets because, in addition to the danger from falling signs and other debris, razor sharp bits of broken glass were flying through the air like bullets. The storm damage hit close to home for us when we returned to the Savoy and found the roof had leaked and allowed water to fill up the beautiful grand piano.

As if this weren't bad enough, only 12 days later, on September 11, another hurricane—this one called "Edna"—blew in. It wasn't quite as bad as the first, but natural disasters like these are no aid to business and club attendance reflected this. Nevertheless, we left on amicable terms and with an invitation to return when it was possible.

FORTY

IN SEPTEMBER we were back at Nick's for the fall season, with a new trombonist, Lee Gifford, in the band. Andy Russo had left and Lee, a powerful player with a lot of technique, was molded by Billy Maxted into a tremendous asset to the band's ensemble sound.

During the day, I resumed my work in the recording studios and, in particular, began doing house dates for two new companies, Waldorf Music Hall and Grand Award Records, both headed by my old friend Enoch Light. Always playing in the brass section with me were Charlie Margulis and Bobby Byrne (the young trombonist discovered by Jimmy Dorsey as a replacement for Tommy in the Dorsey Brothers Orchestra). We were doing remakes of a lot of the big-band music of the 1930s, along with a series of recordings that sold very well called "The Roaring 20s" and "The Flirty 30s." Enoch Light was very successful with these records, and I greatly admired his insight.

Like several other successful recording executives—Ben Selvin, Ed Kirkeby, Archie Bleyer—Enoch had an extensive background of experience in the band business, combined with a strong commercial sense. He seemed to know what would sell, yet at the same time he made every effort to turn out a quality product. He used the best recording equipment available, a good studio, and he hired one of the best recording engineers, Bob Fine. His staff arranger was the very proficient Lew Davies. But, above all, he supervised each of his recording dates himself, making sure of excellent results from every session.

Enoch was an easy-going man, and never seemed to get excited, but he had an expression which always amused everybody. In the middle of a recording he would come out of the control room, stop us, and say something like, "Can we change such-and-such a measure or phrase? The excitement seems to leave in that spot. It just seems to lay there like a cold latka."

Nor did he ever leave things to chance. With three or four albums on the shelf to sell, he would take to the road and travel the country setting up distributors to handle them. He followed through on the process from start to finish.

Enoch was always looking for better recording fidelity, too. After he had helped his company establish two very successful labels in Waldorf and Grand Award, he used his own money to buy new equipment and experiment in high-fidelity recording. He used the name "Command Records" for his new product and launched it with an album he called "Persuasive Percussion." It was a huge success and a million seller. With success assured, his company reimbursed him for the money he had spent. I had the pleasure of recording three albums for Enoch, which I will talk about later.

I was also a frequent visitor to the Long Island studios of Everest Records, where I enjoyed another great musical experience, recording an album with one of the foremost brass-band conductors, Merle Evans, leader for generations of the Ringling Brothers Circus band. We made an album of circus music (Everest 2112; "Music from the Big Top") and if I have ever been over my head in a musical medium, this was it. I have rarely played with concert bands, and I'm not really familiar with the repertoire, but suddenly I found myself surrounded by the absolutely finest players in the field, many of them from the great Goldman Band of New York City.

Two of the trumpet players were all-time kings of the classical instrument. Our first trumpet was the master, Harry Glantz, and his assistant was one of the greatest of cornet soloists, James Burke. Glantz is considered by most musicians to be the greatest symphonic trumpet player America has ever had. For many years, he was principal trumpet with the New York Philharmonic, and it has been said that Toscanini would not sign a contract to conduct the NBC Symphony unless Harry Glantz was guaranteed to be the principal trumpet player.

James Burke succeeded Del Staigers as cornet soloist with the classic Goldman Band and for a great many years he entertained audiences with all of the great cornet solos, dazzling them with his great facility and the beauty of his tone.

Need I say what a great thrill it was for me to be in such distinguished company? And something else impressed me tremendously—this band played more softly than any danceband I'd ever worked in but due to the vibration of embouchure permitted by the soft playing, the facility and resonance of the band was superb. When we heard the playback of the recordings, the sound had the impact of a Howitzer.

Between takes, Evans told stories of circus life from his vast experience of years under the big top. One concerned an offended animal trainer who went to a great deal of trouble to ship his offender an entire bale of elephant manure by express. Another was about an inexperienced cornet player who joined the circus band and immediately started off by playing all the cornet solo parts an octave higher in order to impress his colleagues. After three shows like this, ignoring the warnings of his associates, he succeeded in paralyzing his lip and could never play again. The point Evans was trying to drive home is how important proper pacing is to the circus musician.

Merle Evans, by the way, has always been a great cornetist himself. If you have ever seen one of his circus performances, you may remember him directing the band with one hand and playing the cornet with the other. He told another amusing story about a trombone player he noticed behaving oddly during a matinee performance. Instead of playing his part, the man kept staring at one of the spectators. Finally Evans walked over and asked him what the trouble was.

"Oh, no trouble," was the answer, and the trombonist jabbed a finger in the direction of the man he'd been staring at. "I've just been thinking about what a great job I could do on that man over there." Off season he worked as a mortician.

Charlie Margulis recorded several albums in 1955, and I was involved with two of them. One, produced and directed for the Everest label, was called "Gershwin in Brass," and I recall playing several solos on it. Another was an album of marches for Enoch Light's Grand Award company called "Great American Marches As Performed by Charles Margulis and His Brass Band" (GA33-369). I recall contributing some originals to this, along with some arrangements and playing in the band. He also made a solo showcase album for Grand Award entitled "Solid Gold Horn."

At about this time I did some afternoon subbing and transcription work for MGM with my friend Joel Herron, but all the while I was still performing regularly at Nick's, and several times George Nelson had used our jazz band for background music to jingles. Also the trombone spot rotated again in March, with Andy Russo coming back to replace Lee Gifford. Both were excellent musicians; Lee was a fine trombonist and an asset to any band, but Andy had been with us a long time and had many friends and admirers at Nick's.

One day I received a call from Bob Thiele asking me to come to his office to listen to a tape that Rudy Van Gelder had made of our band the previous year during a performance at Fort Monmouth, N.J., when Kenny John was still our drummer. Thiele liked the tape and wanted to release it as an album on the Brunswick label.

I listened to it and considered the overall performance to be fair, but although the three front-line horns sounded in tune with each other, to my ear they were sharp in relation to the piano and bass. I objected to this, but Thiele argued that the intonations didn't offend him and that the feeling and spirit on the tape far outweighed my objection. The tape couldn't be redone, and since recording was Thiele's domain I figured his judgment was better than mine and gave him the go ahead. As it turned out, his opinion was justified because the sales of this particular record ("Pee Wee Erwin in the Land of Dixie," Br BL 54011) were greater and lasted longer than any other record the band ever made.

During that spring I became acquainted with Helen Burbidge, a lady from Canada who spent quite a few evenings in the company of various groups of people at Nick's. On a couple of occasions she took my daughter Merrily to entertainments during the day, since she lived nearby. While on a visit to my apartment, she noticed a long, gray cabinet I had assembled for hi-fi components, and after admiring my handiwork told me that she had the

252

perfect objects to complete the appearance of my cabinet. Her husband, who had passed away, had been the representative of an English tea firm and, over a period of many years, had been presented with a herd of ebony elephants with ivory tusks and toenails. If we could get them cleared through customs, she would make me a present of them. She very kindly arranged with some relatives in the States to get the figures to me, and they still grace various places in my home. I have always been grateful to Mrs. Burbidge for such a lovely gift, and we have kept in touch since.

On Monday evenings (my night off at Nick's) I worked on an interesting radio show for NBC. The conductor was Skitch Henderson, and the fairly large orchestra played Broadway theater music. I mention it mainly because it was the only time I ever played the music for a one-act operetta by George Gershwin entitled "125th Street." The show also offered a good opportunity to appreciate the considerable talents of Skitch Henderson as a conductor while watching Cliff Leeman's efforts to play tympani—the percussion assignment was very distasteful to Cliff.

Sidney Gross, recording supervisor for a European company, Urania Records, worked out a deal for the band to play a recording date on May 16, 1955, the day following our last night of the season at Nick's, and the beginning of our next road tour. I learned a lot about worrying beforehand. On our last night at the club many of our friends came in before the 11-hour session to bid us farewell. Andy Russo was really celebrating and so stoned that I was worried about his making the record date, but as it turned out Andy played fine—I made most of the clams on the record.

We recorded some of our more interesting tunes and arrangements for Urania, especially the routines on "Dixieland Shuffle" and "Memphis Blues." Charley Treager doubled on trombone, so Billy Maxted wrote second trombone parts for the flag-waving out choruses on "Glory Glory" and "Hindustan." Consequently, this made our ensembles very effective. Then too, Tony Spargo played some very cute kazoo choruses.

I find it very interesting that every ten years or so this record has been re-released with a new cover. I'm still partial to the original. The photographer took a picture of me in Times Square standing in the rain and wearing the most forlorn expression I could muster. (My original idea was to have my picture taken with my horn sticking out of a garbage can, but the photographer didn't think it was funny.) Anyway, the rain picture was used for the first album cover.

Phil Napoleon put together a new band—Kenny Davern, clarinet; Harry DeVito, trombone; Johnny Varro, piano; Pete Rogers, bass; and Phil Failla, drums—and took them into Nick's while we were on tour. We were scheduled to open on May 17 at the Savoy in Boston, and it was a tight squeeze for me. I recorded in New York with George Nelson until 6 p.m., and then, thanks to that marvelous invention, the airplane, was in Boston in time to open at the Savoy at 9 p.m.

After a month in Boston, we moved on again to the Grandview in Columbus, and this time I took Merrily with me because she had been invited to stay with friends, Dr. Richard Vance and his family. The Vances had a daughter of Merrily's age, and they lived in an interesting location—on the edge of a golf course which belonged to a country club attended by a growing number of people who came to watch a very young genius of the game, Jack Nicklaus.

Also of particular interest this trip was the annual Fourth of July parade held in Arlington, a suburb of Columbus. This is pretty much like other parades, except it features a fantastic collection of antique automobiles. The fact they are in the parade indicates that they are still running well and maintained in excellent condition. This is the only time I have ever had the opportunity to see and be allowed to inspect that great classic of automotive engineering, the Dusenberg.

Bob Thomas, a close friend in Columbus, decided to produce with us an album dedicated to the Grandview Inn and arranged for an engineer with portable equipment to record on-site tapes of the more unusual material in our performances, including "Peter and the Wolf," "American Patrol," "Big Noise From Winnetka," and "After You've Gone." It was released by Cadence Records, a firm run by the fine arranger Archie Bleyer, and—music aside—had one of the most attractive covers I've ever seen on an album, a lovely picture of the Grandview Inn. Under it, in unobtrusive lettering, were the words "Pee Wee Erwin at the Grandview Inn."

From the musical standpoint, we met with some adverse criticism regarding our selection for the album of things like "American Patrol" and "Peter and the Wolf." Some critics thought we had overstepped the boundary of the jazz repertoire and the arrangements were too contrived. This may be true, for that matter, but the arrangements were fun to play and a relief from countless renditions of "Muskrat Ramble" and "The Saints." (The defense rests.)

After this stint we had a month's vacation before returning to Nick's after Labor Day, 1955.

John Varro

254

FORTY-ONE

MY PERSONAL STAY at Nick's that fall was of comparatively short duration. Once again I fell off the wagon and on a Saturday night, in a fit of drunken candor, I advised the management that I was unfit for the job and was leaving. I further advised them that if they had any sense they'd forget about me and make Billy Maxted leader of the band which, in view of all his musical contributions, he more than deserved. So they took me at my word, and Billy started building the interesting groups which he continues to lead to this day.

That September I went through a pretty rough session in my bout with booze, and I finally hospitalized myself in Nebraska to dry out. I could go for extended periods without taking a drink, but when I did I was progressively less able to stop drinking and my toleration for alcohol of shorter duration. I did dry out, though, and went back to New York and free-lancing but every now and then I'd have an off-period and wind up fighting myself and the booze. During these times I was saved from making a complete spectacle of myself simply because I became helpless so quickly I couldn't work after drinking. I have always been very lucky to have enough work when I needed it and good friends to help me when I needed them.

I was back in time to do a telethon with Tony Cabot on WOR on October 22, and once more I became heavily involved in the recording studios. Almost every weekend I'd wind up at the Central Plaza, and I can remember working there on New Year's Eve for less money than usually demanded on that night. I also became good buddies with Martha Kaiser, a TWA stewardess, and several of her associates. Very often she would sample my dinners, sometimes bringing a friend or a roommate, and then go to Central Plaza with me. She was a friendly person who enjoyed music and the sociability.

Two jobs stand out in my recollections of this period. I played some concerts at a bowling alley on Sunday afternoons with a fine trio headed by pianist John Coates, and I made an album with clarinetist Tommy Reynolds. I have never heard this record, but I know that Billy Butterfield and I played some of the great Louis Armstrong classics, such as "Cornet Chop Suey."

Although I had no way of realizing it at the time, 1956 was to be something of a milestone year in my life, in spite of the fact that my bouts with alcohol often made it stormy.

While working at the Central Plaza I heard a very impressive trombone player from Alton, Illinois, named Sam Moore, and for the first time I met Kenny Davern, one of the most creative musicians I have ever known. At that time he was only 19 years old and already a brilliant clarinetist. Then a friend of mine, Allen Herman, offered to become my personal manager and, for starters, came up with a weekend at a place called the Melody Lounge, in Woodside, Long Island. So I put together a six-piece unit with Sam Moore, Kenny Davern, and Bobby Donaldson on drums; Johnny Varro, piano; and Jim Thorpe, bass. It was immediately obvious that we had the potential of a great band. Kenny was a superb player, and Sam Moore (who was 6' 4") was commercially impressive on the bandstand, especially to the ladies, as well as playing sensational trombone. Bobby Donaldson was a great drummer, and Johnny and Jim were excellent musicians. Altogether, the band offered a much greater latitude for expression and freedom of improvisation that the highly organized arrangements I had been accustomed to playing at Nick's.

Allen Herman knew people who were involved in opening a new hotel in Las Vegas, The Tropicana, and he brought them to hear the band, with the result we wound up with a contract to open at the lounge in the new hotel in July.

However, strictly from personal viewpoint, the most important development from our stay at the Melody Lounge came about through Martha Kaiser, who always brought her pals to listen to her friend Pee Wee wherever he was playing. This time she brought a young lady named Caroline May, a ground hostess for the U.S. Immigration Service at Kennedy Airport. Right from the start, I was more than casually interested, although no one could have foreseen that she would become the future Mrs. Erwin. As a matter of fact, I've never been very forward in my dealings with the opposite sex, so I doubt if I gave Caroline even the slightest indication that I was interested in knowing her better. It took several meetings before she must have become aware of this.

Then Allen Herman, giving us a goal to work for, set up a series of engagements beginning on April 10, involving a week at the Windsor Park Hotel in Washington, D. C. where we were the back-up group and part of the show which headlined the marvelous Connee Boswell. It was a most enjoyable engagement, not only because Connee was so nice to work with but also because I was visited by Caroline May, who was staying with her parents in Chevy Chase. Our relations were still on a cordial basis only, of course, since I had no idea whether she might be interested in getting to know me better—more than likely at that point she wasn't.

Tony Spargo had joined us on drums, replacing Bobby Donaldson, but otherwise the band was the same as at the Melody Lounge, and I honestly believe it was the most commercial, as well as one of the most musical, groups I'd ever had. Jim Thorpe had been with Ray McKinley's band for several years. He was an excellent bass player and very good on tuba, but equally important he was a terrific showman—a real fun guy on and off the bandstand. When he went through his antics with the tuba—very often winding up the ensemble chorus flat on his back on the floor with the tuba on top of him—the audience loved it. And like it or not, Tony Spargo had a very unusual novelty instrument in his kazoo. Sam Moore was a great salesman, and Kenny has always been a great crowd pleaser because his playing has so much intensity people readily recognize what a great musician he is. All in all, we had one helluva band, and it was accepted as such wherever we went.

From Washington we went to the Preview Lounge on Randolph Street, in the heart of downtown Chicago. We opened on April 23 and stayed for three weeks. The Preview was the top spot in Chicago for our kind of music and had a set-up similar to the Metropole's in New York, except they didn't leave the doors open to let the people outside hear the music. It did, however, have large glass panels which fronted on Randolph Street so the bandstand could be seen from the street.

We had a variety of experiences in Chicago—some good, some bad. We were staying in the famous Chelsea Hotel, on the northside, a popular hangout for musicians and show people. One night we were having an after-hours snack in a small restaurant near the hotel, when Sam Moore, who was feeling pretty good, had the bad judgment to make a few remarks to a girl who was in another booth with a quartet of obvious hoods. The remarks in themselves were not too bad, but almost anybody is bound to resent a stranger making passes at a girlfriend, and these guys were no exception. What made it worse, Sam combined too much to drink with a hot temper, and he wasn't about to take a backward step so we had quite a job getting him out of the place before he had his head smashed. It's quite easy to get your head smashed in Chicago—in any big city, for that matter—and we needed our trombone player.

We ran into another problem when the band Lothario, Johnny Varro, fell head-over-heels in love with a beautiful young lady named Jackie. We thought we were going to lose him when we moved on, but instead she married him and came along.

One night I was on the bandstand minding my own business when a customer walked up behind me and swatted me on the head with a folded newspaper. When I recovered from my natural indignation, I recognized my assailant as an old friend, Mike Riley, of Riley-Farley and "The Music Goes 'Round" fame. Thereafter, Tony Spargo and I had many hours and sessions with Mike, along with another friend of long standing, Phil Dooley, recalling the old days of the Thirties when we were all having a lot of fun. Another good friend to visit with was Vic Engle, who had played drums with Red Nichols before settling in Chicago, where his popularity made him the honorary mayor of musical circles.

Jazz Limited was still the choice spot on Rush Street, and owner Bill Rinehart, the clarinetist, was ably assisted by the wonderful Miff Mole on trombone and two excellent musicians from Detroit, Nappy Trottier on trumpet and Doc Cenardo on drums. Another good jazz band played in the

Brass Rail, which was only a block from the Preview on Randolph. Chicago in the Fifties was still holding its own as a good music town.

When we moved on, our next run was a four-week engagement at the Grandview Inn in Columbus and we were launched with a very impressive opening on May 14, followed by a very successful engagement, which lasted until my birthday on May 30. On that day I was invited to a cook-out at the house of very good friends, and I discovered a bottle of whiskey sitting on a counter top in the kitchen. I guess things were going too well, and my masochistic tendencies couldn't take it. I drained the bottle.

After that, things went downhill in a hurry. Despite the good efforts of Mike Flesch and other friends to try and dry me out, I was unable to complete the job at the Grandview. Instead, for several days I wound up in a heap on the floor of my room at the Chittenden Hotel.

When I finally did come out of it, I discovered I had succeeded in frightening Tony Spargo and Kenny Davern out of the band. They had returned to New York. Kenny had come to the hotel to check on me after the band had taken a couple of nights of harassment from the management. He found me lying in a sodden heap on the floor. After trying unsuccessfully to revive me, he sat down and wrote a sad note explaining he had had enough and departed for New York in what had to be sheer disgust.

In addition, Johnny Varro wanted to take a couple of weeks off, and Jim Thorpe had already left the band, although he had replaced himself with a good bass player. So there I was, in the middle of the United States with a string of bookings and a band that consisted of a trombone player, a bass player—and one helluva hangover! We decided that Sam Moore would go back to Chicago and audition musicians to rebuild the band, and I would take Carl, our new bass player, with me back to Falls City and use it as a base of operations. By then it was already June 10, and our next major job was in St. Louis on the 18th, so it was imperative that I straighten up and fly right in a hurry. I was determined to try.

Sam Moore enlisted the aid of Jimmy Granada, a good friend and veteran Chicago clarinetist, and they began shopping around for a drummer and clarinetist, our most urgent requirements. Johnny Varro had covered us on the piano spot by arranging for Charlie Queener to fill in for him for three weeks. In the meantime, anticipating that it might be a good idea to break in the new men on another location before we opened at the Congress Hotel in St. Louis, I booked us for the weekend of the 15th, 16th, and 17th at my old stomping ground in Kansas City, Wildwood Lakes.

On the 13th Sam called to tell me he had lined up a drummer and a clarinet man, and they would meet us on the job on the 15th. So we had a full complement of musicians when we opened at Wildwood Lakes. The only problem was the clarinet player didn't know any of the dixieland tunes. Although he was a very nice guy, he might as well have come from outer space as far as playing the kind of clarinet we needed was concerned. Afterwards Sam gave me a rather humorous account of the method he had used to audition men in Chicago. The drummer had come highly recommended and, as a matter of fact, stayed with us for a couple of months, but when it came to looking for reedmen, Sam merely went looking for a sax player who could double on clarinet and hired the first guy who showed any interest.

Now it was necessary to find a clarinetist in time for the St. Louis opening—only three days away—and, although I don't remember how we did it or who recommended him, we came up with a young man from St. Louis named Bob Schroeder, who fit the bill and knew our repertoire. We were lucky, because by now it should be obvious that a wide choice of categorized musicians is not readily available away from the major urban centers. The greatest concentration of competent musicians is in the larger cities, simply because this is where the work is. Then too, when part of the players are in Ohio and others in Nebraska, communication is not as easy as calling down the street. If you happen to be in New York, Chicago, or Los Angeles, and a replacement is necessary, you might have as many as a dozen people to choose from, but if you are in a small Midwest town, you may have one—or none.

Anyway, after a frantic weekend spent in breaking in a new band and new material, we opened at the Congress on schedule on a bill with popular singer Sylvia Sims (who had a hit record on "I Could Have Danced All Night") and a very entertaining hypnotist, Ted Boyer. Again we were lucky, because this strong entertainment took the pressure off the band. Sylvia Sims is one of the all-time great club singers, and with her in the show it was an assured success. The hypnotist used people from the audience in his act, which always establishes a strong bond between spectators and performers. So the engagement turned out to be a successful one, and to make things even more pleasant, I had a nice suite of rooms at the Congress so I was able to send for Merrily to come out from New York to spend the summer months with me.

Shortly after the Congress opening, a call came in from Allen Herman in New York. He explained that because the Tropicana Hotel in Las Vegas was not ready to open on schedule we were being rerouted to open at the Dream Room on Bourbon Street in New Orleans on July 10 for a six-week run. I didn't know whether to laugh or cry! My big chance had arrived, and here I was in St. Louis with a green band!

I was thrilled with the thought of playing in the original birthplace of our music and on the most famous jazz street in the world, but I was brought down by the knowledge that I also had the most mediocre band of my career with practically no opportunity to improve it. And for this I had nobody to blame but myself. It was all a very sobering proposition.

Our scheduled itinerary gave us a week off at the end of the Congress job. Through my buddy Bill Muchnic, I booked the band to play on Friday, July 6, at the Atchison Country Club in Atchison, Kansas, and on the following night at the Falls City Country Club. We had a hell-raisin' good time in each place, and Johnny Varro came back in time to play the two dates, but in Atchison we played on the club veranda, which turned out to be an experience for Johnny that made him wish he had stayed in New York. As usual in that area of the country, the summer brings a fantastic harvest of insects. Johnny had never seen bugs in such vast numbers before, and when he discovered the piano and surrounding area were completely covered by thousands of these harmless but ugly things, we had some difficulty persuading him to play.

But on Sunday, July 8, we piled into the car for the non-stop 1,000-mile drive from Falls City to New Orleans, with Merrily charged with the job of keeping me awake and Carl sleeping off a hangover in the back seat. We stopped for breakfast in Natchez, Mississippi, and that chicory-filled, black, southern coffee sure hit the spot with grits and eggs. We had hit the dear old southland for sure!

FORTY-TWO

AS LOCATIONS GO for New Orleans nightspots, it would be hard to beat that of the Dream Room. It was on Bourbon Street, about two blocks in from Canal and across the street from Prima's 500 Club. We were only one block south of the corner where the Old Absinthe House and the Famous Door were located, and only another block south of us was the Court of the Two Sisters and Pat O'Brian's. So we were as centrally located as we could be, despite the fact that strip joints were gradually taking over the street.

The Dream Room was operated by three partners, each of whom had interests in other clubs. As was customary in New Orleans clubs, our band alternated with another—in this case, a fine group led by drummer Paul Barbarin, with Alvin Alcorn on cornet and Louis Cottrell on clarinet. These gentlemen had a great band and are among the most illustrious of the musicians who carry on the marvelous New Orleans musical tradition.

Working hours at the club were from 11 p.m. until 4 a.m., so we were able to enjoy the fascinating New Orleans nightlife. We alternated 45-minute sets with the Barbarin band, and this gave us plenty of time to get around to other places, particularly since we had a lot of help from Helen Arlt, a lovely young lady I had met at Nick's. She was very active in the New Orleans Jazz Club, and graciously introduced us to the local people who were active in traditional jazz.

I leased an apartment on St. Charles Street, and Sam Moore, who had his wife and child with him, followed suit. This worked out quite well, because it allowed me to relax in the knowledge that Merrily now had a safe place to sleep while I was working, with Sam's wife close by in case of any emergency. In addition, the building management maintained good security with a locked outside entrance, which was important because it was usually well after 5 a.m. when I got home. I really enjoyed the nostalgia of riding the open streetcar home after work. These are open on both sides, just like the cable cars of San Francisco, and were very popular around the turn of the century, especially in warm weather. They have a great charm and, of course, provide good viewing for sight-seers as well as lots of ventilation for nature lovers.

Helen Arlt introduced me to Joe Mares, the brother of Paul Mares, who had played trumpet with the famous New Orleans Rhythm Kings. Paul was dead, but Joe was very active on the New Orleans music scene. He was in the produce business and had a large warehouse on St. Louis Street, where he had built a recording studio. It was here, during the frequent jam sessions, that I first heard some of the New Orleans musicians. One of these was Al Hirt, relatively unknown at that time but obviously a great trumpet player; another was Raymond Burke, the marvelous clarinetist. I was told that Burke operated a news and sundries store, and if the urge struck him to go fishing he'd just close the store and go. This, to me, exemplifies a great love of life which I think comes out in the creative playing of the New Orleans musicians.

Joe Mares was instrumental in our meeting many of the local musicians, and in no time it was brought home to me that I didn't need the greatest band of all time to be accepted by these gracious people.

The Famous Door also had a two-band policy, one led by the well-known trombonist Santo Pecora and the other by a tremendously talented young trumpet player, George Girard. Both bands played in the New Orleans tradition and included some of the best players available. Santo was a master of the tailgate style of trombone, and he surrounded himself with musicians of comparable stature such as Monk Hazel on drums and Roy Liberto on trumpet.

Tragically, it was to be the last season for George Girard, who died when he was only 27 years old—a terrible loss of a fine talent. He was not only an outstanding jazz player but had exceptional stage presence as a singer and entertainer. I'm sure that had he lived he would have achieved the commercial acclaim of performers like Louis Prima or Al Hirt. He had a very good band too. Although I didn't realize it at the time, the marvelous trombone player Bob Havens was part of it.

Above the Famous Door, Papa Celestin's band was still holding forth at The Paddock, where New Orleans jazz in its purist form was played, and every Sunday afternoon Tony Almerico headed an open jam session in a hall on Royal Street that was well supported by both musicians and the public. It was during one of these sessions that I heard a very young trumpet virtuoso who was so good I spoke to his father about his coming back East with us to do some guest appearances. His father informed me that his schooling had to come first, but afterwards he was free to do all the playing he wanted to. A few years later I saw the young fellow making a guest appearance on the Lawrence Welk show, introduced as a student at one of the California universities. He was a terrific player, and I only recently learned that he is a very successful studio musician in California. His name is Warren Luening.

In the mid-Fifties the established New Orleans trumpet players were Tony Almerico, Sharkey Bonano, and Roy Liberto, and all of them were active. Joe Mares also introduced me to Pete Fountain and Al Hirt, both very obviously outstanding musicians, but they were working at day jobs. It was really a thrill when Al Hirt came over to sit in with our band, and sometimes he would play a whole set for me around one in the morning—a welcome rest.

It wasn't long after this before Pete and Al started their stints with the

262

Lawrence Welk band on TV, and the rest is history. My only comment on this, aside from their great musical ability, is success couldn't happen to two nicer guys.

Joe's recording studio on St. Louis Street, in the middle of his warehouse, was where he recorded many of the fine, local jazz players for his Southland record label, contributing a number of classic sides to our jazz heritage. It was in this studio that I met Joe Rotis, the trombonist, a fine player in the classic tradition. At a dinner Joe gave for the musicians I became acquainted with some of the more classic New Orleans gastronomic treats. Joe traveled through the bayou country in the process of transacting his business of collecting and trading in hides, so he came into contact with good sources for fresh ingredients. At his dinner he served venison as the main course, with an orange wine I never knew existed, and a great fish caught in Lake Ponchartrain which the locals call "lake trout," although in reality it is a salt-water fish. The outstanding treat of the evening was a "New Orleans Crab Boil." I understand this means a bushel of crabs are boiled in an old-fashioned clothes boiler with bags of seasoning floating in the water. The crabs are then cooled, cracked, and served cold. Al Hirt proved to me that he was not only a great trumpet player, but a good eater as well. I also had a nice visit with trombonist Jack Delaney at this dinner.

Tony Almerico went out of his way to introduce us around, and also arranged for me to be interviewed on the New Orleans radio station, WWL. Along with Joe Mares and Helen Arlt, he made sure I was acquainted with the inner circle of New Orleans musical life. At one point I picked up a virus and was treated for it by no less than the great authority on New Orleans jazz, Dr. Henry Souchon himself.

Because Merrily was staying with me, I made it a point to get moving during the daylight hours so we could take in some of the historical sites and landmarks. Of these, New Orleans has more than most cities, as well as a unique charm of its own. It was particularly significant to me to visit the sites of Storyville and Congo Square—now the location of the Municipal Auditorium. Another fascinating little place, only one of many, is the little coffee shop located in the French Market where they serve the bagnets (square doughnuts) with your coffee. The ancient oyster bars and other excellent restaurants serving the almost universally good food of New Orleans—plus the bars which remain open 24 hours—maintain its reputation as a great pleasure city.

As mentioned earlier, we were working opposite the Paul Barbarin band—great musicians and fine gentlemen. Paul was especially nice to me, and he invited me to attend a funeral procession in which he was playing, to further acquaint me with the great musical traditions of New Orleans. It was a great honor for me, too, to share the bandstand with legendary musicians like Alvin Alcorn and Louis Cottrell. In 1956 it was still possible to hear many of the giants of New Orleans jazz—George Lewis and his associates; Jim Robinson; and not to forget Raymond Burke, Armand Hug, Johnny Wiggs, and Monk Hazel. All were still active and very much a part of the local scene.

In the meantime, it had become a certainty that our job in Las Vegas was not going to materialize, and we would most likely have to return to New York and regroup for the next season, the fall of 1956. Since there was no job in our immediate future, at the end of the Dream Room engagement our drummer decided to return to Chicago, the clarinetist went back to St. Louis to wait until we sent for him, and the rest of us pointed the radiators of our autos in the general direction of New York, ending one of the most interesting periods in my life.

That drive, by the way, is an education in the makeup of our country. We came up by way of the industrial area of Birmingham into the lush and beautiful territory of Tennessee around Chattanooga and the famous battlefields of the Civil War, one of the most beautiful sections of the country.

FORTY-THREE

WHEN WE GOT BACK to New York I had a long talk with Allen Herman, with the resulting conclusion that fall booking prospects were not too promising. We did a few club dates in order to scrape up some ready cash, and then I had to advise the guys to hole up some place to wait for further work. I had brought a very good drummer back with us from New Orleans, a youngster named Paul Ferara. It was a big thrill for him just to be in the Big City, but I had promised his older brother I'd look out for him and I couldn't foresee much opportunity for a brilliant future with a band that wasn't working, so I sent him back home. I'm happy to say I have since heard him playing very well with Al Hirt's band.

On September 8 we played a real fun job in Newark. An old friend of mine from Nick's, Tom Celantano, opened a beautiful new market and hired us to play for the formal opening. When we got to the location we were surprised to see huge banners stretched across the street proclaiming: GRAND OPENING CELANTANO'S MARKET—ALL WELCOME— FEATURING PEE WEE ERWIN DIXIELAND BAND.

Nevertheless, my band didn't seem to have anything like a future, and early that October I again took refuge in a heavy drunk. I must have presented a sorry sight to the outside world, but fortunately for me, while I was in the middle of it, Martha Kaiser came calling and brought Caroline May with her. I have an idea that Martha, observing my lapse, enlisted Caroline in helping to keep an eye on me.

She proceeded to do just that, and since I was very fond of her I tried as best I could to contain the debacle within reasonable bounds. I'm not really qualified to judge whether I did or didn't succeed, but at any rate we became pretty well acquainted—not a bad thing in itself. The truth is simply that she took pity on me, and I'm also sure that even in my fog I did my best to convey that I could be more than just casually interested in her. As a matter of fact, I had never met anyone quite like her. She was an interesting conversationalist, but much more than that she had firm and great principles which I found admirable, and by present-day standards almost unbelievable. As far as I was concerned, I suppose it's very obvious I was hooked—but on the other hand, in my wretched state I was hardly in a position to impress anybody with my interest.

Then Al Herman managed to get us a week's booking at a club in Philadelphia, beginning on October 29. In spite of the shakes and practically no embouchure, I managed to make it through the opening night. Caroline's sister was attending the University of Pennsylvania, studying medicine, and her brother-in-law, James Donald, was working for DuPont in Wilmington, so they lived in Philadelphia. This made it easy for Caroline to visit them and bring them to hear the band. As things worked out, it proved to be a wonderful opportunity to have a marvelous time with Caroline because by then I had dried out enough to be halfway decent company. Toward the end of the week, she returned to New York, and when the Donalds visited the club again I told them how fond I was of her. I was delightedly shocked when her sister Mary, never one to waste words, stared me straight in the eye and asked, "Why don't you marry her?"

Quite frankly, until that moment the thought had never occurred to me, because no matter how attractive I found her to be I was very much aware that I was a full 20 years older. On the other hand, I wasn't at all unhappy to learn that Caroline's relatives didn't consider me too undesirable as a prospect—even if they were only kidding.

When I stopped shaking from my hangover, we had a terrific band for that week in Philadelphia. With me were Kenny Davern, Sam Moore, Phil Failla, Johnny Varro, and Pete Rogers, and if I do say so, we turned in one helluva job—which only compounded the aggravation and inconvenience of being handed a check by the management at the end of the engagement, which couldn't be cashed until the following Monday. Even then the check had to clear before the bank would credit it, and when I asked them to call at my expense in order to rush the money everyone needed, the word came back that the check was no good.

Caroline's presence had made the week one of the most enjoyable of my life but not getting paid for the band's work cured me of leading a band—at least for the time being. I released everybody and went back to free-lancing.

In November I got a call from the management of the Metropole to come in for a conference. My relations with them had always been cordial, and now they made me an offer that luckily came at a time when I needed work, and it eventually turned out to be one of the most lucrative and convenient jobs I've ever had. It seemed that business at the Metropole had expanded to the point where they were now presenting jazz from one in the afternoon until four in the morning, seven days a week. The main night attractions played from 9 p.m. until 4 a.m. One group, under the leadership of Henry "Red" Allen, included J. C. Higginbotham, Claude Hopkins, Buster Bailey, and various drummers like "Sticks" Evans, Cozy Cole, and others of note. The other was a quintet headed by clarinetist Sol Yaged, featuring the vibraphone artist Harry Sheppard.

This schedule left the sessions from 1 p.m. to 9 p.m. wide open, to be filled by other groups—very often trios and quartets made up of excellent musicians like pianist Marty Napoleon, drummer Mickey Sheen, and others of similar caliber. What the Metropole management was offering me was the job of titular contractor. The musicians' union had refused to deal directly with the management and insisted on a contractor. Although there were many musicians working at the place, none wanted to assume the responsibility of collecting the union tax. The management had done this for a year, but now they wanted someone to act as go-between and comply with union regulations.

As the proposition stacked up, I would lead a five-piece band on Saturday and Sunday afternoons and fill in for one of the night groups on a Monday and for the other on Tuesday. Working on Saturday and Sunday afternoons and the off-nights of Monday and Tuesday, the job wouldn't interfere with anything I did free-lancing. What's more, it was very lucrative and gave me the opportunity to play with some of the greatest jazz musicians of all time—men like Charlie Shavers, Coleman Hawkins, Big Chief Russell Moore, Tony Parenti—as well as just about every other New York musician you can mention.

In many ways, Tony Parenti was one of the most interesting, both as a man and as a musician. He was a true son of New Orleans, and his playing followed the patterns of the great tradition. He was particularly proficient in the ragtime idiom and he played many of the old rags as clarinet solos.

Tony was a sociable man and he loved to drink—a pastime at which he could hold his own in any situation, but I never really saw him show it. He had a cute habit of looking at me once in awhile and saying, "Jeez, I'm stinkin'!" Then he'd pick up the clarinet and play like a demon. He was also a terrific cook, and gave me some of the recipes for Creole cooking he had learned in New Orleans. I was lucky to know Tony because he had relatives still living there who would send him seasonings, and every now and then he would pass some on to me, such as bags of file, or the strong coffee.

Tony started his New York career working in the theaters with the well-known conductor Erno Rapee, before returning to his own field in the clubs. In later years he became quite a fixture at Jimmy Ryan's.

Big Chief Russell Moore was a very colorful man and a good trombone player. He was a full-blooded Pima Indian from Central Arizona and got his start playing with some of the Indian bands in the Southwest. He always remained active in national Indian affairs. Most of the time he weighed in at around 300 lbs. and the extra weight seemed to give him extra steam on the trombone.

The Chief toured Europe a number of times with various groups, including Louis Armstrong's. On one tour he met the Duke and Duchess of Windsor, who were much taken by his music. The Duchess asked him where he played in New York, as they would like to hear him again on their next visit to the States. The Chief obligingly invited them to attend a session at Central Plaza. The Central Plaza was a catering hall on New York's Lower East Side with a large ballroom on the top floor. Here Jack Crystal presented jazz bands every Friday and Saturday from 9 p.m. until 1 a.m., and the place would be filled with close to 1,000 young people drinking beer, milling around, and screaming their heads off for their favorite musicians or whenever they approved of the music. A visit by the Duke and Duchess of Windsor would have been very interesting, to coin a masterpiece of understatement.

For many years the Chief worked with Lester Lanin's society orchestra, which included two other extremely heavy men, Jerry Packter, a saxophonist, and Chubby Silver, a bass player. Both weighed well over 200 pounds. One night during an intermission, these three goliaths were walking together across the dance floor and they were spotted by George Jaffe, a trumpet player with a flair for words. "There they go," he said, with a nod in the direction of the trio, "on their way to the elephants' graveyard."

At one time I traveled to Baltimore with the Chief and Tony to do a TV show sponsored by a local beer company. We worked with a rhythm section from the area, and after the show the producer came backstage to congratulate our front line. In the course of complimenting us, he came up with the dubious comment, "This may not be the best jazz band I've heard, but it sure is the funniest-looking." If we had any inclination to feel insulted, all we had to do was look at each other. Tony was bald and had heavy bags under his eyes, standing in the middle was dumpy little me, and rounding out what must have looked like a comic trio on the tube, was the mountainous Chief, holding his trombone like a toy.

Once the Chief took a vacation and went home to visit his relatives in Arizona. He sent me a card which read, "It's great to visit home and be chased by real squaws again." This tickled my imagination so much I laughed for a week. The Pimas are Pueblo Indians, and they live in houses carved into sides of cliffs with very small openings for door and windows, and the only means of access is by ladders. I had a hilarious mental picture of the 350-lb. Chief standing on the top of a ladder presenting his prodigious rear to the world as he tried to squeeze through a tiny door, while half-a-dozen pretty Indian maids danced around the bottom of the ladder.

The Chief used to live on 8th Avenue before he got married, and he kept a huge St. Bernard. They made a massive pair whenever he took the dog out for a stroll.

The alternating policy at the Metropole was designed to maintain interest. Each band played a half-hour set and then was joined by the new group for a fifteen-minute jam session, after which the second band would play for a half hour, and so on. This format continued throughout the operating hours and furnished an exciting program for the listening customers. It also proved to be very interesting and worthwhile for me, because mixing the bands in this manner enabled me to enjoy the great privilege of working and listening to Coleman Hawkins—one of the giants of all time. Above all, it gave me the opportunity to play with and observe one of the greatest musicians ever to pick up a trumpet, Charlie Shavers. I admired this man as much as any musician I have ever played with, and I learned a great deal from him.

It didn't matter to Charlie whether one customer or 500 were listening.

When he got on a bandstand he played at the top of his considerable ability. I truly believe that aside from his amazing technical accomplishment he was one of the greatest ballad players of all time. In addition to this, he was such a fine gentleman that he never made the other guy look bad—and, believe me, he could have very easily. Today, these genteel qualities are shared by Clark Terry, I find, way beyond comparison as a man and a musician.

On Saturday, December 1, 1956, I took part in a televised memorial program presented by Jackie Gleason in tribute to Tommy Dorsey, who had just passed away. Many of the ex-Dorsey musicians were invited, including Johnny Mince, Carmen Mastren, and Bud Freeman. Ironically, earlier in the year I had worked on a record album commemorating Paul Whiteman's 50th anniversary in music, which reunited many of the Whiteman alumni, including the Dorsey brothers, Jimmy and Tommy. Little did any of us realize it would be TD's last record date.

FORTY-FOUR

THE YEAR 1957 BEGAN with a very heavy schedule. Besides the work at the Metropole, I was busy recording, particularly with Enoch Light's labels as part of his house band. The Cha-Cha was at the peak of its popularity, and I think Enoch decided to corner the market completely with records designed for cha-cha dancers. We did two or three dates weekly for about six months, adding cha-cha rhythm to every composition known to man from Bach to Stravinsky. I never heard any of the records, but I'm sure Enoch sold them by the ton.

Early in February I did a telethon with Tony Cabot, a good friend since the Venezuelan trip in 1949, and he came up with an interesting proposition. He had a band on a daytime radio show for NBC called "Bandstand," and he asked me to recruit a three-man front line to play some dixieland tunes on the program. I recommended Kenny Davern, who was able to double on baritone sax in the big band, and Sam Moore, who could do the same thing on trombone. We were scheduled to do a dixie tune on each show, and since Tony had a good rhythm section, which included Marty Napoleon on piano, we would have a good jazz band.

About a week before the broadcasts were to begin I learned that in conjunction with the radio show Tony had booked his band into the Arcadia Ballroom on Broadway. I told Tony I didn't mind working at the Arcadia, but I would have to be off for the Saturday and Sunday matinee sessions because of my obligation at the Metropole, but he wouldn't hear of it. He said he wouldn't permit any substitutions in his band under any circumstances.

This, of course, would jeopardize my job at the Metropole, and I told Tony it didn't seem worth it for one week's work—aside from the "Bandstand" broadcast, which I had agreed to do. Nevertheless, he insisted that I work the Arcadia job, and left me with the chore of asking for time off at the Metropole. This I did, and in contrast to Tony's hard-nosed attitude, the Metropole management very graciously told me I could be absent for the matinee with their good wishes. I would have made more money, by the way, for the four sessions I missed at the Metropole than I received for the "Bandstand" show—not to mention playing the Arcadia for strictly scale—

but as a favor to Tony I agreed to work the radio show and the ballroom. So I lost money on the deal, placed my Metropole job on the line and, as things developed, I was one of the very few guys in the Arcadia band who didn't send a substitute. Instead, the Arcadia band turned into a parade of different guys for each session.

All of which was bad enough, after what Tony had put me through, but then he never had the good grace to offer an apology or even an explanation. All he would have had to say was that he was sorry but the men had taken advantage of him, or that he particularly wanted to be sure I would always be on the job—in fact, he could have said anything, but he didn't. I guess more than anything else my feelings were hurt, but there is no question I was put upon, and I've never forgotten it.

Early in March, however, I was offered a rather unusual opportunity—a chance to be part of a Broadway stage production. A very successful set designer, Frederick Fox, called me in to make a record for him which was to be used in a production he was working on at the Broadway Theater. It seemed that in the play there was a scene in which one of the characters, an ex-soldier and bugler, had a dream about his early exploits. In the dream he started to blow a bugle call which was abruptly cut off (a la Gunga Din) when he was wounded. The record I was to make was to be played off-stage for the duration of the play's run, and I was to receive a weekly salary for the entire period. Needless to say, just when I had worked out extensive plans for a luxurious vacation in the Caribbean based on this potential bonanza, the play folded after three days.

Meantime, in spite of all this activity I was steadily becoming more emotionally involved with Caroline and getting to rely more and more on our relationship as the main reason for my existence. To me she was everything wonderful. Even from an intellectual standpoint I found her to be the most stimulating person I had ever known. I kept toying with the idea of marriage, but I was still very much aware of the 20-year difference in our ages and, looking back at it now, I might even have been using this as a handy, if feeble, excuse to postpone things for fear that if I were to bring things out into the open I might only succeed in ruining our whole relationship. The risk was too big to take, so I was content to let the situation drift.

Around this time my recording work took a couple of interesting turns. I made a couple of albums with society bandleader Meyer Davis, among others, but the one that stands out in my mind as exceptional was recorded for Pickwick Sales with Claude Hopkins, issued on their Design label. Design was a volume label which enjoyed large sales because it was marketed through supermarkets and department stores at discount prices. Because of the late hours worked by the men Claude wanted to use on the session, he decided to split it in two, each one starting at 4 a.m. It's the first time I can remember going to work around the same time farmers feed the chickens. The result was an album called "The Golden Era of Dixieland," and besides Claude and me, it featured Buster Bailey, Vic Dickenson, Milt Hinton, and George Wettling. It was a fun album to make, and I'm inclined to think the odd hours helped

271

contribute to it.

My life at this time was relatively happy and was, at least, going along on a reasonable level, so even if I could remember much about what happened next I would be hard put to think of an excuse. All it boils down to is that Caroline went out of town for a short visit to some place, and while she was gone I hit the bottle again. This time it was bad—a binge that lasted for a couple of weeks and I was in pretty sorry shape. Caroline came back to New York but had to leave almost immediately due to prior commitments to go to Nassau. I believe she had made plans to introduce me to her parents, but I was certainly in no condition to meet them—and if they found out why, I'm sure they were hardly impressed. So my state of mind, such as it was, was hardly improved by the knowledge that I was doing a great job of botching the best thing that ever happened to me, and I drank more.

When I finally managed to pull out of this siege, on a gradual basis, it was mainly through the help and good offices of my friend Merrill Kaye. He opened the campaign by visiting the neighborhood bars and liquor stores and warning them not to sell me any booze—threatening to report them to the A.B.C., which might result in their being closed. They cooperated, whether or not the threat had any real impact or not, and at the same time Merrill showed up at my apartment with a couple of bags full of food and did everthing he could to sober me up. He even went to the extent of encouraging me to go along with him on jobs, to sit in the 4th trumpet chair and play when I wanted to. I will be forever grateful to Merrill for this kindness and consideration.

The drinking finally stopped, and within a few days I had regained my composure. But now I missed Caroline terribly. Although she had probably told me where she was going, I was too confused to remember and I began to panic. Suppose she had given up on me in disgust? Suppose she didn't intend to come back—ever? Not that I could blame her, but what would I do without her? I tried frantically to get in touch with her at her home in Chevy Chase without success, and then went on to try every place I could think of. She wasn't at any of them. Meanwhile, I couldn't sleep. I was still shaky from my recent bout with the bottle, and finally the combination of these things caught up with me.

After two successive sleepless nights I was walking down 6th Avenue, only a few blocks from my apartment, when I suddenly experienced the strangest feeling of my entire life. It was more than a mere sensation of dizziness—I had the impression the world around me was rocking from an earthquake. I was in front of a drugstore, so I managed to stagger in and ordered a cup of coffee, thinking it might help. Instead it seemed to make me feel worse.

I tried to make the druggist understand how I felt, and he gave me a whiff of ammonia—probably thinking I was having a heart attack—and then was good enough to place a phone call to Harold Meyers, whose office was only a block away on 53rd Street. Harold picked me up in a cab and rushed me to my doctor, the good overseer of the acting profession, Dr. Meylackson, whose diagnostic abilities were beyond compare. After checking me over thoroughly, he accurately pinpointed my trouble as acute vitamin deficiency of the central nervous system.

In analyzing what had brought on this condition, the doctor finally narrowed things down to a new trick I had resorted to during my last drinking bout, one I had never tried before. Usually I drank scotch or brandy, neither of which were intended to be consumed at the rate of three fifths a day, but even so I had weathered many rough seas at this rate, and as long as I stuck to these fluids I suffered no dire consequences. At least, nothing like my present state. But this time I began to run out of money toward the latter part of my drinking, and by that time I was too far gone to write a check. Since I knew my finances to be limited, and at the same time, even in my fog, beginning to have a desire to taper off, I started drinking white wine.

I have since been told that white wine is sometimes artifically aged by chemicals and in excess these chemicals will attack the nervous system. For several days I had been consuming over a gallon a day of cheap sherry, and although the full effects didn't catch up to me until a week after I had stopped drinking, there was no doubt this was the reason for my illness.

I was sober, but mentally I was as low as I could get. I was convinced that Caroline had given up on me, and physically I was in no shape to work, so I asked the doctor if I could fly home to Nebraska. I could at least get some rest there and, even if I croaked, I'd be with home folks. He gave it some thought and finally came up with a solution. He said he could give me a massive dose of medicine to hold me for awhile. Then, if someone could put me on a plane, and somebody else would meet me at the airport in Kansas City to take me home to Nebraska, and a doctor waiting to take care of me there, it would be possible.

With the help of Harold Meyers the arrangements were made, and I was loaded on a plane at Laguardia Airport which was met in Kansas City by Al Maust. He took me to Falls City, where my lifelong friend Dr. Bob Cook was waiting to check me over. By then I was so helpless I was afraid to walk alone, and my coordination was so bad I couldn't even reach my handkerchief pocket. I hadn't slept in three days.

The medication prescribed by Dr. Meylackson was standard in treating cases like mine and met with the full approval of Dr. Cook, but at this stage the most important therapy was sleep, so he gave me an injection of a sedative that barely left me time to get into bed before it knocked me out for a full ten hours. After that he proceeded to give me two shots daily of liver extract, iron, and Vitamin B1. At the end of three weeks, I was finally able to function normally. I was also completely convinced at last that I had three options open to me for the rest of my life: 1) I could keep drinking until I was a physical wreck; 2) I could keep drinking until I found an early grave; or 3)I could stop drinking. And if I didn't follow the third option, I deserved either of the first two.

I was with my family and among good friends and gradually getting back my health, but I wasn't happy. I felt as though I just didn't care to go on without Caroline May, but there didn't appear to be anything I could do about it. I had no idea where she was and, even though my mother and Aunt Hazel kept assuring me I would hear from her sooner or later—that such a fine person was bound to get in touch—I was too depressed to accept this. After all, I had disappeared from all my regular hangouts too, so who knew where I was—or cared? Besides, I was firmly convinced that Caroline had every reason for never wanting to see an old drunk like me again.

They did everything possible to cheer me up. I went on a picnic in the country in the company of two fine couples, Buck and Katie Badunah, and Albert and Helen Maust, and I was probably the most forlorn excuse for a companion they had ever had to put up with.

You can just imagine my joy and delight that Friday, July 12, when without any warning a phone call came from Caroline, who told me she was in Pennsylvania visiting friends. I was so excited the only thing I could think of was to plead with her to get on a plane for Kansas City, and I would meet her at the airport. I could hardly believe it when she readily agreed and said she would arrive on Sunday evening, the 14th—her birthday—but it was the greatest news I could have had.

Now that I knew she was coming, I suddenly felt strong and healthy, except that when I began to think the situation over I was once more saddled with doubts. What would I do with her when she arrived? What could I say to her? Then common sense took over and made me realize there was only one thing I was absolutely certain about—I never wanted to be separated from her again. In light of that conviction, there was only one course of action to consider.

I went into a conspiracy with Albert Maust about ways and means of smoothing the way so Caroline and I could get married as quickly as possible. Albert, Richardson County judge for many years, knew the right people to facilitate such matters and was more than willing to help. The big gamble, of course, was that I was putting the cart before the horse—I had never had the slightest indication from Caroline that she might even consider marriage. In view of recent circumstances, it was expecting a helluva lot. But I didn't have much in the way of an alternative. Even if, by some miracle, she consented, we were at a disadvantage just being located in Falls City, which is 90 miles from Lincoln, the state capital, where it was necessary to have a blood test before a marriage could be performed, and sending samples through the usual channels would take days. Judge Maust called the necessary agencies in Lincoln and obtained their agreement to give Caroline and me the blood tests on Monday, if we could get to Lincoln. They would phone the results to him. Once that was accomplished, he told me, we could retain the proper clergyman in Falls City and most likely get the marriage under way by Wednesday. I promptly replied that I had no intention of doing any such thing—that he and I had been born one week apart in May 1913, had been friends and played music together for years (in fact, all of our lives) and if anyone was going to perform the marriage ceremony for Caroline and me, it would be Judge Albert Maust. He squirmed and argued that being married by the clergy was the best way, but I stuck to my guns and he finally, but

Caroline and Pee Wee

reluctantly, agreed.

Now the only obstacle to the final success of my plot was to get the girl to say yes! I couldn't see why she would, but I was determined to try.

I met Caroline at the airport about 6 p.m. that Sunday, and afterwards we drove north until we came to a roadside lunchroom where we stopped for coffee. It wasn't the most romantic spot in the world, but there was nothing to distract her attention while I unfolded the details of my plot and asked the big question. When she agreed to accept my proposal I was happier than I had ever been in my life, and I wasted no more time. We drove to Lincoln (in a car borrowed from Judge Maust), had the blood tests, bought two wedding rings, and then headed back to Falls City with the temperature around 103° — something that happens in Nebraska every now and then.

On Wednesday, July 17, we assembled in the Judge's chambers at the Richardson County Courthouse, and Judge Albert Maust tied a strong knot to unite two very happy people. My friend Robert Hoban gave the bride away, and my mother, Chloe Erwin, happily gave away her son.

A few hours later the Judge, the Best Man, and the groom, assisted by Buck Badunah, took part in one helluva jam session prior to the bride and the groom taking off for a marvelous one-night honeymoon at the historic Robidoux Hotel in St. Joseph, Missouri.

FORTY-FIVE

I HAD PULLED OFF A MINOR MIRACLE, and Caroline and I were married. However, now that my dream was an accomplished fact, I had some serious breaks in the fence to mend. In my whirlwind courtship of their daughter, I had never stopped to consider how Caroline's family might view the whole thing—especially since I had practically abducted her, or so it might appear in their eyes—and they are very genteel people. So now it was up to me to attempt to make amends. I didn't expect this to be easy. After all, I had side-stepped all such formalities as asking for their daughter's hand, a reasonable period of courtship, and letting them get to know me to the extent of expressing their approval or disapproval. Instead I had proceeded with poor taste and effrontery, without saying anything to anybody, including those very close to Caroline. I hadn't even given them the option of attending or declining to attend the wedding.

Back in Falls City, after our one glorious night at the Robidoux, we talked it over, trying to decide the best way to handle the matter. Caroline had made a date to meet her folks in Chevy Chase on Friday, the 19th, and we finally agreed it might be best to convince her family that she hadn't married a worthless alcoholic. Afterwards, we would meet in New York. I'm certain that the way we went about things hurt her family, but they had the good grace to pass it over. As it was, Caroline's mother had little left to her but the small consolation of mailing announcements that her daughter was married. I'm equally certain it took quite a few years for them to get over the idea she had married some kind of a savage.

Before my illness, I had made an agreement with my associate Danny Lapidos to play the month of August with his band at Kutsher's Country Club, in Monticello, New York. The job included room and board, but now that I was married it was out of the question. After I got back to New York, I called Danny to explain why I couldn't do the month with him and, in the middle of the conversation, he asked me to hold the phone a few minutes while he told the owner what had happened. Then when he came back he said the situation had been resolved—Mr. Kutsher had said to come ahead and

277

bring my bride with me.

I met Caroline on the following Monday and together we went to Monticello, where for the entire month of August the good people at Kutsher's provided us with a honeymoon cottage and marvelous food and drink at their expense. It isn't often you hear of a free honeymoon, and we will always be grateful for the perfect time we had, thanks to Danny and the other wonderful people at Kutsher's. It was especially appreciated since our assets at the time consisted of a sickly bank account of $44, although we were far too happy to worry about finances.

After Labor Day we returned to New York, and again I ran head on into a lucky break. Wild Bill Davison, who had been working at Eddie Condon's club on West 3rd Street in Greenwich Village, left on a trip to Europe, and I was invited to take his place. Just like that I became a member of the Condon mob, and my musical life as well as my personal life was off to a new start.

My marriage immediately changed my life for the better. I could see no place for alcohol in the scheme of things from that point on. I was happy, contented, had a wonderful wife, and there was no reason for ever taking another drink.

Caroline's parents had been divorced many years before so she actually had two sets of parents. Her father, George E. May, M.D., lived in Wellesley, Massachusetts, and had remarried. We took a couple of days to visit them. Her father was a very nice man, and with his wife and a small son, Elliot, greeted me very cordially. So now, at least, I was acquainted with one half of Caroline's family. Meeting the other half, her mother and stepfather, the Thompsons, would have to wait until they returned from a trip to the Far East.

We had a lot of catching up to do on the financial end, too, so I wasted no time in getting back into the full swing of things. In addition to playing at Condon's, I began doubling some at my old job at the Metropole and once more became very active in the recording studios. I made some albums with the society bands of Ted Straeter, Ben Cutler, and Meyer Davis; a lot of transcriptions with George Nelson; and was usually good for two or three sesions a week for Enoch Light. Enoch was still trying to record every tune ever written as a cha-cha.

Working at Eddie Condon's, I soon discovered, was an experience in itself and one that provided me with a completely new view of the music business—the world of Eddie Condon. The clientele in the Condon club was quite different than at Nick's. Eddie was on a first-name basis with hundreds of people with a variety of artistic talents, had put together the first jazz shows for TV, and was a favorite of all the New York writers and artists. It wasn't uncommon for the club to be graced by the presence of people like Bing Crosby, Johnny Mercer, Lee Wiley, Charles Adams, and numerous other celebrities. One night, for instance, I looked up after playing a solo to find Errol Flynn leaning on the rail beside the bandstand, watching me. In addition, the club drew a lot of young people and the regular tourist crowd, but there was always a representation of the more talented people in New

York.

Eddie was one of the most humorous men I have ever known. Drunk or sober, he was a very funny man and a great conversationalist. I doubt if he ever met anybody who didn't like him. He had millions of friends and fans. He had been the prime mover of the Austin High Gang in Chicago, was in on all of the activity of the Twenties involving Frank Teschmacher, the McPartland brothers—Jimmy and Dick—Bud Freeman, Bix Beiderbecke, Mezz Mezzrow, Wild Bill, Pee Wee Russell, and anybody else who had anything to do with jazz in Chicago. He could tell endless stories about the mobsters of the Capone era he and his friends had worked for.

Eddie's sharp wit was ever present, but I'm afraid he was by no means a great guitarist. He started out playing banjo, but when he switched to guitar very few ever heard much coming out of it. Saxophonist Larry Binyon, something of a wit in his own right, once said that Condon fell asleep on the bandstand one night with his hand under his chin and leaning on his guitar. After awhile his hand slipped out from under his chin and fell across the strings on the way down, and that was the only time anyone ever heard a sound come out of Eddie's guitar.

I first met Eddie in 1934 when he was running around New York trying to organize various places as showcases for Condon and Friends, but the first time I really became aware of his activities was at a session—or gathering of musicians—at a party in the Decca studios. From this I came to appreciate his vast ability to organize great jazz groups, probably his most important asset. Attending and participating were Pee Wee Russell, George Brunis, Jack Teagarden, Frank Signorelli, Dave Tough—in short, practically anybody who had anything to do with the jazz scene in New York at that time. Sessions such as these were the forerunners of the concert concept which Condon and

Bandleader Ben Cutler

279

Eddie Condon

Ernie Anderson were to promote in the Forties. The Town Hall concerts really paved the way for the future, just as the Condon recording sessions for Commodore and Decca opened the door to jazz albums.

The band at Eddie Condon's was a good one. We had Herb Hall on clarinet; Cutty Cutshall, trombone; Gene Schroeder, piano; Leonard Gaskin, bass; and George Wettling on drums. We were all under the direction of Eddie Condon. Cliff Jackson played intermission piano. When Eddie personally conducted the sets there's no doubt he inspired a lot of extra fire from the band, and yet his manner on the bandstand was very relaxed and he was always ready with a quip to suit any occasion. Caroline hit on the best description of a Condon-led set: She said his direction of the musicians presented a rather loose routine of improvisation giving great latitude to the individual, which had a tendency to bring the listeners into the performance.

I don't really know what this faculty was, but for certain it was there, and it could be very stimulating to an audience, his great success as an impresario certainly indicates that he had a lot to offer. I'm very grateful for the opportunities I had to be associated with him.

At Condon's I played for the first time with Herb Hall, who, like his brother Ed, is one of the great exponents of the Albert-system clarinet. Both brothers improvised with tremendous sound and feeling in the New Orleans tradition. Every now and then when you work with somebody new it gives you the chance to learn and gain from the experience, and working with Herb was no exception. Playing with new musicians always results in an expanded repertoire, at the very least, because they generally play tunes that are unfamiliar to you. In addition to his great musical ability, Herb is one of the finest gentlemen I know. Playing with Cutty Cutshall offered many rewards, too. As everybody knows, he was one of the giants of the trombone. Altogether it was a real thrill for me to be a part of that front line.

A book could—and perhaps some day will—be written about the drummer and painter George Wettling, an exceedingly talented man. He was from Topeka, Kansas, but he became part of the Chicago groups in the Twenties. His style on drums was very similar to that of Dave Tough, and during my Condon stay he was a part of a fabulous rhythm section. Gene Schroeder, a marvelous pianist, was from Madison, Wisconsin. He came to New York in the early Forties to play with Joe Marsala and, after a short time, joined Eddie. He took part in all the early concerts and recording sessions, including the Commodores and the Condon trips abroad, and had a unique approach to the keyboard. Leonard Gaskin, a Brooklyn-born bass player, worked with Dizzy Gillespie, Eddie South, and Charlie Shavers before joining Condon, and rounded out the section nicely. All in all, the stint at Condon's provided a lot of musical latitude and was a very memorable period.

There's no question about it—1957 was a banner year in my life. I married a lovely girl, gave up alcohol for good, and managed to pull my career back together and regroup my finances. I was, indeed, a very lucky guy!

FORTY-SIX

THE BEGINNING OF 1958 saw me back at my old stand, the Metropole, and also extremely busy with recording. I was doing quite a few sessions each week and making out quite well. At one point I had the fun of making some commercials with Billy Maxted's new band. I hadn't worked with a truly organized outfit since leaving Nick's, so the arrangements were a bit complex for me, but Billy made allowances for the fact that I didn't know his library. I also did a good bit of TV background work, and I recall in particular two shows based on music from the Civil War, directed by folk music authority Oscar Brand. One show depicted experiences of General Grant and the sequel was based on those of General Lee. What made them so outstanding to me was the authentic Civil War music, most of which I had never heard before. They were aired on "Camera Three," over CBS.

On March 30, I was playing a job with Danny Lapidos at Manhattan Center when I received word that I was the father of a baby girl, born at 12:30 a.m. at Doctors Hospital. I couldn't get to the hospital until 2 a.m., and although they were kind enough to show me the baby, they wouldn't awaken Caroline. I went back the next morning and was delighted to find that both mother and daughter were doing fine. During this time I was free-lancing, so I had ample time to see my family. My mother-in-law, Mrs. Thompson, paid us a visit to see the newest member, Georgine. It was a very happy time.

On June 18 my sister-in-law, Mary Donald, finished her term of internship in Philadelphia and was awarded her M.D. from the University of Pennsylvania.

Billy Maxted wanted to take his band on the road. He had recently made a hit record, and he felt its popularity would bring in very profitable audiences on a swing around the country. I agreed to organize a band to take his place at Nick's, and for the most part took over a group that had been working as a unit with Phil Napoleon but very familiar to me—Kenny Davern, Harry DeVito, Johnny Varro, Charley Treager, and Mousie Alexander on drums. For certain it was a great little band, and it was a pleasure to be back on the bandstand at Nick's with such a versatile and musical group.

We were there until December 7, when Maxted's bunch came back to pick up the chores. But we had a two-week vacation from August 23 to September 16, and we took advantage of it to record the first of two albums contracted for with United Artists. Kenny Davern, whose musical judgment I have always appreciated and trusted, did most of the groundwork.

At Nick's he had perfected an unbelievably successful solo on "Over the Waves," using a straight, heavy, four-four beat behind it. The pitch and intensity he built up would literally drive the audience into a frenzy, and to this day I consider it to be the most consistently sensational solo ever heard on a bandstand. We naturally picked it as a must for the album, but cutting the number to comply to normal record length destroyed its effect.

Kenny also gave me some material from the Jelly-Roll Morton "Red Hot Peppers" repertoire and, by a stroke of luck, when I approached the E. B. Marks publishing company—who had taken over the original Melrose catalog—they were able to supply several of the Morton arrangements which had been copied from the original scores. Since then, of course, much of the Morton repertoire has been recreated, but I believe we were among the first to attempt it. In addition to the Morton tunes, we played a couple of rags—one, an original, could have been deleted without any great loss to the overall effort. We used a banjo, and on some tracks a tuba, which I believe enhanced our effort to authenticate the Jelly-Roll material. I was quite pleased with the result. Besides Kenny, the personnel included Lou McGarity, Dick Hyman, Tony Gattuso, Jack Lesberg, Harvey Phillips, who played the tuba tracks, and Cliff Leeman. The album was called, "Oh, Play That Thing!" As far as I'm concerned, it's the best album I have ever had my name on. Even the cover design won an award.

On the day after the date for United Artists, I took my family back to Falls City so Georgine could be christened in the Episcopal Church there. Her godparents were Albert and Helen Maust, and I felt very gratified that we were able to get home for this ceremony because all of the big events in my family history, dating back to the middle of the last century, took place in that area. Needless to say, it was a momentous occasion and a very pleasant visit.

After our brief vacation we continued into the fall season at Nick's, but Charley Treager left us. He was in the last year of engineering school at Columbia and felt it was no longer possible to work six nights a week until 4 a.m. and still do justice to his studies. So Irv Manning played bass with us for the rest of our time at Nick's.

That last quarter of 1958 was a hectic one for me, working at Nick's at night and at the recording studios in the day. It was one of the busiest periods I've ever had, but I wasn't drinking so I could cope with it, and I'm happy to say I succeeded in reestablishing myself in the confidence of the management at Nick's. It was a great feeling and, except for the baby disturbing my sleep, everything was in great shape.

One evening I went to work at Nick's and found Grace Rongetti entertaining her friend Mrs. Sinatra. I stopped at their table to pay my respects, and in the course of conversation griped a little bit about the baby having colic and interfering with my sleep. Mrs. Sinatra promptly informed me that she had once been a nurse in a maternity ward, and if I would put two drops of gin in the baby's bottle it would cure her colic. After I had thought this suggestion over for a second, I couldn't resist asking, "If I feed my baby a bottle with gin in it, will she grow up able to sing like your son Frank?"

FORTY-SEVEN

THE NEW YEAR began with something a bit out of the ordinary—playing with Meyer Davis for Nelson Rockefeller's first Inaugural Ball in Albany. I enjoyed it immensely.

Also on the positive side, my recording commitments carried over, and around this time I worked on a dixieland album with Bobby Byrne for Grand Award. I recall we had a pretty good line-up, including Peanuts Hucko and Billy Maxted, and it reminded me that it was time I started thinking about the second album I owed United Artists.

Kenny Davern had introduced me to a talented singer from Pennsylvania, Chet Ely. Chet sang blues and spirituals with the relaxed feeling of Jack Teagarden, so we decided to play a number of spirituals on the album, using Chet on the vocals and the jazz band in the background. With this idea in mind, I got the inspiration to take it a giant step further. Along with many other people, I had always been impressed with the fine choral work of a famous singing group of the Twenties and Thirties, led by a most accomplished gentleman named Hall Johnson. The Hall Johnson Singers interpreted spirituals and chorales on a number of radio shows and were favorites of mine. I asked Mr. Johnson if he would be interested in furnishing a group to back Chet Ely on our record.

He agreed to become part of our effort, and this led to my attending several preparatory sessions with him and his singing group. I had collaborated with the fine composer Willard Robison, a man with an outstanding talent for writing music with a spiritual flavor, and we turned out several numbers, two of which we considered good enough to include on the album: "Everybody Needs a Helping Hand," and "Camp Meeting Friends." In addition, we planned to do "Walkin' with the King," "Lord, Lord, You Sure Been Good to Me," and others of a similar nature. So I worked out sketch sheets on the tunes for the musicians to follow and then watched in amazement as Hall Johnson developed wonderful choral backgrounds for the selections—a unique experience in itself. He had the marvelous ability to master a score himself and then orally convey to the individual singers the parts he wanted them to sing. Of course, this was the best way to give them the widest possible latitude for personal expression while at the same time conforming to the overall pattern.

Altogether we picked 12 numbers for the record, four of them to be vocal presentations, and planned to use the same front line that had recorded "Oh, Play That Thing,"—Kenny on clarinet, and Lou on trombone, with the rest of the band consisting of Dick Hyman, Milt Hinton, Ossie Johnson, and the great banjo player who had worked with Jelly-Roll Morton, Lee Blair. In my opinion, Lee had the prettiest sound on banjo I've ever heard. In planning the instrumental part of the album, we decided that on some of the numbers we would attempt to recreate the sound of the early New Orleans bands. They used a straight, unaccented four-four rhythm which had a regular, strong pulse, and when played by a four-man rhythm section it lent a certain resonance to the overall sound. This was the same rhythm, with its tendency to build and build to a climax, that Kenny had used so successfully on "Over the Waves."

For additional tone-color we intended to use a muted trumpet with the clarinet, playing melodically and exchanging the melody line back and forth, sometimes with the harmony line above it, and with an organ background played by Dick Hyman, who happens to be a master of this instrument.

It should be evident that we put a lot of thought into the project, and I'm certain that if all had gone well the results would have been exceptional, but, as is so often the case, unforeseen problems arose. When we got to the studio we were greeted with the disastrous news that Chet Ely had such a sore throat he couldn't sing a note. It was disastrous because without Chet we couldn't use the background of the Hall Johnson Singers and, without either, the entire character of the album as we had planned it was changed. Inasmuch as we were all in the studio, the company paid the artists anyway, and the band went ahead and recorded an all-instrumental album called "Down by the Riverside." Some of the tracks turned out well, especially a beautiful version of "Careless Love" as a lovely trombone solo by Lou McGarity, spelled by a sensitive blues clarinet solo by Kenny. Milt Hinton contributed an outstanding bass solo on "Swing Low Sweet Chariot," and we came up with a nice cut on "Just a Little While to Stay Here," a duet for trumpet and clarinet. So go the plans of mice and men!

As I've mentioned several times, I did a lot of recording for Enoch Light's labels, long before I agreed to make records for United Artists. I only jumped at the United Artists offer because the deal was based on higher royalty rates than Enoch offered. Which only shows the kind of a businessman I am, because I forgot to take into account that he sold records in tremendous quantities, while many of the other companies producing records lacked proper distribution. Even worse, their products failed to sell for lack of promotion. However, I felt indebted to Enoch, and since he wanted some dixieland albums in his catalog, I told him I would play on them if he didn't use my name. I would make the albums for production cost and no royalties.

He accepted my offer (although I still receive royalty checks for some of my original tunes he used), and I made three albums for him—"The Charleston City All-Stars Play Dixieland," which was issued on the Grand Award label, and two others which came out on Command under the name of "The Dixie Rebels." These are all fairly good albums and feature a number of fine musicians—Kenny Davern, Lou McGarity or Harry DeVito, Johnny Varro or Gene Schroeder, Milt Hinton or Jack Lesberg, and either Cliff Leeman or Mousie Alexander. On some tracks we also used Lee Blair on banjo. But the most unusual thing about them has nothing to do with the music. Because I had asked Enoch not to use my name, he dreamed up the catchy pseudonym of "Big Jeb Dooley" and then proceeded to write liner notes establishing a fantastic pedigree for this "legendary" trumpet player that should qualify as a masterpiece of modern fiction.

In the meantime, Phil Napoleon was back on the stand at Nick's and he had developed dental problems. I finished a couple of nights for him when things got too bad, and then on March 24, I took over to give Phil a three-week rest, winding up on April 12. May and June were saved from boredom by Joel Herron. He was conducting a CBS show starring Jimmie Dean, and arranged for our jazz band to make two guest appearances. Both were a lot of fun, and Jimmie Dean was a friendly guy and a pleasure to work with.

New York can broil during the summer months, as anybody who has lived there will attest. Caroline was about to have our second baby, so we took a month's rental on a place on Long Beach, Long Island, in the hope of keeping cool near the beach. We consumed a lot of seafood and our stay resulted in some pretty good jam sessions. Lee Blair lived nearby, so we entertained the Long Beach residents with our free music.

On July 28, we opened again at Nick's for a run that took us well into the fall season, and during the Sunday afternoon session of August 9, my daughter Cathy was born at Doctors Hospital, arriving at 5:30 p.m. I went to the hospital during our break—from 8 to 9:30—and saw Caroline and Cathy, and when I got to the bandstand at 9:30 I discovered that the whole joint was ready and waiting to help me celebrate the birth of my little girl. Grace and her daughter Judy had dressed a cute baby doll which was prominently displayed on the intermission piano for all to see and admire, and the drinks all around had to be on the proud father.

The band for this session at Nick's included Kenny Davern, Harry DeVito, Johnny Varro, Tony Spargo, and Charley Traeger. With the job at Nick's and plenty of activity in the recording studios from July well into February 1960, my career in music was lucrative but routine.

FORTY-EIGHT

IT WAS AROUND THIS TIME that Caroline and I learned that the apartment building where we lived was going to be torn down, which meant we had to start looking for a new place to live. Rents in the city were already very high, but even if we were willing to pay a premium merely for the sake of convenience, we now had to take into consideration two small children and the latest addition to the family, a cocker spanial named Jiggs. So instead of hunting for another apartment, we decided to look for a house.

I had no experience at all in house-hunting. The last time I had been involved in anything like real estate was when I rented the house on Long Island with an option to buy. It had ten rooms and a price tag of $8,500—in 1935. For a number of years I'd known friends who had moved to Bergen County in New Jersey, and I liked this area better than any other within easy commuting distance of New York. It was higher and dryer than most, and the commuting couldn't be much easier unless they ran a subway across the river. So we checked around and the first house we heard about being offered for sale belonged to a friend, Charlie Queener, the composer-pianist, and it was located in Hillsdale. Caroline and I made a trip to Hillsdale to look at Charlie's house and we were very favorably impressed. It was a lovely place situated on a nice plot of ground, with trees, shrubs and all the things that go with life in the suburbs, and certainly very adequate for our family needs. So we asked the price.

When Charlie quietly answered, "Twenty-seven thousand dollars," I ran back to the city in a state of shock and didn't recover for at least three weeks.

After I came out of my near collapse, we started looking again, and it wasn't long after the usual rounds when we fully realized that Charlie's house was a very good buy. But in the meantime we found a house in New Milford which offered excellent potential for expansion, and we stated negotiating in mid-February. I wound up buying that house—our present home—and I can assure you that in the long run it cost considerably more than the shocking $27,000.

We finished up at Nick's in February, followed again by Billy Maxted's band, and on February 11 I started work on a new CBS series starring Kate Smith. This turned out to be an unusual experience because the band—especially for a studio outfit, and one backing a conservative performer like Kate Smith—included many new faces and a novel approach. It was conducted by the trumpet-playing arranger Neil Hefti, who had earned a considerable reputation as an innovative writer for the Woody Herman band. He was assisted on the arrangements by Bill Stegmeyer, whose reputation had been made writing and playing for jazz bands.

Kate Smith, a very gracious and friendly person, often visited with the band during rehearsals and once told us something about her personal design for living that impressed me a lot. Anyone who has ever heard her sing knows the great power of her voice—she had always been capable of singing above an orchestra of as many as 30 pieces, while still retaining the quality in her tonality. She told us she bought her country home at Lake Placid because of the swimming facilities it provided—that she had been swimming at least one mile a day, winter and summer, ever since she was 14 years old. To me this accounts for the enormous breath control necessary to sustain such vocal prowess.

Doing this show, along with my usual free-lance work, gave us some time to move to our new home in New Milford. On April 1, 1960, we made the eventful step, bag and baggage, children and dog, and it has been our home ever since. Actually, when I remember how busy I was during this time, I marvel that we managed to pull it off.

Among other activities of the moment was making the album "Tubby the Tuba," for Golden Crest Records, featuring the tuba playing of Harvey Phillips and directed by composer George Kleinsinger. Several others come to mind such as a Decca session with Bing Crosby doing Irish songs and novelties like "Who Threw the Overalls in Mrs. Murphy's Chowder." Bing's tremendous sense of humor put the zest of life into such things. There was another Decca session with the McGuire Sisters, which resulted in their first hit, "Mr. Sandman." Speaking of hits, I also played on Perry Como's first smash for Victor, "If I Loved You." The orchestra was directed by Russ Case and, although I never knew why, I believe it was the only record he did for Como. On the melancholy side, April 18 marked the date of the very last concert I was ever to play with the great trombonist Miff Mole, at a school in Melville, Long Island.

On May 24 I played a date for Muzak (the wired music system) in a first-class quartet with Dave McKenna, Milt Hinton, and Sonny Igoe, and around the same time, I worked on a vocal "dixieland" album with Eydie Gormé. She used a good-sized dixie-styled band which included Yank Lawson and me, and it's the only time I ever heard anybody sing lyrics for "Muskrat Ramble," and "South Rampart Street Parade."

On June 23, the Erwin family made another trip to Falls City, this time for the christening of Miss Cathy Erwin—a ceremony performed during persistent warnings of a nearby tornado. And we also found out that my grandfather, George Prater (who was almost 90), was in poor health, so we decided to send him to relatives in California in the hope the climate would help. This accomplished, Caroline and I headed back to our haven in New Jersey.

In July it was back again to Nick's with my old standbys Kenny, Harry DeVito and Johnny Varro, all set for the summer season, a pleasant prospect. I also decided to put my old woodworking hobby to practical use by framing out a back porch on our house. I would work like a beaver on the porch all day and play every night at Nick's—and once more my stupidity caught up with me. The last week in July I pulled the muscles in my back, the most painful injury I have ever had, and wound up in traction in Holy Name Hospital. While I was there my grandfather died in California on July 30, 1960, two days before his 90th birthday.

In two weeks I was back on the stand at Nick's but all strapped up like a mummy. The back was painful, but the big worry was the constant fear of overdoing and going into another muscle spasm. After awhile, though, it wore off.

In mid-August my mother and aunt and uncle came East to visit us. They had decided to make the trip after bringing my grandfather from California to Nebraska for burial. It was a very welcome visit, and I was particularly pleased to see my uncle because it gave me a chance to talk to him about the evaluation of our house and to make notes on his suggestions for the construction jobs I planned to expand our facilities.

Just to make sure I would keep busy, on September 19 I started work as a staff musician at CBS. It's hard now to explain what I had in mind, considering the work load I was already handling, but I had always been very strong and, until my back was injured, I guess I considered myself just about indestructible and my body capable of fulfilling any demands I made of it. I was about to learn again that I wasn't Superman. After five weeks of playing the full schedule at Nick's every night and then putting in full days at CBS—to be exact, from September 19 right through until October 23—I had to give up working at Nick's.

Kenny Davern took over as bandleader and immediately started to rebuild it, so when I finally got back to hear it again he had the best small band I'd heard since John Kirby's. With him were Johnny Windhurst on trumpet; Cutty Cutshall, trombone; Dave Frishberg, piano; Jack Six, bass; and Cliff Leeman, drums. I'm not one to go out of my way to listen to music when I'm not working, but this band impressed me every time I heard it.

After putting up with the strenuous work and long hours of jazz-band jobs, the CBS staff position took on the atmosphere of a perpetual vacation— except for the annoyance of my still aching back. The main show I worked on was the one-hour Garry Moore variety show, which aired on Friday nights, and consisted of a two-day rehearsal—a three-hour reading rehearsal on Thursday, and an all-day full-cast rehearsal and the show on Friday. As a rule these shows were put together in segments. Each segment rehearsed with the orchestra, and when each had been covered, the final dress rehearsal took place. The Garry Moore Show was scheduled so the dress rehearsal went on about 4:30 to 5:30 and then the show was taped from 8 to 9.

Besides Garry Moore, the principals were Durwood Kirby, Carol Burnett, and a group of six or eight dancers. The format called for a guest star each week, usually people like Alan King, Gwen Verdon, Chita Rivera, or Katrina Valente. The full company took part in the skits as well as taking turns in the solo spots. The orchestra was under the direction of a very talented orchestrator, Irwin Kostal, and was generally around 25 pieces but was sometimes augmented if special instrumentation was called for. The men were all high caliber musicians. In the trumpet section with me were Bernie Privin, Chris Griffin, and Jimmy Nottingham, and the trombonists were Joe Bennett, Wayne Andre', and Jack Rains. The reeds were Ray Ekstrand, Artie Drellinger, George Dessinger, and Hal McKusick. The eight strings were headed by Aaron Rosand, a virtuoso, and the rhythm section included Hank Jones on piano; Trigger Alpert, bass; Chuck Wayne, guitar; and Sonny Igoe, drums. Without fear of exaggeration, you could assess this as a band capable of playing anything from Stravinsky to Ellington—and quite often it did just that! Irwin Kostal, who was to go on to win awards (including an Oscar for scoring the music for the movie, "The Sound of Music"), demanded nothing short of musical perfection, and usually got it.

In addition to the Moore Show, I was on call for special shows produced by CBS. One was called "The Right Man," a flashback to the political scene of Teddy Roosevelt's time and another was an elaborate production of "The Great Waltz." These were backed by studio orchestras under the prestigious leadership of guest conductors like Jay Blackton or Elmer Bernstein. Also, for most of my years at CBS, I worked on a show called "American Musical Theater," under the direction of Alfredo Antonini. This was a weekday broadcast presenting a thumbnail version of a current or a past Broadway show, utilizing the stars of the production itself. Thus we would have people like Zero Mostel, Sammy Davis, Jr., or Florence Henderson, doing the most popular numbers from such original productions as "Fiddler on the Roof" or "Most Happy Fella." We also did operatic shows featuring various opera stars, and these, too, were always under the direction of Antonini.

I usually had a few nights free, so I would nearly always play one or two nights a week on jazz jobs—very often Saturday nights at the Central Plaza. There was very little call for jazz of any kind on CBS.

FORTY-NINE

BY THE TIME 1961 rolled around Caroline and I had agreed on plans to finish our house with the addition of a large bedroom and a studio on the second floor. However, since I had injured my back I wasn't up to such heavy construction so we had to get a contractor to do the work, except for some built-in cabinets I was able to make. Because we were so satisfied with the contractor's work, we decided to have him complete the lower floor as well, adding a double playroom area and a bedroom on the basement level. This still left ample room for both a laundry and a workroom for me. By the summer we finally had our living quarters completed to our satisfaction.

That year my friend Dick Hyman joined the Arthur Godfrey radio show as conductor and asked me to arrange a dixieland library for the Godfrey band. They had an excellent front line of jazz players—Johnny Mince on clarinet, Lou McGarity on trombone, and Johnny Parker on trumpet—so I arranged about 20 dixie standards for them and had the additional pleasure of hearing the group do a superb job of playing them on the air.

In March, CBS sent the Garry Moore Show to Winter Haven, Florida, for one week, and this gave me the oportunity to visit Caroline's remarkable grandmother, Mabeth Hurd Paige, who spent her winters there. In the 1890s Mrs. Paige had been an art student, developing into a relatively good painter. She even spent a year studying abroad, but in 1895 she married James Paige, a law professor at the University of Minnesota and, after the marriage, her Victorian husband refused to let her continue her painting career. Possibly in revenge, she attended his law classes and earned a law degree. In the 1920s she became an associate of Carrie Chapman Catt and other women interested in the suffrage movement. She was also elected to the Minnesota Legislature, where she served from 1922 until 1944, building a lot of respect for her efforts in the Urban League and the provision of proper housing for single women. She is listed among the first 100 citizens of Minnesota. I enjoyed my visit with her immensely.

I also had an aunt and uncle living nearby, in Mt. Dora, Florida, so I went to see them too. My Aunt Jean was my father's sister, and her husband was Charles G. Grau. They were both interesting people, and Aunt Jean was

292

something of a family historian as well as a great storyteller. She told me that in the early Twenties she had lived on a homestead in Montana near Havre, when it was still a wild and remote area, and she would commute 30 miles every night to play piano in a movie house in Havre. During this period she met and married Charles Grau, an engineer from Pennsylvania. Aunt Jean said that when she was living on the homestead it was sometimes necessary to climb out a window in order to get out of the house, because so many rattlesnakes were sunning themselves on the front porch!

I had a soft spot in my heart for Uncle Charley. In 1924 he sent me my first radio, which he had built himself. During this visit in 1961, Aunt Jean trotted out several family keepsakes and an album of photographs of the Erwin grandparents and ancestors from the Carolinas. The foremost exhibit was a night cap and a pair of slippers which had belonged to Abe Lincoln, a relative by marriage.

At one point in their married lives, Aunt Jean and Uncle Charley had located in Rhinelander, Wisconsin, where he became affiliated with a gas company. Aunt Jean had a falling out with a neighbor, and when the neighbor died she specified in her will that she be cremated and her ashes sprinkled on Aunt Jean's lawn, just to get even.

These visits to relatives were worthwhile in themselves, but aside from them the trip to Florida turned out to be a great experience. Garry Moore had brought his tugboat overland all the way from Long Island to Florida to be used on the show, which was being filmed on a Winter Haven lake. In addition, he took over an entire club (Garry is a very nice guy!) and stocked it with all the goodies for our four-day stay—it was open house for all.

Not long after this, another interesting musical wrinkle came along. Lou Shoobe, the musical contractor for CBS, had been an associate of mine ever since we played together in the Raymond Scott Quintet. He liked jazz and managed to convince the CBS radio execs to permit him to put together a small group to work with disc jockey Ed Joyce on a live jazz show for CBS radio. Lou would schedule whatever jazz players he could spare among the staff musicians to play in my jazz band on this once-a-week broadcast—usually Ray Ekstrand, clarinet; Morty Bullman or Joe Bennett, trombone; and a rhythm section with Hank Jones, Chuck Wayne, and Sonny Igoe. The show became so popular it lasted on the air for two years.

Ed Joyce was very personable in his presentations, and during the summer months we would do the show live from "Freedomland," an amusement complex in the Bronx. I tried to keep the broadcasts interesting by constantly changing tunes, which required a wide variety of the kind of material played by traditional bands. The problem was, I never knew in advance who would be in the band or whether the majority of musicians in the band would know the tunes I picked. So I prepared lead sheets with the chord changes for improvisation on each instrument, and put them into some green music notebooks. One night I went to the studio to do the broadcast, and Joe Bennett greeted me with: "Did you bring the Mouldy Library tonight?" I never did know if he meant the music or the color of the books.

293

In May I was recruited by Bob Crosby to travel to Miami Beach and take part in one of those "Timex Jazz" extravaganzas which the Timex Watch Company sponsored for several years. This was a lot of fun and gave me a chance to spend some time with a fine jazz band made up of old pals. I was with Yank Lawson, Chris Griffin, and Cutty Cutshall in the brass section, and Peanuts Hucko, Bud Freeman, Bob Haggart, Cliff Leeman, and Lou Stein made up the rest of the band. The show went on in one of the biggest ballrooms I have ever seen. The Crosby crew was also the backup band for Louis Armstrong, and working and kibitzing with Louis thrilled us all. The other groups included the Les Brown and Lionel Hampton bands. Added to these were vocalists and commentator John Cameron Swayzee. All in all, it was a great show for jazz and a marvelous experience.

I was entitled to a three-week vacation at CBS in July, but because of my commitment with the Ed Joyce show I had to stay in New York while Caroline and the children spent a couple of weeks with her parents in Texas. She made arrangements with my old friend Bill Muchnic from Kansas to spend a week with me while she was gone to keep me busy playing duets. Little did she realize we had several fests with nonalcoholic champagne. Caroline had also made arrangements to return to school and earn the credits she needed for a teaching certificate in New Jersey, but before she could get started her grandmother died and she had to attend the funeral in Minneapolis.

As for the fall schedule at CBS, it filled up quickly. In addition to the on-going Garry Moore Show, Jackie Gleason had returned to New York, and I was part of the orchestra conducted by Sammy Spear, who in his trumpet-playing days had worked on many shows with me, including the "Let's Dance" program. So these chores, along with some outside dates, kept me pretty busy, especially since the popularity of the Ed Joyce radio program seemed to go along at a steady pace.

And so the year hurried to a close. The New Year was approaching and our third baby was due but reluctant. Caroline's sister, the doctor, told her: "If you want the tax deduction for 1961 you better take a walk around the block."

Caroline followed the advice, and Caroline Howe Erwin was born at 7 a.m. on December 31—a helluva time to have a birthday, so close to Christmas and on top of New Year's Eve. It was three degrees below zero on the day she arrived, but she has since shown definite signs of having a very warm heart.

FIFTY

MY SCHEDULE AT CBS didn't change in 1962, because the shows always remain on the air from October until the following May—unless, of course, they bomb, in which case they go off at the end of 13 weeks or sooner. This means that the commercial shows are booked in two segments of 13 weeks each, for a total of 26 in all. But the Garry Moore and Jackie Gleason shows were stayers.

Early in the year I made a record for Decca, "Henry Jerome Plays Dixieland With Strings." Jimmy McPartland and Max Kaminsky were featured too, and we each did two or three jazz-band tunes with the standard jazz-band format plus strings in the background. The recording sticks in my mind because one of the tracks I made was of "South Rampart Street Parade," and the composer, Bob Haggart, played bass on it. He had also written the arrangement and had nicely scored it in a different key than the original, making it a lot easier to play. This tune, in its original key of E^b is one of the hardest of all the jazz band standards to play, for the simple reason that the routine is long and there is very little chance for the trumpet to rest. I have always wanted to get this album but have never succeeded.

Caroline was pretty busy at this period, taking care of the children and going to school, so Marie Fields (who was to remain with us for a number of years, literally becoming a member of the family) came to live with us to help with the kids and give Caroline time to pursue her studies. Marie was a lovely lady from Texas who had worked for Caroline's mother when Caroline was a young lady, so she had been a friend of the family for many years. She soon became an important member of our family group, and we are still close although she has long since returned to Texas.

Two things are always uppermost in the minds of staff studio musicians. One is the regularity of the paycheck on a solid 52-week basis, often sweetened with overtime pay (during my stay at CBS overtime was plentiful, making it a very lucrative job), and therefore, automatically, the other thing is mostly worry about the first. The main topic of conversation among staff men centered around the big question: "When am I going to lose this job?"

Now, once the idea enters your mind, it can grow to become uppermost in your thoughts, and after awhile it inhibits your actions. It becomes a habit of thought and conversation almost like a hypnotic suggestion, and keeps eating away at your peace of mind. On top of this, working a staff job does nothing to add to your feeling of musical security because you're seldom exposed to an audience of any size. After awhile you begin to feel as though you're in hiding from the world. Then too, there is a sameness to the music you play to the extent it becomes more of a habit than anything creative. It's easy for atrophy to set in. I have never worked a Broadway theater job, but I'm told it has the same psychological effect.

In my case the CBS schedule began to interfere considerably with my work in the recording studios. Staff work demanded priority at all times, and, as time went on, not being readily available for recording work had the usual result—out of sight, out of the minds of the recording contractors. I tried to do as much work on the outside as possible, but for most of 1962 and well into the fall of 1963 I did very little. I guess it was part of the insidious laziness setting in.

Nevertheless, in 1963 I started making mood albums with Jackie Gleason. This sensational and best-selling series of recordings put out by Capitol Records had begun quite some time before, and the story of how they were started is another one of those classic tales of the entertainment industry. Jackie Gleason greatly admired Bobby Hackett's cornet stylings, so at his own expense he financed a recording session and the production of an album featuring Bobby's horn. But when he tried to sell one of the record companies on issuing the album, nobody would touch it. A year later it was still in the can when Capitol approached Gleason about doing something else for them. Jackie knew an opportunity when he saw one and told them he was only available if they would issue his album. So the deal was made and the result was a runaway best-seller, "Music For Lovers Only," followed by a long series of albums under Jackie's name.

Bobby Hackett for a long time continued to be the featured soloist on these recordings, and then one day I got a call from Lou Shoobe asking if I would like to make one. I was delighted with the offer. It would be hard to find a more ideal setting for a soloist—the largest string section used in recording (48 strings), marvelous arrangements, and the latest in recording techniques. You couldn't ask for a nicer background. But through the years it has never been my policy to cut anybody out of anything, so I told Lou I wanted to think it over, and as soon as I got the chance, I put in a call to Bobby Hackett. Bobby assured me that he and Jackie had parted on friendly terms, and only because Bobby had been offered a deal to make a series of albums under his own name. He told me to take the offer, and I made six albums for Jackie.

I also began to experiment tentatively with private trumpet teaching, which eventually led to my interest in teaching on a larger scale—all brought about, in my estimation, as the result of staff work and the feeling it generates of being left behind and out of the mainstream of things—an atmosphere of semiretirement.

Later on a call came in from Columbia Records. They wanted to do a couple of dixieland-styled albums based on folk tunes. Epic Records had put out some big-selling records by a group called The Washington Square Stompers, using two banjos and a three-man front line in a loose dixie format, but playing folk music. I suppose Columbia figured it could be turned into a money-making fad. I enlisted the services of Bob Wilber to assist in some of the writing, and between the two of us we turned out about 30 arrangements—enough material for two albums designed to sound exactly like The Washington Square Stompers.

We recorded all of these numbers for Columbia, obviously involving quite a financial outlay for the company, only to have the entire project turn out to be a dud. I can only report from hearsay, but as I understand it The Washington Square Stompers were on hand to hear the playback of our tapes and immediately took steps to prevent Columbia from releasing the records. This wasn't too difficult, I suppose, since Epic Records was a subsidiary label of Columbia—in the same family, as it were—so they were probably able to bring strong pressure to bear. The albums were not to be released under my name so I wasn't bothered too much—especially as I had made quite a bit of money on the deal. I never did hear any of the tapes.

1963 was notable to me in a very personal way. I started taking treatment for my chronic back problem from Dr. George A. Schroeter, a great authority on podiatry, who had perfected a method of hydrotherapy which in innumerable cases worked seemingly miraculous cures. In my case, he succeeded in relieving me of a constant dull pain in my back and in addition showed me ways of improving my general health.

When 1964 and 1965 offered little more than the same rather monotonous staff work at CBS, I began to get restless and started looking around for greener pastures. This led to my working about two dates a week for a club-date booking office, Steven Scott, which handled music for private parties—weddings, bar mitzvahs, etc.—on the supermarket principle. I worked in small groups, always under the direction of a musician-singer, who followed a set format in playing for every party. In theory—in practice too, I guess—this was a pretty good idea for doing party work on a volume basis, and the office was successful at it for quite a few years.

The office was headed by a group of six club-date leaders who had done quite well in this field and decided to combine their efforts and move into the business on a large scale. They employed a sales force and an office staff and wrote exclusive contracts authorizing them to provide music in some of the largest catering halls, as well as with the smaller caterers and establishments specializing in private parties.

In 1965, I joined the band of Sy Menchen, one of the Steven Scott partners, on a more-or-less permanent basis. At that time he had the best club-date band I had ever heard. Sy was an excellent salesman on the bandstand, and he built his band around his own unique talents, but, more important to me, he had a great admiration for the better big-band sounds, and as a result his was the only club-date band I knew of that played the material in the proper tempos. He also had a nucleus of excellent musicians. Vincent LeRose I consider to be one of the best tenormen in this field, and the other men were polished professionals, also—Johnny Knapp (piano), Buddy Christian (drums), and Jimmy Stanley (bass). Menchin played trumpet and, with Mickey Gravine on trombone, we had an impressive three-man brass section. I can honestly say this was the only club-date band I ever played in which made it a pleasure to go to work.

By the end of 1965, the six albums with Jackie Gleason were behind me, and I had logged some interesting experiences. Early in the year, Bill Muchnic asked me to put a band together to play for the opening of a new mall complex in his home town of Atchison, Kansas. I had lived there briefly in the late Twenties, when I was playing with Roland Evans, and I was pleasantly surprised and honored to be presented with a plaque as a former citizen of the community.

We played for a tremendous crowd that night, working opposite Harry James's big band (which featured Buddy Rich) at the other end of the hall. Our band included Bob Wilber, Lou McGarity, Dave McKenna, Sonny Igoe, and Roland Evans, my former bandleader, on bass. It was a pleasurable job and we all enjoyed it, with the possible exception of Sonny Igoe. Because of the high cost of excess weight on board the plane, Sonny had brought only his cymbals. When we mounted the bandstand, he was considerably brought down by the sight of a rented, cheap set of Japanese drums. He sounded fine to us, but he was more than a little perturbed to have to play mediocre drums opposite his idol Buddy Rich.

Even CBS staff work still provided an occasional chuckle. Once on a Candid Camera Show (which I worked for a long period), I was sitting next to great trumpet virtuoso Ray Cresara. He looked at me mournfully as he took out his horn and remarked, "You know, I'm getting awfully tired of opening this case and never knowing whether I'll find a friend or a bag of worms."

1965 also saw the release of another one of my projects—one I had been working on for a long time—a "do-it-yourself" method book entitled, "Pee Wee Erwin Teaches You to Play the Trumpet." This involved a step-by-step text, combined with a recording to illustrate the lessons, and was designed for the student who didn't have access to a real live, breathing trumpet teacher. Theoretically, a diligent, hardworking, and talented person could teach himself or herself to play pretty well. The book and the record were published by Prentice-Hall, and they certainly turned out a beautiful package. On the other hand, I don't think anything ever came of it. The only report that filtered back to me regarding its use was when somebody told me the Eastman School of Music in Rochester was using the book in their brass department for *transposition studies*. Oh, well . . . .

FIFTY-ONE

I LEFT CBS IN 1966 to take a fling at an undertaking I had been considering for some time. Working on a staff job seems to promote a feeling of uncertainty and insecurity, and after awhile you develop a pit-of-the-stomach hunch that it might be smart to move on to something else or consider retiring before the axe falls—preferably something that offers a secure income. You lose contact with reality and everything that takes place outside of the small sphere comprised of the studios tends to become remote and scary.

A number of the staff musicians developed phobias, particularly the nagging fear of being let go, having to face the cold outside world without prospects and the necessity of promoting new contacts all over again. Many of them tried other business ventures. One I knew bought himself a liquor store. Another bought into a trucking business. Several tried my idea (and were successful) of teaching young musicians. A lot of them looked around for greener pastures and wound up investing in things they knew very little about. In retrospect, I think I can safely state I was one of them.

As you know, Chris Griffin and I went back a long way together—all the way to the time we played in the Goodman band—and we lived in the same town and often commuted to New York together for many of the jobs we worked. In addition, we both taught privately, so it was only natural that we began to discuss the feasibility of a joint teaching venture. After we kicked this idea around for awhile, it developed into the more ambitious plan of opening a music school. The more we talked about this, the more logical it became. We reasoned we had each established reputations of some stature as performers (when you work studios you tend to labor under the illusion that you have attained some sort of high pinnacle in your chosen profession), and we thought this would inspire confidence in a comfortably large number of people and cause them to seek us out for study. We also figured that since we lived in an area loaded with elementary and high schools, there would automatically be a lot of music students looking for private instruction. In our naive analysis of the situation we anticipated all kinds of great and intense interest in musical instruction—not only on the trumpet, but all instruments. At the time, it was true, a lot of kids were gravitating to guitars and drums, but that was about the size of it.

Nevertheless, our talking finally resulted in the deicision to open a music school, and from there we went on to assess what we needed in a physical plant. We outlined the earning capacity of one studio operating eight hours a day and somehow arrived at the conclusion we could operate a solvent business by utilizing four studios. I suppose we assumed we could sign up enough students to keep four studios busy for eight hours a day—a major assumption in itself and an indication of how unrealistically we approached the situation.

This done, we began to look for a location to rent, and Chris was very patient with me at this point, leaving me to do most of the talking to the real estate people. We looked at empty buildings in Dumont, Edgewater, Hackensack, and finally settled on a vacant store in Teaneck that had once been occupied by a hardware dealer. This place had 4,000 square feet of area, and this is when someone should have run a check on my personality before allowing us to continue. When I eat it is always too much, and if I drink (alcohol or otherwise) it is always too much, and this should have been the tip-off. In other words, I have a big tendency to overdo everything I attempt.

Relating this to our music school, I guess we both had illusions that all we had to do was open the doors and we'd immediately sign up several hundred students eager to take private and class music lessons, completely unaware we'd have been a lot smarter to open a small retail store with three or four small studios in the rear. The retail operation would have given us another means of supplementing our income and would have allowed us to build a business from the ground up. Instead we started at the top, with a physical establishment large enough to handle more students than the average conservatory, and a very limited chance to realize enough profit to support it.

We had some good breaks, though, and the best advice and help anyone could hope for. One of our prime considerations had to be soundproofing since we were located next to a beauty parlor with only a thin wall between. For this we had the expert engineering advice of Bill Leek, one of the top acoustic men with the Owens Corning Fiberglass Corporation, and Tony Monk supplied all of our construction materials at nominal cost.

So I got my hammer, lined up a crew consisting of Paul Griffin (Chris's son), two young seniors from Bergen Technological High School, and a TWA pilot, Don Roquemore. I brought my power tools to the job site, and we went to work converting 5,000 linear feet of 2 x 3s, 3,000 feet of 2 x 4s, and several tons of sheetrock, insulation, wire, nails, and other assorted material into a music school at 951 Teaneck Road, Teaneck, N.J. We started in June, and by the time we were finished we had constructed eight small studios and two large ones, a large foyer 30' by 24', which provided office space and a showcase area, and a large recording studio and practice area in the rear, complete with a soundproofed control booth. Everything was completely soundproofed, and we installed an air conditioning and heating system with fiberglass ducts. We looked and worked like beavers and finished everything down to the last detail, even to equipping the recording studio with professional quality tape recorders and control panels, in time to open the doors in October.

It was a truly beautiful teaching facility, right down to the wall-to-wall carpeting, and very comfortable. Following the advice of another real friend, Henry Adler, we put in a small stock of retail musical merchandise. He even provided us with an opening inventory of guitars, drums, and accessories, and then arranged a credit standing for us with musical suppliers.

We incorporated the business, launched it with a quite respectable ad campaign based on the expert advice of another old friend, Ed Prodigo, and then stood back ready and willing to take care of the anticipated rush of students to our door. We estimated we would start with a few hundred, and we recruited a staff of 14 teachers capable of teaching practically all instruments. This involved a profit ratio that required far more students than actually appeared—although now that we know the area's potential we didn't have a bad turnout. Experience would show it was costing us from $800 to $1,000 a month just to turn the key in the door. After a few months of really hard work it became very evident we weren't going to make it.

We spent every waking minute in the pursuit of business, but even after we reduced our teacher-student ratio, we still found it impossible to operate on a profit basis. On the theory that we could supplement the school business with other means of income, we tried emphasizing retail sales—only to find out very quickly we couldn't begin to compete with the big dealers who, due to their ability to buy in volume, were able to discount as much as 40 percent from list prices. When this became evident, we turned to the school instrument-rental business, and with the help of two gentlemen from Connecticut, Bill Ratzenberger and Frank Banko, we were able to build another source of income. However, this involved a great amount of time and work, and in some instances it meant handling all the details, from supplying the instruments to actually teaching in the parochial schools—all in addition to making our regular calls in the public schools for sales and rentals.

Just to make sure we touched all bases, we began recording and producing records for students, schools, and private groups. Putting everything together we managed to come up with a situation that practically assured that we had to work around the clock without a vacation every year, with all the effort expended on a losing proposition. This in spite of the fact that along with our investment of time and work, we had committed ourselves for a great deal of money, even bringing in a third partner, Jack Ruppel.

After five years of steady endeavor, during which time we were successful in getting the business from six school systems, we decided to sell the business. We did this by selling the physical premises (the business facilities and studios) to two of our teachers, and the inventory to a larger retail concern Rondo Music of Union, N.J. This included the stipulation that I work for Rondo as a salesman and liaison man for awhile, in order to retain the rental and sales programs in the schools that we had agreed to supply. In itself this proved worthwhile in furthering my personal education in sales and methods of musical demonstration, but after a little more than a year things reached a point where the demands on my time were making it difficult for me to continue any kind of playing career, so I had to give it up.

FIFTY-TWO

I RECORDED MY LAST ALBUM ("The Last Dance for Lovers Only") for Jackie Gleason on June 30, 1966. During the year, I played my first jazz concert of many under the direction of radio personality Jack Sterling, in New Canaan, Connecticut. Jack always used the fine trombonist Tyree Glenn, along with Bernie Leighton on piano, and a number of other excellent musicians for his early morning radio show.

Other memorable dates that year included the wedding of book publisher John G. Powers' daughter Jean in Greenwich, Connecticut, and a job in Rockville Center, Long Island, on September 3, which turned out to be Peanuts Hucko's last one as a New Yorker. Right afterwards he made a permanent move to the West. Almost every weekend was filled by dates with the Sy Menchin band, and these, combined with my activities for the music school, were more than enough to fill my time so the year slipped by in a hurry.

In February 1967, at the invitation of the Rutgers University Institute of Jazz Studies and the University Concerts and Lectures Department I produced a concert program for them depicting a cross-section of jazz history, and it was presented four times. The first concert took place in Carnegie Hall and drew a rave review from *New York Times* critic John S. Wilson. The second was on the Rutgers Newark Campus. The third and fourth presentations took place on the Rutgers home campus in New Brunswick. All four were well received. In the band I had Bob Wilber, Lou McGarity, Dick Hyman, Sonny Igoe, and Bob Haggart on string bass alternating with Harvey Phillips on tuba where a brass bass was more appropriate. Harvey at that time worked for the Rutgers Concert office.

Later that same month Wilber, McGarity, and I traveled to Aspen, Colorado, where we joined forces with three fine local musicians, Bert Dahlander, an excellent Swedish drummer, pianist Walt Smith, and bass player Dean Billings. We all thoroughly enjoyed ourselves as the guests of John Powers and his lovely wife, Kimiko. It was our introduction to the beautiful settings at Aspen, a marvelous winter resort. While there we were joined for most of the sessions by one of the most colorful performers of all time, Freddie "Schnicklefritz" Fisher, who played pretty fair clarinet. He is also the only man I have ever heard who could insert profanity after every other word and make it sound like acceptable language. He got away with it because everyone was so fond of him they paid no attention to it. For years he led a very successful band that convulsed audiences with their crazy antics, winding up, I believe, in a hofbrau in Cincinnati.

Freddie spent a lot of time outdoors around the Aspen countryside, and he perfected a way of coating Aspen oak leaves with metal in various hues. So treated, the leaves were permanently preserved and made very attractive pins and other ornaments of costume jewelry. Tragically, the day after the jam session with our group, he was taking a walk in the mountains and died of a heart attack.

An impressive treat on any visit to Aspen in those years was the work of the "Boss of Solo Piano," Ralph Sutton. Ralph and his beautiful wife, Sunny, operated a nice restaurant called "Sunny's Rendezvous," where Ralph played every night. They had a policy of augmenting Ralph's music quite often with well-known musicians for two weeks or a month during the ski season. Recordings were made of some of these sessions, featuring artists like Ruby Braff, Bob Wilber, Jack Lesberg, George Barnes, Cliff Leeman, and others. We found Aspen a very pleasant place to visit; we enjoyed it so much we repeated it a month later, in March.

Other concerts in unusual settings that year included several quite successful appearances with a local group under the direction of pianist Charley Holland at the famous New England seaport museum at Mystic, Connecticut. In April I played a show in Westbury, L. I., with a very good group led by Bob Crosby. We did a jazz program in the theater-in-the-round. It was the first time I heard Bob's son, Chris Crosby, who is a very good contemporary singer.

In 1968 I worked on a program of preseason preparation for school bands similar to preseason football practice. I would take a lower brass teacher, a reed teacher, and a percussion teacher into a school to prepare the students in advance for the coming fall season in the marching and concert bands. This system was developed by Mr. Burt Bluhm, musical director of the Westwood Regional High School in northern New Jersey, whose musical units were always among the best in the state. He also recommended private instruction to his students whenever possible. The football season begins very early in the school year so, just like the coaches started running their teams through their paces in preseason workouts, we did the same for the marching bands and gave them a head start on the strenuous fall programs.

Around this time Tommy Gwaltney, a musician from Washington, D.C., well known for his work on clarinet and vibes—especially in the fine little band Bobby Hackett put together for the Voyager Room of the Henry Hudson Hotel in New York in the Fifties—opened a jazz club in Washington called "Blues Alley." For some time, I had been talking to him about appearing there. A lot of my friends had played there and I wanted to, but we were having trouble getting together on a price because my commitments at home were such that I had to get a good price to make a week away from home worthwhile.

Finally Tommy came up with a solution. He had booked his band for one of the inaugural balls (Nixon-Agnew, Jan. 20, 1969), and told me that if I played in his band for this affair on a Monday night, his profit from the job would enable him to meet my salary for playing the rest of the week at Blues Alley. The arrangement worked out very nicely. The club had a great group of musicians in the house band and I had a marvelous time playing with them.

I took advantage of my week's stay in Washington to have lunch and visit with a friend of my earlier years, Hal Marley, who during his college days at Columbua had played trumpet. We had become good friends when I was working with Tommy Dorsey. He was now a colonel in the air force, and we had corresponded quite a bit while he was on some of his assignments in Europe. At one time I sent him a batch of dance-band arrangements which he turned over to Polish and Czeck bands, thereby earning their everlasting gratitude because such music was completely unavailable to them.

Incidentally, the present-day inaugural balls are a bit of a farce, but they do create work for musicians, at least for one night. About three or four balls are held in Washington on the same night, and the victorious president and vice president spend a brief time at each of them, making it possible to appear before a much larger group of supporters than they could otherwise. After this particular Inaugural Ball, I went back to Blues Alley to become part of a group of trumpet players who were relaxing after playing at the numerous balls around the city. Sitting at one table were Doc Severinson, Yank Lawson, Bobby Hackett, and Billy Butterfield. If the roof had fallen in, the world would have been deprived of many of its most talented trumpet players all at one time.

Later in the year I received a call from Peanuts Hucko. He was now running a nightclub in Denver, and he wanted me to join him and Murray MacEachern for a night of jazz. Of course, I didn't hesitate, especially since I hadn't seen Murray (a great musician) since our days together in the Goodman band. I flew out and joined Murray in doing full justice to a terrific barbecue that Peanuts had prepared for us on his terrace, and then, instead of going to his club to play as I had expected, we got on another plane and flew to Colorado Springs to play for a party.

I don't think anybody at that party knew, or cared, who was playing for them, or that any advance publicity had announced that Peanuts, at great expense, was importing a trumpet player from New York and a trombone player from California. In fact, although I've never asked Peanuts, I have an idea the job simply paid well enough for him to send away for a couple of pals so he could play in a band to his own liking. So he just went ahead and did it—and we had a lot of fun.

On the way home I stopped off in Atchison, Kansas, to attend the 50th birthday party given for my old schoolmate Bill Muchnic.

Also that year I played a date with Chris Griffin and his jazz band at the

Dutchess County Fair in Rhinebeck, New York. This has since become an annual concert, still taking place after all these years.

Then one day I received a call from a man I shall call Charlie Wall, asking if we had facilities suitable for copying records. I told him we did, and he immediately made an appointment to come to the studio to have copies made of a number of acetate recordings of original material he had produced in Florida. When we got around to discussing what he wanted and the best way to go about it, he decided he would prefer to redo the records with a large orchestra in a style of the Paul Whiteman orchestra of the Twenties, and asked if I had any ideas on how this could be done. I told him that in order to get anything near the sound he wanted he would have to have orchestrations made utilizing the proper instrumentation, and the first step would be to hire an orchestrator capable of doing the writing.

Mr. Wall then said he had a recording studio in his home suitable for the making of demo-quality records, and what he had in mind was organizing such an orchestra for the purpose of playing his music and recording it in his studio so he could evaluate its merit. After a couple of conferences, I gave him an estimate of how much this would cost, and he told me he wanted to produce the session. I contacted a first-rate arranger, George Williams, who had contributed most of the scores for the Jackie Gleason albums, and introduced him to Mr. Wall, who in turn explained to him exactly what he wanted the music to sound like. George turned out twelve arrangements in accordance with Mr. Wall's ideas.

Next I assembled a ten-piece band for the session at Mr. Wall's house and recorded demo records of quite a few of the orchestrations. On some of the sides we used a very good vocalist, Molly Lyons.

The records were quite good. In fact, the only trouble with our demos was that Mr. Wall, after listening to them over and over, concluded that we didn't have a large enough orchestra to produce the sound he was seeking. Up to this point, the venture had already cost him quite a bid of money—considering the cost of the orchestrations and hiring the musicians—at least several thousand dollars. Nevertheless it was decided to rewrite the library for a larger group.

With everything going forward on a much more ambitious level, after the rewriting was finished we rented the Capitol Recording Studios for the independent production of a full-scale album—and in the meantime Mr. Wall came up with another idea. He decided that each track on the record would begin with a vamp background while a joke (vintage of the Twenties) was told, after which the band would play the music. His reasoning was this would gain the listener's rapt attention to what followed. The jokes were told by Neil Stanley, a young man with a voice that bore a remarkable resemblnce to Jimmy Durante's, and Dardanelle, a young lady with a strong southern accent. The vocals were by Bernie Knee and Molly Lyons.

In the orchestra we used four reed players—Ray Ekstrand, Lennie Hambro, Bob Wilber, and Romeo Penque; three brass—Carl Poole, Buddy Morrow, and me; and two pianos—Joe Cribari and Bernie Leighton. On banjos we had Al Caiola and Art Ryerson, and Buddy Christian was on drums, with Joe Tarto alternating between string bass and tuba. From the musical standpoint we turned out a good album. It had a good jazz feeling throughout—only to be expected from a band made up of such excellent players—and certainly no expense was spared in its production. I would guess the total cost must have been around $25,000, but just how successful it was from the sales standpoint, I have no idea. The album was released and distributed by Jay Gee Records and, to say the least, it was different.

The most important thing, of course, was that Mr. Wall was pleased with the results. He informed me that he was the head of a large business concern and wanted me to assist him in the production of a show to be presented at the annual Christmas party to be held at a New York hotel. I performed this function for three of these annual affairs, and I must say that when Charlie Wall had a hand in a production everything went first class.

FIFTY-THREE

IN 1970 BASSIST RED BALABAN produced a jazz concert for the Lions Club in a Connecticut town close to his home, using two bands. This was the last date I would ever play with both Eddie Condon and Gene Krupa. Eddie and Gene spent most of the intermissions talking over old times, and it made for some interesting listening.

That May I got my first invitation to attend a unique event that takes place every year in California. Essentially, it is an eight-day horse ride and camp out that takes place on the first week in May in the area around Santa Barbara and is a recreation of the cattle drives that took place in the early days of California history, making their way from one mission to another to rest the herds and enjoy the hospitality of each place. The custom was revived about 50 years ago by a group of local ranchers as "Rancheros Vistadores," and it has become a tradition.

It begins with a ride of several miles from the first campsite to Solvang, California, where the participants are blessed at the mission there. Then after three days of camping, the ride travels over the mountain trails for 20 miles and winds up at the final campsite in the San Marcus Mountains outside of Santa Barbara. Taking part in the expeditions are approximately 500 members and 500 wranglers—all men. No women are allowed. Actually, the "ride" is made up of 15 individual camps surrounding the central facilities, and at various places along the way the riders participate in sporting events like horse races, rodeos, and other equestrian contests like all-day rides in the country. It's a perfect outing for a horseman. Everybody eats three meals a day in the central dining tent, and each of the 15 smaller campsites has a large campfire, a bar open to all, and, in most cases, music of some kind.

Each day of the ride one of the smaller camps has a special cocktail hour where special treats are offered. One camp, for instance, will feature a barbecue, another Mexican food, and a camp with hunters will have wild game such as antelope, venison, or wild boar. Musical entertainment can be heard every evening in the central dining tent which serves all the Rancheros—one night a western group, the next night a jazz band, and so on. Finally the eight days wind up with an amateur rodeo featuring the members of the ride, and then the camps disband until the next year. This is one of the most congenial gatherings of men you can imagine, and all for the simple enjoyment of the great outdoors and the pleasure of each other's company.

Back home again, the Erwin family enjoyed our second vacation in Maine, with the entire crew present during July, and we appreciated the outdoors and each other as much as anybody.

I also had the pleasure of playing for a night at the Delgado Art Museum in New Orleans, in my first return to the city of jazz since my stint on Bourbon Street. We entertained at a true southern-society ball for the patrons of the Museum, one of the great art institutions of the South.

By the time 1971 came around I was playing more jazz dates than at any time since starting at CBS, especially while devoting so much time to the music school. I played a number of park and school concerts with Sal Pace, the clarinetist, in groups which included his son Gary on piano, Miff Sines on trombone, and Eddie Locke on drums, and these had a lot to do with rekindling my interest in jazz.

This year saw the end of my long association with my favorite trombone player, Lou McGarity. I worked with him for the last time on May 28, in Wilmington, North Carolina. He and I had been imported to play with a local band for the Cape Fear Jazz Society, and we were met by Dr. Harry Van Velsor, who cordially entertained us until performance time. Dr. Van Velsor not only plays fine clarinet—he has the only doctor's office I've ever been in where one entire wall is a mural of a jazz band.

Just before the start of this concert, a tall, elderly gentleman came up to the bandstand and introduced himself to me. In one hand he was holding a cornet case and in the other a jug of whiskey, and he said. "I can't blow a note above E above middle C, but I'm the best damn second-cornet player you ever heard." And he lived up to his brag.

The 800 or more jazz fans present heard a very good band. Lou McGarity was in peak form and, from the very first tune, did his best to blow the roof off. He didn't let up for the entire evening, and it was a memorable performance from a man who, in my estimation, was one of the greatest trombonists who ever lived. This is not to downgrade in any way the many other great trombone players, but to me the lines that Lou played in ensembles were beyond compare. Only a short time after our Cape Fear appearance Lou had a massive coronary attack while working at Blues Alley in Washington, never regaining consciousness. It was a sad day for music.

On another occasion I was invited by my friend Zack Cullens to play an afternoon concert at Ruby Red's Underground in Atlanta, at that time the scene of once-a-month jazz sessions with guest appearances, sponsored by the Atlanta Jazz Society. I walked in to play with one of the best organized bands in the country—Ernie Carson's—and it's always a genuine pleasure to be able to do a guest appearance with a band that plays well and knows any tune you call. I consider Ernie Carson a great cornet player who has never received the recognition he deserves, and the same thing goes for Herman

Foretich, the clarinetist in the band, a superb player in the Fazola tradition. The other excellent members of the group included Harry Hagen, trombone; Julius Wimby, piano; Shorty Johnson, tuba; and Spider Ridgeway, drums.

Incidentally, the Atlanta Underground is one of the most interesting areas I have ever visited. When Atlanta was burned during the Civil War, some of the warehouse and city center buildings were not destroyed, but when the city was rebuilt an elevated section was created over the original streets and buildings. A few years ago these buildings—now "underground"—were refurbished, and an area of approximately twelve square blocks of fine restaurants, stores, and amusement areas, complete with old-fashioned gas-burning street lights, an old streetcar, and other decor of the period, resulted. It's a fascinating area to visit.

Back in 1962, a great friend of jazz, Dick Gibson, and his wife, Maddie, took over the Jerome Hotel in Aspen, Colorado, for the Labor Day weekend, and then invited 14 of their favorite musicians and 40 couples as guests. They launched the first three-day jazz party in history. The party was budgeted, with the cost split up among the guests—so much per person—with the Gibsons making up any deficits. It was such a huge success that it was repeated the following year with a few more musicians and a few more guests. Each year the party, still held every Labor Day weekend, continued to grow until finally it was too large for the facilities at Aspen. One year it was moved to larger quarters in Vail, but it is now quartered at the beautiful Broadmoor Hotel in Colorado Springs. By the time I received my first invitation to attend the ninth party in 1971, it included 41 topflight musicians and 500 guests. And it's still growing! In 1979 the total was 55 musicians and 700 guests for the 17th annual party.

I believe the Gibsons have contributed more to the cause of jazz in the past decade than any other individuals I can think of. Dick has always been a sincere follower of jazz and knows the music and musicians. He realized one of his lifelong ambitions when he organized the musicians who formed the nucleus of the jazz party at Aspen into a band he called, "The World's Greatest Jazz Band." Under the coleadership of Yank Lawson and Bob Haggart and with its original personnel, the band was probably just that. Besides Yank, the other trumpet player was Billy Butterfield. Lou McGarity and Cutty Cutshall were the trombonists; Peanuts Hucko was on tenor and clarinet; Bud Freeman, tenor; Ralph Sutton, piano; and Cliff Leeman, drums; with vocals and banjo by Clancy Hayes. Haggart, of course, was the bass player.

It was a great band that made a strong impression on everybody who heard it, and Dick Gibson did a marvelous job of promoting it; but the payroll alone is astronomical in supporting a band like this, so he finally had to sell his interest to other people. They have continued to expand and promote the original concept, but many personnel changes have taken place.

Nevertheless, the concept of the Gibson jazz parties caught on, and now there are quite a number of similar affairs taking place in other parts of the country. The Odessa (Texas) Jazz Party, the Midland (Texas) Jazz Party,

310

and the Paradise Valley Jazz Party (Scottsdale, Arizona) all started along the lines of the Gibson party. As a result of this stimulation, a number of other jazz festivals have also come into being. So for certain, everyone associated with jazz owes thanks and appreciation to the Gibsons.

By the time 1972 arrived, my jazz activities were steadily increasing, and this meant the phasing out of my connections with the music school, as well as the instrument rental program in association with Rondo Music. I thoroughly enjoyed working with the people at Rondo, particularly Carl Zentmaier and Ann Placko, two of the nicest people I have ever met. I was truly sorry I couldn't continue with them, but duty lay elsewhere.

The year started off with an interesting date in January—a "Viennese Ball," held in New York City. Featured, of course, was the music of Vienna and the Court of Franz Joseph—Strauss waltzes danced by colorfully dressed people to whom this music was the music of home. This is an outstanding social event for the people of Viennese heritage who live in or are visiting New York for the occasion, and it is lavishly catered, with special pastries flown in from Vienna for the party.

However, what made this particular ball of special interest was the orchestra, which was under the direction of American-Viennese Max Hamlisch, who had his son play piano with us. It was obvious that Max was very proud of his son, and with reason, but none of us could know then what outstanding success young Marvin Hamlisch would achieve as one of America's most prolific composers. His first truly big contribution was to score the hit motion picture "The Sting," in which he brought about a latter-day revival of the music of Scott Joplin. He was also responsible for the score of another hit movie, "The Way We Were," starring Barbra Streisand and Robert Redford, and he composed the music for the Broadway stage hit, "A Chorus Line."

A close associate of mine from Tenafly, N.J., Dr. Sanford E. Kaps, was on the Board of Directors of the Bergen County Cultural Society that year. A multitalented man, Dr. Kaps is an optometrist, but he came to me with a rather unusual idea for a show he wanted to produce for the Cultural Arts Council. This was to present a historical synopsis of the development of American music and dancing from 1900 to 1972, highlighted by the use of photographs projected on a screen from the rear and with live dancing on the stage.

Once we got involved with this, it turned out to be a project of major proportion. None of us realized how big it would be, however, until we were well into the planning stage, and then we began to have inklings of what we were in for. The dance sequences were under the direction of Ed Verso, a member of the Joffrey Ballet Company. I orchestrated the music and put it into logical order for the various eras, and Dr. Kaps had charge of the most exciting part of the show, the lighting and photo effects.

We put the whole thing together, drawing-board style, without a dress rehearsal. The orchestra put in several hours of reading the music on the day of the show, and Ed Verso coached his dancers separately. On Friday evening, April 14, we put it all together for the first time with the metromedia effects dreamed up by Dr. Kaps, at the Orrie de Nooyer Auditorium in Hackensack, in front of a packed house. Entitled "Cakewalk to Rock," the show offered musical segments with dancing to match for four periods: 1900 to 1910—Cakewalk through ragtime to the Castle Walk and the Tango; the 1920s—Fox Trot, Charleston, and Black Bottom; the 1930s—big-band, swing and jitterbugging, and Latin; and, finally, the 1950s—and rock.

We used six dancers, a 16-piece orchestra, and with the rear-projected movie clips, it turned out to be one of the nicest productions I have ever been associated with. Of course, nobody knew beforehand if the thing would make it or fall apart in the middle. Just before the downbeat for the overture my buddy Chris Griffin inquired conversationally, "What would you give to be somewhere else?" His question broke up the band, but it also served to relax the atmosphere, and in spite of the scant apology for a rehearsal—only a fraction of the time really needed—the orchestra played the two-and-a-half hours without a flaw.

Mr. John Everett, the director of the Bergen County Cultural Council, scheduled us for another rather novel concert in August in the same auditorium, but this time we used the standard six-piece jazz band. In it with me were Kenny Davern, Mickey Gravine, Milt Hinton, Marty Napoleon, and Sonny Igoe, with Harry Sheppard as an added attraction on vibraphone. Near the close of the program we invited all comers from the audience to sit in for a colossal jam session, and this turned out to be a great crowd-pleaser. What's more, some of the musicians who came forward were quite good. I think we played one of the longest versions of blues in B^b in musical history.

The previous September I had joined the Fine Arts staff at Fairleigh-Dickinson University, Teaneck campus, as director of the band instrumental music programs. With the second semester in January 1972, my activities were expanded to teaching classes in music history and theory. The job required that I present one instrumental concert each semester, and we were more or less expected to play for the June graduation exercise. Because of the small enrollment of instrumentalists, this wasn't easy, so I came to rely on some friends—especially Warren Vache' Jr., his brother Allan, Effie Resnick, and Mark Heter—to attend regularly our instrumental sessions and to augment our sections into a respectable complement for a concert-band repertoire. I did the concerts in conjunction with a staff professor, Dr. David Saturin, and we were able to present some interesting programs.

The class I enjoyed the most was the one on jazz history. Each 16-week semester I managed to cover the subject fairly well, using the lecture format reinforced by records from my own collection and those of friends, to offer a chronological history of jazz. It was almost like reliving my own life each semester. I consider myself very fortunate to have known perhaps 70 percent of the people—or at least, to have met them—who have created the history of jazz, from King Oliver to the present day.

My class in this subject averaged about 30 to 35 students each semester, and during the three years I taught it very few were musicians. Since the subject was elective, it drew from a wide variety of students. We had business students, dental students, etc., and it was gratifying to me to see so much interest in jazz from such a varied group.

While on the subject of my nonplaying musical activities, I should mention that I was doubling as recording engineer in the studios we operated in conjunction with our music school. I produced an album for two folksingers, "Wright and Keller," who were quite good. They wanted to introduce a friend who played banjo on the second side of the album, so they made arrangements with me to record him.

This turned out to be a gentleman named Paul Cadwell, who had been president of the Princeton banjo club in 1910. He showed up at the studios one Saturday afternoon accompanied by his wife, who carried a rather large bag of refreshments sufficient to carry Mr. Cadwell through the rigors of a recording session. The first thing he did was try the studio piano, promptly informing me it was badly out of tune. He insisted I have it tuned at once because on a couple of numbers he required piano accompaniment, and I had to scramble around for a piano tuner before we could begin.

After the piano was tuned, Mr. Cadwell told me that he was a classical banjo player and that his banjo was unique because it was strung with nylon fishing line. He then proceeded to record eight classical or semiclassical tunes, like "Melody In F" and the "Rockozy March." Before each number he made a brief speech about the selection, for instance, "I will now play a number dedicated to Admiral Dewey's steaming into Manila Bay—it's called 'Blaze Away.' "

No question about it, Mr. Cadwell made one of the most unusual and interesting sides I have ever been associated with.

Another pleasant assignment was recording Chuck Slate and his "Traditional Jazz Band," a group playing at the historic Chester Inn, in the little western New Jersey town of Chester. Chuck had an excellent lineup, including Marv Ross on clarinet (one of the Bayonne gang of youngsters who sat in at Nick's years before); Larry Weiss, cornet; Marty Bergen, trombone; Red Richards, piano; and Warren Vache' on bass. Chuck plays drums. They turned in a fine album of twelve standard tunes well played by a great band, and I had the added pleasure of joining them on one number, "That's A-plenty," on the first side.

And speaking of Nick's, around this time I made my first guest shot with Red Balaban's Sunday-afternoon jazz concerts at a place called "Your Father's Mustache," which was a banjo-parlor the other six days of the week, featuring sing-alongs, sawdust, and peanut shells on the floor. This location had formerly been Nick's, and although entering the doors brought back a flood of memories, they were considerably saddened by the contrast between what it had been and what it had become.

In March I made another guest appearance, as a soloist with Ken Morgester's orchestra at a country club in Hartford. In the middle of a set a man carrying a trombone case came up to us and asked Ken if his friend could sit in on trombone. The friend, he said, was parking his car but would be in soon and would really enjoy playing with the band. He went on to tell us that his friend was a very good trombone player who had been a soloist with the great Jean Goldkette band in Detroit.

I didn't say so, but I thought the guy was either badly misled or telling us a cock-and-bull story, because I knew the trombonists with Goldkette had been Bill Rank and Speigle Willcox, and I didn't think either of them was anywhere near Hartford. So imagine my surprise when the friend turned out to be the real Speigle Willcox, who proceeded to charm us all with his marvelous personality and fine trombone playing.

A short time later, I took part in a "Fats Waller Concert" promoted by Jack Kleinsinger at the DeLise Theater in Greenwich Village. The concert featured Fats Waller's son, Maurice, who played piano on some of his father's compositions. Dick Hyman, who has the fantastic ability to emulate the keyboard styles of other pianists with such authentic realism you would swear you were listening to the original, was brought in also, this time to recreate the organ solos Fats had recorded. Fats Waller alumnus Al Casey played guitar with us and did a few vocals, and the rest of the lineup included Dickie Wells on trombone, Phil Bodner on clarinet, Milt Hinton, and Cliff Leeman. This performance was so successful it started a whole series of concerts produced by Jack Kleinsinger, continuing to the present time. However, the location has been changed to the Loeb Auditorium at New York University.

On March 14, I took a group that included Johnny Mince, Mickey Gravine, Sonny Igoe, Hank Jones, and Milt Hinton into the Dwight Morrow High School in Englewood, N.J., to play a concert on the same program as Dizzy Gillespie's band for the benefit of the high school band. The benefit was to raise funds for the band to make a trip overseas. Dizzy's group included Al Gaffa, guitar; Mike Longo, piano; Earl May, bass; and Mickey Roker, drums. We turned out a pretty good mixture of modern and traditional jazz that went over quite well with the audience.

The best part about the concert for me was the programming session Hank and I had with Dizzy beforehand. It's the only time I've been in a position to work closely with him, and his knowledge and experience soon becomes very apparent. It was obvious why his contributions to music are so important.

FIFTY-FOUR

BY 1973 MY LIFE-STYLE was falling into the pattern which it still follows. Primarily this is a routine geared to the jazz parties and festivals that have proliferated around the world in the past decade or so. And I love it! Not only have I practically toured the world with a horn in my hand, I've played with many of the finest musicians the world has ever seen, and at the same time I've made hundreds of new friends. Typically, in '73 I was invited to the Gibson party for the third time, made my annual visit to the Rancheros Vistadores, and in addition directed several concerts of my own, putting together various combinations to suit specific jobs.

One of these was my first concert for the New Jersey Jazz Society, the beginning of a long and pleasant association with a fascinating group of people dedicated to the preservation of jazz. We put on a three-hour program at The Watchung View Inn, which is owned and operated by former musician and bandleader Bill Sayre, in Pluckemin, N.J. We had a full house and a most enjoyable afternoon. With me were Kenny Davern, Dick Wellstood, Mickey Gravine, Sonny Igoe, and Bill Stanley on bass and tuba. The superlative Maxine Sullivan was our vocalist. The only departure from jazz came about accidentally when I introduced Mickey Gravine to the crowd and he began to tell anecdotes about Joe Venuti. His stories were so well received that he held forth for a half hour or more. I must admit the great Venuti was the source of some very funny material.

Dick Gibson called to book me to play in Denver on April 25, for the opening of a new restaurant called "The Spaghetti Factory." This was located in "The Denver Tramway Cable Building," a downtown Denver historic site, the last structure to be used as a carbarn for streetcars. The owners spared no expense in trying to recreate an appropriate 1890s atmosphere, even going to the expense of importing all the way from the Yukon an authentic, antique mahogany bar. We started off with an excellent band—Kenny Davern, Dick Wellstood; Carl Fontana, trombone; Dr. Lyn Christie, bass; and Alan Dawson, drums. But it became a truly memorable night for me when my old buddy Billy Butterfield came in and played a couple of sets with us. Of course, a lot of spaghetti was served, and I'm told the restaurant turned out to be a big success.

On April 29, I returned to my old stamping grounds, Kansas City, to take part in a huge jazz festival being held in the Municipal Auditorium. Also appearing were such stars as Clark Terry, Arnie Lawrence, Bill Chase, Conte Condoli, Bob Havens, Frank Rossolino, and Joe Pass, all playing with Kansas City bands, winding up with the Thad Jones-Mel Lewis orchestra.

It was a great treat to return to the scene of my early days, as well as enjoying the marvelous festival. One of the nicer aspects of this visit was being the house guest of my very dear friends Dr. and Mrs. Louis Forman. Louis, you will recall, played lead trumpet with Eddie Kuhn's band at the Kansas City Athletic Club, so he was just the one to assemble many of our mutual friends for a reunion. I must admit I was thrilled to be invited upstairs to a smaller room in the Auditorium where 30 members of my high-school graduation class were gathered. I thought then—and still do—that it was quite remarkable that so many in a class that numbered only 45 students to begin with were still able to attend a reunion, and some of the women were still beautiful. All of which, I suppose is a testimonial to the life, health, and longevity of those who live in the Midwest.

Among those present was our former bass player, Charley Knox, the man who introduced me to Joe Haymes. I also had a chance to visit with the Patterson brothers, Norman and George, and their lovely wives, Lois and Marge, to reminisce about the many jobs we had played together in the late Twenties. Norman had become a successful dentist in Kansas City, and George was the postmaster of Bremer, Missouri. I also met newspaper writer and record collector Robert Morris, with whom I still correspond.

This year brought my first invitation to the Odessa Jazz Party, an affair put together by one of the best-liked persons I have ever known, Dr. O. A. Fulcher. Thanks to the wonderful hospitality of the Texas people, this is one of the more relaxed and friendly jazz parties, and—following the original pattern set by Dr. Fulcher—of the longest duration, six days. This tends to encourage an attitude of relaxation and enables the musicians to give tension-free performances. Each evening the music lasts for four hours, entertaining about 400 guests, and since there are always plenty of musicians invited, 25 or so, it's easy to make up four bands of six pieces, with a soloist or two still in reserve. Every evening special gourmet dinners are prepared for the guests and musicians, served in a private dining room, that adds much to the pleasant, sociable atmosphere. As another attractive aspect of the Odessa Party, the good people of Odessa give at least two or three after-hours parties, with varied menus for each.

The year 1973 saw my return to the recording studios, too. I had the pleasure of playing on "The Music of Jelly-Roll Morton," an album for Columbia (M-32587) by Dick Hyman, featuring Joe Venuti. Dick used a large orchestra on some tracks, and a small group on others.

With the advent of 1974, the trend established the previous year began to pick up speed, resulting in the busy schedule which has been the pattern of my life ever since. Essentially this comprises guest appearances with various groups around the country, as with the Drootin brothers at the Scotch and Sirloin in Boston, my repeated visits to Atlanta, and a variety of promotions by bandleader Parke Frankenfield in the Allentown area of Pennsylvania. Parke, like the Atlanta musicians, has one of the finest musical aggregations in the country, and it's always a pleasure to make a guest shot with a fine band able to play flawlessly in the traditional repertoire.

In March I made a trip to the United Kingdom with a musical package designed to recreate the music of Tommy Dorsey. The program, under the joint direction of singer-trombonist Warren Covington and the great arranger Sy Oliver, presented a number of the big hits associated with Tommy. The vocal group "The Pied Pipers," featured ex-Dorseyite Lil Clark in some superb solo spots, and Warren Covington's beautiful trombone playing did full justice to Tommy's solos. He also doubled on vocals, backed by the Pied Pipers. Of course, the segment directed by Sy Oliver was highlighted by the originals he arranged for the Dorsey band, like "Yes, Indeed" and "Opus One."

Also included and well received—was a reconstituted "Clambake Seven," with three of us from the group which recorded the original records—Johnny Mince, Skeets Herfurt, and me. We used a four-man front line, with Warren playing Tommy's part. Panama Francis and Peck Morrison were in the rhythm section.

Chris Griffin was with us in the brass section of the big band, and Bob Levine was part of the sax section, so lots of fun was connected with the tour, which was promoted and well handled by a British agency, Kennedy-Masters. They provided nice accommodations and transportation facilities for us. On the other side of the coin, however, I was the victim of an oversight that annoyed me quite a bit. About three or four days into the tour I happened to pick up a copy of the program booklet that was being circulated among the audience at each concert. After reading it through I became aware that it contained a biography and picture of everybody in the company—except me. I was barely mentioned. Now I'm not usually one to make waves, and I was being well paid, but I think I was justified in this instance to resent the neglect. After all, I had been one of the original members of the Dorsey band and recorded with it extensively, and many of our English fans knew this very well. So I saw red and proceeded to raise so much hell with Warren Covington and Ed Kennedy it's a wonder they didn't drown me, but the only thing I accomplished was establishing a close friendship with Ed Kennedy, who really felt bad that I had been passed over in the program.

Of much greater importance, I met a number of people on this tour who became good friends—Jerry Dawson and Max Jones from *Melody Maker*, the English music paper; Marion Gillies, a newspaper gal from Southport; Sinclair Traill, founder of *Jazz Journal International*, the fine English jazz magazine; writers Eric Townley and Derek Colliar; and several media men with whom I did radio interviews, among them Peter Clayton in London and John Featherstone from Radio Manchester.

I also had the pleasure of meeting the legendary British trumpet player

Nat Gonella. It was Nat's solos of the early Thirties that I used to play with Ray Noble when Ray came to America, and I have always admired his contributions to our music, both in his writing and his playing. Other noted musicians there were John Chilton, and the musicians from the fabulous Palladium orchestra—Jack Parnell, Bob Burns, and the dean of English trumpet players, Tommy McQuater.

The tour was unusual in that for once we had time to visit some of the great historical sites. The first concert was in southwest England, at Paignton, which happily took us past Stonehenge and through Exeter, where Caroline had gone to school for a year. On the following night we were on the south coast at Bournemouth, and our first Sunday was at the New Theatre in Oxford, which gave us the opportunity to tour the University. Our quarters were in a very ancient and charming country inn at Abingdon, where fortunately we had a day off and could spend several hours viewing the sights at Windsor Castle. After a couple of days in the London area, we went to Edinburgh, Scotland, for a concert in Usher Hall, and here again we had plenty of time to visit Edinburgh Castle and shop in Prince Street.

I had broken a small brace on my trumpet, so I took it to a music store in Edinburgh and asked if they could resolder it. They said they could, if I'd wait "just a minute," and sent word to someone in the back of the store. In a few seconds a giant with a great mop of red hair and a beard to match appeared, carrying the biggest blow torch I've ever seen. He held out his hand to me and said, "Let me see the horn." After eyeing the break for a minute, he lit the torch, which sent out a flame at least a foot long, and proceeded to do the neatest soldering job you could ever ask for. When I asked, "How much do I owe you?" he gave me a broad grin and said, "That's your Christmas present, Sonny."

On Sunday, March 24, we played the theater in Southport, which is where I met Nat Gonella and Marion Gillies, who interviewed me for the local newspaper. After concerts in Bristol and Croyden we played at a theater in Manchester on Thursday. After that concert I left the theater by the wrong exit and bumped my head on a low pipe. When I got to the bus, Chris Griffin took one horrified look at me and then ripped off his shirt to bandage my head. Without realizing it, I had opened a large gash in my scalp and it was bleeding profusely. Ed Kennedy drove me to an infirmary where two doctors painlessly sewed 14 stitches to close the cut, and, when they had finished, and I again asked, "How much?" They told me I owed them nothing, that I was a guest, and to go to any hospital in a week's time and have the stitches removed. It was part generosity and a large measure of British socialized medicine.

That Saturday we did our show at "Ronnie Scott's," the famous London club in Soho, and on April 3 we enjoyed the considerable thrill of playing in London's Royal Albert Hall, where I renewed acquaintance with an old London friend, Monty Montgomery. For many years Monty played trumpet with the Mantovani orchestra, and we had first met during one of their American tours. Many times since we have renewed our friendship in

England and in America.

The rest of our tour was spent in the London area, a city I enjoy very much. After the tour was over, I took advantage of the fact that I was in Europe, and continued on to visit some other countries. My first stop was Paris, and I arrived there just in time to appreciate fully the meaning of the song "April In Paris," because suddenly it was shirt-sleeve weather. I put in several days of museum-hopping and getting acquainted with places of historical significance, and then went on to Rome for more of the same. The trip was like a thumbnail excursion backward through time—from Westminster Abbey, Notre Dame, and the Vatican, all the way back to pagan Rome. It was a short but rewarding experience.

FIFTY-FIVE

BACK IN THE STATES, I quickly picked up on my old routine, starting with a second return to the Odessa Jazz Party and then a visit to St. Joseph, Mo., to play for the wedding of Nancy Schreiber, daughter of my good friends Allen and Mary Schreiber. After another Gibson Party, I played a concert with Dick Hyman at Carnegie Hall that would establish a new concept in jazz concerts.

This is worth a note of explanation. Dick wrote arrangements based on the famous solos of Louis Armstrong, scoring them for three trumpets and a full orchestra and presenting them in the context of a musical history of Armstrong's early years. The Carnegie concert was promoted by George Wein, who conceived the idea of projecting film clips of Louis on a movie screen behind the orchestra, edited to give the impression that he was announcing or explaining the numbers we played.

The concert was a huge success and so was the recording that was made of the performance. Both received excellent reviews, and these paved the way for a worldwide presentation of the program. Because of prior commitments, however, especially a projected tour of South Africa, I was unable to go with the group on their first swing, which included a tour of the Soviet Union. I did rejoin them at a later date, though, for a series of thirty concerts in Europe. More about this later.

Following this, the Kennedy-Masters office in London gave me the opportunity to make a European tour with carte blanche to organize the best concert band I could put together. Taking advantage of the option, I assembled a group we called "The Kings of Jazz," which included Kenny Davern and Johnny Mince on reeds, Bernie Privin and myself on trumpets, and Ed Hubble on trombone, backed by Dick Hyman, Major Holley, and Cliff Leeman. We toured northern Europe for the first half of the swing. We started with Iceland, then went on to Stockholm, Sweden, and, finally, a very successful concert at the Hanover Jazz Festival, in December. The second half was played entirely in the British Isles, with an appearance at Usher Hall in Edinburgh, Scotland, and another at the famous 100 Club on Oxford Street in London. Our last concert was in Manchester, neatly timed so we were able to return home on December 24, just in time for Christmas.

The "Kings of Jazz" European tour, 1974. L to R: Eddie Hubble, Bernie Privin, Pee Wee Erwin, Cliff Leeman, Johnny Mince, Major Holley, Kenny Davern, Dick Hyman.

Musically, this was one of the most satisfying tours I have ever taken, but the compatibility of the people involved also made it extremely enjoyable. All those concerned felt the same way, and we were anxious to repeat the tour but, as often happens, this never materialized.

To end the year in style, I picked up a case of the flu, but, even though I still had a low-grade fever, I made a trip to Denver in order to play a two-day stint with a great trio headed by Peanuts Hucko and including those masters of rhythm Ralph Sutton and Gus Johnson.

Almost immediately, the new year, 1975, showed promise of bringing about the most extensive and interesting travels of my career, and this in spite of the fact that I was still playing every weekend in the New York vicinity with Sy Menchin's band. It started out with plans for a tour of South Africa, and, while these were in the making, George Wein invited me to make my first appearance at the jazz festival at Nice, France. So I worked things out with the promoters of the South African trip to do a three-week tour just prior to the Nice Festival, which would coordinate one with the other and make it possible for me to play both. The African trip required inoculations, so I had to get shots for yellow fever, malaria, and cholera.

With the middle of the year already scheduled, the year began with a concert that I presented in my capacity as an instructor in the music department of Fairleigh Dickinson. They kindly allowed me to send in substitute teachers whenever it was necessary, so I was able to maintain this position fairly well. I also did my share of local concerts for the first half of the year, including taking part in the second performance of the Louis Armstrong program at the Kennedy Center in Washington, D.C., and a third visit to Odessa in May. In addition, I worked with Dick Hyman on a James P. Johnson album called "Charleston" and played a party with Peanuts Hucko for the AMA Convention in Atlantic City—brought about because the doctors being installed in the top positions of the organization were all jazz fans and friends of ours.

Of particular interest was a program presented in Carnegie Hall that April by the New York Jazz Repertory Company, dedicated to the music of Bix Beiderbecke. This concert began with a recreation of the "Wolverine Orchestra" of the Twenties, and the classic Beiderbecke solos were played by a young man I consider to be the brightest cornet star to come along in a decade, Warren Vaché Jr. At that time, Warren was exactly 24 years old, the same age as Bix when he made the original records.

The program was narrated by Dick Sudhalter, noted writer, trumpeter, and Bix authority. In addition to Warren, the Wolverines were enhanced by the cornet of Jimmy McPartland, the man who was chosen to replace Bix in the original band. Bob Wilber, who did a marvelous job of transcribing the arrangements from the records, played clarinet as well as the George Johnson tenor solos, and the rest of the group included Kenny Davern on bass saxophone; Effie Resnick, trombone; Howard Johnson, tuba; Dill Jones, piano; and Chauncey Morehouse (who played with Bix in the Jean Goldkette band and on a number of small-band recordings) on drums, aided and abetted by Bobby Rosengarden. Marty Grosz played banjo.

322

Following the Wolverine segment, the stage was taken over by the reconstituted Jean Goldkette Orchestra, playing arrangements originally created by Bill Challis and transcribed for the concert by Dave Hutson, a talented Detroit orchestrator and saxophonist who had been one of the collaborators on the records recreating the music of the McKinney's Cotton Pickers orchestra. The full personnel included Dave Hutson, Kenny Davern, Bob Wilber, and Johnny Mince, reeds; Speigle Willcox and Bill Rank, trombones; Pee Wee Erwin, Doc Cheatham, and Bernie Privin, trumpets; Bucky Pizzarelli, guitar; Chauncey Morehouse and Bobby Rosengarden, drums; Milt Hinton, bass; Paul Mertz, piano; and Joe Venuti, violin. The outstanding emotional aspect was that five members of the original Jean Goldkette band were present—the last time this would ever happen. Tragically, for some undisclosed reason, the concert was not recorded.

All we had to do to realize how good the Goldkette band must have been was play the Challis arrangements, which still make considerable demands on the performers. Yet it was very evident that Willcox, Rank, Mertz, Morehouse, and Venuti were very much at home and hadn't lost a thing in the 50-year interim.

The Wolverine segment was televised, once on NBC's "Today Show" and again for Public TV, and the repertoire included many of the selections recorded by "Bix and His Gang." However, no recordings resulted from this very worthwhile and unique program.

Pee Wee in Zululand, South Africa, 1975.

June 24 came and it was time for my South African trip. I had elected to travel by way of Rio de Janeiro, figuring I could spend a little time there and see some of the sights of that beautiful Brazilian city and at the same time break the monotony of the long air flight. Caroline drove me to the airport and then decided to wait around until my actual departure because the schedules at Kennedy had been badly disrupted by the crash of an airliner at the edge of the field. However, takeoff time finally arrived and the flight was uneventful. We landed in Rio early in the morning, and I spent the day making a trip to Sugar Loaf, with its splendid view of the lovely beaches, the city avenues with mosaic streets, and the 100-foot statue of Christ perched on top of Corcovado Mountain. Without question, this is one of the most beautiful cities in the world, and someday I hope to visit it again. After feasting on exotic Brazilian fruits and coffee, I was back aboard a South African Airways plane that evening for the long trip across the South Atlantic. We landed the next morning in Johannesburg, where another plane was waiting to take me to Durban.

At the Durban Airport I was met by Eric Clewlow, the promoter of my tour, who took me to my quarters in a hotel called the Warwick. I had a very nice suite, complete with a balcony that overlooked Durban and the Indian Ocean, and my meals were served in the hotel dining room where the service seemed to hark back to British colonial times. The menus were extensive and served in very elegant fashion by Indian waiters.

I was scheduled to play three concerts in Durban in the ballroom of the Alangeni Hotel on June 29, July 3, and July 6, all of which were billed as "Kansas City Jazz Concerts." My backup groups were the George Wooler Trio and the Johnny Williams Jazzmen, a quintet, for the first two concerts. The third concert was with a group from Johannnesburg that included Archie Silansky, piano; Dan Hill, clarinet; Gus Eckhart, bass; and Gene Latimore, drums. With each group, I was joined by an excellent Durban trombonist, Ernie Strange. With the last band, I recorded two half-hour radio shows for South African Radio, which were to be aired at a later date on regularly scheduled jazz programs. The radio shows and our concerts were announced and conducted by Wilf Lowe, a well-known South African jazz authority.

In addition to playing good clarinet, Johnny Williams turned out to be an excellent vibraphonist, and I played with his group on two successive Saturdays at the Durban Killarney Hotel for the Jazz Preservation Society of South Africa. The Society made me an honorary member for life. I also played a public concert in the Durban City Hall for those who could not attend the Alangeni concerts and a dance held at the Amanzimtoti Country Club in the Durban suburbs, where I was startled to be greeted at the portico by two huge, blue cranes.

All my life my ideas about the "Dark Continent" were largely conditioned by Tarzan movies. Instead, I found Durban to be a lovely, modern, subtropical city that reminded me very much of Santa Barbara. However, when they told me we were going to play a job about 60 miles out of the city, in the town hall of a place called Pietermaritzburg, I immediately assumed that now we were really going into bush country. Then I found out how primitvie things really were. Just before we started our concert, Eric Clewlow announced he was going out to bring

324

back some food for us, and when he returned he had two large buckets of Colonel Sanders' Kentucky Fried Chicken.

I had plenty of time for social activities and sightseeing, and I was treated very hospitably. Eric Clewlow entertained me in his home, where I met his fine family, and I was invited to the home of Wilf Lowe for a "briefleisch," the South African term for barbecue, which literally translates as "burnt meat." Johnny Williams very kindly acted as my personal tour guide around Durban and made certain I saw the many beautiful points of interest, as well as taking me out to a game reserve located in a geologically interesting area called the "Valley of 1000 Hills."

On this game reserve (where you are advised not to get out of your car) you can find yourself surrounded by all types of animals which are allowed to roam at will, just as they do in the wilds, and it is possible to photograph them in their natural habitat. The only animals I saw penned in were lions, and you can even enter this compound when the lions are being fed and obviously too preoccupied to bother visitors.

On another trip with Johnny, we were accompanied by Val Lowe, the wife of our announcer, to Zululand. Val spoke Zulu and made it possible for us to visit two Zulu villages under very cordial conditions. In one village I joined the Zulu drummers and singers, trying to record a tape playing tunes with them, but I found their music to be too repetitious to allow much latitude for my improvisations.

From Durban they flew me 1,000 miles west to Capetown—a startling contrast. Capetown is located on the Cape of Good Hope, where the Indian Ocean meets the Atlantic, and is so different from Durban that it might as well be on another planet. Capetown resembles a typical English seaport and has an interesting geographical setting. Towering above it is a mountain-top formation appropriately named "Lion Head." As in Durban, I was met by very nice people who showed me the points of interest, including the memorial to Cecil Rhodes and the hospital where Dr. Christian Barnard pioneered the heart-transplant operations.

For most of my stay in Capetown, I was associated with a trumpet-playing bandleader named Gerry Kirkham, who had a very good band. I enjoyed playing with them because they knew the library of standard and traditional songs, and Gerry and I hit it off very well. He had been stationed in the CBI (China-Burma-India) theater of operations with the British army during World War II, and he had a lot of colorful stories to tell about it. This also led to the realization that we had mutual acquaintances in Sinclair Traill, the English journalist, Lennie Felix, the British pianist, and Jack Stine, President of the New Jersey Jazz Society, all of whom had been stationed in the same area during the war.

With a very fine pianist named Jimmy Smith added to Gerry's band, we played two excellent concerts at a place called Weizman Hall, Sea Point, in Capetown. We had a drummer who played very well too, and it wasn't until the first concert was over and I saw him limp off the stage that I found out he wore an artificial leg. Then they told me an amusing story about him. Sometimes the leg would hurt the drummer, so he only wore it during a performance and then afterwards would take it off. They played a job a couple of hundred miles into the back country, and, when they finally got home after a grueling drive, the drummer started looking around in the car for his leg and suddenly realized he had left it on the job. They had to make arrangements with a trucking company that serviced the remote area to pick up the leg and deliver it to the drummer before he could play another job.

My last weekend in South Africa was spent in Johannesburg, playing with Dan, Archie, Gus, and Gene, the same musicians who had played the radio broadcasts with me in Durban. We played for the Johannesburg (they call it "Joberg," for short) Jazz Club, and I met and heard a number of the local musicians. Many of them are quite good, because Johannesburg is the music center of South Africa and it is where the principal studios are located—and, therefore, the bulk of the work.

The city is positioned on a plateau at an altitude of 5,000 feet, completely modern, and designed, so I was told, by an American engineer, and therefore much like an American city. I stayed at the home of Archie Silansky, who was especially kind to me, even including me in a birthday party being held for a member of his family. South Africa is an amazingly beautiful country, and visiting there turned out to be a great experience.

On July 15 I flew on Alitalia from Johannesburg to Rome—6,000 miles with only one stop to refuel in Kinshasa, Zaire, where they wouldn't let us off the plane because of local unrest. I spent one night in Rome and on the very next day took off again for my first appearance at the jazz festival in Nice.

FIFTY-SIX

THE OFFICIAL TITLE is "Grande Parade du Jazz," and it is the world's biggest jazz festival, masterminded by the most successful jazz entrepreneur in the world, George Wein, and held every July since 1948 in the "Jardins des Arenes de Cimiez"—the site of ancient Roman ruins, located above the city of Nice, France. In the United States George Wein is probably better known as the promoter of the famous "Newport Jazz Festival,"—the daddy of them all—an annual event that has been a success for many years, but his international reputation has been established by the Nice Festival, a truly international event produced on a grand scale. Every year, more than one hundred of the best-known jazz musicians perform on three sound stages in the beautiful gardens, with more than 100,000 fans in attendence over the 11-day span of the Festival. They come from all over the world.

One stage, aptly called "The Arena," is built on the site of a Roman arena, with the original rock structure forming the back and sides. The stage was built right into the Roman wall, with seats to accommodate about 2,000 people arranged within the walls. The stage is baffled to contain the sound. About a block-and-a-half away is another stage, called "The Dance Stage," which has a dance floor built directly in front of it. Bordering on three sides are market stands selling records and a variety of foods and, directly behind the stage, is an outdoor arrangement of tables for dining, with chefs imported from New Orleans cooking up gumbo, red beans and rice, and other Creole dishes. Finally, several blocks further along, is the third stage, also appropriately named—"The Garden Stage." This is also surrounded by stands, these selling sandwiches and drinks. Altogether it's an ideal and convenient arrangement for the jazz fans, who can either bring food or purchase it at the stands and then enjoy the music as they picnic in beautiful garden surroundings.

The music begins on each stage at 5 p.m. and continues until midnight. Some groups are organized units—such as the big bands of Count Basie, Woody Herman, and Lionel Hampton, and the smaller groups of Dave Brubeck and Dizzy Gillespie—but others are assembled from the large pool of free-lance musicians invited to the Festival, combined to form blues bands, traditional bands, and modern groups. In fact, eventually you will hear every kind of band

Marian McPartland and George Wein

you want to, just so long as the music is jazz oriented, and, after 11 full days of this, you can't help but feel you have been to the Mecca of jazz.

George Wein and his staff are experts at devising interesting combinations and putting compatible musicians together, and they come up with some excellent groups within the accepted pattern of each musicial style—that is, modern players in one set, mainstream players in another, and so on. Each musician plays two sets each night, and each on a different stage. A typical group, for instance, put together to play a set entitled "Cornet Chop Suey," might include Bobby Hackett, Doc Cheatham, and me, with perhaps Kenny Davern and Vic Dickenson, plus an appropriate rhythm section. Then I might be in another set entitled "The Heritage Hall Jazz Band, featuring Pee Wee Erwin."

George Wein always sends notes to the musicians at Nice, telling them that he wants them to enjoy themselves, and the programming really backs this up. Two sets stand out in my recollection of the 1975 Festival: one with the George Barnes-Ruby Braff group and another with Joe Venuti, Red Norvo, and Teddy Wilson. How could I fail to be inspired to do my very best?

Aside from the great music, Nice is a lovely seaside resort. One of the attractions is the many open-air restaurants, especially along the Rue Massena, a street which is blocked to automotive traffic and is lined with sidewalk cafes, with tables extending right out into the street. Almost every day at noon I had the pleasure of joining a pleasant group of Englishmen at one of these tables for a session of drinks, laughs, and storytelling, all of them regular visitors to the Festival—Sinclair Traill, founder and editor of the fine British jazz magazine *Jazz Journal*, and his friends, George Ebbs, Andrew Gillies, and Lennie Felix.

This was always a lot of fun, and our regular table was out in the street where a number of friends would walk past and exchange a few words. Under a table umbrella shading us from the warm, sunny skies, this was a delightful leisure hour.

When the Festival was over I went back to Italy for a sightseeing trip but after only two days I got homesick, so I took the first flight I could get from Rome to New York. Seven weeks turned out to be just a bit overlong to be away from home.

However, after a couple of weeks in Maine with the family, I was reconditioned for more travel and flew out to Denver for my fourth Gibson Party—thirteenth in the series. This one included 47 musicians and over 500 guests.

In October George Wein lined up an ambitious tour for the Louis Armstrong program that had first been presented at Carnegie Hall in 1974. The swing would cover 12 European countries in 30 days, and the program would be presented in its entirely, including the screen projection of Louis on film behind the band. When this was put together, Jimmy Maxwell and Joe Newman were the other trumpet players, Eddie Hubble was on trombone, and the rest of the group included Kenny Davern, Marty Grosz, George Duvivier, and Bobby Rosengarden, with vocals by Blanche Thomas, and Ruby Braff as an added attraction. It was all under the direction of Dick Hyman, and we certainly had enough cornet players.

The central theme of this tour, from the musicians' standpoint, appeared to be travel—with most of it in a hurry! Nevertheless, Wein's road managers and tour directors—two gentlemen named Bob Jones and Spike Barkin—were experts, and this turned out to be the best-handled tour I'd ever been on, in spite of the necessity for fast moves and long hauls. Obviously, with an itinerary taking in 12 countries to be covered in a month's time we had to move almost daily, and each move entailed a lot of people, a lot of detail, and a lot of luggage and equipment, yet the only thing each of us was required to do was stand beside the luggage ramp in every airport to make sure our bags had arrived with us. Everything else was done for us. Even our bags were picked up from our rooms in one city and delivered to those we were to occupy in the next port of call.

Our first concert was in Umea, Sweden, 500 miles up the Gulf of Finland, north of Stockholm; the second was in Warsaw, Poland, our first trip behind the Iron Curtain. In Warsaw we were part of a good-sized music festival, and we heard some very good musicians. Dick Hyman did the announcing for our show, and after he spoke everything had to be translated into Polish before we could start to play. It slowed our routine quite a bit, but at least the audience understood what we were doing.

Since this was my first trip to Eastern Europe, it was all new and very interesting, but the novelty soon wore off. Upon entry we were required to declare all the money we had on us, to insure, I suppose, that we didn't leave with more than we brought in. Then we were greeted by a representative of the U.S. State Department, who gave each of us a sizeable amount of Polish zlotys, since we couldn't use any other money. In no time at all, it was brought home to us that

The multi-talented Dick Hyman. Cathy Gardner photo

this was a different world. As it turned out, we had little need for money since we were only there overnight, and we were treated to a large dinner by our hotel after the performance. The hotel, by the way, appeared on the surface to be a relatively elegant place, but I noticed the pipes in the bathroom were green with corrosion, and I saw quite a few cockroaches running around.

We had breakfast at the airport the next morning, and a thick fog delayed our flight. It was most likely my imagination, but I had an uncomfortable feeling of suppression and being closed in; I was glad to leave.

Back in Sweden, we played in Gothenburg in one of those ultramodern concert halls that are all concrete and hardwood, with absorbing baffles designed to kill the overtones. Some of these auditoriums provide nice acoustics. The next morning we were loaded on a bus which took us to a pier, and we boarded a large, ocean-going ferryboat for a two-and-a-half hour trip across the North Sea to the northernmost point of Denmark. The ferryboat was equipped with a first-class diningroom where we all had a whopping breakfast and a lot of fun was generated by our humorist-in-residence, Marty Grosz. Marty's quick wit can liven up any situation, especially in combination with Kenny Davern and Ruby Braff at the table.

When we got to Denmark a bus took us south to Aarhus, where we played in a really swinging club called the Jazzhus, and from Aarhus we returned to Stockholm for a performance at the Ballet Theater On the Square, which was televised by national TV for a Christmas replay.

On October 30 we moved on to Brussels, Belgium, where we stayed for three days, playing one concert in Brussels on the 31st, and on the next day traveling by bus for 80 miles to Rotterdam, Holland, to play a joint concert with the Charles Mingus Quintet. On Sunday the bus took us to Ostend, on the North Sea Coast, and after appearing there we continued on to Paris. There we were scheduled to do one televised show in the Theatre Nationale de Chaillot, a beautiful entertainment complex near the Eiffel Tower. This worked out fine because we had four full days in Paris and for three of them we were free to do as we pleased. We had a great time and were even treated to an after-theater banquet in a lively Montparnasse restaurant by our promoter, George Wein.

After Paris, the tour took us to a quaint little town in Germany named Kamen. We landed in Dusseldorf and had to take a bus for the 40-mile ride north to Kamen. We were at least four or five miles on the way before somebody took a head count and discovered that Joe Newman was missing. Since the basis of our entire show was the trumpet trio playing the harmonized choruses of Louis Armstrong, even the loss of one horn was disastrous enough to wreck it, so there was nothing to do but return to Dusseldorf. We went back to the Dusseldorf airport and made a thorough search, but there was no sign of Joe, which left us no alternative but to continue on to Kamen and hope that in some way Joe would manage to get there too. What we failed to take into consideration was Joe's considerable experience in traveling around Europe. When we made our anxious entry into Kamen, we stopped for lunch at the only restaurant in the little town, and when we walked into the dining room we found Joe already enjoying his lunch. He had taken a cab from Dusseldorf.

We stayed in a quaint rural inn on the outskirts of Kamen, where they observe a charming custom. When you are ushered to your room you find a piece of fresh fruit and a piece of chocolate on your pillow as a welcoming gift. We had to arise at 6 a.m. the next morning for our early departure, and were served a hearty breakfast of porridge, varied pastries, jams and jellies, and coffee by the inn's knee-pants-clad proprietor, ably assisted by his children.

From Kamen we traveled south to Baden, Switzerland, which is not too far from Zurich, so that at the concert I met a lovely couple from Zurich, Mr. and Mrs. John Simmen. John is one of Europe's foremost jazz authorities and record collectors.

We left Baden before daylight to fly to Berlin, which involved a quick flight connection in Frankfurt. The connection was so quick, in fact, that our luggage, including the instruments, had to follow on a later plane, a situation that led to the creation of a few more gray hairs. Our Berlin performance at the Philharmonic Hall was set for 2 p.m. and the instruments didn't arrive until 1:30 p.m. As though this wasn't bad enough, when I opened my trumpet case I found the bell of my horn had been bent like an accordian. I did the best I could to roll it out with a drumstick and, since the horn still blew okay, I was a bit broken but not beaten.

We checked into the Schwizerhof Hotel after our concert and had the evening and all the next day to view the points of interest around the city.

After a November 11th concert in the beautiful city of Lausanne, Switzerland, we flew over the Italian Alps for our second trip behind the Iron Curtain, to a festival in Belgrade, Yugoslavia. When I saw several women digging a trench for sewer pipes in front of our hotel, it was again apparent that we were in a different cultural society but, in contrast to the gloomy depression so prevalent in Poland, the Yugoslav people appeared lively and confident. This was the first festival we played where we appeared on the same stage with a Russian jazz band, and we had to admit they were pretty good. Afterwards, Dick Hyman, Marty Grosz, and I stopped into a small restaurant next door to the theater and enjoyed the best yogurt and baklava I've ever tasted.

We played another concert in Zagreb, Yugoslavia, and then we were flown to Bologna, Italy, for a three-day stay. In the meantime, for a good part of the time we'd been skipping from country to country, the European edition of the New York *Herald Tribune* (practically the only English-language newspaper available to Americans traveling on the Continent) had been reporting a revolution taking place in Portugal. Since Portugal was the last stop on our tour, there was considerable apprehension and speculation as to whether it would be wise to attempt to fulfill the commitment. Some of our members didn't care to risk becoming involved in foreign unrest.

However, this didn't stop us from taking advantage of the good food in Bologna, playing a concert in the "Teatro Comunale Dell'Opera" in Genoa, and then flying to Barcelona, Spain, to present another at the 10th "Festival Internacional de Jazz," in a theater built in 1871. After Barcelona, we took one of those superb trains, the *Targa*, for a trip up the Spanish coast to Marseilles, France. Aboard these elegant, high-speed trains they have two sittings, ship-style, for meals in the dining car, and the food is excellent. To get to Marseilles, it was necessary to change at the French city of Avignon, whch for 80 years was the seat of the Pope during the Middle Ages.

In Marseilles we were booked into the "Theatre des Varietes," and the posters that were spread around the city advertising the concert were unique, to say the least. The billboards announced "The Armstrong Show," in huge letters, with all of our names listed below—and then, directly below these, was an advertisement sponsored by the prostitutes of Marseilles who were striking for more money and better working conditions. Fortunately, I was able to take pictures, because how often is one given the opportunity to appear on such an illustrious bill?

By the time we had played our performance in Marseilles, the fear and anxiety generated by the situation in Portugal had reached fever pitch among the members of our company. We kept reading in the paper news stories telling of warring factions taking over the various public buildings, tanks blocking the streets of Lisbon, and other unpleasantries—hardly a happy atmosphere for jazz concerts. Finally, our road manager, Bob Jones, gave us a choice. He told us that although he had to go ahead to Portugal, in his opinion it was the option of each individual to decide what he wanted to do, and if anybody preferred not to go he could return home. Kenny Davern and Marty Grosz elected not to continue and took off for the return to Paris and then New York. Kenny told me later, though, he changed his mind in Paris and tried to rejoin the group, but couldn't swing it.

The rest of us went on to Portugal but, of course, the loss of the clarinet and guitar knocked a hole in us musically. We arrived in Lisbon feeling more than a bit nervous, but the only sign of unrest at the airport was a rather nasty porter. But we didn't hang around there very long, leaving for Cascais, about 40 miles from Lisbon on the beautiful Estoril Coast, where we were to play for the 5th "Festival Internacional de Jazz de Cascais." We were lodged in one of the prettiest hotels I've ever seen. George Duvivier and I had adjoining rooms, and during the night we found out we couldn't turn off the air conditioning, so we wound up freezing even though the temperature outside was warm and comfortable.

The hotel was pretty crowded with entire families, and we learned that many of the people were Angolan refugees, but the only other indications we saw of the revolution were the painting and signs on the buildings we passed on the drive to the hotel from the airport. A bus came to pick us up for the trip to the arena where we were to play for the Festival, and we got as far as the arena grounds when we were stopped by a huge, milling crowd surrounded by police and soldiers. We began to think that we had bulled our way right into the middle of a riot or a part of the revolution, but we were told the crowd consisted of gate crashers who were being held in check by the guards. Nowhere on the tour had we experienced anything like this, and even when we got into the arena proper, we were met by the wildest crowds we had ever played for, and the smell and the smoke of weed hung over the place in clouds.

We had no clarinet, but fortunately the crowd liked us, and we turned in one helluva performance by the brass and the rhythm section for the conclusion of a most interesting tour. Outstanding in my recollection of it is the wonderful job Jimmy Maxwell did in the lead trumpet chair. This man played a different book for a series of 25 consecutive concerts, and I never head him miss, which in my estimation places him among the greatest lead trumpet players of all time. The performances turned in by Ruby Braff, who did a 20-minute solo spot on every program, were likewise superb. Ruby is a very creative musician, and his performances kept me pretty happy musically.

Aside from these pleasant things, I must admit I hated to leave that warm Portuguese coast behind at the end of November, only to face the prospect of the ice and snow of a typical New Jersey winter.

FIFTY-SEVEN

A SERIES OF SINGLE CONCERTS in the New York metro area started off 1976. One of them was with a group put together by Chris Griffin for White Beaches Country Club in Haworth, N.J., with top artists like Sal Pace, Harry DeVito, Marty Napoleon, and Sonny Igoe. I continued to work various engagements with Chuck Slate, a disciple of George Wettling who plays very much like George, and manages to surround himself with such good musicians as Marv Ross on clarinet, Hank Ross on piano, and Alex Watkins or Marty Bergen on trombone. The group plays many of the routines similar to those that Phil Napoleon's and my band used to play at Nick's. I have always enjoyed the many dates I have played through the years under the leadership of Chuck Slate.

In February, Dick Hyman organized a quintet to play a unique program of music for a month's stay at Michael's Pub, a mid-town restaurant in New York. Others in the group were Bob Wilber, Milt Hinton, and Bobby Rosengarden, and, although Dick's fabulous musical talents went into the development of the quintet, the exceptional ability of the individual musicians made the entire concept evolve into an outstanding musical experience. We played the music of Jelly-Roll Morton, Scott Joplin, and James P. Johnson, and although the compositions of these men were written for the piano, Dick wrote leads and routines for the unit utilizing the two horns to enhance the piano themes. The result proved to be a rewarding musical adventure. Our program was very well received, and as a consequence we've been invited back to Michael's for several years running, and each year Dick has expanded the repertoire.

After Michael's, I made a quick trip to Falls City in order to play for the wedding of Teresa Hoban, daughter of my old friend Dr. Hoban. Since we had been so close to the Hoban family for so many years, Judge Maust and I were elected to play during the ceremony along with the church organist, Mrs. Kopetsky. Nothing seems funnier than two old jazz buffs playing serious wedding music, but we came through.

A number of interesting dates followed; an appearance at "Jazz At Noon," in New York, several with Parke Frankenfield, and still another with saxophonist Jerry Jerome on April 4, for the Morristown Historical Society. This proved to be a thumbnail history of jazz narrated by Jim Jensen, the CBS newsman, who did his homework very well. It was an excellent program, with a good band.

April was notable, too, in that I started a once-a-week evening of jazz on a refurbished ferryboat turned into a unique restaurant. Under its original name the *Binghamton*, it was permanently anchored on the New Jersey side of the Hudson River, in Edgewater, providing guests with a great view of the river, the New York skyline, and the George Washington Bridge. I presented a five-piece jazz band on Tuesday nights, rotating the personnel so it was a different band every week. They also permitted me to send a substitute in my place when I had to be away, and this also added to the musical variety. The job continued through that August, and the boat was a nice place to cool off on a hot summer evening. Many of my friends were regular patrons and I found it most pleasant.

In June I played a concert with Joe Venuti for the New Jersey Jazz Society at a place called Farcher's Grove. A date with Joe always brought out a large crowd, in part because of his great sense of humor. The day was made even more memorable by an experience with an entirely new wrinkle, something that had never happened to me before. I was pleased when an old friend I hadn't seen in about ten years, Bob Strachan, came up to shake hands with me, but the big surprise came when he handed me an envelope and I opened it to find it stuffed with money. When I asked what it was for, he reminded me that ten years before I had played an affair at his house in Chappaqua, N.Y., leaving before he had a chance to pay me—now he was rectifying the oversight. For my part, I dimly recalled not expecting to get paid, thinking I was donating my services to a friend, but to say I was astonished at being paid ten years later would be an understatement.

Later in the month the New Jersey Jazz Society collaborated with George Wein's Newport Jazz Festival in cosponsoring the first "Jazz Picnic" at historic Waterloo Village, a quaint and lovely setting near Stanhope, N.J., and I was invited to take part. Actually I did three segments of the Newport Festival, which is now held in numerous locations around metropolitan New York. Besides the Waterloo picnic, I played "Tubby the Tuba" for a program designed for children, produced by Jack Kleinsinger at the Loeb Center of NYU. The principal role was ably handled by Major Holley, and the narration was by Clark Terry, and it all brought back memories of the original record I had made with the composer, George Kleinsinger, many years before. My third appearance was with Dick Hyman's Quintet for a midnight concert at Radio City Music Hall on July 1. We had a lot of company on this program, including Joe Williams and the Count Basie Band, Freddie Hubbard, Clark Terry, and enough groups to provide continuous music until 3 a.m.

Incidentally, the New Jersey Jazz Society's "Jazz Picnic" was such a huge success that it is now an annual part of the Newport Festival, and attendance has grown every year to the extent that it is now one of the most popular events, with a wide variety of musical attractions performing on a continuous basis from noon until dark in a relaxed and congenial atmosphere.

In July I made my second trek to the Nice Festival, this year performing as a member of a number of small groups keyed to various periods in jazz history, like "A Night At Nick's" and a "Clambake Seven," with Bud Freeman and Johnny

Joe Venuti and Pee Wee Erwin

Mince. Still another was called "Windy City Jazz," with Marian and Jimmy McPartland taking part, along with Bud Freeman. Since all the members of the Dick Hyman Quintet were on hand, we were able to do several sets as a unit. Of special interest as a new experience, I enjoyed appearing as a guest with the "Dutch Swing College Band" and the "Barrelhouse Jazz Band," from Frankfurt, Germany. One of the numbers I played with the Barrelhouse bunch was issued on one of their albums.

From Nice I made a side trip to The Hague for a one-day appearance at the brand-new "North Sea Jazz Festival," playing in a very unusual hall called the "Congresgebouw," which was divided into several separate halls, each one presenting a different kind of jazz for the three days of the Festival. The large halls were used to present stellar attractions like Count Basie, Ella Fitzgerald, and Lionel Hampton, and the smaller ones for groups working in such various jazz styles as traditional, modern, avant garde, or the like. I was told that over 6,000 people could be entertained under the one roof.

Back in the States we did a repeat of Jerry Jerome's "History of Jazz," with Jim Jensen, at the historic Earle Theater in Washington, D.C., the scene of many big-band performances in the old days, and a nostalgic return for me. Then I rejoined Dick Hyman for another presentation of the Jelly-Roll Morton concert in a church in Newport, R.I. The church dates back to colonial times and has magnificent natural acoustics. We played some of the music recorded on the original Columbia album by a large orchestra, and trombonist George Masso did an excellent job of calling in proficient local musicians to augment the six men in the original group and play the arrangements. This turned out to be one of the most rewarding concerts of the year.

In mid-August, the jazz sessions on the *Binghamton* came to an end, the management deciding to suspend them until the next summer, and I flew out to take part in my fifth Gibson Party. That year the Gibsons decided to film the proceedings for a full-length movie to be called, "The Great Rocky Mountain Jazz Party." They imported a professional crew from Hollywood to do the job, complete with sound trucks, engineers, cameramen, lighting technicians, and a director, and 24 hours of the party were recorded on film. All of the musical performances were shot, and in addition, sequences of the pre-party happenings were filmed, such as the private party at the Gibson home in Denver, the arrival of the musicians, and a few scenes of the usual pranks and horseplay. They also took pictures of everyone aboard the buses, and some planned sequences at the Broadmoor. All of this footage was edited into a 90-minute film that was introduced at the Cannes Film Festival; it has also had several private viewings for the purpose of lining up distribution. So far it hasn't been placed for showing, but, in due time, it probably will because such films have a habit of becoming priceless documentaries at time goes on, offering rare footage of great jazz artists.

My two very close friends, Bill Muchnic and Bill Seifert, are Board members at Rockwell International, and each is a musician. Muchnic plays trumpet (he studied with Otto Jacobs, father of my teacher, Ferdinand Jacobs), and Seifert is a drummer who plays with a fine group in the Pittsburgh area. They were instrumental in my being invited to attend an outing held by Mr. W.A. Rockwell at a game preserve located south of Pittsburgh, an annual event called the "Nemacolin Encampment." To some extent this is similar to the "Rancheros Vistadores," except in this case the band is called, "The Nemacolin Bird Dogs," and we play for our own pleasure as well as that of the members of the encampment.

October was highlighted by my invitation to take part in a new addition to the "jazz party" concept. This one, in Connecticut, was sponsored by an airline pilot, Ed Ramsey, who had visited the Gibson and Odessa affairs and decided to start one of his own. As with the others, I'm happy to report, it was successful and has been followed by more. Then in November a surprise phone call came in from a man in Minneapolis who asked me if I could supply a band to play for a party to be sponsored by the Dairy Queen organization at the Waldorf Astoria on November 24. The caller identified himself as president of the company and then went on to say he remembered hearing me play 25 years ago at The Paddock Lounge, in Trenton, N.J., when they used to have jam sessions there.

To close out 1976 I worked in two movies, a medium I hadn't been involved with for some time, except for the Gibson Party movie. In one picture I was in a scene filmed on board a ship, the *Christoforo Columbo*, a departure sequence complete with serpentine and confetti, but it was filmed in the rain and it was cold. In the other, I played on the sound track for scenes depicting the French Quarter in New Orleans. Fortunately or unfortunately, depending on how the movies turned out, I can't remember the name of either one.

FIFTY-EIGHT

JANUARY 1977 FOUND the Dick Hyman Quintet—Wilber, Hinton, Rosengarden, Hyman, and Erwin—back at Michael's Pub, but for the second month-long engagement we played a completely new library. Dick Hyman had put together a program he called "Music of the 1930s," featuring the music of Fats Waller, Duke Ellington, and John Kirby and emphasizing tunes that are seldom heard. We played things like "Yacht Club Swing," "Stompy Jones," and "Paswonky," and once again we were well received for the novelty of the program and the unique sound of the group. The sound was mainly achieved by the unusual blend of the soprano sax with the trumpet, and the beautiful sound Bob Wilber gets from his horn.

In the middle of this engagement, I made a quick trip to the Marriott Motel in Providence, R.I., to play in a special memorial concert to Bobby Hackett. I worked with a very fine group that included Dick Johnson on reeds, George Masso, Dave McKenna, Frank Tate on bass, and Ernie Hackett (Bobby's son) on drums. Bobby's wife, Edna, attended, as did many of his relatives. The show was recorded and played all over the country on Public Radio. It was an honor to be invited to participate in this fine tribute to a very good friend and a great creative artist, Bobby Hackett.

February started off with another presentation of the Armstrong Show at the Stratford Theater, in Stratford, Conn., the third one in the United States. On February 20, I flew out to the West Coast to play for Bill Muchnic's 60th birthday party at the San Diego Country Club. I had a terrific band for the evening— Henry Questa, clarinet; Bob Havens, trombone; Ray Sherman, piano; Jack Lesberg, bass; and Nick Fatool, drums—and the party was great fun because Beverly Muchnic managed to surprise Bill completely. She invited about a hundred of his best friends, and then had one of his favorite jazz bands play for the occasion.

Back home, the second season of jazz on Tuesday nights on the ferryboat *Binghamton* began, and I continued the same policy of a new band every week. Also the New Jersey Jazz Society presented an ambitious jazz program for the first time, called "The Strides of March," at the Playboy Club in Vernon Valley, N.J. The festival lasted until May 8, and with me on the program were Joe

340

Williams, Al Green, Barney Bigard, Benny Carter, Vic Dickenson, George Duvivier, Earl Hines, Milt Hinton, Dick Hyman, Ellis Larkins, Jimmy Maxwell, Johnny Mince, Bob Rosengarden, Zoot Sims, Clark Terry, Joe Venuti, Teddy Wilson, and Trummy Young, who acted as host for the entire festival.

In April, I made another trip to San Diego to visit the Muchnics and to check in for a day at the Scripps Clinic for a physical. From there I went on to Honolulu, where I played for a party at the Hawaiian Village Hotel on the 30th. This was followed on May 2 by the jazz festival sponsored by Kool Cigarettes, which offered such attractions as Woody Herman's Orchestra, Chuck Mangione's Quartet, and Wallace Davenport's New Orleans Band. The impressive lineup for the weekend of jazz included Ruby Braff, John Bunch, Al Cohn, Kenny Davern, Vic Dickenson, George Duvivier, Micky Gravine, Marty Grosz, Major Holley, Dick Hyman, Ed Hubble, Cliff Leeman, Bobby Rosengarden, Zoot Sims, Jack Six, Fred Stoll, Warren Vaché Jr., Dick Wellstood, Bob Wilber, Wayne Wright, and vocalist Carrie Smith. Again it turned out to be a very rewarding experience from the musical standpoint, with a variety of combinations producing some unusual sounds.

I also had a nice reunion with my old friend Charley Knox and his wife, who were on a Honolulu vacation. We had a good time talking over our Kansas City days in the Thirties, and what a long way we have come since.

On Sunday afternoons, Honolulu visitors can hear dixieland jazz at the Hawaiian Hilton played by a good band led by trumpet player John Norris. They work from a well-rounded repertoire and made for pleasant listening when I got the chance to hear them. I did, because I stayed in Honolulu for four more days after the festival was over, so altogether I was able to enjoy almost two weeks of the beach and lovely weather. The big treat, however, was the privilege of recording an album with "Trummy Young and Friends"—Paul Madison on tenor, Barney Bigard, Milt Hinton, Dick Hyman, and Bob Rosengarden. It was a very relaxed session and I'm happy to have been a part of it. Trummy was one of my very best friends and he played and sang wonderfully. Paul Madison was also a pleasure to play with and listen to, and, of course, it was an honor to record with Barney.

Back on the mainland, I stopped in San Diego for a one-night session and then flew to San Antonio, Texas, where I had been invited to do a guest shot with Jim Cullum's "Happy Jazz Band," featuring Allan Vaché, my young friend from New Jersey, on clarinet. The Happy Jazz Band is a good one, and once again I will repeat that it is a genuine pleasure to be able to walk into a club so far from New York and find a band that is so well-equipped to play all of the standard repertoire. Their home base for many years has been a club called "The Landing," which has the double advantage of being located in San Antonio's beautiful Hyatt-Regency Hotel, at the center of the city's most beautiful attraction, the "Paseo del Rio" (the River Walk), a magnificently landscaped stretch along the San Antonio River, removed from the noise and bustle of the city by being situated a story below street level. The band has established a national reputation for excellence and backs it up in every sense of the word, entertaining customers and conventioneers from all over

The front line of The Happy Jazz Band—Allan Vache', Jim Cullum, and Randy Reinhart.

the country.

From San Antonio I moved on for my fifth visit to the Odessa Jazz Party. A week later, I attended an event that has to be rated as the most unusual, and probably the most ambitious, musical affair in the country, the "Sacramento Jubilee." This takes place in the old, refurbished section of the city, "Old Sacramento," which dates back to the colorful days of the Gold Rush. There are a lot of bars, restaurants, and nightclubs which do their best to retain the flavor of the "Forty-niners" period in California history, and in addition, there is a large open-air arena that can accommodate a few thousand people, as well as a couple of theaters capable of handling good-sized audiences.

To this novel setting, once a year, bands from all over the world, as well as a number of "guest" musicians, are invited to play and entertain for almost 24 hours a day. Huge crowds attend and enjoy the carnival atmosphere. Whole families join in the festivities. In 1977 there were more than 50 traditional jazz bands at the Jubilee and more than 20 guests to play with them. You could have jazz for breakfast, jazz for lunch, jazz for dinner, and all the time in between, for the entire three days.

A touching experience made this visit unforgettable for me. I had finished playing a set in the main arena with a very good band and was about to leave the bandstand when the entire audience of several thousand people stood up and sang "Happy Birthday to You." It was May 30, my 64th birthday, and I don't believe I've ever been more surprised or thrilled.

My visit was greatly enhanced by the hospitality of my old friends Ed and Dottie Lawless, who entertained me in their home before and after the Jubilee, taking me on a tour of San Francisco that included a great night at Earthquake McGoon's, the home of the Turk Murphy Jazz Band. They also gave me a birthday party in Sacramento, with music provided by a remakable teenage jazz band called "The Jazz Minors." The Lawlesses are true jazz lovers, and Ed, an excellent photographer, has since been elected president of the New Orleans Jazz Club of Northern California.

The Sacramento Jubilee is undoubtedly the largest jazz festival in the country, and with such great music and fun involved I'm convinced it is a cinch to grow every year.

I was home in New Jersey for only a few weeks, then back to California on June 19 to join Peanuts Hucko at a Sunday session for the San Diego Jazz Club, followed by a very special event in San Francisco on the 22nd, the AMA Convention. Our favorite doctor, Dr. John Budd, was installed as president. We had a terrific band for the installation—Peanuts, Dick Cary, Eddie Miller, Abe Lincoln, Ray Leatherwood, Nick Fatool, and me—and at the reception after the ceremony we had the added pleasure of having Dr. Budd sit in with us on piano.

When July 5 came up on the calendar, I took off for my third Nice Festival, going to work immediately upon arrival. By Thursday I began to notice an uncomfortable swelling of my upper lip, and on Friday it was worse. For that half of the Festival I was unable to play. The doctors I went to see in Nice seemed to think the problem was caused by an allergy, but whatever it was, they weren't able to help. Obviously, to a trumpet player nothing is more upsetting than having something happen to his lip; not only his livelihood but his entire mode of artistic expression is in jeopardy.

The promoters of the Festival were very cosiderate, and the musicians were expecially helpful, sometimes finishing the evening for me. One of these was Benny Carter, who noticed me suffering and insisted on taking over for me. Whatever was causing the swelling, it was very slow to respond to treatment, and the Festival was well along before I could play again, and then not too comfortably. I had agreed to go to Holland after the Festival to make an album with the Ted Easton band, but under the circumstances this was out of the question and I had to cancel.

After a week or two back in the States my lip returned to normal, but I have never quite lost the fear that it might, at any time and without any reason, swell up again. It's an extremely disturbing possibility.

In August I returned to Sacramento for a Sunday session. For this one, they had the equivalent of about four bands among the guest musicians, and about 1,000 people in attendance. The Sacramento fans are certainly among the most enthusiastic I have ever played for. I stayed at the home of a very gracious couple, Mr. and Mrs. Jack Weaver. They invited me to join them in attending a marvelous church service, and enlisting the help of the Old Man Upstairs probably went a long way in making certain we'd have a great session that afternoon. It was also a treat to see again so many of the friends I had made at the Jubilee.

The year brought two rather unusual experiences. One was engineered by John Worsley, a teacher at Rhode Island Junior College, and jazz promoter in the area, who initiated the jazz series at the Marriott Hotel in Providence as well as establishing the scholarships and other benefits in the name of the city's favorite son, Bobby Hackett. John, never one to pass up an opportunity to provide work for a jazz band, arranged for us to play on a chartered boat hauling yachting enthusiasts around Newport Harbor while they watched the trial runs for the America's Cup Race. We met on the dock of John's yacht club at 10 a.m. on the beautiful morning of the trials, and everything went along as scheduled except that our drummer, Alan Dawson, failed to show up on time and we had to leave without him. Boat races allow no leeway for tardiness. Kenny Davern and I had to play our nautical duets without drums, tapping our feet for rhythm.

The other date was a jazz concert under the direction of Lou Stein, held on a Westchester estate called "Caramoor." This is the home of a fabulous collection of art treasures assembled by the Rosen family, the original owners, who have donated it to Westchester County. Caramoor is now dedicated to the presentation of a wide variety of musical programs, primarily chamber music and opera. Ours was the first jazz band ever to play in this lovely setting, but I don't think we disgraced the people who invited us because they heard Kenny Davern, Al Klink, George Masso, Bob Rosengarden, and Bob Haggart, along with leader Lou Stein and me, and vocals by the tiny but graciously talented Maxine Sullivan.

Labor Day brought the 15th Gibson Jazz Party and my sixth visit to the Broadmoor. Again the guest list had been expanded because the locale had been

344

moved to the convention center of the Broadmoor, which could accommodate more people. There's no question about it—this party handles the participants first class all the way. The Broadmoor is one of the most attractive hotels in the world. It nestles at the foot of the Rocky Mountains on the shore of a beautiful lake. There are promenades all around the lake, and the hotel has magnificent facilities. The six dining rooms feature the finest cuisine, and the guest rooms are spacious and private. All of this, plus a private bar, are at the disposal and enjoyment of the artists. In 1977, there were 68 musicians on the roster.

This year also saw three new places added to my itinerary. After the Gibson Party I had to pass over my invitation to the Nemacolin Encampment in order to fill my first engagement at Disney World, Lake Buena Vista, Florida. Along with Vic Dickenson, I played with the house trio at the "Village Lounge," an unbelievably flexible group of musicians. They seem equipped to handle any possible musical concept. Under the leadership of pianist Bubba Kalb, the trio with Louise Davis on bass and Harvey Laing on drums offers all that can be asked of a backup group. The press notices were terrific! One said that Vic Dickenson looked like a mortician and I looked like a CPA.

But the best part of the job is the fringe benefits. You're provided with a beautiful villa in a garden setting, the use of an automobile for the entire stay at Lake Buena Vista, and if, for any reason, you're not happy with the great music at the Lounge, at least you can live like a king.

My next flight was to Windsor, Ontario, for a night with a great band from the Detroit area, with my old friend Doug Woods on drums. Most of the patrons were from the Detroit vicinity, which gave me the opportunity to renew acquaintanceship with Jim Taylor, the guiding light of jazz in Detroit, plus a visit with another old friend, Bill McQueen. These Windsor sessions are under the direction of a young man named Hugh Leal and deserve all the support they can get.

I also worked for a week at "B. J.'s Lounge," a room in Toronto that was the home of the Climax Jazz Band. The management decided to initiate a guest policy, and, for my stay, I was backed by a fine local group that included Phil Antonello on tenor, Bernie Sinensky on piano, and Jerry Fuller on drums. The Toronto press was very kind to us. While in Toronto I joined trombonist Frank Rossolino for a Saturday session in the Toronto Hotel. It was the last time I would ever see famous Canadian trumpet player and singer Trump Davidson, who passed away shortly after.

In November, I went south again to take part in the first jazz party held in Midland, Texas, which, like the others, has become an annual event. This one, sponsored by Max Christensen, is held at the Midland Hilton, continues for six days, and entertains over 400 guests. The program of four or five sets each night is played by a variety of combinations and small bands put together from the available personnel. Since the combos and musicians are rotated from night to night, everybody gets a chance to play with different people through the week.

Taking part in this first party were George Barnes, Bucky Pizzarelli, Dave McKenna, Derek Smith, Dick Hyman, Red Norvo, Jack Lesberg, Milt Hinton,

Mousie Alexander, Jack Hanna, Cliff Leeman, Kenny Davern, Johnny Mince, Flip Phillips, Eddie Miller, Scott Hamilton, Carl Fontana, Ed Hubble, Bill Watrous, Ed Polcer, Warren Vache' Jr., Ruby Braff—and me. And this proved to be a very relaxed and sociable affair, with a good many of our friends from Odessa, as well as those from Midland, in attendance.

In addition to the big party at the Hilton, we received a number of private invitations to smaller ones, like the open-house offered by our recording engineer and supervisor, Max Howard, an open-house lunch sponsored by Mr. and Mrs. Foy Boyd, Mr. and Mrs. Bobby Crues, and Mr. and Mrs. Max Christensen, and a special farewell party at Luigi's Restaurant given by Louis and Zelda Hockman. Bucky Pizzarelli and I were further honored by being selected to play for the wedding reception of good friends George and Trina Conly—a great party.

The incomparable Cliff Leeman.   Kathy Gardner photo.

FIFTY-NINE

YOU MIGHT SAY THAT 1978 started off with no waiting. On January 3 the Dick Hyman Quintet opened for another month at Michael's Pub, with the same personnel as before—Hyman, Wilber, Rosengarden, Hinton, and Erwin—but this time Dick featured the music of George Gershwin. This, of course, lends itself very well to a performance such as ours where the piano is the predominant voice. We played some of his lesser known compositions, things like "Rialto Ripples Rag" (which you may remember from the early days of TV when Ernie Kovacs used it as his theme song), thumbnail versions of his preludes, and gave particular attention to the music from *Porgy and Bess*. On one evening, we had the pleasure of being joined by George and Ira Gershwin's sister Frances, who sang some of their songs. This created enough interest that NBC sent in a TV camera crew to film a shot for the nightly news.

On January 14, we took a night off from Michael's Pub and flew to Baltimore, where the Quintet was booked to appear with the Symphony at the Lyric Theater to perform a rather ambitious program. The format called for each of us to play a solo accompanied by the symphony orchestra during the first half of the program, and during the second half to play our regular repertoire as the Quintet.

After the overture, Rob Roby McGregor, a trumpet player with the Symphony, led things off with a solo on "I Must Have That Man," in memory of Bobby Hackett. Bob Wilber followed with his original composition dedicated to Johnny Hodges, "Johnny Was There." Then it was my turn. For the occasion Jackie Gleason had graciously loaned me the arrangement I had recorded with him of "Hello, Dolly." After this, Dick Hyman played the Third Movement of his "Concerto Electro for Organ and Orchestra," and the last soloist was our guest, the wonderful Joe Venuti, playing his composition "Venutiana." The conductor for this half of the program was Andrew Schenck. For me it was a great thrill to solo with a full symphonic background, and it was a memorable evening.

In February I reformed a version of the "Kings of Jazz" for a four-day stint starting in Pine Bluff, Arkansas, where we played at the Arts Center, sponsored by a grant from the National Foundation For the Arts. And while we were there

Pee Wee Erwin's Kings of Jazz, featuring the three trumpets of Ed Polcer, Warren Vaché, Jr., and Pee Wee Erwin on Dick Hyman's arrangement of Panama. Waiting to see how it comes out—Bob Wilber and Johnny Mince. In the back row, Jack Lesberg, Derek Smith, and Bobby Rosengarden.

we were royally entertained by the White and Nixon families, B. A. Wilkens, and Connie Roscoe—all good friends.

In this reconstruction of the "Kings," I had Kenny Davern, Bob Wilber, Ed Hubble, Marty Napoleon, Milt Hinton, Cliff Leeman, and Warren Vaché Jr., and we played two concerts at the Arts Center on Friday and Saturday, and on Sunday we played for a party in honor of Al White's 50th birthday. As the saying goes, "a good time was had by all," and for icing on the cake we had the guest sit in on drums.

On the 13th we drove from Pine Bluff to Jackson, Mississippi, to play for the Jackson Jazz Society, and on the way we passed through the city made immortal by the song Al Jennings used to sing with Joe Haymes. In spite of the fact that we were in the middle of the road I couldn't resist the temptation to take my horn out of its case and blow one chorus of "I'm a Ding Dong Daddy," for at least one time in the real Dumas. Still later we stopped at Vicksburg, and our host, Merle Harris, treated us to a seafood banquet in honor of Milt Hinton, a Vicksburg native son. Arriving at Jackson, we had a good turnout of the Jackson Jazz Society for our Monday-night concert. Charley Knox and his wife were there—

the first time I had seen them since Honolulu. Charley always had a terrific sense of humor, and this night it cropped up while I was playing a solo. He leaned over to Warren Vaché Jr. and commented, "You know, I used to play with Pee Wee 50 years ago—and he still doesn't play any better."

March saw the birth of another jazz party—the Paradise Valley Jazz Party—sponsored by Don and Sue Miller and held in the Scottsdale Conference Center in Scottsdale, Arizona. This turned out to be a great musical happening for several reasons: the beautiful setting, the lack of pressure to play, and the desire of everybody to join in and make it a success. Musically it was outstanding, and so was the lineup: Roland Hanna, Dick Hyman, Bob Rosengarden, Jake Hanna, Milt Hinton, Major Holley, Joe Newman, Bill Watrous, Carl Fontana, Flip Phillips, Kenny Davern, Bob Wilber, and Herb Ellis.

The proceedings got off to a head start with a bang-up jam session and buffet at the Miller home on Friday night, and this was followed by sessions at noon on Saturday, another at 5 p.m., and still another at midnight. On Sunday there was a concert at noon, and the wind-up session took place at 5 p.m.— altogether a very judicious beginning for jazz in the glorious climate of Arizona.

The month went out like the proverbial lion on the weekend of the 31st, because back in New Jersey the New Jersey Jazz Society staged the second edition of the "Strides of March" at the Playboy Club at Great Gorge, with another impressive roll: Kenny Davern, Bob Wilber, Eddie Miller, Zoot Sims, Warren Vaché Jr., Ruby Braff, George Masso, Ed Hubble, Vic Dickenson, Bill Crow, George Duvivier, Slam Stewart, Dick Hyman, Dave McKenna, John Bunch, Bucky Pizzarelli, Marty Grosz, Bob Rosengarden, Connie Kay, and Cliff Leeman. Of course, I was there, too, and I must say some superb musical moments took place. With such a wealth of talent, this is only to be expected.

April brought another revival of the Armstrong Show as a part of the New Orleans Jazz and Heritage Festival. We played in the ballroom of the New Orleans Marriott Hotel, joined by Wallace Davenport and his all-star New Orleans band. Carrie Smith recreated her original vocals, and the rest of the personnel consisted of Jimmy Maxwell, Bernie Privin, and me playing the trumpet parts, and Vic Dickenson, Kenny Davern, Dick Hyman, Bob Rosengarden, Milt Hinton, and a veteran from New Orleans, Emanuel Sayles, on guitar. However, the high point of this concert was a solo spot on three numbers by Barney Bigard, who on this visit to his hometown turned in the greatest performance I ever heard him play. It was also nice to see some of my old New Orleans friends again—Helen Arlt, Myra Menvile, Frog Joseph, Freddie Kuhlman—and to enjoy a special visit from Don Albert, the San Antonio bandleader, who was related to Barney Bigard and Natty Dominique.

Shortly before this New Orleans jaunt, I played a job with Danny Lapidos at a ball held in the New York Hilton for the U.S. Air Force. Among those receiving awards that night was Carter Burgess, my friend since the Isham Jones band played for his graduation prom at VMI in 1934. He has one of the best musical memories of anyone I've ever met, and when he became assistant secretary of defense, I'm sure the walls of the pentagon often echoed with his recollections of "Dallas Blues," "Blue Room," and other tunes from the Jones library.

349

Major Holley

Pee Wee, Doc Cheatham, George Masso

On May 1 I got a call from Bill Seifert of Rockwell. He told me the Rockwell Board of Directors was having a meeting on Cat Cay in the Bahamas, and the regular group led by Reid Jaynes was unavailable for the trip to furnish entertainment. Bill wanted to know if I could put together a group to play for dinner and then furnish a concert on Friday the 3rd—and of course I told him I could. On May 3 the Rockwell Sabre Jet picked up Kenny Davern, Phil Flanigan, Marty Napoleon, and me and flew us to Bimini, and from there we were ferried by boat to Cat Cay. Bill Seifert joined us on drums, and we played for the dinner and concert, and the following morning we were flown back home.

That same month I made another trek with the Rancheros Vistadores in California and immediately afterwards boarded a plane in Los Angeles that was supposed to fly me to Chicago so I could play at the "Big Horn Festival" in Gurnee, Illinois. One hour out of L.A., the plane burned out an engine, and we had to return to change planes. This operation cost us two hours, but finally we were on the way again, with the first stop scheduled for Kansas City—except that in keeping with the rest of my luck on this trip, Kansas City experienced a tornado during our stop. This delayed our take-off for another hour, so by the time I arrived in Chicago and then drove out to Gurnee I was just in time to play the last set of the Big Horn Festival that night.

The Big Horn offered more high-powered talent: Milt Hinton, Art Hodes, Dave McKenna, Bob Wilber, Kenny Davern, Marty Grosz, Ed Hubble, Barrett Deems, Pug Horton, Chuck Hedges, Sid Dawson, Jerry Fuller, Bob Cousins, and Don McMichael. The Salty Dogs, a well-known traditional group, also played: Lew Green, cornet and leader; John Cooper, piano; Mike Walbridge, tuba; Wayne Jones, drums; Kim Cusack, clarinet; Jack Kunch, banjo; and Tom Bartlett, trombone. Featured on vocals was the dynamic Carol Leigh.

This festival ran for three days, May 12 to 14, under the direction of Buzz Snavely and his charming wife, Jackie. The event turned out to be an unusual treat for me because my brother Jim brought two of my nieces, Janice and Diane, and my nephew, Jim Jr., to visit me. This also gave me a chance to meet for the first time Janice's husband, Clyde Doepner, and Jim Jr.'s wife Linda. It ws a real family reunion to the accompaniment of great music.

I was also introduced to a young trumpet player, Tommy Bridges, age only 14.

From the Big Horn I went directly to Odessa, Texas, for my fifth jazz party there, and this time my fellow trumpet players were Wild Bill Davison, Clark Terry, and Ed Polcer. Odessa was followed by another glorious week at Disney World in the Lake Buena Vista Lounge. In addition to the house trio, I was joined by a very fine soprano sax and clarinet player, Rick Fay.

I returned home on Sunday morning, June 7, just in time to play a benefit performance with Ed Polcer, Major Holley, Vic Dickenson, Clarence Hutchenrider, Red Richards, and Cliff Leeman at Waterloo Village.

Later in the month I was back there as part of the Newport Jazz Festival in a program featuring the music of King Oliver, as arranged for groups and orchestras of various sizes by Dick Hyman and Bob Wilber. The early music was played by a relatively small group featuring the two-cornet duets of King Oliver and Louis Armstrong that have become immortalized in jazz history. For these I was teamed with Jimmy Maxwell and we did things like "Snake Rag," and "Dippermouth." Then the orchestra was augmented and Joe Newman came in for a three-trumpet rendition of later Armstrong solos, and finally a full-fledged orchestra played Dick Hyman's arrangements of fully scored Armstrong numbers.

I was again part of the New Jersey Jazz Society's Jazz Picnic segment of the Newport Festival on Sunday.

On July 4th I took off once again for my fourth "Grande Parade du Jazz," in Nice. I was told that this year more than 110,000 people attended over the 11 days, and taking part were the bands of Buddy Rich and Lionel Hampton, the Dizzy Gillespie Quartet, the Jonah Jones Quartet, the World's Greatest Jazz Band, the Stan Getz Quartet, the Kenny Burrell Trio, Bill Doggett's Sextet, and numerous individual musicians—Eubie Blake, Mary Lou Williams, Carrie Smith, Clark Terry, Illinois Jacquet, Shelly Manne, Wild Bill Davison, Stephane Grappelli—the complete list would fill a page. Altogether, more than one hundred musicians. On this occasion I was given the chance to play with the great Jonah Jones group for a couple of sets and to hear for the first time—and to sit in with—the fine Alex Welsh band from England. But I think the thing that amazed me the most was seeing the venerable Eubie Blake, beautifully dressed, sitting in the lobby of our hotel (the Mercure, on Boulevard des Anglais) waiting for midnight so he could hang out with the night people.

The Riviera in July is magnificent, and at that time of the year France can't be topped for its luscious cheese and fruit. The open street restaurants offer the best locations to congregate and hold gab sessions, and almost every day I would join my English friends—Sinclair Traill, Andrew Gillies, George Ebbs, and Gill and Mike Baille—for prelunch drinks while we watched numbers of our colleagues pass by.

On the last day of the Festival I made my customary jaunt to The Hague for the North Sea Festival and played with the Ted Easton band.

Back home again, on July 28 I played a concert in the Art Park, an amusement center on the banks of the Niagara River near the mighty Falls, with the "Perfect Jazz Repertory Quintet" (the new name for the Dick Hyman Quintet), with Kenny Davern filling in for Bob Wilber. We had a great "feel" in the group and enjoyed ourselves musically.

On August 22 the Erwin household was shaken by terrible news. Caroline's sister, Mary Donald, was involved in a serious automobile accident with her three children, Amy, Wiley, and Elliot. The kids were slightly injured, but Mary was hurt worst of all and for a month her condition was touch-and-go. Eventually she recovered, but the initial shock of the news and the following days of concern made it a difficult time for us all.

The annual Gibson Party took place during the first four days of September, and it was my seventh. Again the sessions were held in the International Center, across the street from the main entrance of the Broadmoor. More than 50 musicians were on hand (among them quite a number of new faces) to entertain over 500 guests. A note of sadness colored the proceedings because Joe Venuti, who had been scheduled to appear, died shortly before. Dick Gibson, who was instrumental in bringing Joe out of retirement to enjoy a marvelous revival of his career, paid a moving tribute to his memory. The music world had lost another giant.

That September also brought the first "Great Northeastern Jazz Festival," held in Greenville, N.Y., under the promotional efforts of Skip Parsons. It took place at the Rainbow Lodge in Greenville, and a number of jazz bands took part, augmented by some individual musicians; the Salt City Six (with Jack Maheu and Will Alger), the Morgan Street Stompers, the Jazz Locale, the Bearcat Jass Band, the Soda Ash Six, Skip Parsons' Riverboat Band, and "Doc Cheatham and the Kings of Jazz," with Chris Griffin, Ed Hubble, Kenny Davern, Bob Wilber, Major Holley, Bobby Pratt, Cliff Leeman, and yours truly.

We had a lot of fun at this festival, and when a couple of the men were late we permitted the world's most travelled jazz fan, Bill Bacin, to join us for some of his vocals on Jelly-Roll Morton tunes.

This year I was able to accept an invitation to the Nemacolin Encampment as part of the Nemacolin Bird Dogs: Benny Beneck and Bill Muchnic, trumpets; John McKean, and Jim Tucci, trombones; Ernie Matteo and Jim Pellou, reeds; Frank Mazur, banjo; Reid Jaynes, piano; Bill Seifert, drums; and Burr Wishart, bass. One of the highlights of any year is being able to join in the good fellowship of this great group. It's the only band I've ever played with that will eat their own dinner and then turn around and play for anybody still in the dining room.

However, due to a misunderstanding, I almost missed my travel connection out of Nemacolin, and I was operating on a very tight schedule. I was due to open the following night in Geneva, Switzerland. When Dick Spence, the Rockwell coordinator, heard about my problem he called the Pittsburgh airport to reserve a private Sabre Jet and then put me on a helicopter to take me to Pittsburgh. The jet flew me to Newark Airport, and I still had enough time to go home and pack my luggage for the Geneva trip on TWA at 7 p.m. It all worked out beautifully, but I must admit I did sweat a little.

SIXTY

I OPENED WITH JOHNNY MINCE at a jazz club in Geneva called the "Popcorn." This was the beginning of a 1978 tour, during which we were to play with local groups in a variety of locations. The Popcorn is owned by Tommy Graf, a pretty good trumpet player in his own right and a Louis Armstrong fan, who spent a lot of time in the States and was well acquainted with the jazz clubs of former years, like the Metropole. In his club he had featured many of the top American musicians: "Sweets" Edison, Eddie "Lockjaw" Davis, Oliver Jackson, and Carrie Smith. We followed Earle Warren, so we knew we were among friends—and in a restaurant where the food was excellent.

The backup group we worked with was fine. Henri Chaix, probably the best traditional pianist in Europe, was in it, and I don't think I called anything that Henri didn't know. He is also a fine soloist and a nice person to work with, and although at first we had a small language barrier, we

Bobby Rosengarden

managed to overcome it. On drums we had George Bernasconi, a Swiss, and a very tasty drummer with good time, and the bass player was Jimmy Woode. Jimmy had once played with Duke Ellington, but elected to stay in Europe and lived in Munich, using it as home base for European dates.

The Popcorn has a built-in jazz trade, and, with the combination of an enthusiastic reception and marvelous treatment, we had a ball. Every day we had lunch at the Club, a daily treat, and Tommy Graf provided each of us with an apartment located about five minutes' walk from the Popcorn's front door. The Club is located in a nice section of the city, and another five minutes' walk brought us to the shore of beautiful Lake Geneva.

A couple of other things added to the pleasure of our Geneva stay. One evening we were visited by Alex Ischer and his son Yvon—good friends we knew from Nice and New York—and another night a note was passed up to us from the audience asking what a member of the Rancheros Vistadores was doing in Geneva. You might think that California and Geneva are many long miles apart, but just to prove how modern travel has shrunk the world, sitting in the audience was a fellow Ranchero, Don Tognazzini, a California friend who lives in Geneva.

While in Geneva, I visited a tobacco shop where genuine Havana cigars are readily available, but when I tried to buy chewing tobacco all they could sell me was some stuff made in Germany. These were small pellets of tobacco preserved in some kind of oil, and they didn't taste anything like real chewing tobacco.

Our next stop on the tour was Vienna, and we were met at the airport by Christian Zahn, leader of a Viennese group called the "Classic Swing Company." Christian and his lovely wife not only met us, they gave us our first sightseeing tour of the ancient Austrian capital. And on our first evening we were entertained by our promoter, Axel Melhardt, and his wife, Tillie, who treated us to a fabulous dinner at a Greek restaurant—which probably gave me a headstart toward gaining the 16 pounds I put on during this tour, and it didn't end there! Tillie Melhardt may very well be one of the finest cooks in all of Europe. The Melhardts occupy an apartment on the fourth floor of a building without an elevator, and Axel told us that when Eddie "Lockjaw" Davis came to town and Axel issued his usual invitation to dinner, Eddie said, "I appreciate the invitation, but I'm not going to a fourth-floor walk-up for any meal." However, after some persuasion Axel succeeded in getting him home for dinner and, when the meal was over, Eddie looked at Tillie and asked, "O.K. What time is breakfast?"

We played at a place called "Jazzland," which has to be one of the most unique clubs in the world because it's built into the catacombs of a 1,000-year-old church and jammed with the most exuberant jazz fans to be found anywhere. So long as things are swinging, nobody goes home. The cave-like interior and the large wooden tables also provide a distinctive atmosphere. Johnny and I were backed by two groups who took turns playing behind us. One was called the "Red Hot Pods" and the other was Christian Zahn's "Classic Swing Company."

Inquiries about the tobacco situation in Austria evoked the information that it is state controlled. But when I got down to specifics and asked about chewing tobacco, Christian Zahn laughed, and that evening he came to work with two pouches of chewing tobacco that had been packaged in New Jersey. As it turned out, this was the only tobacco I was able to find in continental Europe.

The Red Hot Pods were Dieter Beitak, cornet; Harry Jirsa, trombone; Claus Nemeth, clarinet and vocals; Lothar Reichold, piano; Erwin Frassine, banjo; Michael Libowitzky, bass; and Gerhard Sondermann, drums. The Classic Swing Company included Christian Zahn on vibes; Peter Marinoff, guitar; Alex Spaeth, bass; and Gerhard Sondermann. Obviously, in working with both groups Gerhard Sondermann had all he could handle, but these musicians were so happy to play they were willing to go on forever. Gerhard was originally from Frankfurt, Germany, and was an excellent drummer.

It has always been amazing to me how many of the early jazz numbers these men are acquainted with. Dieter Beitak was able to play duets with me on the Oliver-Armstrong tunes, and Harry Jirsa had a strong trombone sound very much like George Brunis. In addition, Claus and Johnny did great duets on the standards. Erwin Frassine, the leader of the Pods, has a great collection of tapes and records, too. We played a date that involved a long trip by car, and Erwin played Jabbo Smith tapes for us almost all the way to Salzburg.

Aside from the music, Vienna is a fascinating city in many ways, and luckily we had ample time to visit historic sites like the Hofburg and Schoenbrun palaces, the homes of the Hapsburgs. Both palaces have been well preserved and cared for, and still reflect the splendor of the court of Franz Joseph, and the influence of Marie Theresa. Johnny and I enjoyed the visit immensely.

We played for a large festival on October 6 and 7, which was mainly due to the efforts of the Viennese Musical Fraternity and took place in the Vienna Konzerthaus. These concerts were under the supervision and promotion of Vienna's premier radio personality, Mr. Gunther Schifter, who also functioned as Master of Ceremonies. There were a number of good bands present—the usual thing at these European festivals—the "Barrel-house Jazz Band," the "Original Storyville Jazz Band," the "Blue Devils," among others, plus our friends the Red Hot Pods and the Classic Swing Company. Johnny Mince and I were joined by Kai Winding, Carrie Smith, and Oscar Klein. Klein is a fine jazz trumpeter and guitar player who was the original trumpet player with the Dutch Swing College Band. He now lives in Bern, Switzerland, and is very popular at festivals and jazz clubs in central Europe. I see him at Nice every year.

On Sunday we played a mini-concert at a hotel in Vienna, mainly arranged as a sort of farewell party for those who had taken place in the festival. The audience consisted of the families and friends of the musicians, and I was reminded of the fun at an old-fashioned midwestern get-together. Everyone played when he felt like it, lots of people danced, and there was a great feeling of fellowship.

London was next on the tour, and again we were given red-carpet treatment by Peter Boizot, owner of the "Pizza Express," where we appeared. Peter loaned us an apartment across the street from the Pizza Express, which we were told had once been occupied by the Porno King of Soho. It was very comfortable and had the added advantage of being close to the job. We worked two nights at the Pizza Express, and our stay was made delightful by visits from old friends—John Chilton, Derek Colliar, Eddie Kennedy, Wild Bill and Anne Davison, Kenny Davern, plus my guide in London and very good friend, trumpet player Monty Montgomery. Pat and Len Mash also came, and they extended an invitation to visit them in the country, which we reluctantly had to decline because of our tight schedule.

As always, whenever I'm in London I make certain to buy a bottle of Gordon's Green Gin for my Pittsburgh pal Bill Seifert, and while I was on this errand I visited Dobell's, the famous record shop on Charing Cross Road. Then I noticed a Snuff Shop across the street, and since I'm always on the alert for a source of chewing tobacco, decided to check it out. I entered the shop (which has been there for a hundred years or more) and asked the gentleman behind the counter if he had any chewing tobacco in stock.

Without any hesitation he replied, "Yes, we do. Do you want it mild or strong?"

This was something I'd never had to decide before, so I told him I didn't know, since I hadn't tried his tobacco, and suggested he give me a little of each. First he handed me a tightly wrapped rod of tobacco about the size of a fat cigar, informing me that this was the mild tobacco and I could cut chewing-sized pieces from it, and then from under the counter he brought out a large, round, tin can. He took off the lid and began to pull out a continuous rope of dark tobacco, and said, "This is Cornish Twist. How much of it do you want?"

I told him to give me a section about a foot long, which he did, along with a gratuitous pricelist and brochure describing the advantages of using snuff.

When I was outside I decided to sample the Cornish Twist to satisfy my curiosity. I took a good-sized bite—and immediately discovered how it must feel to bite into a red-hot coal! What's more, two minutes of chewing that tobacco was the equivalent of drinking four boilermakers—it sent me high as a kite. So the Cornish Twist has withered away on my desk, and I satisfied my filthy habit with the mild tobacco.

At the Pizza Express we were accompanied by the Brian Lemon Trio. Brian is a marvelous pianist with great taste, an excellent example of the high quality of musicianship in Europe. These days the visiting American jazz musician can work with his European colleagues with complete ease, and more often that not the musicianship is superior to much of what we are exposed to in the States—proving to me that artistically, at least, we have only one world.

Johnny and I were booked next to play at the "Club Jazzland" in Amsterdam, Holland, on October 13 and 14, so we made sure we got to Victoria Station on the morning of the 13th (Friday) in order to catch a train for Gatwick Airport, where we were to take a plane for the 30-minute flight to Amsterdam. But during the cab ride to the station, it became very obvious we were getting our first taste of a genuine London fog, and at Victoria they told us at the office for the shuttle train to the airport that all flights had been cancelled. Nevertheless, since we had no alternative, we took the one-hour train ride to Gatwick and then sat around the airport from 11 a.m. to 5 p.m., sweating out a flight and wondering if we would ever reach Amsterdam in time to play the job.

Finally the weather cleared enough for us to take off, and we arrived in Amsterdam around 6 p.m., which still gave us plenty of time because our contract stated that we were to start playing at 9. We checked in at our hotel and relaxed, confident that we would be on time and that we would be working with a good band, because we had been told we were the guests of the Ted Easton Band. I had played with them twice before, at the Northsea Jazz Festival, and I was looking forward to working with them again. But around 8 o'clock a call came from the Club, and we were told that we were not to start until 10 p.m. and that we would not be working with the Ted Easton group after all. However, the man said that someone would pick us up at the hotel and take us to the Club.

Now we were a bit nervous. Aside from being Friday the 13th, the day hadn't started off too well, and now our contract was showing signs of not being worth the paper it was written on, but there was nothing we could do except play along. Around 9 o'clock a mysterious young lady called for us at the hotel and directed us to the Club, which was within easy walking distance of the hotel, and turned out to be an attractive restaurant. It had a seating capacity of perhaps as many as 400 people, with tables surrounding a large, circular dance floor, and a bandstand large enough to accommodate a good-sized band. We were invited to have dinner, and the food was excellent.

The Club Jazzland is a first-class restaurant with a respectable clientele, but it was a bit startling for us to discover during our walk that it is located on a street resembling New York's 42nd Street, lined with porno shops and suggestive pleasure palaces. Furthermore, since I'm naturally the apprehensive type, I began to worry a bit more after meeting the owner, who spoke very little English, thereby creating a communication problem. Our contract had been signed by Ted Easton, who was nowhere in evidence, and now we were going to work with a strange band I had never heard. As far as the contract was concerned, nothing so far had complied with it, so it could very well be worthless. Mainly, I must admit, I was concerned about being paid. I don't recall how much money was involved but I do know it was a pretty fair-sized amount because it included our pay for the two nights, plus round-trip fares to England.

We were given our playing schedules, introduced to our fellow musicians, and continued to sweat out developments. The place started to fill up early, and by 10 p.m. the tables were full. It had been decided that the house band would start playing, and then Johnny and I would be introduced, one at a time, to play a solo. I looked out at all those people and crossed my fingers.

Then the Dutch band began to play—and Johnny and I looked at each other in pleased surprise. This wasn't just a good band, this was one of the best I've ever heard—both individually and collectively. You can believe me, before the job was over, Johnny and I were calling on every bit of our talent and ability to keep pace with these guys. The leader of the group was Fritz Kaatee, a sensational reed player—and in this case "reed" means all of them, clarinet, soprano, alto, tenor, and baritone. The bass player, Koos Sluis, in addition to playing fine bass, proved to be a terrific flugelhorn player. But the greatest of them all was the pianist, Cees Slinger, to me the most tremendous piano player I've heard outside of the United States.

The music was terrific! But that didn't prevent me from worrying about being paid and the lack of a binding contract. Around the middle of the second evening, in fact, the worry kept getting stronger the closer we came to the close of the engagement. I was approaching the desparation stage of wondering what we would do if no money materialized, when the owner's girlfriend, who had been our mysterious guide of the day before and spoke English, came up to the bandstand and said, "Franz Tol, the owner, wants to know how much he owes you." I gave her the figure in American dollars, including the air fare, and she simply said, "Thank you," and went away.

After we played the last set, Mr. Tol took me into his office, and without any hesitation or quibblig paid me the entire amount in Dutch guilders, counting it out very carefully. Then he handed me an additional one hundred guilders, and explained this was in case we lost money in exchanging the guilders for American dollars. When the financial end was taken care of, he asked a question that's always nice to hear and understand, even in broken English: "When can you come back?"

Our last day of the tour we played in Brighton at the King & Queen Tavern, where we had a wonderful time working with another great band and great guys, Bennie Simkins and his band, with Pete and Geof Simkins. A most appreciative audience was spurred on to enthusiasm by Sinclair Traill and George Ebbs, many pints were passed, and the hosts did everything possible to make us welcome.

We stayed overnight at George Ebbs's house, and the next monring he drove us all the way to Heathrow Airport outside London, where—after a fine English breakfast—we caught the noon plane for New York. It had been a very successful and enjoyable tour.

SIXTY-ONE

HOME AGAIN I teamed up with Dick Hyman's Perfect Jazz Repertory Company to play some rather unusual dates for the balance of October and November. On October 29, 1978, we did a program at a small dinner in honor of "The International Advisory Committee" of the Chase Manhattan Bank. We were invited as dinner guests to meet the people we were playing for. Adding Maxine Sullivan to the group for the evening, we met some interesting people from the world of international finance, and our program was well received.

Following this we traveled to Scottsdale, Arizona, to play for Young and Rubicam at the Carefree Inn for the international meeting of the executives of this advertising giant. On our return, we gave a concert at a "length of service" dinner for the people at Reader's Digest in Pleasantville, N.Y. The members of the literary fraternity seemed to enjoy our presentation, and we were accorded special recognition from Mr. John O'Hara, president of the organization.

We gave another concert of George Gershwin's music for the Renaissance Advisors at Scarsdale High School. The reason I call particular attention to these affairs is because they were played for organizations and gatherings where you might not expect to hear jazz presented. Although you might tend to classify the Perfect Jazz Repertory Quintet as a polite musical group with jazz overtones—rather than as a dyed-in-the-wool barrelhouse unit—I believe these concerts prove that although jazz may have had humble beginnings, today it has achieved concert-hall respectability on a par with chamber music societies.

Sandwiched in between these engagements, I managed a visit to the Muchnics in San Diego, stopping off on my way to do a solo stint for the Traditional Jazz Society of Oregon, in Eugene, on November 5. Jazz clubs like this one are very popular throughout the country but especially in the Pacific Northwest—Portland, Seattle, Sacramento, etc. A very high level of

360

musical performance, plus great audience appreciation, is the rule and that afternoon's concert was typical. I played four sets of one-half hour duration, and each set was with a different group of musicians. Every musician there was of high caliber too, especially "The Jazz Minors," the little band known as the "Pride of Eugene." For the past two years this group had been a major attraction at Disneyland, and under the leadership of the trumpet-playing leader, Rusty Stiers, they've played all over the country, including a concert on the White House lawn for the president of the United States. The group is supervised by Sheri and Tony Otten, a couple dedicated to jazz, and under their guidance has appeared to enthusiastic reception at many of the major jazz festivals.

From Oregon I moved on to the second jazz party in Midland, Texas, and this year I was joined by Bill Seifert, who attended the party. Also appearing for the full week of jazz was a large coterie of friends and peers: Ralph Sutton, Dick Hyman, Derek Smith, Mundell Lowe, Red Norvo, Joe Wilder, Warren Vache' Jr., Jack Lesberg, Milt Hinton, George Mraz, Mousie Alexander, Bob Rosengarden, Jake Hanna, Bill Watrous, Al Grey, Carl Fontana, Bob Wilber, Kenny Davern, Johnny Mince, Al Cohn, Al Klink, and vocalist Mavis Rivers.

The lineup was impressive, the music was sensational, and our host, Max Christiansen, provided Warren and me with our own suite of rooms adjoining the party facilities, fully equipped, even to a milk bar.

I played an interim date sponsored by the Monmouth County Library Eastern Branch, located in Shrewsbury, N.J. with Ed Polcer, Kenny Davern, Derek Smith, Jack Lesberg, and Connie Kay, and we were joined on several numbers by Al Duffy on violin. Al, an outstanding exponent of jazz fiddle, worked for many years with Paul Whiteman, and we were also associated for a long time in the studios.

Warren Vache' Jr.   Photo by Bernard Long

The "Kings of Jazz" were reconstituted for a concert sponsored by the New Jersey Jazz Society—Kenny Davern, Warren Vache' Jr., Ed Hubble, Major Holley, Derek Smith, and Cliff Leeman—and we played for a sell-out crowd at the Watchung View Inn on November 19.

On Saturday, December 2, the Perfect Jazz Repertory Quintet, augmented by trombonist Urbie Green, appeared for a second time with the Baltimore Symphony Orchestra. The program opened with the string section of the orchestra playing an arrangement by Dick Hyman of Jelly-Roll Morton's "Shreveport Stomp," dedicated to Joe Venuti, who had been with us for our first performance with the Symphony. Following this, Bob Wilber played a solo on "My Man's Gone Now," from *Porgy and Bess*, and then Urbie Green played "Willow Weep For Me." I was next, with "Buddy Bolden's Blues," and then Milt Hinton was featured playing a special composition written for him by Dick Hyman called "The Judge Meets the Section." The "Judge," of course, referred to Milt's nickname, and he played with the Symphony's bass section. Dick then played his composition called "Organix For Organ and Orchestra," and we topped everything off with a well-put-together arrangement combining the Quintet and the orchestra, entitled "Friendly Conversation For Jazz Band and Symphony Orchestra."

These concerts have proved worthwhile with enthusiastic public acceptance, so we have a number of them on the calendar for the future, playing with other symphony orchestras. Just to round things out in pleasant style, we went back into Michael's Pub which, in addition to the more obvious advantages, offered a very nice bonus—being home for the holiday season.

The new year, 1979, started off with a very pleasant recording session, an album with the lovely and talented Helen Ward. The date was rather nostalgic because among other things, we did a remake of Bernie Hanighen's "The Dixieland Band," orchestrated by Deane Kincaide, which we had both recorded 45 years earlier as members of the newly formed Benny Goodman band. As related to my career in later years, the tune was somewhat prophetic. Helen today sounds as great as she did with the Goodman orchestra, and the result of this session has been packaged in a beautiful album, "The Helen Ward Song Book—Vol. I," and issued on the Lyricon label.

A week later the members of the Dick Hyman Quintet were in Phoenix, Arizona, to play for the Paradise Valley Jazz Party, and while we were there it provided a perfect opportunity to record the group for the first time. During every one of our three month-long sessions at Michael's Pub we had played the music of different composers. Dick Hyman loves to diversify the repertoire, providing as much opportunity as possible for spontaneity, so we didn't know what music we were going to record until we were in the studio. Then he told us we were going to make an album of Irving Berlin's music. The result is definitely fresh improvisation, an album on World Jazz by Dick Hyman and the Perfect Jazz Repertory Quintet, called "Say It With Music."

After the recording session the Quintet played at a dinner sponsored by the International Council of Shopping Centers, at the Phoenix Biltmore. My old associate Albert Sussman heads this organization.

Over the weekend, January 12 to 14, we were part of the second Paradise Valley Jazz Party, held at the magnificent Camelback Inn, in Scottsdale, Arizona. This party was in honor of Milt "The Judge" Hinton, and offered a great lineup: Dick Hyman, Roland Hanna, Ralph Sutton, Major Holley, Ray Brown, Jake Hanna, Bobby Rosengarden, Shelly Manne, Bucky Pizzarelli, Joe Newman, Clark Terry, Carl Fontana, Bill Watrous, Bob Wilber, Kenny Davern, Zoot Sims, and Buddy Tate.

The Camelback Inn is probably one of the really great showplace hotels in the United States. It consists of a complex of Spanish-style buildings—a large building housing the dining rooms and lounges, several lesser buildings with convention rooms and ballrooms, and at least 40 smaller buildings with suites for the guests—and all set in beautifully landscaped gardens. The jazz party presents two sessions on Saturday and a noon-to-six session on Sunday.

On my return to cooler climes, January 31 found me in Providence, R.I., with the second Bobby Hackett Memorial Concert. Early in February, I joined Bob Wilber, Ed Hubble, Milt Hinton, Dave McKenna, and Bobby Rosengarden to form a unit that Bob dubbed the "East Coast All Stars." We performed as a feature of the Central Illinois Jazz Festival, playing a standard jazz band set followed by a presentation from Bob Wilber and his wife, singer Pug Horton. This group was so well received that it resulted in the format being booked for a series of concerts for eight Mid-west jazz clubs for the fall.

Another interesting date that month took place at the Brooklyn Academy of Music, where the Twyla Tharpe dance company presented a program of eight dances to the music of Jelly-Roll Morton. A seven-piece band comprised of Dick Hyman, Phil Bodner, Jack Gale, Marty Grosz, Major Holley, Tommy Benford (who played and recorded with Jelly-Roll on some of the original records) and me, played a number of the Morton titles—"Bugaboo," "Shreveport Stomp," "Smokehouse Blues," "Strokin' Away," "Blue Blood Blues," "If Someone Would Only Love Me." The arrangements were transcribed by Dick Hyman from the records and in style-concepts as close to the originals as we could muster. The degree of authencity is a great testimonial to the technical adaptability of the musicians involved. A similar group, with the substitution of Bob Wilber for Phil Bodner, and Warren Vache' Jr. on cornet, had played many of the same titles at a concert for the Smithsonian Institution on Febrary 26, 1978, which was recorded and issued in an album as part of the Smithsonian Collection.

Nostalgia seemed to be the keyword for 1979, with Benny Goodman stepping back into the picture after many long years. Benny asked me to do some concerts with him in March, the first of which was to be at the "Kennedy Center for the Performing Arts" in Washington, D. C. We had a rehearsal in New York to familiarize the group with the music that was going to be played, and this included several of the Goodman hits of his early years such as "Let's Dance," "Stompin' At the Savoy," and "Sing Sing Sing."

I asked Benny if lead sheets were available for these tunes, and he looked at me in surprise. "You were there when they brought this music around so what do you need lead sheets for?" I couldn't help a chuckle when I reminded him, "That was 44 years ago, so I may need a little refreshing."

After the Washington date we did a series of concerts in the Pacific Northwest, beginning in Vancouver, B.C. The group included the Canadian vibraphonist Peter Appleyard; Cal Collins on guitar; Wayne Andre', trombone; Bill Ramsey, a very good Tacoma, Washington, tenor saxophonist; John Bunch, piano; Connie Kay, drums; and Michael Moore, bass. This area of the country has an awful lot to offer, in picturesque scenery as well as marvelous seafood. When we hit Seattle, I had a chance to visit and reminisce with Roy Wager, my sidekick in the Joe Haymes brass section. Then we moved on to Portland, and after our concert Benny called me into his dressing room and introduced me to two lovely young ladies who turned out to be the daughters of Nate Kazebier. Nate, who had passed away some time ago, was with me in Benny's 1936 band, and as I have said many times, never received the recognition he deserved.

Between my trips away from home, I was working as a regular at Eddie Condon's, Red Balaban's club on 54th Street in New York, for the Friday lunch sessions, which were building up a large following. I was also substituting once or twice a week in the regular night sessions for Ed Polcer, the regular cornetist.

For March 23 and 24 I was booked for the third edition of the "Strides of March" weekend sponsored by the New Jersey Jazz Society, joined by an illustrious cast: Doc Cheatham, Ruby Braff, George Masso, Vic Dickenson, Jack Gale, Kenny Davern, Bob Wilber, Bobby Gordon, Buddy Tate, Zoot Sims, Remo Palmieri, Herb Ellis, Dick Hyman, Dick Wellstood, Derek Smith, Cliff Leeman, Jake Hanna, Bob Rosengarden, Jack Lesberg, Milt Hinton, and Mike Moore. To complete the month, I played a concert with Dick Hyman and the PRQ at Allegheny College in Meadville, Pa. Afterwards we were royally entertained by the well-known record collector, Joe Boughton, and his wife Emmy, at their home in Meadville. The following night we played for a great private party given by our Pittsburgh buddy Bill Seifert at a Pittsburgh country club.

After a couple of weeks of part-time playing at Eddie Condon's, Caroline and I, taking advantage of a gracious invitation from Don and Sue Miller, the principal hosts of the Paradise Valley Jazz Party, made a trip to the Southwest. Along with several other musicians and their wives, and friends of the Millers, we had been asked to join them for a weekend in Mexico. We flew to Scottsdale, Arizona, and that evening played a private concert at the Arts Center, along with Bob Wilber, Bucky Pizzarelli, Milt Hinton, Roger Kellaway, and Bob Rosengarden. This turned out to be one of the best concerts of my experience, mainly due to the fact that the stage was equipped with a Bosendorfer concert grand piano, one of the most beautifully toned pianos I have ever heard. The piano inspired Roger

Kellaway to an outstanding performance, and in turn his playing was an inspiration to the rest of us. At the time I didn't realize it, but the progrm was taped. Several months later I heard the tape, and in my opinion it is good enough to be a commercial record.

Caroline and I were the weekend guests of a very gracious Scottsdale couple, Sam and Pollie Ross, who were also invited to be guests of the Millers in Mexico. We spent the night of the concert at the Ross home, and the following day drove with them to Mexico, about 90 miles away.

Puerto Penasco, located on the Gulf of California, is a small shrimp-fishing village. There is an American colony of vacation homes on the beach, where we were entertained for the weekend. On our first evening, we were invited to a dinner in our honor given by the Mexican dignitaries. We were served a wonderful seafood meal of indigenous fish and treated to an unending supply of Margaritas and hospitality by the friendly Mexican people, after which we reciprocated with a mini-concert.

On Saturday, after swimming, sailing, and other beach activities, we were entertained by a mariachi band and treated to a Sonora specialty, barbecued goat. Ending with a late jam session, it was indeed a fun-filled weekend.

SIXTY-TWO

ON MY WAY to the Odessa Jazz Party in mid-May, I made a detour to play two nights at "The Landing" in San Antonio with Jim Cullum's "Happy Jazz Band." This is a truly fine band, and it is always a pleasure to guest with a group like this. We seem to have been playing together for years.

The San Antonio stop also gave me a chance to accept a long-standing invitation from Caroline's parents, Dr. and Mrs. Milton S. Thompson, to stay at their home in the city. I thoroughly enjoyed my stay and the guided tour of the San Antonio points of interest. We also had the opportunity to visit with my nephews, Peter and Jeremy Neesham, my daughter Georgine, a student at the University of Texas in Austin, as well as Caroline's sister and her husband, Mr. and Mrs. Jack Judson, also residents of San Antonio. Incidentally, this was the last time I would see my father-in-law, Dr. Thompson, who passed away the following July.

Dr. Thompson was a most interesting man, with a great interest in history, especially American history. After graduation from Harvard Medical School in 1925, he went on to acquire a worldwide reputation as an orthopedic surgeon. He entered the Army Medical Corps at the beginning of World War II and remained until his retirement with the rank of colonel. After this, he and Mrs. Thompson traveled extensively in Europe, Africa, Australia, and the Far East, where he devoted his services to training others in orthopedic procedures.

Jim Cullum, a fine cornetist, does a superb job in both his management of The Landing and the nightly presentations at the club. When I first arrived, I told him I had been looking forward to meeting him for some time, and to my surprise he replied, "Oh, we've met before!"

Somewhat taken aback, I said, "Really? That's strange—strange, because I have an excellent memory and I can't see how I wouldn't remember our meeting."

"Well, I think it's understandable," he explained with a grin, "we met in Venezuela when I was seven years old."

Allan Vache', who used to help me out with my Fairleigh-Dickinson concerts, is the featured clarinetist with the Cullum Band, a talented young man who adds a lot to the presentations at The Landing, helping Jim select guests and arranging tours for the band.

After my San Antonio session I moved on to Odessa for the 1979 Jazz Party and joined a great lineup: John Best, Ed Polcer, Ken Davern, Bob Wilber, Johnny Mince, Eddie Miller, Peanuts Hucko, Ashley Alexander, Bob Havens, Al Grey, Herb Ellis, Bucky Pizzarelli, Dave McKenna, Lou Stein, Dick Hyman, Milt Hinton, Red Callender, Jack Lesberg, Cliff Leeman, Jake Hanna, Gus Johnson, and Red Norvo. The greatest contributing factor to the success of this six-day party is the support and enthusiasm of the audience. Since the advent of this affair, the spirit of the listeners and patrons have been beyond compare. What's more, it's like a visit home. The musicians know and enjoy the folks in attendance, so the result is a party for all concerned.

On June 15 I had a really thrilling experience. I played a concert with Benny Goodman and the octet for the Playboy Jazz Festival in the Hollywood Bowl, and, as Benny stated during our performance, this was quite an anniversary for us—43 years after our first appearance in Hollywood at the Palomar Ballroom in 1936.

Besides Benny and me, the octet included Michael Moore, bass; Bill Ramsey, tenor; Mickey Gravine, trombone; John Bunch, piano; John Pisano, guitar; and Frank Capp, drums. We were on a bill with Count Basie, Joe Williams, and Sarah Vaughan, with Bill Cosby as Master of Ceremonies, and over 25,000 people in the audience. I've heard Benny play for many years, of course, but I never heard him play better than he did that night. Which proves, as far as I'm concerned, that even now he is still "king of the clarinet."

On July 3 I again departed for the Nice Jazz Festival—this time as a member of the New York Jazz Repertory Company, presenting the music of Duke Ellington, Jean Goldkette, and Benny Goodman. We had a large company—Joe Newman, Ernie Royal, Dick Sudhalter, Jimmy Maxwell, Eddie Bert, Britt Woodman, Michael Zwerin, Haywood Henry, Arnie Lawrence, Norris Turney, Budd Johnson, Bob Wilber, Bobby Rosengarden, George Duvivier, Bucky Pizzarelli, and Dick Hyman, director.

Each daily concert in Nice was a two-hour presentation of the music from the chosen period of the band being recreated. For instance, one concert offered music from Duke Ellington's 1920s period, another from the 1930s, and so on. One program was devoted completely to the music of Jean Goldkette, and another to Benny Goodman. All in all, we had five different libraries for use during this tour.

Nice in July is just about the nicest place to be that I can think of. The produce stalls are just bursting with Cote D'Azur fruit of all kinds, and very often the festive atmosphere of the Riviera is such that it seems that all of France has gathered on the Coast. Then, too, the site of the Festival, Jardins des Arenes de Cimiez, offers a perfect setting for picnicking under the trees while listening to good music.

On July 15, I left the Repertory Company for one day in order to make an appearance at the Northsea Jazz Festival taking place at The Hague, where I played again with the Ted Easton band. On the 16th, I rejoined the Repertory Company for a night at a festival in Munich, Germany, held in the Munich Stadium, built for the Olympic Games and scene of the 1972 massacre of Israeli athletes.

From July 17 to 22 we were part of the first Capital Jazz Festival, held that summer in London. It was staged in a park in the northwest part of the city affectionately called "Ally Pally" by Londoners. This is the location of a huge building called Alexandra's Palace, named for Princess Alexandra of Denmark, who married Edward VII when he was Prince of Wales, later becoming queen, after the death of Queen Victoria. The building was on a hill, the highest point in London, and was used by the BBC for transmitting the first TV shows broadcast in London.

On the sloping lawn in front of this gigantic building, two soundstages were built, leaving room in between for the many food stalls, and record stands. From these stages, the Festival music was presented to the throngs of listeners. After the balmy weather of Nice, we were treated to the very cold and windy weather of England. Really cold for July, the wind blew our music off the racks. Our performances were still geared to 2½-hour concerts, but we were lodged at the Kensington Close Hotel in the heart of central London, and it was at least an hour and a half each way to and from the Festival site. Shuttle buses ran from the hotel for our convenience, but sometimes they would wait for two or more hours on the return, which made it very inconvenient. Even if we used the efficient London Underground it still took us 1½ hours to get back to the hotel.

On our evening off, I made an album for Ted Easton at a studio far out in southeast London with some British musicians. I have never heard the results of this session, but some day I would like to—especially to hear the trombonist Roy Williams and the pianist Brian Lemon.

I have always enjoyed my visits to London, and this one was no exception. I had the chance to visit with my British trumpet-playing friends Tommy McQuater, John McLevy, and Monty Montgomery, and also had the pleasure of meeting for the first time the fine London trumpeter Digby Fairweather.

I suppose it's fashionable to drink beer in London, but I had quite a start when I got on the bus for Ally Pally one day and saw Dick Sudhalter with a bottle of milk. I asked him where he got it, and he led me across the street to a parked milk-delivery wagon. "Help yourself to a liter," he said, "and leave 37 pence by the driver's seat." I did as I was told, and the milk was delicious. As a milk addict, I had to ask questions, and I was told it was Channel Island milk—as rich as any I have ever tasted.

Back in the States, early in August I appeared at the second Great Northeastern Jazz Festival in Greenville, N.Y. This festival, sponsored by Skip Parsons and his Riverboat Jazz Band, is presented under a tent next to the Rainbow Inn in Greenville, with guest soloists and a number of New York State jazz bands.

Digby Fairweather   Photo Bernard Long

Also during this month, Caroline and I were the guests of Pug and Bob Wilber at their home on Cape Cod. Strange to say, in all the years of my touring New England, this was my first trip to the Cape. I played two dates there with Bob's quartet, featuring Pug's vocals, one at the Linnell House in Orleans and the other at a charming country Playhouse in North Truro. Here we had the pleasure of playing with the accomplished pianist Marie Marcus; I had first met when she was playing with Preacher Rollo's band in Miami. During this visit we spent an evening at the home of Jack Bradley, official Louis Armstrong photographer, and were treated to a showing of many interesting movie clips of Armstrong, Fats Waller, Bunny Berigan, and others, including a short I was in and had forgotten. It was made by a Will Bradley band in 1944, and it was interesting to see what I had looked like in my younger days.

On August 30, I was in Buffalo to do a concert with the Repertory Quintet at the beautiful Art Park, nearby to Niagara Falls. We played an all-George Gershwin program which was taped by Public Television for national release, but although I have spoken to a number of people who have seen this on PBS, I have never seen it myself. This was followed in quick order by the 17th annual private jazz party held at the Broadmoor in Colorado Springs (September 1-2-3). Still expanding, this huge event boasted 55 or more musicians, plus somewhere between 600 and 700 guests.

The program printed for the occasion listed: Trumpet—Clark Terry, Ruby Braff, Pee Wee Erwin, Harry "Sweets" Edison, Red Rodney, Joe Newman, Doc Cheatham, Billy Butterfield. Trombone—Carl Fontana, Vic Dickenson, Bill Watrous, Al Grey, Trummy Young, Slide Hampton, Roy Williams, Britt Woodman. Tenor Sax—Zoot Sims, Flip Phillips, Buddy Tate, Al Cohn, Scott Hamilton, Eddie "Lockjaw" Davis. Baritone Sax—Budd Johnson (also tenor). Clarinet—Peanuts Hucko, Buddy De Franco. Piano—Ralph Sutton, Dick Hyman, Roger Kellaway, Teddy Wilson, Ross Tompkins, Jay "Hootie" McShann, Derek Smith. Bass—Milt Hinton, George Duvivier, Ray Brown, Larry Ridley, Major Holley, Chuck Domanico. Drums—Cliff Leeman, Gus Johnson, Alan Dawson, Bobby Rosengarden, Jake Hanna, Jackie Williams, Shelley Manne. Guitar—Chuck Wayne, John Collins. Other—Splendid musicians. The program also stated: "Music will begin on stage at 2:45 p.m. on Saturday and end around 9 p.m. on Monday. Over that 55 hour span, approximately 53 sets of music will be presented encompassing about 28 hours of actual playing time.

"Sunday will be black-tie. The hotel requires the wearing of coat and tie in any of its dining rooms after 6 p.m. Afternoons at the party dress is casual; guests go barefooted and wear clothes almost as frayed and bizarre as those worn by Jake Hanna and Carl Fontana."

A month working around the New York area was next. Then I attended the Festival of Traditional Jazz presented at the Holiday Inn O'Hare, in Rosemont, Illinois, by the Preservation Jazz Fest Society, which honored Milt Hinton and featured some great "second line" performances by Danny Barker. Danny, as well as being a great banjo player is one of the most entertaining speakers around, with a tremendous sense of humor. In November I was back in Texas for the third Midland Jazz Classic. This six-day affair offers a great deal to the musicians who play it and the Odessa party. I, for one, feel as though west Texas is a second home where friendliness and hospitality reign supreme. The music is always superb, and the social life matches it.

After Midland, a number of us went on tour, making the rounds of several midwestern jazz clubs under the banner of the "East Coast All Stars," the name tagged on us by Pete George from Illinois. The tour was made financially possible because we were able to take advantage of the unlimited mileage ticketing offered by Allegheny Airlines, which enabled us to make all of our stops for the price of one master fare. The only disadvantage involved was that we had to return from whereever we were to the main Allegheny terminus before moving on to the next stop. For example, to go from St. Louis to Minneapolis we first had to fly from St. Louis to Pittsburgh, and then board a flight from Pittsburgh to Minneapolis. Actually, this worked out quite well for me. Every time we stopped in Pittsburgh, my friend Bill Seifert would show up for a short visit and bring along a fresh supply of my favorite chewing tobacco.

Incidentally, this group was unique from a jazz standpoint, because we had the foundations of two completely different presentations, allowing us to offer a diversified program. On the tour were Bob Wilber, Urbie Green, Dave McKenna, Major Holley, Bob Rosengarden, and vocalist Pug Horton, and we played a program divided into three parts. The first segment was the jazz band, with ensemble and solo performances on typical jazz standards, followed by the Bob Wilber Quartet in the second segment, including a solo spot for Pug Horton. The final part of the program offered more band ensemble and solos and wound up with a complete ensemble finale. Altogether it provided a nice show, tastefully paced, and we presented it in Indianapolis, St. Louis, Grand Rapids, Minneapolis, Cincinnati, Pine Bluff (Ark.), and Charleston.

SIXTY-THREE

ON THE FIRST AND SECOND DAYS of December 1979, one of the greatest events in my entire life took place: The good people of Falls City, Nebraska, threw a big celebration in my honor!

Caroline and I were invited to be the guests at a round of testimonials offered by many of my lifelong friends. It began with a concert and dance at the Vets Club, where a number of my former schoolmates, along with people from near and far, took part in the presentation of a plaque which proclaimed "Pee Wee Erwin Day" in Falls City. Pictures of Caroline, my mother, and of me were taken for the next editions of the local and neighboring-town papers. On Sunday morning, a brunch was held at the Elks Club, and I was presented with the keys to the city by Mayor Shaeffer. This was also attended by many out-of-town guests.

That afternoon, they put on a concert in the high-school auditorium, and I wound up taking part in it with a group representing not only Falls City but a number of other towns around the state—Judge Albert Maust, tenor sax; Dr. Robert Hoban, guitar; Bob Shields, guitar; Dave Jones, drums; Jeff Barker (from Shubert, Neb.), bass; Rod Schmidt (from Bellvue, Neb.), trombone; Dennis Schneider (University of Nebraska, Lincoln), trumpet; Russ Gibson (Lincoln, Neb.), piano; Riley Duryea (Houston, Tex.), clarinet; Dr. James Seeley, (Holton, Kan.), tenor sax. And don't think I wasn't proud to be able to play with all of these stalwarts!

In the audience were John Sheridan and Dr. Louis Forman, who had played with me in Eddie Kuhn's band at the Kansas City Athletic Club 50 years ago, Phyllis Forman and Mr. and Mrs. Howard Turtte, good friends from Kansas City, and Mrs. Lois Patterson, wife of Norman Patterson, with Mr. and Mrs. George Patterson. George, you may remember, was the drummer brother of sax player Norman.

As part of the proceedings, I was presented with a citation of welcome to my home state from Charles Thone, governor of Nebraska. I won't deny I was thrilled by it all. It was really a great honor to be the subject of such a celebration, and for much of the festivities I owe special thanks to Harriet

Falter, Merle Stalder, and my lifelong associate Albert Maust.

In comparison, the rest of 1979 was spent under fairly tame circumstances, working with the Perfect Jazz Repertory Quintet at Michael's Pub in New York and playing the music of George Gershwin.

The New Year started off sticking fairly close to format, with my staying close to the New York metropolitan area and working intermittently at the Eddie Condon Club on 54th Street. They always have a good band there, and the atmosphere is nostalgically comparable to Nick's and the original Condon clubs. The place serves as a watering hole for many of the New York musicians after they have finished work at various spots around town, and it has become the social mecca to go to when you want to see your friends among the musical night people. Prices at Condon's are reasonable, the management is cordial and very jazz oriented, and they offer the best in traditional music.*

In addition to filling in one or two nights a week, for some time I have been performing as a regular in the band led by Tom Artin, a good trombonist, at the Friday noontime "Brunch Session." This takes place from 12 noon until 3 p.m. every Friday, and music is supplied by the traditional six-piece lineup. Besides Tommy and me, the personnel usually includes Jack Maheu on clarinet; Bobby Pratt, piano; Ernie Hackett, drums; and Dick Waldburger, bass. The jazz luncheon policy has really caught on, with a large clientele of jazz fans and business people from the neighboring office buildings, so it has become a unique jazz institution with a very close relationship between the band and its friends. This feeling has been rather well captured by an album of the group, produced by Tom Artin, and called "Condon's Hot Lunch," recorded for Slide Records.

On the subject of records, you may have noticed that it has been quite a few years since I last made an attempt to record under my own name. I had made a whole series of recordings in the Fifties, some of which I consider were quite good, but by 1980 they were all out of print, with the exception of the one made in 1954 for the Urania label with the band from Nick's, called "Accent on Dixieland." This has been reissued four times, each time under a different label.

Bill Muchnic had been talking to me for several years about recording a solo album of ballads, which he thinks I do well, and after watching me procrastinate about the project for a long time he finally decided to take charge. He asked Bob Wilber to arrange 12 numbers which we agreed on, and on January 22 and 23 we recorded them with an eight-piece group at the Vanguard Studios in New York. In the band were Bob Wilber, Johnny Mince, and Frank Wess (reeds); Ed Hubble, trombone; Derek Smith, piano; Milt Hinton, bass; and Bobby Rosengarden, drums. The album has a distinct dance-band flavor and presents some very nice solo spots for the

---

*"Eddie Condon's," and "Jimmy Ryan's," the jazz clubs located on W. 54th Street in Manhattan, are no more. The buildings where they were located, along with others on the same block, were torn down in 1986 for a redevelopment project.

all-star lineup. It is called "Pee Wee in New York" (Qualtro Records, 1020 Prospect St., La Jolla, CA 92037).

Incidentally, our trombonist, Ed Hubble, had been in a very serious auto accident that almost cost him his life and did injure his legs. This recording session took place just before he was to undergo further surgery, and he played the session with his injured leg propped up on a chair!

On February 2 and 3, I made my second appearance at the Central Illinois Jazz Festival in Decatur, Illinois, fronting the "East Coast All-Stars." Hubble was unable to make this date, so Tom Artin filled in with our group and was well received. Like George Masso, trombonist with "The World's Greatest Jazz Band," Tommy is one of the younger generation of trombone players which is slowly building a well-deserved reputation for talent and musicianship. With us were Bob Wilber, Dave McKenna, Milt Hinton, Bob Rosengarden, and Pug Horton; others on the program included Tom Saunders, Bob Hirsch, Dan Williams, Chuck Hedges, John DeFauw, Barrett Deems, Pud Brown, Conrad Jones, Jimmy Haislip, Monte Mountjoy, John Ulrich, Don DeMichael, Jerry Martin, Armand Toscett, and Lee Parsons; plus a band from Boston (Bob Connors and the Yankee Rhythm Kings) and another from Detroit (Chet Bogan and the Wolverine Jazz Band with "Dixiebelle").

While we were there I enjoyed greeting old friends, like Jim Taylor from Detroit, the Bill Yorks and John Clements from Indianapolis, and the Clay Kennedys from Brownville, Nebraska. This is what adds a lot of satisfaction to attending these jazz festivals—the chance to see old friends again.

After Decatur, Milt Hinton, Bob Rosengarden, and I traveled to Indianapolis to play a one-night date for the Indianapolis Jazz Club. It turned out to be a very enjoyable concert in which we were joined by Willie Baker on tenor and clarinet; Lon Young on trombone; and John Ulrich on piano. I was the house guest of Mr. and Mrs. John Kercheval during my stay.

On February 12 I was back in New York to join a marvelous group of performers for a three-week stint at Michael's Pub. Carol Sloane, the personable and versatile vocalist, was the featured attraction, backed by a quartet led by pianist Jimmy Rowles. With us were Michael Moore on bass, and Joe LaBarbara on drums; the theme of the program was the music of Frank Loesser.

In my opinion, Carol Sloane has one of the sweetest and most flexible voices I have ever heard. Her intonation and vocal quality are superb but, beyond that, her musical conception is tremendous. The program format presented her in solo spots alternating with vocals by Jimmy Rowles, and they also sang some duets. I was given the opportunity to do a few numbers with Carol as well as a couple of solo turns. While I'm handing out compliments, let me say that I consider Jimmy Rowles to be one of the freshest and most creative pianists of our day. Working with this group provided a never-ending challenge and pleasure.

On March 5, I once more became part of the New York Jazz Repertory Company, playing the music of Louis Armstrong and journeying with them to Washington, D.C. to attend a formal state dinner at the White House, given by President and Mrs. Carter in honor of Helmut Schmidt, the chancellor of West Germany, and Mrs. Schmidt. Our group included Budd Johnson, tenor sax; Kenny Davern, Lou Stein, piano; Milt Hinton, Bob Rosengarden. Jimmy Maxwell and Joe Newman were with me in the trumpet trio. We were fortunate to be chosen for this honor, because a state dinner is a very select and exceptional function, conducted with highly formal procedures, and among the more colorful of White House events. We were also invited to take part in the reception and dinner prior to our concert.

At the reception, the president, the first lady, and the honored guests were heralded into the dining room by an impressive Marine Corps orchestra and a military guard, after which they formed a receiving line and the guests filed in to be introduced to the presidential party. We enjoyed taking part in this very colorful procedure.

After the dinner, the guests filed into the East Room and were seated to hear our concert. At first the social secretary, Gretchen Posten, expressed some apprehension about the arrangement; she was afraid our music might be too loud. But when we began to play and President Carter, who turned out to be a jazz fan, started clapping his hands and singing the lyrics to "I'm a Ding Dong Daddy," all fears concerning too much volume evaporated. Our presentation was an unqualified success.

The Paradise Valley Jazz Party in Arizona came up next, and this year they were kind enough to make me the Guest of Honor. I must admit that it gets very emotional when such nice people do so many nice things for you, say so many kind words, and go out of their way to make you feel like somebody special. Besides getting a very warm sensation inside, you begin to think that maybe your life has been worthwhile after all, and material gain becomes relatively unimportant compared to the good wishes and high regard of your friends.

Musicians participating included: Dick Hyman, Roger Kellaway, and Jay "Hootie" McShann, piano; Milt Hinton, Ray Brown, Brian Torff, bass; Bob Rosengarden, Shelly Manne, and Jake Hanna, drums; Herb Ellis, guitar; Joe Newman, Clark Terry, Pee Wee Erwin, trumpets; Buddy Tate, Kenny Davern, Bob Wilber, and Zoot Sims, reeds; Carl Fontana and Bill Watrous, trombones.

To close the party, Don Miller gave a summary of my life in the music business, using records and a slide-projector to present a review of some of the bands I've been fortunate to work with. This all left me quite wrought up and pretty tongue-tied but extremely grateful for all of the well-wishers—not to mention the great honor of being made an adopted citizen of Arizona by Governor Bruce Babbitt.

A trip to Dublin was next on the itinerary—Dublin, Georgia, that is—to play for the last day of a week-long St. Patrick's Festival, an annual affair. But first I flew to Atlanta to spend the weekend with good friends, Zack and Dot Cullens, and in line with prior arrangements made an album on March 22 with the great ragtime-piano authority Knocky Parker.

Knocky Parker is a professor of English at the University of Florida, but in addition to his academic work he has acquired a reputation as one of the foremost living authorities on ragtime music. More than that, he is equally proficient as a ragtime piano player, and it was quite an honor to play on one of his albums, produced by George Buck. Also in the eight-piece band on the record are Ernie Carson on cornet, Herman Foretich on clarinet, and Charley Bornemann on trombone.

The afternoon's celebration in Dublin took place on March 23 in a nice public park, and we played on a beautifully decorated flatbed truck. Our leader was the popular Dr. William Dodd of Wrightsville, who plays a swinging jazz piano, and the others were Charley Lodice, Pete Fountain's drummer from New Orleans, Harry Hagen, a trombonist who is very active in the studios of Atlanta and Nashville, Jerry Rousseau, Al Hirt's bass player in New Orleans, and Pud Brown, a very fine tenor and clarinet man—also from New Orleans—with whom I had worked in California. Altogether it was a gala event to wind up a St. Patrick's celebration.

We drove back to Atlanta on Sunday night, and on Monday I made another album for George Buck—this time one of standard jazz band tunes (Jazzology J-80 "... Swingin' That Music"). I had been talking with George about an album for some time, but this was the first time my schedule had brought me close enough to Atlanta. The rest of the musicians on the record are from Atlanta—Herman Foretich, clarinet and vocals; Harry Hagen, trombone; Freddie Deland, piano; Ike Isaacs, bass; and Hal Smith, drums— and I think it is a nice album.

Home again, it was time for a repeat of the Jelly-Roll Morton program behind the Twyla Tharpe dance group, presented for this performance at the Winter Garden on Broadway. On April 12 I took part in an evening of jazz produced by Don Marino at The Inn at Longshore, in Westport, Connecticut. Don offered two bands alternating on the bandstand, with vocal entertainment by Peter Dean between sets. It was a very successful promotion. Taking part were Ed Polcer, Al Cohn, Al Klink, Kenny Davern, Johnny Mince, Vic Dickenson, George Masso, Mickey Crane, Derek Smith, Jack Lesberg, Bill Crow, Cliff Leeman, and Mousie Alexander.

After this, I had a very nice three-day engagement at the Board of Trade Country Club on the outskirts of Toronto, where I appeared with a quartet. During the dinner period, I presented a nostalgic program which was a review of the various bands I played with during the Thirties. Since most of the diners were middle-aged and my music was aimed at the big-band era, it was very well received. After dinner we played for dancing, and it proved to be one of the most pleasant sessions of the year.

Toronto was followed by a one-night presentation of the Armstrong Show at the Sheridan Hotel in St. Louis, where we played for a convention. It was here that symptoms of a severe bladder infection first manifested themselves. I went to my doctor when I got back to New York, and after the usual routine of tests and conferences, the obvious conclusion was that I would have to undergo an operation eventually, but in the doctor's opinion I would be able to fulfill my immediate playing comitments first.

SIXTY-FOUR

I LEFT NEW YORK on April 27 to appear with a group called "The American Dixieland All Stars" at the International Jazz Festival in Bern, Switzerland; that is, Johnny Mince, George Masso, Ralph Sutton, Jack Lesberg, and Gus Johnson.

On our first evening in Bern we were treated to a "get-acquainted" dinner to meet the press and enjoy the company of other performers at the Festival. Among these were Wild Bill Davison, Jay McShann, Peanuts Hucko, Teddy Wilson, Dick Wellstood, and Sammy Price, and later in the week we were to see more of our friends—Earle Warren, Budd Johnson, Leonard Gaskin, and Oliver Jackson—plus Joe Newman, Wallace Davenport, Curtis Fuller, and Ritchie Pratt, who were appearing with Lionel Hampton.

Without any question Bern is one of the most picturesque cities in Europe, retaining the atmosphere of medieval Europe to this day. Buildings with turrets, arcaded sidewalks, a sixteenth-century clock tower, and a beautiful Gothic cathedral from the fifteenth century all add to the charm of the place. This is especially true during festival occasions when the old streets are lined with hundreds of varicolored flags, and street markets and music in the squares make for a real holiday spirit.

Our first concert was at the Kursaal, a lovely auditorium across the bridge in the new section of the city, which was presented for school-age children, and I'm sure we collected a few future followers of jazz music. On Wednesday, the All Stars—plus Wild Bill Davison and Jay McShann— drove over the border north of Zurich for an evening concert at a festival in Germany. This one was sponsored by two German cities, Villegen and Schwenningen and, to Ralph Sutton's surprise and delight, the concert hall boasted a marvelous Bosendorfer piano that made him sound like a full orchestra all by himself.

On the trip into Germany, Wild Bill wondered about the feasibility of buying a bottle of scotch whiskey, because in Switzerland the price was $25, so when we arrived at the concert hall the promoter obligingly did provide Bill with a bottle. However, in the social atmosphere of the dressing room the entire bottle was soon drained. Luckily for Bill, the promoter was able to get him another bottle. After the concert we were taken to a large ballroom for an excellent buffet, plenty of free beer, and a jam session.

The following morning we were driven back into Switzerland in time for a 10 a.m. concert in a school at Langenthal, a little Swiss village and, when this was over, we were driven back through Bern to another village, named Thun, where we played a 3 p.m. concert in another school. The Swiss really make certain the young people have ample opportunity to see and hear visiting artists.

Our Friday night concert was presented for the general public in a suburban shopping center called "Shoppyland." We certainly couldn't complain about being overworked. On Saturday night, which seemed to be the culmination of the Bern Festival, we performed in the Kursaal and the concert was recorded for Swiss radio. We followed the usual jazz-band format, with ensembles and each member of the group performing a solo during the show. Since we'd played several concerts during the week our ensemble had evolved into a very solid unit.

On Sunday morning, at 10 a.m., we repeated our night concert in one of the most unusual halls I've ever seen. This was a place called Kornhauskeller, a huge hall built to resemble a barrel and about the equivalent of two stories underground. There were about 2,000 people there on Sunday morning, and to our amazement our concert seemed to drive them to a fever pitch of excitement and enthusiasm. There were people literally hanging from the rafters, and I think you'll agree that it's a pretty rare thing to see such great spirit generated so early in the morning.

That night—our last in Bern—we were invited to play a set in a lovely new night club which had just opened in our hotel (the Kaiserhoff). This has since become a regular stop for American groups appearing in Europe.

On my return to the States, Caroline joined me, and we took off for our second weekend in Mexico. As we did the year before, we stopped off in Arizona to do one concert; this time it was at Arizona State College at Tempe. Our entourage included Bob Wilber, Bucky Pizzarelli, Derek Smith, Michael Moore, and Bob Rosengarden.

Our visits to Puerto Penasco offer a lot of pleasure, especially since Caroline accompanies me on the trip, and she proved herself to be quite a sailor aboard the Miller's catamaran. The beach is beautiful, too, and for a brief time it's like visiting another world.

On the way back Caroline stopped in San Antonio to visit her mother and our daughter Georgine, who by this time had pretty well established herself as a Texan. In addition to her studies at the University of Texas in Austin, she had been working part time for a real-estate firm, a field she seems to be well suited for.

I went on to Odessa for the annual Jazz Party, May 19 to 25, and this year the roster was as distinguished as ever: John Best and Ed Polcer were the other trumpets; Kenny Davern, Bob Wilber, Johnny Mince, Buddy Tate, and Flip Phillips, were the reeds; Carl Fontana, George Masso, and Ashley

Alexander, trombones; Herb Ellis and Bucky Pizzarelli, guitars; Dave McKenna, Lou Stein, John Bunch, on piano; Milt Hinton, Jack Lesberg, and Michael Moore, basses; Cliff Leeman, Gus Johnson, and Bob Rosengarden, drums; and Red Norvo on vibraphone.

After talking things over with Bill Muchnic, we decided that since I was scheduled for an operation in July it might not be such a bad idea to make a sequel recording to follow the one we'd made in New York in January, this time using West Coast musicians plus Kenny Davern on clarinet. So Kenny and I flew to Hollywood after the Odessa Party, and on May 27 we recorded an album of standard tunes with Eddie Miller on tenor; Bob Havens, trombone; Dick Cary, piano; Ray Leatherwood, bass; and Nick Fatool on drums. This was to be our second album for release in 1981 ("Pee Wee in Hollywood," Qualtro Records).

I returned home from California just in time for our youngest, Caroline, to graduate from high school, finishing up the string. Our other two girls, Georgine and Cathy, graduated in 1976 and 1977 in regular order.

It also appears I'd been bitten by the recording bug during this period. For some time I'd been discussing a trio album with Bucky Pizzarelli, so at last, July 2, we decided to try our hand at it. We managed to tape enough material in one evening for one side of an LP ("Pee Wee Playing at Home," Qualtro Records).

After a swinging night at the Princeton Reunion, on July 6, with Johnny Mince, Scott Hamilton, George Masso, John Bunch, Connie Kay, and Frank Tate, I made arrangements to enter White Plains Hospital on July 9 for corrective bladder surgery. The operation necessitated a two-month rest and recovery period afterwards, so Caroline took advantage of my convalescence to spend more time on the care and maintenance of her family's summer home in Maine. My time off from work gave us a chance to make a couple of trips to Maine for housecleaning, having the house painted, and other odd jobs. Aside from these occasional necessary chores, the house in Casco, Maine, is a perfect retreat for spending part of the summer away from metropolitan New York.

My first playing dates after the operation included the one at the Dutchess County Fair, which I do every year with Chris Griffin's band, and one on the following night for a concert conducted by Hal Davis at the Galli Curci Theater in Margaretville, N.Y.

Then on August 24 the New Jersey Jazz Society sponsored one of the nicest things that has ever happened to me—a huge testimonial in my behalf at the Downtown New York Athletic Club. Before this, I never knew I had so many friends and supporters in the world. The music started at 2 p.m. and was still going at 8 p.m. on a continuous basis and supplied free by a huge group of my talented friends, all donating their services in my behalf. The ballroom was filled with friends and well-wishers, and the entire affair was completely wonderful—and overwhelming. At this stage it would be impossible for me to recall and list the names of all those who contributed, but I will be forever grateful to each and every one.

Pee Wee performing for the New Jersey Jazz Society. Jim Andrews, pno; Walt Levinsky, sax and clnt; guest Don Watt, clnt; Pee Wee, Warren Vache' Sr., bass, Sonny Igoe, drums, (out of picture).

On August 27, I left for Colorado, three days earlier than necessary for the start of the Gibson Jazz Party. I had accepted an invitation from Bill and Beverly Muchnic to be their house guest at their lovely summer place in Cascade, and I particularly enjoyed the visit because a number of my friends from the Midwest were also present—John and Jane Byram, from Kansas City; Wendell and Violet Lehman, from Atchison, Kansas; and Ruth Crawford, from Sun Valley, and later we were joined by Bill Seifert. After a couple of days at Cascade a nice mood was in order for the 18th Gibson Party in Colorado Springs.*

On my return home to New Jersey, Caroline and I were honored by a week-long visit from Sinclair Traill, the eminent British jazz writer and founder of England's foremost jazz magazine, *Jazz Journal*. We enjoyed Sinclair's visit immensely, and, along with keeping us entertained by accounts of his many and varied experiences, he treated us to some samples of his first-class culinary accomplishments.

In mid-September I made the annual trek to the Nemacolin Encampment, once more joining the "Birddogs" for a weekend of music and fun, and then Caroline and I made one more trip to Casco, Maine, this time accompanied by Bill and Martha Leek. Bill hauled along a large amount of fiberglass insulation which he used to insulate our attic in layers at least 12 inches deep.

*AN INVITATION   July, 1980

We are pleased to invite you to our 18th annual private jazz party, to be held in The Broadmoor Hotel, in Colorado Springs, over the Labor Day weekend of Saturday, Sunday and Monday, August 30, 31 and September 1.

At least 57 of the world's finest jazz musicians will play. They include:

TRUMPET: Clark Terry, Pee Wee Erwin, Joe Newman, Snooky Young, Billy Butterfield, Sweets Edison, Doc Cheatham, Red Rodney, Joe Wilder

TROMBONE: Vic Dickenson, Trummy Young, Bill Watrous, George Chisholm, Bob Havens, Al Grey, Carl Fontana, Slide Hampton

TENOR SAX: Al Cohn, Buddy Tate, Frank Wess, Scott Hamilton, Flip Phillips, Lockjaw Davis, Jimmy Forrest

ALTO SAX: Benny Carter, Phil Woods, Marshall Royal, Richie Cole, Chris Woods

BARITONE SAX: Budd Johnson (also Tenor)

CLARINET: Peanuts Hucko, Kenny Davern, Bob Wilber (also Soprano)

PIANO: Ralph Sutton, Jay Hootie McShann, Dick Hyman, Roland Hanna, Dave Frishberg, Roger Kellaway, Ross Tompkins, Derek Smith

BASS: Milt Hinton, George Duvivier, Ray Brown, Major Holley, Michael Moore, Chuck Domanico, Carson Smith

DRUMS: Cliff Leeman, Gus Johnson, Alan Dawson, Grady Tate, Jake Hanna, Bobby Rosengarden, Jackie Williams

GUITAR: John Collins

VIOLIN: Claude Williams

OTHER: Another

Music will begin on stage at 2:30 p.m. on Saturday and end around 9 p.m. on Monday. Over that approximately 55 hour span, about 54 sets of music encompassing nearly 28 hours of actual playing time will be presented.

From October 10 to 13 I was once again a member of the Perfect Jazz Repertory Quintet, and we appeared with the Pittsburgh Symphony for the opening of the Pittsburgh Pops Series. This time the program was based on the music of George Gershwin, and we followed the format we had developed in our previous concerts with symphonies. The conductor of the Pittsburgh Symphony was Michael Lankester. We each played a solo number with the orchestra during the first segment of the program, and then the Quintet played the second half alone. My solo was "I've Got a Crush on You," nicely orchestrated by Dick Hyman, and I must admit it is always a thrill to play with a full symphony orchestra behind you, especially for a player who is essentially a saloon cornetist.

During this visit to Bill Seifert's hometown, we also played for a private dinner he gave for some of the people associated with the Pittsburgh

Symphony and, of course, all of the Nemacolin Birddogs.

Two weeks later I was back in West Texas for the Midland Jazz Classic, and Max Christensen again provided the suite of rooms complete with the milk bar.* To end October, Caroline and I made a final trip to Maine to prepare the house for winter. On the way home, we stopped in Providence so I could play at a concert for the Rhode Island Junior College, held to dedicate a beautiful auditorium in the name of Bobby Hackett. A number of Bobby's other associates took part: Bob Wilber, Vic Dickenson, Mike Renzi, Ernie Hackett, and Frank Tate. This auditorium, plus an annual scholarship established in his name, will forever perpetuate the name of Bobby Hackett in his native Rhode Island.

*MIDLAND JAZZ CLASSIC 1980

Oct. 21 through 26

The invited musician list is as follows:

Clarinets:	Abe Most, Bob Wilber and Kenny Davern
Tenor Sax:	Zoot Sims and Al Cohn
Piano:	Dick Hyman, Derek Smith and Ralph Sutton
Bass:	Jack Lesberg (Musical Director), Milton Hinton & George Mraz
Vibes:	Red Norvo
Trumpets:	Warren Vache', Billy Butterfield and Pee Wee Erwin
Trombones:	Al Grey, Bill Watrous and Carl Fontana
Guitar:	Mundell Lowe
Singer:	Sue Raney
Drums:	Jake Hanna, Jackie Williams and Gus Johnson

In mid-November I took part in a weekend series of concerts sponsored by the International Art of Jazz, presented at the lavish Guernee's Inn in Montauk, Long Island. A full complement of prominent performers was present, and the event is planned as an annual affair, part of the concert series offered by New York University at Stony Brook.

Following this I joined Kenny Davern, Ed Hubble, Milt Hinton, Dave Frishberg, and Bob Rosengarden for a brief road tour in the Midwest, making a swing of the various jazz clubs. This was probably the most musically enjoyable group we could have got together, and it resulted in a very pleasant time for the musicians, which I'm sure was communicated to our listening audiences—they had to feel the fun this band had playing together. We played St. Louis, Decatur, Minneapolis, Cincinnati, and Charleston (W.V.). A radio station in Minneapolis made a tape of the group, and I hope, because of the musical spirit involved, a record will eventually be produced from it.

December was notable for the fact that I made my first appearance at the Manassas Jazz Festival in Virginia. This event is promoted by jazz enthusiast Johnson McCree, better known to his friends as "Fat Cat." It is a happy affair, presenting music in the traditional jazz styles. I had the pleasure of working again with two fine trumpeters and very special friends, Billy Butterfield and Connie Jones. The month then settled into the pattern of recent years and I was back again at Michael's Pub with the Perfect Jazz Repertory Quintet—this time with a program designed by Dick Hyman as a musical salute to the great Irving Berlin.

EPILOGUE

ONE DAY MY PHONE RANG, and when I picked it up a familiar voice said, "I've got a problem."

"Who hasn't?" I replied in the same conversational tone. "What makes you any different?"

"Well, my problem's different, that's why. I've got two guys who are after me about material for an article in the *International Musician* and for a book. I can't bring myself to say no to either one of 'em. What should I do?"

"That's easy. If one of the guys is me, say yes."

"It's not that easy. If I say yes to you, what do I tell the other guy? I don't want to turn him down either. So here's what I'm going to do—take your pick. Which do you want to do, the article or the book?"

"You mean I have a choice?"

"Yeah. Somebody has to break this thing, so it might as well be you. If you decide to write the book—which doesn't speak very highly for your intelligence because I can't imagine anybody wanting to read a book about me—then I'll tell my other friend he can do the article."

"Fair enough. Tell him to go ahead."

"In other words, you're going to write the book."

"That's right."

"Have you any idea what you're in for?"

"No, do you?"

"I think I have a better idea than you do about it. Don't say I didn't warn you."

And so it all started. I was delighted that Pee Wee had given me the option to make a choice because I was already familiar, in a general way, with his fabulous career, and I was firmly convinced it was a story that belonged in the archives of American music as an integral part of our heritage.

384

In the beginning, we tried to work by means of cassette recordings. Whenever he had the opportunity, Pee Wee talked into a recorder and mailed me cassettes—two or three at a time. Then I would carefully transcribe what he said. But as time went by, a number of disadvantages about this method became clear. For one thing, unless Pee Wee remembered to spell out a proper name, I was left with no option except to spell it the way I heard it—in most cases, of course, incorrectly. For another, transcribing the tapes was not only tedious but very time-consuming. But the main problem was one of continuity. As most people do in the course of conversation, Pee Wee often wandered away from the main trend of thought, punctuating his narrative with long parenthetical asides and sometimes forgetting to get back to the point. Or quite often a whole new train of thought would emerge, as interesting as the first but better suited to be included somewhere else in the narrative.

Of course, none of these things were taken too seriously because Pee Wee and I had agreed that the first step was a long way from the final one. As I told him often, the first draft was like assembling a skeleton that we had to put together before we could add the meat to the bones. On his part, Pee Wee kept insisting that he was just attempting to put the events of his life into chronological order. He was sure that once this had been done, his memory would be prompted into supplying a wealth of additional details.

Nevertheless, the cassette system was discarded as too cumbersome. Pee Wee began sending me material he had jotted down in longhand, and this immediately proved more practical. Aside from giving him all the time he needed to think about what he wanted to say, it also enabled me to do some editing beforehand, thus eliminating a lot of repetition and at the same time making it easier to spot omissions and contradictions. It also proved to be a big help in the spelling of proper names, and I soon found that Pee Wee was very reliable in this regard. He had a remarkable memory for such details, but if there was any doubt, he didn't hesitate to take the time to check with an authoritative source.

Early on in our work, I was very impressed by Pee Wee's amazing gift for recall—not only for proper names and places, but for people and events—so that even when he was remembering his very early years he did it with the sharpness and authenticity of someone describing a recent happening. He and I were not so far apart in age that I couldn't appreciate this gift.

In the meantime, weeks would go by and our only contact would be an occasional telephone call or a new batch of scribbled notebook pages in the mail. Sometimes his international bookings tied him up for weeks, even months, and then our project would practically come to a halt. He seldom found time to work at his notes on the road. Thus, while we were still at the cassette stage, he toured South Africa and took along a batch of blank cassettes. He anticipated having a lot of time on his hands and a fine opportunity to get some work done. As he put it, "What else is there to do in South Africa?"

As it turned out (and you will read for yourself), South Africa kept him just as busy as any other place, and when he reached his next stop, Nice, France, he sent me a card which read:

"First off you're going to shoot me, because I've used up all my tapes recording various bands—good and bad—from Capetown to Nice. I hate to admit it to my fuddled brain, but I've been so damn excited and carried away by the various activities that I haven't done a single thing constructive toward our venture. I had a wonderful time in South Africa. It's beyond doubt one of the most beautiful countries on earth and so much of the scenery is breath-taking . . . ."

So, the book progressed by fits and starts. Because my own schedule didn't permit me to devote all my time to working on the manuscript, I had to burn a lot of midnight oil and practically all my available free time was spent at the typewriter. Even when the opportunity presented itself to combine a two-week vacation with a visit to my son Allan's house in San Antonio and a week's engagement with Jim Cullum's Happy Jazz Band at The Landing, I took along the necessary writing materials, set up office in the garage, and worked every day.

We did make progress and on the occasions when Pee Wee and I would grace the same bandstand, he'd usually start things off by apologizing for not doing his "homework," and promising to do better, even though I never criticized him too seriously telling him many times that such a big project was bound to take a long time. His intentions were always good. Once, on a tour of Europe, he took along a notebook, explaining he expected to be able to jot down random thoughts during dull hours in hotel rooms. Needless to say, the "dull hours" never materialized, because Pee Wee was lionized everywhere he went. He was lucky to find enough time for the selfish purpose of sleeping.

Still, in spite of everything, we persevered and the book progressed. I mailed off sections of the manuscript to Pee Wee from time to time, as I completed them, and eventually they would come back with corrections— and so many additions that he devised a system of coding them for insertion in the proper places. Sometimes the additions added up to more than the original manuscript.

I was into rewriting long before Pee Wee got around to writing his notes for the later chapters, and one day he called me to say a few words that were very gratifying, though offered in the usual offhand Erwin manner.

"I haven't had a chance to read this mess we're working on, but Caroline looked over some of the new copy you sent, and she's revised her opinion."

"That so? What was her first opinion? I don't recall ever hearing about it. And how did she revise it?"

"Well, she glanced over some of the stuff I was writing for you, and she told me my writing style had all the excitement and suspense of a composition by a tenth-grade pupil. At least she rated me in high school, though, which isn't too bad, I guess."

386

"And now?"

"Well, now she seems to think it's pretty good. She even went so far as to say she liked it."

"Well, I'm very glad she does. That's quite a compliment, I gather."

"You know it is."

Toward the latter part of 1980, Pee Wee's doctors finally convinced him that another operation was needed to alleviate a problem he described as "a clog in my rusty plumbing." A year earlier, he had undergone surgery for a urinary difficulty and for awhile everything seemed to be working out well, but then he developed abdominal pain and the decision eventually was made, after a variety of medicines had failed—that only another operation would clear up the problem. From all indications, it would be major surgery.

Pee Wee talked about it freely, in the same wryly humorous way in which he approached everything, and he refused to admit to any misgivings.

"This doctor of mine is the best there is. He tells me the operation is a tough one and I'll be a long time recuperating from it, but he also says it should straighten out whatever the hell is wrong with my plumbing. He also says I can rest easy on one point—there's no cancer involved."

"That's good to hear."

"Yeah. But it wouldn't be me if other complications didn't enter the matter. Because of my damned emphysema they're worried if I can take being completely anesthetized."

"Come again?"

"Well, the last time they gave me a local anesthetic, I was awake the whole time during the operation. I even watched them in a mirror."

"Yuk!" I commented.

"No 'yuk.' It was very interesting. I didn't feel a thing, and it was like watching them work on somebody else. But this time a local won't be enough. They'll have to put me completely under, and with my lungs they're afraid I might stop breathing altogether."

"Hells bells!" I gasped. "What can they do about it?"

"I dunno—yet. They're going to give me some tests to see what my chances are. My breathing is pretty good lately, so I'll be all right, I think. Anyway, there's a good part to all this."

"I hope so. So far you've done a good job of hiding it, whatever it is."

"Well, first of all, I'm told the operation should correct whatever's making my life miserable down below. But aside from that, I won't be able to blow a horn for a long time afterwards, probably not until April, so I'm going to have a lot of time to work on the book with you. Maybe, with some reasonable luck, we might even get to finish the damn thing."

Then, as an afterthought, he added something I didn't like. "One thing is sure. We better hurry up and get it done while I'm still around."

At the time, and every time later on when he made similar remarks, I refused to take him seriously. We had long discussions on aging, physical and mental health, and a myriad of subjects that had nothing to do with the book. But now, in the light of later events, I can't help but wonder if Pee Wee had a premonition that his days were numbered. If so, other than such rare comments dropped offhandedly into a conversation, he managed to hide it very well. As serious as the operation was (with some anxious moments for everybody concerned) he seemed to come out of it in good shape, with none of his zest for life and living even slightly diminished. True to his promise, he started sending me material for the book at a great rate, and almost every day we were on the phone.

"The operation was supposed to take care of my pain," he would growl, "but I feel just as lousy as ever."

"Well, I'm no doctor, but it seems to me that after a major operation like yours, this is only normal."

"Normal! What's normal about feeling miserable?"

"Well, let me ask you something. If a few weeks ago the doctors had cut off one of your legs, or sliced away a piece of your hide, would you expect to be all healed by now and operating as though nothing had happened?"

"I guess not," he grudgingly admitted, "but . . . ."

"No 'buts,'" I cut in. "Just because they did their carving where you can't see it doesn't mean it's any the less difficult for your body to get over it. You have to give yourself time to heal."

"I suppose so. But I still feel lousy."

"You'll feel better as time goes on. Just be glad the operation is behind you."

And he did feel better—or pretended to, at the same time admitting to a nagging pain that refused to leave. As the winter months dragged by, he began to speak more frequently of getting back to work, with growing impatience. His voice had a familiar urgency—the same inflection I'd heard in voices of GIs anticipating the day they would be discharged. He also began talking about the advance bookings he had accepted. From what he was telling me, he intended to hop aboard the old merry-go-round with both feet and without waiting for it to stop or even slow down. I tried to inject a word of caution.

"Are you sure you're going to be up to all this? You're reeling off a schedule that would make a strong man blanch."

"I will be when the time comes," he said confidently. "My doctor says I can begin to practice around the first of April. So don't worry. I'll be in good shape for our trip to Breda."

"I'm not worried about Breda," I told him, "because there's still a lot of time before the last week in May, and if you pace yourself you should be feeling pretty good by then. It's all that other stuff you have lined up beforehand. Can't you cancel any of it?"

"How can I?" he demanded. "I've had some of these dates booked every year for years. People are expecting me, and I can't disappoint them."

I didn't argue the point. The training ingrained in Pee Wee by a lifetime of meeting commitments was not to be denied. As long as he could stand up, he would fulfill his obligations. And at least there was hope that one of his jaunts would prove beneficial: He was booked to play a jazz festival in

Hawaii and was able to take Caroline with him. They both needed the change and the rest, and they would be getting plenty of sun and fresh air.

They came back just in time for Pee Wee to play at a concert on May 24 for the New Jersey Jazz Society at the Watchung View Inn in Pluckemin, and I was delighted to see him climbing on the bandstand looking sun-tanned and healthy, wearing the old familiar grin. If the operation had slowed him down in any way, it hadn't taken away any of his fire on the horn. As always, he gave it a 100 percent effort.

Originally, it had been Pee Wee's intention to play this concert with the same group that was slated to play for the Breda Jazz Festival in the Netherlands, from May 28 to 31, but prior commitments on the part of some of the men had made this impossible, and only three of us—Pee Wee, pianist Jimmy Andrews, and I—were also in the Breda band. Kenny Davern was on tour in Europe and would meet us in Breda; Ed Hubble was living in Ontario Canada, and would fly to Holland from there; and Johnny Blowers was playing another job. On the other hand, inasmuch as pickup jazz groups are more the rule than the exception on today's music scene, there was nothing unusual about all this, and we had a good band at Watchung. Harry DeVito, a veteran of Pee Wee's band at Nick's, filled in for Hubble on trombone, and Walt Levinsky, Artie Shaw's choice to play his parts on the recorded recreation of the famous 1938 band, was on clarinet. Sonny Igoe was in Johnny's place on drums. We had a star group and nothing to worry about.

But when I got the chance to talk to the tanned and fit-looking Pee Wee in private and asked how he was feeling, he shook his head glumly. "Tired. Damned tired! I'm still trying to recover from ten hours of jet lag."

"Aside from that," I insisted.

He met my gaze with no hint of his usual evasiveness. "Lousy."

"Uh-huh. Well, I hope you're going home tonight to get some rest."

"Not much," he grunted. "I have to make that plane for Sarasota."

"Sarasota? What's going on in Sarasota?"

"That new jazz festival. I told you about it, didn't I? As a matter of fact, Warren is there already and I'll be playing with him. I promised the guy who's running the thing that I'd show up for one night anyway, even if I couldn't make the whole thing."

"Well, I'm glad Warren's there. Let him do most of the work. You take it easy."

"I intend to," he assured me. "I'm gonna lean on that kid all night."

I recognized this as smoke, too. Pee Wee Erwin never leaned on anybody—not even Warren, although I sometimes wondered if Pee Wee wasn't more of a father to my son in some ways than I was. He had been a prime factor in Warren's development on the horn, and they had great mutual respect and affection.

On the morning of May 27, I got to Kennedy at what I considered a reasonably early time, fully expecting to find other members of the band already there. Nobody was, so I checked in at the gate and sat down in the waiting room at a spot where I could watch the passengers as they arrived.

After a half hour or so Pee Wee showed up and checked in at the desk. He was towing a folding baggage carrier with one little floppy bag on it, not even a suitcase.

He spotted me and came over to sit in the nearest vacant seat, a few removed from mine, and said without preamble, "Women are funny, you know it?"

I nodded. "So I've heard. What's funny about 'em now?"

He laughed wryly. "I got home late last night from Sarasota, and when I walked in the house Caroline took one look at me and said, 'That's it!'"

"That's what?"

"Meaning she didn't want me to make this trip. She wanted me to cancel out, stay home and rest. Women just don't understand. You can't do things like that. You just can't decide at the last minute you're not going to do something. An agreement is an agreement."

"Uh-huh. But how do you feel?"

He shook his head and admitted, "I'm tired. It's been a rough week. Do you think we'll be able to get some sleep over there? Do you know what time we're supposed to go on?"

I reached for the papers in my inside pocket. "We arrive in Amsterdam at 8:05 a.m. their time, and we're not scheduled to go on until 9 p.m. So we should have plenty of time to settle in and rest up."

He looked relieved, and then I felt obligated to tell him about Jimmy. Jimmy's wife Elena had driven me to the airport. The original idea had merely been that I would hitch a ride with Jimmy, because Elena would be free to drive him to the airport whereas I had been unable to scare up any volunteers. Instead, Elena reported distractedly that Jimmy had worked his steady job at Eddie Condon's in New York but had never gotten home. When she checked to find out if anybody knew where he was, they told her he was last seen getting into his car to drive home. Further attempts to find out more, with both Elena and I making frantic phone calls to the police and hospitals, as well as to mutual friends, resulted in absolutely no word as to Jimmy's whereabouts. On the drive to the airport, Elena was so upset that I drove, both of us hoping without much conviction that Jimmy would either be at the airport already or would call home and report in. Immediately on our arrival Elena went to the phone to call her son and find out if Jimmy had been heard from.

I was just getting my luggage organized on the sidewalk when she reappeared, and I knew without being told that Jimmy was still unaccounted for. "Warren," she said, all in a rush, "excuse me for not waiting with you. I want to get back home in case somebody calls—in case they heard something. Do you mind?"

I told her I didn't and she gave me a distracted peck on the cheek and fled out the door.

After I had told Pee Wee, exploring all the empty theories and possibilities in the process, he looked at me fatalistically and shrugged.

"So the worst thing that can happen is he misses the plane, isn't it? I don't think any harm has come to him, in spite of all the excitement. And piano players will be a dime a dozen in Breda, I imagine, so it shouldn't be too difficult to get one to work with us. It's too bad, but these things happen. Believe me, they happen."

"Well, I don't understand it," I grumbled. "Jimmy's been looking forward to this trip, I know he has."

Johnny Blowers, a resident of Westbury and therefore not too concerned with getting tied up in traffic on the way to Kennedy—an ever present worry to those of us from New Jersey—showed up, bubbling with enthusiasm as usual but quickly upset when I told him about Jimmy. "Goodness gracious!" he commented. "That's terrible. I wonder what happened to him."

The conversation went on to exhaust all theories and possibilities while we all kept an urgent lookout for Jimmy, but when our plane began loading, he still hadn't put in an appearance. We were all feeling pretty glum about it.

I had managed to reserve seats for Pee Wee and me in the only section of the plane where two seats were in the row, and since I preferred the window and Pee Wee liked the aisle, we were perfectly accommodated. Johnny was in the aisle seat in front of us. I sat down and busied myself stowing the box of records I was hand-carrying to a dealer in Breda, working it under the seat in front of me, when I overheard Pee Wee talking to somebody. When I looked up, it was to see Jimmy Andrews standing there, smiling and casually tapping a cigaret on his thumbnail.

"I just wanted you guys to know I made the plane," he said easily. "But I changed my seat to the smoking section."

He explained that his car had conked out on the way home from Condon's, and since it was early in the morning and no place was open where he could get help, he went to sleep in the car and overslept. By the time he got home, we had already left for the airport so he had his son drive him over.

From there on, all went well. We were met at the Amsterdam airport by a smiling couple representing the Festival and then ferried by a Volkswagen minibus to a very nice hotel, the Mastbosch, in Breda, where we were assigned big, comfortable rooms. Pee Wee wasted no time in taking advantage of the huge bed, informing me of his intention of getting some rest and requesting that I wake him in time for our first appearance that evening.

I was happy to see that he seemed fairly well rested when we assembled in the marvelous auditorium called the Congreszaal, in the huge entertainment facility named the "Turfschip," designed to house several simultaneous events, and, as though to prove it, he turned in a performance that was well up to anything he had ever done. I'm sure that nobody in the audience was aware he wasn't feeling up to par. This held true for our two other appearances—one a little later that same evening in the Turfschip, and the final one the next day in a downtown location. This was all that was required of us, although the Festival would continue for another two days, and we would remain in Breda five more days until June 2 because we had taken advantage of the excursion rates for our plane tickets.

However, we were invited to the formal reception held at the Town Hall on May 30, and after the welcoming speeches were made, Pee Wee was called to the podium so the assemblage could sing "Happy Birthday" to him. He made a gracious little acceptance speech for the bottle of champagne they gave him, thanked everybody for their good wishes, and walked off with the bottle tucked into the crook of his right arm.

Outside he told me, "Well, I wasn't going to come to this thing, but I'm glad I did. I decided it was the proper thing to do. They're very nice people. But what am I gonna do with this?"

He held out the bottle, and I had to laugh at the look on his face. To a reformed alcoholic like Pee Wee, it was a bottle of poison.

"Take it home. What else? Somebody will enjoy it."

Jimmy Andrews, Johnny Blowers and I had flown over with Pee Wee, and Jimmy and I would be returning with him, Kenny Davern had already left on the next leg of his tour which would take him to London; Ed Hubble had decided to take an early plane back to Canada, and Johnny would follow Kenny to London, also making an appearance at the Pizza Express, although he wasn't due to leave until our last day and would actually accompany us to Amsterdam airport.

After the reception at the Town Hall, Pee Wee admitted to being tired and said he wanted to return to the hotel. The rest of us stayed in town to take in the local scenery, but when we got back I checked in on Pee Wee and he

The "Giants of Jazz" in Breda Holland. Jim Andrews, pno; Warren Vache' Sr., bass; Kenny Davern, clnt; Johnny Blowers, drums; Pee Wee, and Ed Hubble, trb.

Photo courtesy of Rene de Pater

392

seemed considerably perked up. He said he was quite surprised and gratified that room service at the hotel was able to supply him with the kind of foods he was able to eat on his very limited diet, and the quantities were more than generous. In particular he was happy they had cornflakes, lots of fresh milk, and plenty of fruit. Then he said that he wanted me to wake him the next day in time for him to go with us to take in the final day of the Festival.

So he was with us the next morning, a delightfully pleasant Sunday, when we rode into town again and established ourselves in comfortable chairs in the town square, the "Grote Markt," for the last day of the Festival. We sat around listening to the music, and it was very enjoyable. Jimmy and John were already experts on the merits of good Dutch beer, and at one point Pee Wee went off in search of a milkshake, which he found at the local McDonald's. He looked and acted reasonably well, but he had developed a terrible cough—a dry hack that sometimes lasted a full minute and left him looking haggard and breathless. Once he dozed off in the warm sun, and I was glad to see him getting the rest.

The crowd increased considerably as the afternoon progressed and as the time approached for Doc Cheatham and Franz Jackson to make their appearance on the elevated stage at the end of the square, seating became the rarest commodity. Several times our chairs were almost whisked away under our noses. All we had to do was stand up or leave on a short errand. Nevertheless, it was a beautiful day and Pee Wee seemed to enjoy it.

After the Festival was officially over he spent the remaining days in his room, calling room service for his food orders and staying in bed. He told me he had everything he needed, including a plentiful supply of the medicines the doctor had prescribed for him. But now he admitted that he could no longer keep anything in his stomach, wasn't sleeping much, and felt terrible all the time. While he was talking to me, he coughed constantly. He was obviously a very sick man, but when I suggested seeing a local doctor he shook his head.

"It won't do any good. What could he do, prescribe more pills on top of all those I already have? No, I'll wait until we get home and I can see my own doctor."

On the day we were to leave for the airport he was up and ready in plenty of time, but unusually quiet and on the ride to Amsterdam he sat in front next to the driver and was silent during the entire 60-mile trip. On the plane he dozed most of the time, or seemed too, keeping his head down and his eyes closed, and when we arrived at Kennedy he wasted no time in getting off the plane and lining up to go through customs. I was right behind him so we had the chance to say a few words, and once more I asked how he was feeling.

"Rotten," he answered promptly, and with none of the wry lilt in his voice that always typified his manner. "I can't wait to get home and into bed. Caroline is supposed to meet me, and I hope she isn't late. Then I suppose the first thing I'll have to do tomorrow is see the doctor."

I said the usual things and asked him to keep in touch, feeling the helplessness everyone experiences in such situations, and he said good-bye the instant the customs man handed him back his passport. I watched him move with surprising speed through the gate and into the crowd, towing his little folding cart behind him.

I called Caroline later to find out how he was, and she told me he had an appointment with the doctor in the morning. The doctor diagnosed his cough as pneumonia and made arrangements for Pee Wee to be admitted to the hospital. Word came that the pneumonia was cured, but there were other complications. Pee Wee was very weak and barely conscious. Caroline said that he hardly recognized her. Another operation seemed inevitable, and in view of his condition, combined with his emphysema, it was doubly dangerous.

Finally, the agonizing news. Pee Wee had terminal cancer. His body was riddled with it. Now it was only a matter of time.

Pee Wee Erwin died on Saturday, June 20, 1981.

Much has been written to eulogize him—all of it deserved and all of it well-intentioned—but only in this book is the story told with the clear perception with which Pee Wee Erwin viewed his world and the people in it. It will remain a lasting tribute to the man, and to the remarkable time in which he lived.

It was a great privilege to be part of it.

Warren Vache'
Rahway, N.J.
1981

PEE WEE ERWIN:
A SELECTIVE
DISCOGRAPHY

By Warren W. Vaché
assisted by Dan Morgenstern

Why a "selective" discography? Why not a "comprehensive" discography, if not a "complete" or "definitive" one?

The best answer to this very reasonable question is the one Pee Wee gave me. I was willing to undertake the momentous job if he would be my guide. But he wasn't very encouraging. "I'd hate to push that job on you, and I'm not so sure I'd want to get involved myself, because I simply can't remember all the records I've played on. And I can tell you this: a lot of the present discographies are wrong."

So the project was postponed indefinitely, with the ultimate result that we never got around to it as a team. That is, we never got further than correcting some of the mistakes in the published Joe Haymes and Isham Jones discographies, and such tidbits as a casual mention by Pee Wee that he is the soloist on Raymond Scott's "Just A Gigolo" (Columbia 35363), plus an off-hand present of the 78 that resulted from his association with Joel Herron (Avalon 7220), one of the earliest experiments in high fidelity recording. Pee Wee described the result as "my first experience with underwater music." I gather he meant the echo-chamber effect so frequently used later on.

There is little likelihood that anyone will ever accurately trace the many sides Pee Wee made for Brunswick with various studio groups, or all of those he made with Freddy Martin when Martin's was the house band at Brunswick and ARC. Martin's insistence on muted trumpets complicates identification on the basis of tone. Nor is anyone likely to sort out all the studio sessions for Enoch Light's various labels in which Pee Wee participated during the LP era, many of them only marginally related to jazz, if at all.

Yet there is a wealth of recorded material listed here, and it offers Pee Wee in a wide variety of musical settings. We hear him as a brash, talented youngster with the great Joe Haymes Band of the early 30's, displaying the stamina and iron lip developed from his years with road bands. We can follow him up the ladder as he went from one name band to the other — Isham Jones, Ray Noble, Benny Goodman, Tommy Dorsey. And after the Second World War, we have more than adequate representation of his years at Nick's

395

leading a small jazz band, his many known sessions for Enoch Light (including the famous "Jeb Dooley" albums), and as featured soloist on the Jackie Gleason LPs for Capitol. We also have Pee Wee's word that he was part of the Merle Evans Circus Band that recorded "Music From the Big Top" for the Everest Tradition series.

Altogether, these records add up to an impressive legacy, and at the same time offer solid evidence of Pee Wee's versatility. We may never have a "complete" Pee Wee Erwin discography, but there are many hours of listening pleasure to be had from the list that follows. —WWV

Note: The sources consulted in the compilation of this discography include the standard works (Brian Rust's Jazz Records: 1897-1942; *5th ed.; Jorgen G. Jepsen's* Jazz Records: 1942-1962/69; *and Walter Bruyninckx's* 60 Years of Recorded Jazz, 1917-1977, *plus various specialized discographies, among them D. Russell Connor and Warren W. Hick's* BG On the Record *(soon to be published in fully revised and greatly enlarged form by Scarecrow Press). In addition, the archives of the Institute of Jazz Studies yielded considerable information on records not listed in any discographies.*

JOE HAYMES

This band, with which Pee Wee made his recording debut, recorded extensively for Victor (including its sub-labels Elektradisc, Sunrise and Bluebird) as well as Columbia and the ARC labels while Pee Wee was in its ranks. The two-record set listed below, with liner notes by Warren Vache' Sr., includes four titles from Pee Wee's first session and is an excellent showcase for the talents of this young band and its gifted leader-arranger. The last two tracks are without Pee Wee. The personnel, listed collectively, remained fairly stable. Drummer Jimmy Underwood died in July 1932 and was replaced by John Riley Scott.

Joe Haymes and his Orchestra: 1932-35   Bluebird AXM2-5552
PWE, Roy Wager (t); Les Jenkins (later Ward Silloway) (tb); Mike Doty (cl, as, vo); Johnny Mince (cl, as); Dick Clark (ts); John Langsford (bar, vn); Paul Mitchell (p); Larry Murphy (p, vo); Carl Snyder, Chris Fletcher (g); Stan Fletcher (bb, sb); Jimmy Underwood, John Riley Scott (d, vo); Haymes (arr, vo).
Old Fashioned Love / He's the Life of the Party / Pray For the Lights to Go Out / Let's Have A Party / It's About Time / Ev'ry Little Bit of Me / When I Put On My Long White Robe / If It Ain't Love / Hummin' to Myself / Lullabye of the Leaves / Is I In Love I Is / Am I Wasting My Time / There's Oceans of Love by the Beautiful Sea / Can't Do Without His Love / Get Cannibal / Here's A Little Package / The Yes Habit / Little Nell / I Would Do Anything For You / Toll / Hot Jazz Pie / He's A Curbstone Cutie / Limehouse Blues / Shine On Harvest Moon / I Never Knew I Could Love Anybody / Modern Melody / Just Give Me the Girl / Ain't Gonna Grieve No More / Lenox Avenue / Can This Be the End of Love / The Lady In Red / Honeysuckle Rose.

Joe Haymes and his Orchestra   IAJRC 46
Despite the personnel listings on this album, only five of the performances include Pee Wee in the personnel; these are all from Columbia masters: **When I Put On My Long White Robe / Let's Have A Party / The Old Man of the Mountain / Uncle Joe's Music Store / Gotta Go.** The arrangements are similar to the Victor recordings, but the solos are different.

ISHAM JONES

Pee Wee states that he joined this fine band in March of 1934, replacing George Thow (who'd left to become a member of the newly organized Dorsey Brothers' Orchestra) on second trumpet, making his first recording date with Jones on May 10. He was with the band for the summer season of 1934 in Atlantic City. When the band returned to New York City, Jones changed his recording affiliation from Victor to the new Decca label, for which he re-recorded a substantial portion of his library on August 31 and September 4. Aural evidence confirms that Pee Wee was present for these dates. He specifically stated that the other members of the trumpet section during his Jones tenure were Johnny Carlson (lead) and Clarence Willard, and offered other corrections to the personnels given in most discographical sources. The LP listed below contains six titles from Jones' last two Victor dates, on which Pee Wee is present. He takes a notable solo on **The Blue Room.**

The Great Isham Jones and his Orchestra   **RCA Vintage LPV-504**
Johnny Carlson, PWE, Clarence Willard (tp); Red Ballard, Sonny Lee (tb); Milt Yaner, Victor Hauprich (cl, as); Saxie Mansfield, John Langsford (cl, ts); Eddie Stone, Joe Martin, Nick Hupfer (vn); James "Jiggs" Noble (p, arr); George Wartner (g); Walt Yoder (sb); Wally Lageson (d); Joe Bishop, Gordon Jenkins (arr). Jones played tenor sax, but probably not on these recordings.
China Boy / Dallas Blues / Ridin' Around In the Rain (5/10/34); **For All We Know / The Blue Room / Georgia Jubilee** (7/16/34). (Tracks without PWE not listed.)

The Jones Deccas have yet to be issued on LP. Of those 78s available for auditioning by the compilers, the following contain trumpet solos that sound like PWE; the arrangements differ from those used for the same titles on Victor — for example, the solo on **Blue Room** is much shorter.
August 31, 1934:

38469	**Blue Room**	**Decca 493**
38499	**Tiger Rag**	**Decca 262**
38502-A	**Dallas Blues**	**Decca 569**

September 4, 1934:

38523-A	**When You Climb Those Golden Stairs**	**Decca 220**
38525-A	**Rock Your Blues Away**	**Decca 662**

There may well be other PWE solos from these two sessions, which yielded a total of 25 issued sides. The muted trumpet on **Blue Lament** (Decca 569) is probably Carlson.

BENNY GOODMAN

We depart from strict chronology to list all of PWE's recorded work with Goodman in one segment. He was playing with Freddy Martin's band at the St. Regis Hotel when Goodman approached him about joining him on the "Let's Dance" radio program. PWE is present on Goodman's last three dates for Columbia and the first two Victor sessions by the band, as well as on the famous NBC Thesaurus transcription date and a number of airchecks from this period, for which precise personnels are problematic. The studio recordings have been issued in many and varied LP formats; those listed here are the most comprehensive and available as of this writing.

Benny Goodman and his Orchestra, 1934-35:
The Early Years   **Sunbeam 140**
PWE, Jerry Neary, Art Sylvester(?) (tp); Red Ballard, Jack Lacey (tb); Goodman (cl); Toots Mondello, Hymie Schertzer (as); Art Rollini, unknown (ts); Frank Froeba (p); George Van Eps (g); Harry Goodman (sb); Sammy Weiss (d): (11/26/34). Ralph Muzillo (tp) replaces Sylvester; Dick Clark (ts) replaces the unknown; Gene Krupa (d) replaces Weiss: (1/15/35 and

2/19/35). The vocalists are Helen Ward, Buddy Clark and Ray Hendricks.
I'm A Hundred Percent For You (HW) / Cokey / Like A Bolt From the Blue
(BC) / Music Hall Rag (11/26/34) / The Dixieland Band (HW) / Blue Moon
(HW) / Throwin' Stones at the Sun (HW) / Down Home Rag (1/15/35) /
Singing A Happy Song (HW) / Clouds (RH) / I Was Lucky (HW) / Night
Wind (HW) (2/19/35).
The Let's Dance Broadcasts, 1934-35: Benny Goodman and his Orchestra,
Vol. 1 (Sunbeam 100) and Vol. 2 (Sunbeam 104), and B.G. On The Air!
(Sunbeam 105) contain a number of performances with PWE in the band.
  Goodman's entire output for RCA Victor is contained in the double-LP
series on Bluebird, The Complete Benny Goodman. Those including PWE
are listed below:

The Complete Benny Goodman, Vol. 1: 1935.   Bluebird AXM2-5506
*Personnel as for 2/19/35: (4/4/35). Nate Kazebier (tp) replaces Muzillo; Jack
Teagarden (tb) replaces Ballard; Allan Reuss (g) replaces Van Eps: (4/19/35).
Vocalists are Ward and Clark.*
Hunkadola / I'm Livin' in A Great Big Way (BC) (two takes) / Hooray For
Love (HW) (two takes) / The Dixieland Band (HW) (4/4/35) / Japanese
Sandman / You're A Heavenly Thing (HW) / Restless (HW) / Always
(4/19/35). (Other tracks without PWE.)
  In early 1936, Pee Wee rejoined Goodman at the Congress Hotel in
Chicago. Though opinions differ, we agree with Pee Wee that he was present
for the 1/24/36 Victor session, remaining through the session of 8/21/36, as
below:

The Complete Benny Goodman, Vol. 2: 1936   Bluebird AXM2-5515
*Personnel as before, except Harry Geller (tp) replaces Neary; Red Ballard and
Joe Harris replace Teagarden and Lacey; Bill De Pew (as) replaces Mondello,
and Jess Stacy (p) replaces Froeba (1/24, 3/20 & 4/23/36); Chris Griffin (tp)
replaces Geller and Murray McEachern (tb) replaces Harris (5/27, 5/15 &
5/16/36). Helen Ward is still the vocalist.*
It's Been So Long (HW) / Stompin' At the Savoy / Goody-Goody (HW) /
Breakin' In A Pair of Shoes (1/24/36) / Get Happy / Christopher Columbus
/ I Know That You Know (3/20/36) / Star Dust / You Can't Pull the Wool
Over My Eyes (HW) / The Glory of Love (HW) / Remember / Walk, Jennie
Walk (4/23/36) / House Hop / Sing Me A Swing Song (HW) / I Would Do
Anything For You (5/27/36) / In A Sentimental Mood / I've Found A New
Baby / Swing Time In the Rockies / These Foolish Things (HW) (6/15/36) /
House Hop / There's A Small Hotel (HW) (6/16/36).

The Complete Benny Goodman, Vol. 3: 1936   Bluebird AXM2-5532
*Personnel as last above, except Manny Klein (tp) replaces Kazebier
(8/13/36); Sterling Bose (tp) replaces Klein, and Vido Musso (ts) replaces
Clark (8/21/36).*
You Turned the Tables On Me (HW) / Here's Love In Your Eye / Pick
Yourself Up / Down South Camp Meeting (8/13/36) / St. Louis Blues / Love

Me Or Leave Me / Bugle Call Rag (8/21/36). (The remaining tracks on this LP are without PWE.)

During his final months with BG, Pee Wee participated in the filming of "The Big Broadcast Of 1937." The soundtrack performance of **Bugle Call Rag** from this picture has been issued on **Extreme Rarities EX 1002.**

We now backtrack slightly for what is perhaps Pee Wee's most famous recording date with BG, and certainly the longest studio session in jazz history. This is the 6/6/35 date for NBC's Thesaurus electrical transcription service, 16-inch ETs distributed on a lease basis to radio stations. The policy for such ETs was that the bands were pseudonymous; these recordings were issued variously as by "Rhythm Makers Orchestra" and "The Rhythm Makers." Fifty-one selections were cut between the hours of 9:30 a.m. and 5:30 p.m., with a one-hour lunch break at 1:15. The sidemen were paid $1 per tune, and there were no second takes. For many years, Pee Wee's solos on this session were credited to Bunny Berigan. There have been various LP issues of this material, but the complete session can be found on the three LPs listed below:

Thesaurus: Rhythm Makers Orchestra featuring
Benny Goodman, Vols. 1, 2 and 3   **Sunbeam 101, 102, 103**
(Personnel is as for Goodman's 4/19/35 session, except that Red Ballard (tb) replaces Teagarden.)
Vol. 1: Makin' Whoopie / Poor Butterfly / Ballade In Blue / Beautiful Changes / I Would Do Anything For You / Medley: Sophisticated Lady and Mood Indigo / I Can't Give You Anything But Love / Yes, We Have No Bananas / Rose Room / I Never Knew / Love Dropped In For Tea / Farewell Blues / Pardon My Love / I Was Lucky / If I Could Be With You / Darktown Strutters Ball.
Vol. 2: St. Louis Blues / Indiana / I Surrender Dear / Bugle Call Rag / Can't We Be Friends? / Life Is a Song / Sweet Little You / Between the Devil and the Deep Blue Sea / Royal Garden Blues / Sweet and Lovely / Three Little Words / Sugar Foot Stomp / When We're Alone / There Must Have Been a Devil In the Moon / Jingle Bells / Restless.
Vol. 3: Sometimes I'm Happy / Wrappin' It Up / Rosetta / You Can Depend On Me / Anything Goes / I Get a Kick Out Of You / King Porter Stomp / Digga Digga Doo / Down By the River / Every Little Moment / Star Dust / Dear Old Southland / Ding Dong Daddy From Dumas / Lovely To Look At / She's a Latin From Manhattan / I Know That You Know / Stompin' At The Savoy / Down South Camp Meetin'.
Finally, several tracks from Pee Wee's 1936 period with BG are included on **A Jam Session with Benny Goodman, (Sunbeam 149)**, an album of airchecks. We now resume the chronology:

HENRY 'RED" ALLEN

Among Pee Wee's many "house band" dates for the ARC labels, mainly of a non-jazz nature (he may well be present on some Chick Bullock and Dick Robertson dates from this period, however), this one stands out. For some reason, Pee Wee was asked to play the opening choruses on the first three selections in the manner of Henry Busse, but he does get eight non-muted bars at the end of **Believe It, Beloved,** and is heard in the ensemble only on the last selection. All four titles have been issued on the LP listed below, but an alternate, non-vocal take of **Believe It** appears on **Epic LP LN3252** **("Trumpeter's Holiday").** This is correctly listed by Rust, though he wrongly indicates a vocal, but though Rust lists a vocal take of It's **Written All Over Your Face,** all 78 and LP issues checked by the compilers have no vocal, so this is probably a "phantom" take.

Henry "Red" Allen
and his Orchestra, 1934-1935   Collector's Classics CC13
Allen (tp, vo); PWE (tp); George Washington (tb); Buster Bailey (cl); Luis Russell (p); Danny Barker (g); Pops Foster (sb); Paul Barbarin (d). 1/23/35.
Believe It, Beloved (HA) / It's Written All Over Your Face / Smooth Sailing (HA) / Whose Honey Are You? (HA). (PWE is not present on the remaining tracks.)

RAY NOBLE
   While working with Goodman's "Let's Dance" band, Pee Wee became a charter member of the all-star band put together for the British arranger-composer Ray Noble when he settled in the U.S. The band played regularly at the Rainbow Room in Rockefeller Center and recorded for Victor. Pee Wee is present from the band's first session on 2/8/35 through the one on 2/23/35. In January, he left to rejoin Goodman. He is present on all but five tracks on the LP listed below:

Ray Noble   RCA Vintage LPV-536
Charlie Spivak, PWE (tp); Will Bradley, Glenn Miller (tb); Milt Yaner, Johnny Mince, Jim Cannon (later Mike Doty) (cl, as); Bud Freeman (ts); Nick Pisani, Fritz Prospero, Danny D'Andrea (vn); Claude Thornhill (p); George Van Eps (g); Delmar Kaplan (sb); Bill Harty (d); Al Bowlly (vo). 1935-36.
Slumming On Park Avenue / Way Down Yonder In New Orleans / Dinner For One, Please James / Top Hat / Where Am I / Dinah / Down By the River / Bugle Call Rag / Why Dream? / Where the Lazy River Goes By / Double Trouble / With All My Heart / Chinatown, My Chinatown. (PWE is not present on **Big Chief De Sota, The Touch Of Your Lips,** and **Yours Truly Is Truly Yours.**)
   Pee Wee rejoined Noble in October of 1936 and is well represented on three LPs on London Records, **The Radio Years: Ray Noble and his Orchestra, 1935-36,** (London HMG 5027), culled from airchecks and transcriptions not previously available to the public. They offer a comprehensive study of this great band from start to finish of its career and contain a number of titles not issued commercially.
   Material taken from the radio broadcasts for the Coty program (April 17, 24, and May 1, 1935) is available on **JAZZ ARCHIVES JA-22, Ray Noble**

and His American Dance Orchestra. Pee Wee is featured on two titles in particular, **Dese Dem Dose,** and **An Hour Ago This Minute,** on which he plays muted horn behind the vocal.

Just before leaving New York for Chicago, Pee Wee made a little-known small group jazz date for Decca. One of the two sides was reissued on LP, on an IAJRC album dedicated to Joe Marsala's memory; the other remains on 78 only, at this writing.

SIX BLUE CHIPS

PWE (tp); Joe Marsala (cl); Frank Signorelli (p); Carmen Mastren (g); Artie Shapiro (sb); Stan King (d). 1/17/36.

60356-A	Steel Roof	Decca 740, IAJRC 38
60357-A	Cheatin' Cheech	

TOMMY DORSEY

In terms of recording sessions, Pee Wee's two tenures with the Tommy Dorsey band date from 3/10/37 to 7/25/38, and from 2/9/39 to 6/15/39. Like Goodman, Dorsey was then under contract to Victor, and was recording even more prolifically. Thus, complete details of Pee Wee's output with Dorsey would consume far too much space. Fortunately, it is all available in "The Complete Tommy Dorsey" double-LP series on the Bluebird label, which had reached Vol. VIII when the Bluebird project was discontinued in 1982 — up to the first tune recorded on the session of 3/8/39. Late in 1986, the Bluebird label was revived, with Vol. IX of the Dorsey series scheduled for the third release, in the spring of 1987. That volume should account for Pee Wee's remaining Dorsey sessions.

During most of Pee Wee's first stint with Dorsey, the featured soloists were (in addition to the leader) Johnny Mince (clarinet), Bud Freeman (tenor sax) and Pee Wee himself, supported by an excellent rhythm section of Dick Jones (soon replaced by Howard Smith), piano; Carmen Mastren, guitar; Gene Traxler, bass, and Dave Tough, drums. These players also made up the "Clambake Seven," Dorsey's band-within-a-band. We have listed below the tracks on each album on which Pee Wee can be prominently heard in solos; significant personnel changes are also noted. Edythe Wright and Jack Leonard were the singers.

Vol. III (Bluebird AXM2-5560): Black Eyes / Blue Danube (obbligato to TD) / **Jammin'** (leads collective improvisation after vocal). Pee Wee is present only on the last nine tracks of this LP.

Vol. IV (Bluebird AXM2-5564): Beale Street Blues / That Stolen Melody / Barcarolle / Hymn To the Sun, and a number of Clambake Seven tracks, particularly **Twilight in Turkey.**

Vol. V (Bluebird AXM2-5573): Stardust On the Moon / Smoke Gets In Your Eyes / Who? and eight Clambake Seven tracks.

Vol. VI (Bluebird AXM2-5578): Little White Lies / Oh Promise Me / Shine On Harvest Moon / Yearning / Oh! How I Hate To Get Up In The Morning / Comin' Thru the Rye, and two Clambake Seven tracks. Tough plays on the first track only; he was replaced by Maurice Purtill; Artie Shapiro subs for Traxler on all but the CB 7 session, which is also Freeman's last with Dorsey; Skeets Herfurt replaced him.

Vol. VII (Bluebird AXM2-5582): Without My Walking Stick / I'll See You In My Dreams / The Sweetheart Of Sigma Chi / Symphony In Riffs, and six CB7 tracks. (Note: Lee Castle takes the trumpet solo on **Copenhagen.**)

Vol. VIII (Bluebird AXM-5586): Pee Wee is present only on the last seven tracks; he takes no solos. Dorsey's featured trumpet soloist was then Yank Lawson, and no PWE solos are likely to be included on the projected Vol. XI in the series. A possible exception is the brief and pretty muted solo on **Got No Time (Victor 26195).** Some discographies credit PWE as the arranger on Dorsey's **Blue Orchids,** but the label of Victor 26339 reads "arranged by Paul Wetstein" (i.e., Paul Weston).

In 1985, the Sunbeam label issued six LPs drawn from transcriptions of a 1936-37 series of weekly broadcasts featuring the Dorsey band, sponsored by Raleigh-Kool and starring comedian Jack Pearl. These are in excellent sound quality, and while the band performances are generally shorter than on 78s from the period, they also include much material never recorded commercially. The first two volumes feature Max Kaminsky and Bunny Berigan, Pee Wee's predecessors in the Jazz trumpet chair; he makes his first appearance on Vol. 3. As before, we list only tracks on which Pee Wee is well featured.

Tommy Dorsey and his Orchestra:
Rare Broadcast Recordings, Vol. 3 (Sunbeam 236)
Ja Da / Way Down Yonder In New Orleans
Vol. 4 (Sunbeam 237): Jammin' / You Took Advantage Of Me / I've Got Beginner's Luck / Mr. Ghost Goes To Town / Song Of India / Down South Camp Meetin' / How Could You?
Vol. 5 (Sunbeam 238): Dark Eyes / 52nd Street / Big John Special / Diga Diga Doo

Pee Wee was present on one track on the final volume in the series, but does not solo. It's interesting to hear him on **Song of India,** broadcast on 3/29/37, two months to the day after the studio recording featuring Berigan.

While with Dorsey, Pee Wee was borrowed by Glenn Miller for two Brunswick sessions on 11/29 and 12/13/37. There are no trumpet solos.

RAYMOND SCOTT

Though the discographies do not include him in the personnel, Pee Wee was present on arranger-composer Raymond Scott's first big-band date. (Prior to this, Scott had recorded with a quintet.) He can readily be identified as the soloist on the first item recorded; the other two have not been available for audition. It is our conjecture that Pee Wee replaced Gordon "Chris" Griffin, one of the three trumpeters listed by Rust and other discographers.

PWE, Mike Meola, Willis Kelly (tp); Irving Sonntag, Joe Vargas (tb); Pete Pumiglio (cl, as); Reggie Merrill (as); Art Drelinger, Dave Harris (cl, ts); Walter Gross (p); Vince Maffei (g); Lou Shoobe (sb); Johnny Williams (d).

10/18/39.

26178-A	Just A Gigolo	Columbia 35363
26179-A	Mexican Jumping Bean	Columbia 36211
26180-A-B	The Peanut Vendor	rejected
26181-A	Get Happy	Columbia 37359

This session concludes Pee Wee's first decade in the recording studios. Though he may be present on some non-jazz dates with the Johnny Green Orchestra from the early '40s, his involvement with his own band and the AFofM recording ban kept him out of the recording scene until early 1945.

Thus we move from one Scott to another:

HAZEL SCOTT

Hazel Scott (p, vo), acc. by Toots Camarata and his Orchestra: PWE, Nat Natoli, Yank Lawson, (tp); John Owens (tp, tb); Hymie Schertzer, Joe Dixon (reeds); four unknown strings; Carl Kress (g); Leonard Gaskin (sb); Johnny Blowers (d). 5/3/45.

72849	I'm Glad There Is You	Decca 23551
72850	Fascinating Rhythm	- 23429
72851	The Man I Love	- -

We've not been able to audition the first item, and there is no solo work by the accompanists on the second. But **The Man I Love** contains a beautiful five-bar interlude (between the Scott piano and vocal segments) and a brief coda by Pee Wee.

On 6/29/45, Pee Wee cut two sides for Victor with Jess Stacy's big band, strictly a studio outfit since the pianist didn't consider his own road crew good enough to record. There are no trumpet solos. Nor does Pee Wee solo on four sides cut by guitarist-arranger Brick Fleagle's big rehearsal band for the HRS label on 7/19/45. Next, Pee Wee participated in the last record date by a great name from the past:

FRANK TRUMBAUER

PWE (tp); Jack Lacey (tb); Bill Stegmeyer (cl); Trumbauer (C-melody saxophone); Dave Bowman (p); Carl Kress (g); Trigger Alpert, Bob Haggart (sb), Johnny Blowers (d). 3/25/46.

| 932 | China Boy | Capitol H328, F15857 |

Haggart omitted.
(matrix unknown)

| | Between the Devil and the Deep Blue Sea | Capitol W2138 |

Only one of the two bassists plays in the ensemble on **China Boy**, but they take a duet break and both join in on the ending. Capitol H328 is a 10-inch LP, "Sax Stylists," while W2138 is a 12-inch LP titled "The Jazz Story, Vol. 2." It was issued in 1964, but this first appearance of the Trumbauer cut seems to have gone undiscovered by discographers.

Brick Fleagle (see above) no doubt got Pee Wee involved in the next date, since he acted as a&r man for HRS:

SANDY WILLIAMS' BIG EIGHT
PWE (tp); Williams (tb); Tab Smith (as); Cecil Scott (ts, bars); Jimmy Jones (p, celeste); Brick Fleagle (g); Sid Weiss (sb); Denzil Best (d). 6/3/46.

1037	Tea For Me	HRS 1022, Riverside RLP 143
1038	Frost On the Moon	HRS 1023
1039	Sam Pan	-
1040	Sandy's Blues	HRS 1022, Riverside RLP 143
1041	Gee, Baby Ain't I Good To You	HRS 1029, Riverside RLP 145

The titles of the LPs are "Giants Of Small-Band Swing," Vols. 1 and 2. This was a fine session for Pee Wee; his solo on **Sandy's Blues** is outstanding.

An unusual date for Pee Wee, which we've been unable to audition, follows. Jesse Stone, arranger and pianist, made some interesting records with his territory band in 1927 and is perhaps best known as the composer of "Idaho." By 1947, he had turned to r&b and made a number of records for Victor as a vocalist.

JESSE STONE
PWE (tp); George Dorsey (as); Dave McRae (bars); Don Abney (p); Huey Long (g); George Duvivier (sb); Teddy Lee (d); Stone (vo, arr). 11/26/47.

D7VB2500	Bling-a-ling-a-ling	Victor 20-3127
D7VB2501	Don't Let It Get Away	- 20-2988
D7VB2502	Get It While You Can	- 20-3282
D7VB2503	Who Killed 'Er?	- 20-2788

Though the leader of the next date is not particularly associated with jazz, this is an excellent big-band record in an updated Bob Crosby style:

LEROY HOLMES AND HIS ORCHESTRA
PWE, Billy Butterfield, Jimmy Maxwell (tp); Buddy Morrow, Phil Giardina, Will Bradley (tb); Ernie Caceres (cl, as); Toots Mondello (as); Phil Bodner, George Dessinger (ts); Bernie Leighton (p); Ted Kosoftis (sb); Al Seidel (d); Holmes (arr). c. May, 1950.

50S3042	The New Dixieland Parade	MGM 10706, 0159
50S3043	The Sheik Of Araby	- , -

The first issue is 78, the second 45. The trumpet soloist on **The Sheik** is Butterfield, but the one on the other side might well be our man. The discographies give the location for this date as Los Angeles, but these are all New York-based musicians.

We now come to Pee Wee's first sessions as a leader:

PEE WEE ERWIN AND THE VILLAGE FIVE
PWE (to); Andy Russo (tb); Phil Olivella (cl); Billy Maxted (p); Jack Fay (sb); Cliff Leeman (d). 6/24/50.

K6192	Tin Roof Blues	King 15075, EP242, AudioLab A1502
K6193	Shake It and Break It	- 15074, -
K6194	Eccentric Rag	King 15073, EP242, AudioLab AL1502

| K6195 | Tiger Rag | - 15076, | - |

Same, but Patti Dugan (vo) added. 6/30/50.

K6196	Music Southern Style vPD	King 15073
K6197	Meshuga Over You vPD	King 15074
K6198	When the Saints Go Marching In	King 15075, EP242, AudioLab AL1502
K6199	Wolverine Blues	King 15076, EP242, AudioLab AL1502

(Note: The EP is titled "Dixieland;" the LP, "Dixieland Parade: Pee Wee Erwin and Preacher Rollo.")

Pee Wee's "underwater" debut follows:

JILL ALLEN WITH THE TRUMPET OF PEE WEE ERWIN
Allen (vo); PWE (tp); unknown (org); ca. 1952.

| 72201-8 | Hold Me Closer | Avalon 7220 |
| 72202-9 | Melancholy Baby | - |

PEE WEE ERWIN IN THE LAND OF DIXIE
PWE (tp); Andy Russo (tb); Sal Pace (cl); Billy Maxted (p); Jack Fay (sb); Kenny John (d). 9/1/4/53. Rec. live at Ft. Monmouth, N.J.

Brunswick BL54011

At the Jazz Band Ball / Basin Street Blues / Lassus Trombone / Memphis Blues / Panama / Dixieland Shuffle / Satanic Blues.

Pee Wee's final 78 date marked the recording debut of a fine singer:

BARBARA LEE
PWE (tp); Cutty Cutshall (tb); Eddie Barefield (cl); Bill Austin (p); Bill Pemberton (sb); George Wettling (d); Lea (vo); Terry and the Macs (vo). 6/18/54.

| 7000 | I'll Bet You a Kiss vBL,TATM | Cadillac 149 |
| 7001 | Any Place I Hang My Hat Is Home vBL | - |

The first of many sessions produced by Enoch Light in which Pee Wee was involved follows:

BOBBY BYRNE AND HIS ORCHESTRA
PWE (tp); Byrne (tb); Peanuts Hucko (cl); Billy Maxted (p); Eddie Safranski (sb); Cliff Leeman (d). 1954

Grand Award 33-310, Waldorf 33-121

Muskrat Ramble / Basin Street Blues / The Saints / South Rampart Street Parade / Way Down Yonder in New Orleans / Jazz Me Blues.

Same personnel, except Lou Stein (p) replaces Maxted and Jack Lesberg (sb) replaces Safranski. 1954.

Grand Award 33-313, Waldorf 33-131

That's A Plenty / Royal Garden Blues / Indiana / Struttin' With Some Barbecue.

(Note: Grand Award are 12-inch, Waldorf 10-inch LPs. The second and third tracks (from the first session) also issued on Grand Award 33-322, a compilation LP titled "A Musical History of Jazz." All other issues titled "Dixieland Jazz.")

PEE WEE ERWIN: ACCENT ON DIXIELAND
PWE (tp); Andy Russo (tb); Sal Pace (cl); Billy Maxted (p); Charlie Traeger (sb); Tony Spargo (d, kazoo). c.1955.

Urania UJLP 1202

Battle Hymn of the Republic / Washington and Lee Swing / Dixieland Shuffle / Hindustan / Pagan Love Song / Confessin' / Memphis Blues.
(Note: Reissued on Jazztone J-1237).

PEE WEE ERWIN: DIXIELAND AT THE GRANDVIEW INN
Same as above. Recorded live in Columbus Ohio, July 1955.

Cadence CLP1011

American Patrol / Parade of the Wooden Soldiers / Tea For Two / The Whistler and His Dog / Little Rock Getaway / After You've Gone / Peter and the Wolf / The Big Noise From Winnetka.

The next sessions were conceived as a tribute to Louis Armstrong.

TOMMY REYNOLDS AND HIS ORCHESTRA
PWE, Billy Butterfield (tp); Lou McGarity (tb); Reynolds (cl); Abe "Boomie" Richman (ts); Billy Jacob (p); George Barnes (g); Jack Lesberg (sb); Cliff Leeman (d); Gene Gifford (arr). 10/6/55.

King LP510, AudioLab AL1509

Monday Date / Savoy Blues / Cornet Chop Suey / Jazz Lips.
Same personnel, but without Butterfield. 12/12/55.

King LP510, AudioLab AL1509

Satchel Mouth (Swing) / Mecca Flat Blues / Squeeze Me / Arkansas Blues / Gulf Coast Blues / Potato Head Blues / Hotter Than That / Happy Feet.
(Note: Issued as "Jazz For Happy Feet" on King; "Dixieland All Stars" on AudioLab.)

Though pianist Claude Hopkins was the leader on this date, it was issued under a generic title. It was a fine session for everyone involved.

THE GOLDEN ERA OF DIXIELAND JAZZ
PWE (tp); Vic Dickenson (tb); Buster Bailey (cl); Claude Hopkins (p, arr); Milt Hinton (sb); George Wettling (d). 1956.

Design DLP 38

The Saints / Basin Street Blues / Struttin' With Some Barbecue / Clarinet Marmalade / Royal Garden Blues / Muskrat Ramble / Tin Roof Blues / I Would Do Anything For You / Birth Of the Blues.
(Note: This material has been frequently reissued, often scrambled with a later Design session without Pee Wee but some of the same players. International Award AK-164 and Westerfield AKS-164 are among these reissues.

CHARLESTON CITY ALL STARS
This was Enoch Light's "house band" name for a series of LPs featuring

"jazzed-up" 1920s music. The collective personnel is as follows:
PWE, Charlie Margolis (tp); Artie Manners, Mike Doty, Paul Ricci, Milt Yaner (reeds); Dick Hyman, Billy Rowland (p); George Barnes, Don Arnone (g); Jack Lesberg, Eddie Safranski (sb); Terry Snyder, Don Lamond (d). c. 1956-57.

Pee Wee is present on The Roaring Twenties, Vol. 3 (Grand Award 33-353); Vol. 4 (Grand Award 33-370) and Vol. 5 (Grand Award 33-378). Though the music is quite enjoyable, it borders on the corny in interpretation. While issued under the same band name, the following LP is a horse of a different color, offering excellent playing, very well recorded:
PWE (tp); Lou McGarity (tb); Kenny Davern (cl); John Montillaro (p); Lee Blair (bjo); Harvey Phillips (tu); Jack Lesberg (sb); Mousie Alexander (d).

The Charleston City All Stars Go Dixieland   Grand Award 33-411
Some Of These Days / Baby Won't You Please Come Home / Sweet Georgia Brown / When You're Smiling / Sweet Sue / Chicago / Somebody Stole My Gal / Ballin' the Jack / Shine / Alexander's Ragtime Band / Should I / The Sheik of Araby.
(Note: For some reason, Pee Wee is the only musician not identified in the liner notes. His presence, however, is indisputable.)

Before taking leave of Grand Award, we should mention that Pee Wee is present in the band, and also contributed original material to a non-jazz album, "Great American Marches Performed By Charlie Margulis and his Brass Band" (Grand Award 33-369). He also plays on "Tribute To Tommy and Jimmy Dorsey", performed by Bobby Byrne and the All Star Alumni Orchestra, which has not been auditioned:
PWE, Charlie Shavers, Doc Severinsen, Charlie Margulis (tp); Byrne, Bob Alexander, Walt Mercurio, Andy Russo (tb); Milt Yaner, Johnny Mince (as, cl); Boomie Richman, Babe Fresk (ts); Sol Schlinger (bars); John Potoker (p); Carmen Mastren (g); Sandy Block (sb); Cliff Leeman (d). c. 1958

Grand Award GRD382, S206
Marie / Opus No. 1 / I'm Getting Sentimental Over You / Boogie Woogie / Song Of India / Well, Git It / Amapola / I Understand / So Rare / Green Eyes / The Breeze and I / Contrasts.
(Note: Some personnel changes for the Jimmy Dorsey selections, recorded slightly later, were possibly made.)

Though the next two LPs were recorded more than a year apart, it makes sense to list them together, due to similarities in personnel. Both are of very high musical quality.

PEE WEE ERWIN'S DIXIELAND EIGHT: OH PLAY THAT THING!
PWE (tp); Lou McGarity (tb); Kenny Davern (cl); Dick Hyman (p); Tony Gattuso (g, bjo); Jack Lesberg (sb); Harvey Phillips (tu); Cliff Leeman (d). 10/24/58.

United Artists UAL-4010/UAS-5010; reissued on Qualtro OM 103
Kansas City Stomps / The Chant / Yaaka Hula Hicky Dula / Temptation

Rag / Black Bottom Stomp / Dipper Mouth Blues / Grandpa's Spells / Dill Pickles / Sensation Rag / Big Pond Rag / Jazz Frappe Rag / Georgia Swing.

PEE WEE ERWIN AND THE DIXIE STRUTTERS: DOWN BY THE RIVERSIDE
Same personnel, except that Lee Blair (bjo) replaces Gattuso; Milt Hinton (sb) replaces Lesberg; Osie Johnson (d) replaces Leeman. Phillips is omitted, and Hyman doubles on organ. 12/7/59.
 United Artists UAL-3071/6071 Lead Me On / Walking With the King / Swing Low, Sweet Chariot / The Saints / Just a Little While to Stay Here / Down By the Riverside / Marching Into Gloryland / Ev'rybody Needs a Helping Hand / Give Me the Good Word / Careless Love / Lord, Lord, You Sure Been Good To Me / Just a Closer Walk With Thee.

The next item is another we've been unable to hear, but it looks interesting enough to list.

JACK SAUNDERS AND HIS ORCHESTRA: GERSHWIN IN BRASS
PWE, Charlie Margulis, Mel Davis, Rickey Trent, Bill Vacchiano, Harry Glantz, Doc Severinsen (tp); Bobby Byrne, Urbie Green, Will Bradley, John D'Agostino, Thomas Mitchell (tb); Jimmy Chambers, Don Corrado, Abraham Pearlstein, Al Goodlis, Hunter Wiley (frh); Harvey Phillips (tu); Art Ryerson (g); Jack Lesberg (sb), Cliff Leeman (d); Terry Snyder, Phil Krauss (perc). May and June, 1959.
                                                          Everest PRB5047
Fascinatin' Rhythm / But Not For Me / American in Paris / The Man I Love / I Got Rhythm / Summertime / Liza / Strike Up the Band / Embracable You / Rhapsody In Blue / I Got Plenty O' Nuttin' / Someone to Watch Over Me / Clap Yo' Hands.

Another unheard but intriguing item follows:

HANS CONREID: PETER AND THE WOLF IN DIXIELAND
Maxted (p); George Barnes, Tony Gatusso (g); Harvey Phillips (tu); Cliff Leeman (d); Conreid (narrator). 1959.
                                                          Strand SL1001
Grumpy Grandpa / Peter Meets the Wolf In Dixieland / Wild Wolf Wailing / Requiem For a Blue Duck / The Cat-like Cat / In Defense Of the Wolf / Pete's Theme.

The next album is not listed in discographies, but contains some excellent jazz, notably on the four big-band tracks that include Pee Wee (and also on four cuts featuring Charlie Shavers in a small group, by the way). The brief trumpet solos are all by Pee Wee.

JOE GLOVER AND HIS COTTON PICKERS: THAT RAGTIME SOUND!
PWE, Bernie Glow, Paul Cohen (tp); Urbie Green, Larry Altpeter, Bob

Alexander (tb); John Peper, Jimmy Lytell, Sam Marowitz (as); Morty Lewis (ts); Danny Bank (bars); Paul Ricci (bass sax); Irving Brodsky, Milt Kraus (p); John Cali (bjo); Harry London (sb); Chauncey Morehouse (d); Glover (arr). 1959.

Epic LN3581

Alexander's Ragtime Band / Black and White Rag / Little Rock Getaway / Down Home Rag.

We now come to the famous "Big Jeb" Dooley sessions for Enoch Light. "Big Jeb," of course, was a pseudonym for Pee Wee.

PURE DIXIELAND JAZZ STARRING "BIG JEB" DOOLEY

PWE (tp); Lou McGarity (tb); Kenny Davern (cl); John Montillaro (p); Milt Hinton (sb); Cliff Leeman (d). 1959.

Command RSSD983-2

The Saints / St. James Infirmary / Royal Garden Blues / Tin Roof Blues / Clarinet Marmalade / Milenberg Joys / Limehouse Blues / Ja Da / At the Jazz Band Ball / Indiana / Wang Wang Blues / Creole Rag / Nonbody's Sweetheart / Jazz Me Blues / Tiger Rag / Dixieland Band / Hindustan / Basin Street Blues / That's A Plenty / South Rampart Street Parade.

(Note: The above double album combines two previously released Dooley LPs, "The Dixie Rebels Strike Back" (Command RS801SD), and "The Dixie Rebels True Dixieland Sound" (Command RS825SD). This material may also have been recycled on other labels, including Somerset. During this period, Pee Wee appeared on many Enoch Light Command LPs, often only remotely jazz-related, but allowing for occasional solos. These include "Enoch Light and his Orchestra at Carnegie Hall Play Irving Berlin" (Command RS840SD); "Bongos: Los Admiradores" (Command RS809SD), and "Provocative Percussion" (Command 90122), on which Pee Wee is featured on **The Man I Love**.)

Pee Wee often worked at the Metropole in New York City, where the following LP was recorded live. He does not appear on the other tracks, which feature Coleman Hawkins:

SOL YAGED: JAZZ AT THE METROPOLE

PWE (tp); Benny Morton (tb); Yaged (cl); Nat Pierce (p); Arvell Shaw (sb); Bert Dale (d). 5/19/61.

Phillips PHM200-022

Someday Sweetheart / That's A Plenty / Wolverine Blues.

The strings were overdubbed on what is essentially a very nice small-group jazz date; Pee Wee does not appear on the other cuts.

HENRY JEROME: DIXIELAND WITH STRINGS

PWE (tp); Vic Dickenson (tb); Sol Yaged (cl); Bud Freeman (ts); Dick Wellstood (p); Art Ryerson (g); Milt Hinton (sb); Cliff Leeman (d). 1962.

Decca DL4307

Sweet Lorraine / Darktown Strutters' Ball / South Rampart Street Parade / Chicago.

Another Enoch Light production follows:
DIXIELAND ALL STARS: DIXIELAND WITH A TWIST
PWE (tp); Cutty Cutshall (tb); Peanuts Hucko (cl); Bill Ramal (ts); Moe Wechsler (p); Al Caiola (g); Jerry Bruno (sb); Gary Chester (d). c. 1962.
Somerset SF-16700
South Rampart Street Parade / The Saints / Down By the Riverside / Twistin' Dixie / Bourbon Street Fishfry / Rampart St. Stomp / Sunburst Rag / Midnite In Memphis / Lonesome Railroad Blues / Mississippi Mud / Muskrat Ramble / Golden Slippers Twist.

We haven't been able to date the next venture, but it appears to be from this period. The leader's name is a pseudonym:
CHARLIE WALDO'S BAND: RAZZ-MA-TAZZ
Collective personnel: PWE, Carl Poole (tp); Buddy Morrow (tb); Ray Ekstrand, Bob Wilber, Lenny Hambro, Romeo Penque (reeds); Bernie Leighton, Joe Cribari (p); Al Caiola, Art Ryerson (bjo); Joe Tarto (tu); Buddy Christian (d); Molly Lyons, Bernie Knee (vo); "Miss Dardanella" (narrator); Neil Stanley (impressionist); George Williams (arr).
Endura ELP1001
Everybody Step / When I Get You Alone Tonight / Po' Lil Tug / Wanna Go Back to Chicago / Who's Sorry Now / I Ain't Got Nobody / All Alone / Goin' the Wrong Way Honey / Singin' In the Rain / This Is the End.
Yet another indication of Pee Wee's versatility is his participation in "Music From the Big Top," recorded by the Merle Evans Circus Band, probably around this time (Everest Traditional 2112).

Back to straight-ahead jazz. The bassist Leonard Gaskin was leader on this date, though not credited on the cover; a different group plays on the remaining tracks:

(SWINGVILLE ALL STARS): DARKTOWN STRUTTERS BALL
PWE (tp); "Big Chief" Russell Moore (tb); Herb Hall (cl); Bud Freeman (ts); Red Richards (p); Leonard Gaskin (sb); George Wettling (d). 8/23/62.
Prestige Swingville 2033
Darktown Strutters' Ball / It Had to Be You / Farewell Blues.

From 1962 to 1966 Pee Wee was featured on a number of Jackie Gleason's famous "mood music" albums for Capitol; he replaces Bobby Hackett as the comedian's favored trumpet soloist, and his partner in the solo spotlight was Charlie Ventura, who is mostly heard on tenor sax, but also doubles alto and baritone. George Williams was the arranger. Exact personnel and recording dates are not available, but we've provided content details where known. Tracks on which Pee Wee doesn't solo are omitted. All album titles are preceded by "Jackie Gleason Presents":

411

JACKIE GLEASON

1962: Capitol SW1877

Movie Themes — For Lovers Only: Days of Wine and Roses / Call Me Irresponsible / You're All the World To Me / Third Man Theme / My Romance.

1963: Capitol SW2056

Today's Romantic Hits For Lovers Only, Vol. 2: No details.

1963: Capitol SW2144

The Last Dance . . . For Lovers Only: The Last Dance / Hello, Dolly / Who Can I Turn To? / I Wish You Love / Be My Love / Softly, As I Leave You.

1965: Capitol SW2409

Silk 'n' Brass: The Girl From Ipanema / Everything's Coming Up Roses / Starry Eyed and Breathless / You're Nobody 'Till Somebody Loves You / Begin To Love / If I Ruled the World / Somebody Else Is Taking My Place / You.

1966: Capitol SW2582

How Sweet It Is For Lovers: Strangers In the Night / The Shadow Of Your Smile / The Second Time Around / Autumn Waltz / Au Revoir / I Will Wait For You.

1966: Capitol SW2684

A Taste Of Brass For Lovers Only: This features Roy Eldridge as soloist, with Pee Wee in the brass section.

The nominal leader for the next session was producer Juggy Gales:
JUGGY'S JAZZ BAND: HOLIDAY IN NEW ORLEANS
PWE, Bernie Privin (tp); Cutty Cutshall (tb); Hank D'Amico (cl); Joe Mazzu (p); Al Chernet, Don Arnone, Everett Barksdale (g, bjo); Harvey Phillips (tu); Cliff Leeman (d). 1964.

Time 52198

Swing Low, Sweet Chariot / Dixie / Go Down, Moses / Shortnin' Bread / Tom Dooley / At A Georgia Camp Meeting / Rovin' Gambler.
(Note: Pee Wee does not play on the other tracks from this LP, which was reissued as "Riverboat Jazz" (Mainstream M56029).

Pee Wee appears on one track from the first of many LPs issued by the Connecticut Traditional Jazz Society, as "Conn Trad 1:"
PWE (tp); Jimmy Archey (tb); Tony Parenti (cl, leader); Bill Sinclair (p); Noel Kalet (sb); Cliff Leeman (d). 8/16/65.
Oh Baby!   **Conn Trad CTCJ-1**

After a lengthy hiatus — these were lean years for Pee Wee's kind of jazz in the studios — he returns to records as a participant in Dick Hyman's ambitious tribute to Jelly Roll Morton:

DICK HYMAN : FERDINAND "JELLY ROLL" MORTON — TRANSCRIPTIONS FOR ORCHESTRA
PWE, Mel Davis, Joe Wilder (tp); Urbie Green, Vic Dickenson, Paul Faulise (tb); Don Hammond, Harvey Estrin (fl, picc); Phil Bodner (fl, picc, cl); Kenny

412

Davern (cl, ss); Ray Alonge, Jimmy Buffington (French horn); Don Butterfield (tu); Hyman (p, arr); Tony Mottola or Art Ryerson (bjo, g); Milt Hinton (sb); Panama Francis (dm); Phil Kraus (perc). 12/3/73.

Columbia M32587

Grandpa's Spells / The Crave / Pep / Black Bottom Stomp / Buddy Bolden's Blues / The Pearls.

Note: French horns present on **Grandpa's Spells, Black Bottom Stomp** and **Buddy Bolden's Blues** only; Mottola plays on these three cuts, Ryerson on all others.

PWE, Mel Davis (tp); Vic Dickenson, Mickey Gravine (tb); Kenny Davern (cl, ss); Phil Bodner (fl, picc, as); Hyman (p); Tony Mottola (bjo, g); Milt Hinton (sb); Panama Francis (d). 12/11/73: same LP as above.

Fickle Fay Creep / Mr. Jelly Lord / King Porter Stomp.

Pee Wee does not play on the remaining tracks, performed by a trio of Hyman, Francis and Joe Venuti.

Next, a couple of enterprises for veteran producer Bob Thiele:

BOB THIELE AND HIS NEW HAPPY TIMES ORCHESTRA: THE 20s SCORE AGAIN

PWE (tp); Urbie Green (tb); Clarence Hutchenrider (cl); Hank Jones (p); Art Ryerson (g); Richard Davis (sb); Ted Sommer (d). 1974.

Signature BSC1-0555

Wolverine Blues.

PWE (tp soloist) with big band: Bernie Glow, Mel Davis, Jimmy Maxwell (tp); Urbie Green, Warren Covington, Al Grey (tb); Don Butterfield (tu); Johnny Mince (cl); Toots Mondello (as); Clarence Hutchenrider (as, cl); Al Klink, George Berg (ts); Hank Jones (p); Art Ryerson (g); Richard Davis (sb); Ted Sommer (d); Phil Kraus (perc); Glenn Osser (arr). 1974: same LP.

China Boy / Indiana.

Note: Bobby Hackett and Max Kaminsky (tp) added as soloists on **China Boy**. Pee Wee does not appear on other tracks from this LP, which was reissued as: **Doctor Jazz 39876.**

GEORGE SEGAL AND THE IMPERIAL JAZZBAND: A TOUCH OF RAGTIME

PWE, Mel Davis (tp); Warren Covington (tb); Johnny Mince (cl); Hank Jones, Dick Hyman (p); Bucky Pizzarelli (g); John Tropea (el g); Richard Davis (sb); Bill LaVorgna (d); Segal (vo, ukulele); Glenn Osser (arr). 1974.

Signature BSL1-0654

Charleston Rag / Alexander's Ragtime Band / The Moving Picture Ball.

Note: Teresa Brewer (vo) added on **Alexander's Ragtime Band;** Tropea does not play on **Moving Picture Ball.** Pee Wee does not play on the remaining tracks.

The following album was recorded live at Carnegie Hall from a concert in tribute to Louis Armstrong.

SATCHMO REMEMBERED
Collective Pers: PWE, Mel Davis, Ray Nance, Joe Newman (tp); Vic Dickenson, Ephie Resnick (tb); Kenny Davern (cl, ss); William Russell (vn); Dick Hyman (p); Carmin Mastren (bj, g); Bobby Rosengarden (d); Carrie Smith (v)*. 11/8/74.

Atlantic SD1671

St. Louis Tickle / Creole Belles / Flee As A Bird / Oh Didn't He Ramble / Chimes Blues / Cakewalkin' Babies From Home* / Potatoe Head Blues / Weatherbird Rag / Willie the Weeper / S.O.L. Blues.

Pee Wee was featured at the Honolulu Jazz Festival in 1979 and recorded there, "live," at The Sounds of Hawaii, with local celebrity Trummy Young:
TRUMMY YOUNG: SOMEDAY
PWE (tp); Young (tb, vo); Barney Bigard (cl); Paul Madison (as, ts); Dick Hyman (p); Milt Hinton (sb); Bobby Rosengarden (d). April 1979.

Flair 7477

Perdido / I'm Confessin' (vTY) / Struttin' With Some Barbecue / Creole Love Call / Someday (vTY) / If I Could Be With You.
Note: Flair is a Hawaiian label. The album was issued in the U.S. on **Chiaroscuro 2020.**

A reunion with fellow ex-Goodmanite Helen Ward follows:
THE HELEN WARD SONG BOOK, VOL. 1
PWE (tp); George Masso (tb); Phil Bodner (cl); Tony Monte (p); Bucky Pizzarelli (el g, ldr); Steve Jordan (g); Milt Hinton (sb); Butch Miles (d); Ward (vo). 1979.

Lyricon 1007

I've Got the World On A String / Goody Goody.
Pee Wee does not appear on the other tracks from this multiple-personnel LP.

TOM ARTIN AND CONDON'S HOT LUNCH FEATURING PEE WEE ERWIN
PWE (tp); Artin (tb); Jack Maheu (cl); Bobby Pratt (p); Dick Waldburger (sb); Ernie Hackett (d). 3/20 & 3/25/80.

Slide Records (no. cat. #)

Always / Out To Lunch Blues / Mandy, Make Up Your Mind / That Old Feeling / Wolverine Blues / S'posin' / Rockin' Chair / Smiles / Star Dust / I Double Dare You.

PEE WEE ERWIN: SWINGIN' THAT MUSIC
PWE (tp); Harry Hagan (tb); Herman Foretich (cl); Freddie DeLand (p); Ike Isaacs (sb); Hal Smith (d). Atlanta, Ga., 3/24/80.

Jazzology J-80

Swing That Music / Poor Butterfly / When You're Smiling / If I Could Be With You / I Can't Believe That You're In Love With Me / I Want To Be Happy / New Orleans / Royal Garden Blues / Oh! Baby.

Pee Wee was very much involved with the production of the next three albums, and mainly responsible for their format:

PEE WEE IN NEW YORK
PWE (tp); Ed Hubble (tb); Bob Wilder (reeds, arr); Johnny Mince, Frank Wess (reeds); Derek Smith (p); Milt Hinton (sb); Bobby Rosengarden (d). 1/21/80.

Qualtro QM100
For All We Know / What's New / When Your Lover Has Gone / As Time Goes By / Tenderly / Creole Love Call / He Loves, She Loves / Slow Mood / Buddy Bolden's Blues / Someone To Watch Over Me / Sultry Summer Afternoon / Someday You'll Be Sorry.

PEE WEE IN HOLLYWOOD
PWE (tp); Bob Havens (tb); Kenny Davern (cl); Eddie Miller (ts); Dick Cary (p); Dick Hyman (p); Ray Leatherwood (sb); Nick Fatool (d). 4/22/81.

Qualtro QM101
Farewell Blues / Blues My Naughty Sweetie Gives To Me / Shreveport Stomp / There'll Be Some Changes Made / When My Sugar Walks Down the Street / Hindustan / Bye Bye Blues / Old Fashioned Love / Monday Date / Rose Room / It Don't Mean A Thing.
Note: Dick Cary plays piano with the West Coast group. The two tracks with Dick Hyman were recorded at an earlier session (Dec. 1980) in New York.

PEE WEE PLAYING AT HOME
PWE (tp); Bucky Pizzarelli, John Pizzarelli (g). 4/26/81.

Qualtro QM102
September Song / Misty / The Hour of Parting / Jada / The Touch of Your Lips / Avalon / My Inspiration / Moonlight On the Ganges / Black and Blue / Home / In the Dark / Alice Blue Gown.

The next album (with liner notes by Warren Vaché Sr.) was produced in Holland from tapes made at the 1981 Breda Jazz Festival by Pee Wee Erwin and His Jazz Giants — the last concert he would ever play:

PEE WEE MEMORIAL
PWE (tp); Ed Hubble (tb); Kenny Davern (cl); Jim Andrews (p); Warren Vaché Sr. (sb); Johnny Blowers (d). 4/28-29/81.

Jazz Crooner JC2829581
Nobody's Sweetheart / Rosetta / Someday You'll Be Sorry / I Can't Believe That You're In Love With Me / Savoy Blues / I Want to Be Happy / Shreveport Stomp / Indiana.

INDEX

417

420

"Dooley, Big Jeb," pseudonym for Pee Wee, 287

Dooley, Phil, trumpet, vaudevillian, 64-5, 257

Dorsey Brothers orchestra, 53, 94, 104, 111, 154, 250,

Dorsey, Jimmy, bandleader, 59, 78, 137, 232, 250, 269

Dorsey, Tommy, bandleader, 94, 119, 142, 148-54, 156, 159-62, 164-6, 169-77, 184, 187, 203, 232, 234, 245, 250, 269, 305; recreation of the music of, 317-9; "Toots," first wife, 161; children of: Patsy, Tom Jr., 161

Dorsey, W.D. (Bill), trumpet teacher, 20

Doty, Mike, sax, 61-2, 68, 74-5, 79, 84, 110, 120-1, 145-6, 148, 160

Douglas, Ralph, 189

Dowling, Eddie, 130

Down Beat, 103, 129

Downey, Morton, 170

Downtown New York Athletic Club, The, 379

Ftskr, Blue, vocalist, 184

Drellinger, Artie, sax, 291

Drooten brothers, 317

Duffy, Al, violin, 361

"Duffy's Tavern," radio show, 214

Dugan, Patti, vocalist, 213

Duke, Doris, townhouse, 182

Duke Ellington orchestra, 53

"Dukes of Dixieland," The, 246-8

Dumont TV network, 216

Duncan, Hank, piano, 229

Dupont, Roland, trombone, 145-6, 179

Durante, Jimmy, 230

Durgam, Bullets, bandboy, 119

Duryea, Riley, clarinet, 372

"Dutch Swing College Band," The, 338, 356

Duvivier, George, bass, 329, 333, 341, 349, 370, 381

"Earthquake McGoon's," 343

Eastman School of Music, 211, 298

"East Coast All Stars," The, 363, 370, 374

Easton, Ted, bandleader, 358, 368

Eaton, Benny, violin, 104

Ebbs, George, 328, 352, 359

Ebner, Fred, 186

Eckhart, Gus, bass, 324, 326

"Eddie Condon's," original club, W. 3rd St., 278-81, 373; uptown, 373;

Balaban revival, W. 54th St., 364, 373, 390-1

Eddie Kuhn's Kansas City Athletic Club band; Pee Wee's first stint, 38-49; return, 51, 316, 372

"Eddie Kuhn's Song Shop," 14-5

Eddy Duchin's orchestra, 159

Edgar Bergen radio show, 114

Edison, "Sweets," trumpet, 354, 370, 381

Edwards, Eddie "Daddy," trombone, 179

Effros, Bob, trumpet, 213

Egan, Jack, public relations man, 154

Egan, Jack, writer, 166

Eidus, Arnold, concertmaster, 192

Ekstrand, Ray, 183, 291, 293, 306

Eldridge, Roy, trumpet, 97, 112

Ellington, Duke, 53; the music of, 340, 355, 367

Ellis, Herb, guitar, 349, 364, 367, 375, 379

Elman, Ziggy, 90

El Torreon Ballroom, 42-43

Ely, Chet, vocalist, 285

End, Jack, arranger, 211

Engle, Vic, 75, 257

Epic Records, 297

Epstein, Al, sax, 209, 211

Ernie Carson's band, 309

Ernie Holst orchestra, 80

Erwin, Caroline Howe, daughter, 294, 379

Erwin, Caroline May, second wife, 256, 265-6, 271-8, 281-2, 287-90, 292, 294-5, 318, 324, 352, 364-6, 369, 372, 378-80, 386-7, 389-90, 393-4

Erwin, Cathy, daughter, 287, 289, 379

Erwin, Chloe (Prater), Pee Wee's mother, 3, 7, 14-5, 26, 33, 52, 105, 119-20, 126, 136, 169, 222, 237, 274, 276, 372

Erwin, Diane, niece, 351

Erwin, Elizabeth (Oglesby), Pee Wee's paternal grandmother, 8

Erwin, Frank H. Dr., Pee Wee's paternal grandfather, 4-5, 7, 26, 84

Erwin, Georgine, daughter, 282-3, 366, 378-9

Erwin-Griffin music school, 299-302

Erwin, James Jr., Pee Wee's brother, 25, 105, 119-20, 171, 237, 351

Erwin, James Oglesby, Pee Wee's father, 3, 5-6, 8-10, 12-4, 20, 22,

428

Justice, Tommy, trumpet, 243

Kaatee, Krtiz, reeds, 359
Kahn, Leo, 182
Kahn, Tiny, drums, arranger, 209-11
Kalb, Bubba, piano, 345
Kaminsky, Max, trumpet, 155, 295
Kansas City Athletic Club, 38-49, 50, 53, 316
Kansas City Blues, baseball team, 46
Kansas City Monarchs, black baseball team, 46
Kansas City Star, 15, 41
Kaplan, Delmar, bass, 114
Kaps, Dr. Sanford E., 311-12
Karpilovsky, Murray, trumpet, 203
Katz, Mr. & Mrs. Phil, 144
Kaufman, Bernie, 182
Kay, Beatrice, singer, 191
Kay, Connie, drums, 349, 361, 364, 379
Kaye, Danny, 182
Kaye, Merrill, 272
Kaye, Sammy, bandleader, 158-9
Kazebier, Nate, trumpet, 108, 110-11, 129, 131, 133, 364
Kellaway, Roger, piano, 364-5, 370, 375, 381
Kellner, Murray, (Kel Murray), conductor, violin, 107
Kelly's Bar, 154, 160
Kelly, Willis, trumpet, 179
Kel Murray's orchestra, 107
Kemp, Hal, bandleader, 163
Ken Morgester's orchestra, 313-4
Ken Murray's "Blackouts," TV show, 221
Kennedy Center for the Performing Arts, The, 322, 363-4
Kennedy, Ed, 317-8, 357
Kennedy, John F., 196
Kennedy-Masters, British booking agency, 317, 320
Kenny Burrell Trio, The, 352
Kenton, Stan, bandleader, 210
Kercheval, Mr. & Mrs. John, 374
Kincaide, Deane, arranger, 177, 362
King, Alan, 291
"King and Queen Tavern," The, 359
King Cole Trio, The, 226
King record label, 230
"King of Jazz," The, movie, 4, 53, 76
"Kings of Jazz," The, 320, 344, 362
Kirby, Durwood, 291
Kirby, John, music of, 340
Kirk, Andy, bandleader, 55
Kirkeby, Ed, 250

Kirkham, Gerry, trumpet, bandleader, 325
Klatzkin, Ben, bandleader, 103
Klaus, Allen, 185-6
Klein, Ann and Bob, 205
Klein, Dave, 103
Klein, Manny, trumpet, 53, 75, 102-3, 107, 193
Klein, Oscar, trumpet, 356
Kleinsinger, George, 221, 289, 336
Kleinsinger, Jack, 314, 336
Klink, Al, sax, 344, 361, 376
KMBC, Kansas City radio station, 42
Knapp, Johnny, piano, 298
Knee, Bernie, 306
Know, Charley, bass, 52, 55, 316, 341, 348
Kool Cigarettes jazz festival, 341
Kopetsky, Mrs., church organist, 335
Koss, Buddy, piano, 184
Kostal, Irwin, director, 291
Kostelanetz, Andre, conductor, 103-4
Kovacs, Ernie, 347
Koven, Jakie, trumpet, 48
Kraft Music Hall, radio show, 137
Kral, Miss Emma, milliner, 23
Kraner, Sylvia, 183
Kress, Carl, guitar, 104, 193
Krupa, Gene, 71, 88-106, 129, 137, 139-40, 147; wife Ethel, 27, 90, 134, 147, 155, 192, 308
Kuehl, Joe, ball player, 46
"K. U. Footwarmers," 25
Kuhlman, Freddie, 349
Kuhn, Eddie, piano, bandleader, 14, 38, 45, 49
"Kukla, Fran and Ollie," TV show, 229
Kunch, Jack, piano, 351
Kurtzer, Dave, sax, 209
Kutsher's Country Club, 277-8
KVOO, Tulsa radio station, 59

LaBarbara, Joe, drums, 374
LaCentra, Peg, vocalist, 153
Lacey, Jack, trombone, 104, 106, 108-11, 193
LaFarge, Tracey, drums, 10
Lageson, Wally, drums, 94
Laing, Harvey, drums, 345
Lake Buena Vista, Disney World, 345, 351
Lambert, Dave, vocal arranger, 210-11
Lambert, Jack, vocalist, 115
Lamberti brothers, bandleaders, 37
"Landing, The," San Antonio club,

Williams, Dan, 374
Williams, Francis, banjo/guitar, 39
Williams, George, arranger, 306
Williams, Jackie, drums, 370, 381-2
Williams, Joe, vocalist, 336, 340-1, 367
Williams, John, Boston Pops conductor, 202
Williams, Johnny, drums, 179, 181, 201-2
Williams, Johnny, clarinet, 324-5
Williams, Mary Lou, 352
Williams, Roy, trombone, 368, 370
Williams, Sandy, trombone, 204
Williamson, Freddie, 185
Willis, Glenn, piano, 50
Wilson, bass, 30
Wilson, Bill, 201
Wilson, John S., 303
Wilson, Teddy, 129, 132-4, 140, 328, 341, 370, 377
Wimby, Julius, piano, 310
Windhurst, Johnny, trumpet, 290
Winding, Kai, trombone, 356
Windsor, Duke and Duchess of, 196, 267-8
"Windy City Jazz," 337
Winfield, Herb Jr., arranger, 184-5
Wingerter, Ray, promoter, 68
Winterhalter, Hugo, arranger, conductor, 203
Wishart, Burr, bass, 353
Witt Toma's band, 74
Wolfe, Ed and Dick, 246
Wolff, Bill; Jess, 231
"Wolverine Jazz Band, The," 374
"Wolverine Orchestra, The," reconstituted, 322-3
Woode, Jimmy, bass, 355
Woodman, Britt, 370
Wood, Phyllis, vocalist, 210-1
Woods, Chris, 381
Woods, Doug, drums, 345
Woods, Harry, songwriter, 232
Woods, Phil, 381
Woodson, Sammy, 30
Woody Herman band, 327, 341
World Jazz Records, 362
"World's Greatest Jazz Band, The," 310, 352, 374
WOR, radio station, 154, 203
Worsley, John, 344
Wortner, George, guitar, 94
Wright, Edyth, vocalist, 148, 153, 157-8, 160, 172
Wright, Estelle, 172

Wright, Marvin, arranger, 186
Wrightsman, Stan, piano, 64
Wright, Wayne, guitar, 341
WWL, radio station, 26
Wylie, Austin, bandleader, 88

Xavier Cugat's orchestra, 107

Yaged, Sol, clarinet, bandleader, 248, 266
Yaner, Milt, sax, 94, 120, 121, 141
"Yankee Rhythm Kings, The," 374
Yarger, Claire "Sock," drums, 33, 36
Yoder, Walt, bass, 80-1, 94, 97, 145, 183
Yorks, Bill, The, 374
Young and Rubicam, 360
Young, Lon, trombone, 374
Young, Snooky, 381
Young, Trummy, 341, 370, 381
Young, Victor, composer, arranger, recording director, 101, 138
Youngman, Henny, 76
"Your Father's Moustache," 313

Zahn, Christian, vibes, 355-6
Zentmaier, Carl, 311
Zerafkin, Arabic scale, 152
Zudicoff, Moe (Buddy Morrow), 205
Zugsmith, Al, band manager, 64-5, 70
Zululand, 325
Zurke, Bob, piano, 66, 169, 227